FROM ALFRED THE GREAT TO STEPHEN

Elephant from a misericord in Exeter Cathedral
(*Courtauld Institute*)

FROM ALFRED THE GREAT
TO STEPHEN

R.H.C. DAVIS

THE HAMBLEDON PRESS

LONDON AND RIO GRANDE

Published by The Hambledon Press, 1991

102 Gloucester Avenue, London NW1 8HX (U.K.)

P.O. Box 162, Rio Grande, Ohio 45672 (U.S.A.)

ISBN 1 85285 045 0

British Library Cataloguing in Publication Data

Davis, R.H.C. (Ralph Henry Carless, *1918-*
  From Alfred the Great to Stephen.
  1. England, History, 410-1154.
  I. Title
  942.01

Library of Congress Cataloging-in-Publication Data

Davis, R.H.C. (Ralph Henry Carless), *1918-*
  From Alfred the Great to Stephen/R.H.C. Davis.
  Includes index.
  1. Great Britain – History – Anglo-Saxon period, 449-1066.
  2. Great Britain – History – Norman period, 1066-1154.
  I. Title
DA152.D38   1991   91-6729 CIP

Printed on acid-free paper and bound in Great Britain
by Bookcraft Ltd., Midsomer Norton

Contents

Acknowledgements

The articles reprinted here first appeared in the following places and are reprinted by kind permission of the original publishers.

1 *Studies in Medieval History Presented to R. Allen Brown* (Boydell Press, Woodbridge, 1989), pp. 103-116.
2 *Transactions of the Royal Historical Society*, 5th series, v (1955), pp. 23-37.
3 *History*, lvi (1971), pp. 169-182.
4 *English Historical Review*, xcvii (1982), pp. 803-810.
5 *History*, li (1966), pp. 279-286.
6 *Anglo-Norman Studies*, x (1987), pp. 67-82.
7 *English Historical Review*, xciii (1978), pp. 241-261.
8 *The Writing of History in the Middle Ages: Essays Presented to Richard William Southern*, edited by R.H.C. Davis and J.M. Wallace-Hadrill (Oxford University Press, 1981), pp. 71-100.
9 *English Historical Review*, xcv (1980), pp. 597-606.
10 *Domesday Studies*, ed. J.C. Holt (Royal Historical Society and Boydell Press, 1987), pp. 15-39.
11 *English Historical Review*, lxxvii (1962), pp. 209-232; reprinted in second edition of *Gesta Stephani* (Oxford, 1976).
12 *History*, xlix (1964), pp. 1-12.
13 *English Historical Review*, lxxix (1964), pp. 299-307.
14 *English Historical Review*, lxxv (1960), pp. 654-60.
15 *English Historical Review*, lxxxvi (1971), pp. 533-547.
16 *London Topographical Record*, 23 (1974), 9-26.
17 *A Medieval Miscellany for Doris Mary Stenton*, edited by Patricia M. Barnes and C.F. Slade (Pipe Roll Society, 1962), pp. 139-146.
18 *Oxoniensia*, xxxiii (1968), pp. 53-65.
19 *Oxoniensia*, xxxviii (1973), pp. 258-267.
20 *History*, 66 (1981), pp. 361-74.
21 *University of Birmingham Gazette*, 1979, pp. 3-5.
22 *University of Birmingham Gazette*, 1983, pp. 1-3.

Introduction

After I had written my *History of Medieval Europe*, Reginald Treharne said to me 'I think I see what you are getting at', a remark which silenced me because I could not have told him myself. Similarly with this collection of historical pieces, though they are nearly all concerned with English History between the seventh and twelfth centuries, I find it hard to explain what they are 'getting at'. Having now re-read them I can see the origin of the ideas and questions that underlie some of them. Experience of World War II which I saw at close quarters in ten different countries as a member of the Friends' Ambulance Unit prompted several of them. The questions behind 'East Anglia and the Danelaw' were posed when I heard our French colonel explaining to new recruits that when they got to Alsace they must realize that though most of the people spoke German they were nonetheless good Frenchmen. 'Alfred the Great: Propaganda and Truth' is linked to observed problems of morale in the first three years of the war, and some of the problems of the Norman Conquest seemed particularly vivid because I had witnessed half a dozen conquests or reconquests at close quarters. The personal experience which sparked off 'The Ford, the River and the City' was wrecking a punt when it swung across the stream of a river in flood so that it jammed across the piers of a bridge, while I found the Oxford Charter of 1191 by pure chance when the Warwickshire Record Office produced it instead of the document I had ordered. 'Bede after Bede' was the response to a happy holiday in Northumberland, Durham and Yorkshire. Two of the articles have origins which were both remote and half-forgotten. I noticed the charter for Chalgrove and Tebworth which was to be at the heart of 'Alfred and Guthrum's frontiers' in 1953 when I was working on East Anglia and the Danelaw. I showed it to Goronwy Edwards, then Director of the Institute of Historical Research, and after a good and characteristic look he said, 'Still waters . . ., Davis, still waters . . .,' – and there I left it until (in 1981) I mentioned it in an undergraduate seminar in Birmingham, and the solution presented itself to me as I spoke. The other instance concerns the reading (in 1948) of an article by Carl Stephenson in which he explained how helpful it would be for the history of feudalism if one could trace the origin of the medieval warhorse; I know that I read it because I have subsequently found the notes I made, but I had quite forgotten it until, some thirty years later something in my subconscious induced me to start serious research on that subject.

For that reason I feel diffident about making a list of those I ought to thank. I have had so many and such splendid teachers, colleagues and friends that I would be bound to forget some of the most important if I tried to recall them all at once. I therefore limit myself to two – Sir Richard Southern from whose advice and friendship I have benefited ever since he was my tutor at Balliol; and Professor V.H. Galbraith whom I had the privilege of knowing since I was a small boy and who, without ever being my teacher in a formal sense, was a perpetual inspiration.

Abbreviations

Since these articles originally appeared in different journals or books abbreviations sometimes vary from one to the other.

ANS	*Anglo-Norman Studies*, ed. R. Allen Brown, vols i-xi (1978-88)
BT	*The Bayeux Tapestry*, ed. Sir Frank Stenton. London 1957
Cap. Reg. Franc.	*Capitularia Regum Francorum*, ed. A. Boretius, M.G.H. 1883-97
Dollinger, Phillippe	*L'Evolution des classes rurales en Bavière* Paris, 1949
E.H.R.	*English Historical Review*
Fauroux	Marie Fauroux, *Recueil des Actes des Ducs de Normandie* S.A.N. 1961
G.G. or *Gesta Guillelmi*	*Guillaume de Poitiers: Histoire de Guillaume le Conquérant*, ed. Raymonde Foreville, Paris, 1952
GND	see Jumièges
Inventari	*Inventari Altomedievali di terra, coloni e redditi*, ed. A. Castagnetti *et al.* (*Fonti per la storia d'Italia*) 1979
Jumièges or G.N.D.	*Guillaume de Jumièges: Gesta Normannorum Ducum*, ed. Jean Marx. S.H.N. 1914 (G.N.D.), ed. Jean Marx. S.H.N. 1914
M.G.H.	*Monumenta Germaniae Historica*
M.I.O.G.	*Mitteilungen des Instituts für Österreichische Geschichtsforschung*
Migne) MPL)	J.P. Migne, *Patrologia Latina* 217 vols, 1844-55
Orderic, or OV	*The Ecclesiastical History of Orderic Vitalis*, ed. Marjorie Chibnall, 6 vols. Oxford 1969-80
Perrin	C.E. Perrin, *Recherches sur la seigneurie rurale en Lorraine*. Strasbourg, 1935
Reg.	*Regesta Regum Anglo-Normannorum*, ed. H.W.C. Davis *et al.* 4 vols. Oxford, 1913-69
R.H.F.	*Recueil des Historiens des Gaules et de la France*
R.S.	Rolls Series

1

Bede after Bede

Many historians have discussed what Bede intended in his *Ecclesiastical History*. The title, which unlike many medieval titles is authentic, is *Historia Ecclesiastica Gentis Anglorum* and it expresses exactly the double nature of the work. On the one hand it was about God and His Church, and on the other hand it was about the various Anglo-Saxon peoples – Northumbrians, Mercians, East Anglians, Kentishmen or West Saxons – whom Bede treated as a unity and identified as the people or nation of the English. As Dr Stephens has put it:

> He gave the Anglo-Saxons a new name, or gave it currency; that they were one English *gens*. . . . He showed them that their minds need no longer linger 'in the forests of Germany'. He showed them a new home. That was one ancestry. Another was Christian. He showed them that they were descended from God and not from Woden.[1]

The trouble about complex messages is that they are often misunderstood. It is a real question whether subsequent generations understood Bede correctly or not. Did they understand the subtle balance of his work, or did they study his history primarily for religious inspiration, or primarily for the inspiration of the English nation?

If we are to attempt to answer this question, we must try to discover the extent to which the *Ecclesiastical History* was read in the Middle Ages. This is not an easy task, but we can get some idea of the relative popularity of the work by studying the known manuscripts. These are very numerous, about 160 in all, but for the sake of simplicity we will confine ourselves to the 140 discussed by Sir Roger Mynors, in his introduction to the Colgrave and Mynors edition of *Bede's Ecclesiastical History of the English People* in Oxford Medieval Texts (1969).[2] Using the information which he has there presented, accepting all his dates and attributions – though these latter are only to the earliest *known* location of each manuscript – we can construct a table which, for all its imperfections of detail, points unmistakeably to some general conclusions.

It is, for example, evident that over the whole Middle Ages the *HE* was as

---

* This paper was originally read at a Symposium in honour of Professor Denys Hay at Edinburgh on 9 May 1980. Since much of its interest lies in the Norman period, I venture to think that it may interest Allen and hope that he will accept this shared offering.
[1] J. N. Stephens, 'Bede's Ecclesiastical History', *History* lxii, 1977, 1–14, esp. p. 13.
[2] *Bede's Ecclesiastical History of the English People*, ed. Bertram Colegrave and R. A. B. Mynors. OMT 1969, xxxix–lxxv.

Manuscripts of Bede's *Ecclesiastical History*

	8th Cent.	9th Cent.	10th Cent.	11th Cent.	12th Cent.	13th Cent.	14th Cent.	15th Cent.	16th Cent.	Total
England	5	0	0	5	24½	2½	18	11	0	66
Anglo-Norman	0	0	0	1	5	1	0	0	0	7
France	1	8	0	8	10	0	0	1	0	28
German/Italian	0	3	0	7	14½	½	5	8	1	39
Total	6	11	0	21	54	4	23	20	1	140
OE Bede	0	0	3	3	0	0	0	0	0	6

popular on the continent as in England, and if anything slightly more popular in the Medieval Empire (Germany and Italy) than in France. It is also striking that though Bede did not complete his work till *c.* 731, we know of as many as six manuscripts dating from the eighth century, which suggests that the success of *HE* was immediate. Its widening circulation is clearly indicated by the fact that while five of the six eighth-century manuscripts were written in England, all eleven of the ninth century were written on the continent. That was the age of the Carolingian Empire. One group of manuscripts seems to stem from Alcuin since it is clearly connected with the palace school which he organised and the monastery to which he retired at Tours. Another group is based on the monasteries of Germany where Anglo-Saxon missionaries had been so prominent in the eighth century.

It may not be surprising that during the Carolingian Renaissance monastic scriptoria were more active on the continent than in England, but it is surprising that in the three centuries between 800 and 1100 as many as 27 MSS are continental and only 5 English. This is in strong contrast with the situation from the twelfth century onward and requires an explanation. We know that the *HE* was known in ninth-century England, because it was used by the compilers of the *Anglo-Saxon Chronicle* whose D and E texts (which seem to be Northumbrian) take information and dates from Bede's main narrative, while the A, B and C texts (from southern England) rely on his chronological summary.[3] More significantly there is an Old English version of *Bede* – once attributed to King Alfred but now recognised as Mercian in dialect – with three MSS from the tenth century and three from the eleventh.[4] But this translation, excellent though it is, is not complete, one important omission being that it does not even mention the Synod of Whitby. It may be that the translator did not understand, or could not be bothered with, the Paschal controversy: or perhaps that he was anxious not to give offence to the British. But there is no doubt that the general effect of this and

[3] *Two of the Saxon Chronicles Parallel*, ed. Charles Plummer, 2 vols., Oxford 1892–9, ii, lx–lxi.
[4] *The Old English Version of Bede's Ecclesiastical History of the English People*, ed. T. Miller, 4 parts in 2 vols., Early English Text Soc., Original Series, xcv–xcvi, cx–cxi, 1890–8. For a discussion of the translation and the identity of the translator, as also of the MSS, see Dorothy Whitelock, 'The Old English Bede', *Proceedings of the British Academy*, xlviii, 1962, 57–90.

other omissions is to reduce the importance of Northumbria. The same trend is evident in the *Anglo-Saxon Chronicle*, which also fails to mention the Synod of Whitby and in general gives very little space to Northumbria, with not the slightest suggestion that it had been a land full of monks and saints. Though it recognises the Northumbrians as an integral part of the English people, its principal interest is emphatically West Saxon.

This development is taken one stage further in the chronicle of the Ealdorman Æthelweard. Writing for the benefit of his cousin, Matilda abbess of Essen, he translated the *Anglo-Saxon Chronicle* into Latin, abbreviating it considerably and in the process reducing even farther the references to Northumbria. For example both the *Anglo-Saxon Chronicle* and the Old English Bede stated that when King Cynegils of Wessex was converted to christianity, King Oswald of Northumbria was his godfather: but Æthelweard did not mention the fact, presumably because he did not wish it to be thought that a West Saxon king could have been the client of a Northumbrian.[5] On the other hand, so far from wishing to forget that the Anglo-Saxons came from 'the forests of Germany', Æthelweard provided his German cousin with information about the continental homeland which was in neither the *Anglo-Saxon Chronicle* nor Bede.[6] His interest in the *HE* had been narrowed down to those parts of it which were not in conflict with the view that the destiny of England lay in the royal house of Wessex.

If this development had continued unchecked, one would have expected Bede's *HE* to fall into oblivion. But in the twelfth century there is a dramatic change with 54 new manuscripts, of which at least 24 were written in England and another five or six in the monasteries of Normandy. This is followed by a hiatus, for the thirteenth century provides hardly any manuscripts at all. After that there is a modest revival in which the centre of interest shifts from the continent to England, with 18 English MSS of the fourteenth century and 11 of the fifteenth. It may be that this revival was connected with nationalism or Lollardy, in which case the fact that such MSS as do come from the continent are mostly German may suggest a connection with John Hus. For the present I intend to leave that problem to others, and to concentrate on the revival of the *HE* in the eleventh and twelfth centuries. What gave it such a great appeal in those centuries? Was it an interest in early church history or in the origins in the English nation, or in something which we have not yet defined?

What first aroused my interest in this question was the influence which Bede's *HE* appeared to have had on the northern revival of monasticism in the eleventh century. That revival was necessary because the Scandinavian raids and conquests had extinguished monasticism in Northumbria, with the result that by 1066 there was said not to be a single monastic community north of the

---

[5] *The Chronicle of Æthelweard*, ed. A. Campbell, NMT 1962, 19. Cf. Bede, *HE* iii.7. Æthelweard seems to have known the *OE Bede* where Oswald's part in the baptism is faithfully recorded (ed. Miller, i.168–9), as also in the *ASC*, *s.a.* 635.

[6] *Æthelweard*, 6–7 re. Denmark, and 9 when he states that the chief town of Old Saxony was known as Schleswig in Saxon and as Hedeby in Danish. He was making the translation for Matilda abbess of Essen who, like himself, was descended from King Alfred.

Humber.[7] In the years immediately following, monks from south of the Humber, and particularly from the diocese of Worcester, emigrated to the north because, moved by the reading of Bede's *HE*, they were determined to restore monasticism in Northumbria to its former glories. Their success was spectacular and their foundations numerous, the sites which they selected being invariably places which were mentioned as monastic in the *HE* – Monkwearmouth, Jarrow, Tynemouth, Melrose, Whitby, Lastingham, Hackness, York, Lindisfarne and its shrine of St Cuthbert which had subsequently been translated to Durham Cathedral.

The classic account of the revival is to be found in David Knowles's *Monastic Order in England*.[8] In it he lays great emphasis on the fact that the movement had its origins in the one English diocese in which, even after the Norman Conquest the English church remained under English control, the two dominant figures being Wulfstan II bishop of Worcester and Æthelwig abbot of Evesham, both of whom would, in a later age, have been described as successful (and virtuous) collaborators.

Æthelwig played a large part in secular affairs, serving the Conqueror, until his death in 1077, as a sort of super-sheriff or earl, in the counties of the Mercian law – Gloucestershire, Worcestershire, Shropshire, Staffordshire, Warwickshire and Oxfordshire. Knowles pointed out that he was not a mere time-server, because after the Conqueror's harrying of the North (1069), he set up a reception centre and food kitchens at Evesham for the relief of the refugees from Northumbria. Presumably they did not hesitate to describe to him the devastation of the land which had once been Bede's.[9]

Wulfstan II, subsequently canonised as St Wulfstan, was bishop of Worcester from 1062 until his death in 1095. His see had a special connection with the province of York because, for most of the period between 972 and 1062, it had been held in plurality by the archbishops of York. Wulfstan himself had been cathedral prior when Archbishop Ealdred had held the see of Worcester, and in 1062 had been consecrated by him in York. Before returning to Worcester he had served the archbishop as a sort of suffragan in the northern province, and one of his first acts as bishop had been to dedicate a church in honour of the blessed Bede.[10]

It was in this English enclave of the Anglo-Norman church that the plan was formed to revive monasticism in Northumbria. The people most closely involved were hitherto unknown. One was an illiterate Norman called Reinfrid who 'when crossing the province of Northumbria turned aside to the place called *Streoneshalc* [Whitby] and, affected by the desolation of the place then (*deinde*)

---

[7] Dom David Knowles, *The Monastic Order in England*, Cambridge 1946, 100n.

[8] Knowles, *Monastic Order*, ch. ix.

[9] Knowles, *Monastic Order*, 162. His relief of the refugees is described by Prior Dominic (*c.* 1125–50) in *Chronicon Abbatiae de Evesham ad annum 1418*, ed. W. D. Macray, RS 1863, 90–1. Cf. R. R. Darlington, 'Æthelwig abbot of Evesham', *EHR* xlviii, 1933, 1–22.

[10] *The Vita Wulfstani of William of Malmesbury*, ed. Reginald R. Darlington, Camden Third Series xl. 1928, 20.

became a monk at Evesham'.[11] Why he chose Evesham we are not told. He must have arrived there with, or soon after, the English refugees from the North. But the person who impressed him was a visiting monk called Aldwin who, having 'learnt from the *History of the English* that the province of Northumbria had once been thick with numerous choirs of monks and armies of saints', was determined to visit the sites of their monasteries, even though he knew that they had been reduced to a desert. He wanted to 'live a life of poverty there in imitation of those former monks',[12] and so (*ergo*) he came to Evesham. Aldwin was really prior of Winchcombe; his abbot had been deposed by the Conqueror and his abbey was, for the time being (1066–9), under the rule of Æthelwig abbot of Evesham. Aldwin and Reinfrid, in company with a monk of Winchcombe, Elfwy, who was also a deacon, obtained the abbot's permission to set out for the North in order to restore monasticism. They went off on foot 'leading just a little donkey which carried the books and priestly vestments necessary for the divine service'.[13]

If we ask how Prior Aldwin could have obtained a copy of Bede's *HE*, we find that Winchcombe had a copy of it (Bodleian, MS Douce 368), though paleographers date it, not to the eleventh century, but to the early twelfth. At nearby Gloucester, founded in 1058, there was a copy (BL, MS Royal c.v) which is dated to the late eleventh century, while Worcester Cathedral had an Old English Bede (Cambridge Univ. Lib., KK 3.18) of the same date. Either the Latin or the English text would have given Aldwin and his companions the necessary information about the places where they were to settle.

When they reached Yorkshire the sheriff, Hugh fitz Baldric,[14] (who held the lands subsequently to be held by Robert de Stuteville) directed them to Newcastle-on-Tyne, which was then known as Monkchester. But the bishop of Durham, a Lotharingian called Walcher, who had been nominated by the Conqueror and who, at any rate from 1075 till his death in 1080, combined the office of bishop with that of earl, asked them to move to Jarrow.[15] He did this, it seems, in order to move them from land which he held as earl to land which belonged to the bishopric, but Aldwin and his companions must have been delighted to start their revival of monasticism in the place which had been hallowed by Bede himself.

Bishop Walcher also found them a remarkable recruit called Turgot. He was a dispossessed English landholder from Lincolnshire who, if rightly identified among the pre-Conquest landholders of the Domesday Survey, had also been a lawman (*lagaman*).[16] After the Conquest he was 'one of those whom the Normans held hostage in Lincoln castle for the whole of Lindsey', but he bribed the warder, and at great peril fled to Grimsby where he boarded a Norwegian

---

[11] *Cartularium Abbathiae de Whiteby*, ed. J. C. Atkinson, Surtees Soc. lxix, 1878, i, 1.

[12] '*Historia Dunelmensis Ecclesiae*' or 'the *Libellus*' in *Symeonis Monachi Opera Omnia*, ed. Thomas Arnold, 2 vols., RS 1882–5, i, 108.

[13] *Symeon* i, 109. The donkey (*asellum*) carrying the instruments of the sacrament is, of course, a reference to Christ's entry into Jerusalem (John xii.14).

[14] Hugh fitz Baldric is mentioned only in the Durham *Historia Regum, Symeon* ii, 201.

[15] *Libellus, Symeon* i, 109.

[16] *DB* i, 337, 347, 351, 352v, 353, 353v.

merchant ship.[17] The Norwegians hid him below deck, because they had aboard the envoys whom King William was sending to Norway. When the ship reached open sea, Turgot emerged from hiding. The King's envoys promptly ordered the ship to return to England, but the Norwegian crew reached for their arms, and the envoys, being outnumbered, thought better of the matter. Safe in Norway, Turgot soon came to the notice of King Olaf who, being very religious, asked him to teach him the psalms, for Turgot (as we are now informed) was a clerk. Being in the King's favour, Turgot became wealthy, but we are told that he was frequently smitten with compunction and a desire to abandon earthly things, as circumstances eventually dictated that he should do. After some years he determined to return to England with his wealth, but his ship was wrecked, everyone and everything in it being lost, except for Turgot and five or six others. He went to Durham to pray, and Bishop Walcher joyfully sent him to Jarrow in order that he might become a monk there.[18]

Further recruits arrived at Jarrow, but we are told that few of them were local men, most being 'from the remote parts of England, whence they had been drawn by the reports which had reached them'.[19] As a result additional houses were established. The first was at Tynemouth, Bede's *monasterium . . . iuxta ostium Tini fluminis*,[20] where Oswin king of Deira (d. 651) was now reputed to have been buried. This was probably between 1075 and 1080, but in the confusion following Bishop Walcher's death the monks of Jarrow seem to have lost Tynemouth, and soon after 1090 the new earl, Robert de Mowbray, gave it as a priory to St Albans.[21] There still survives at Pembroke College, Cambridge a twelfth-century manuscript of Bede's *HE* which had belonged to Tynemouth under this latter regime.

The second attempt to found another abbey from Jarrow was at Melrose where, according to Bede, St Cuthbert had been prior under Abbot Eata.[22] The two monks who went there were Aldwin the former prior of Winchcombe and Turgot the exile from Lincolnshire. It was not surprising that there were political difficulties, for Melrose, being in Scotland, was subject to King Malcolm III whose wife, Margaret, was sister of the Ætheling Edgar, the sole remaining English claimant to the Conqueror's throne.[23] Any Norman might have suspected trouble when a character such as Turgot crossed the border to found a monastery under such a king. In fact, Turgot seems to have remained loyal, for the Durham *Libellus* states that King Malcolm did the monks many injuries because 'holding to the precept of the gospel' they would not swear

[17] *Historia Regum*, in *Symeon* ii, 202.
[18] The story of Turgot's early life is found only in the *Historia Regum* (*Symeon* ii, 202–4).
[19] *Historia Regum* (*Symeon* ii, 202).
[20] *HE* v, 6.
[21] The history of Tynemouth is not easy, but it has been unravelled convincingly by H. S. Offler, *Durham Episcopal Charters, 1071–1152*, Surtees Soc. clxxix, 1968, 5 and 41–2.
[22] *HE* iv, 25.
[23] The marriage had taken place 'not later than 1081' (A. A. M. Duncan, *Scotland, the Making of the Kingdom*, Edinburgh 1975, 119).

allegiance to him .[24] But Bishop Walcher's fears are revealed in the very next sentence; 'with frequent letters and commands he asked, told, commanded and finally, with the clergy and all the people in the presence of St Cuthbert, threatened them with excommunication unless they returned to dwell under the authority of St Cuthbert'.[25] Rightly or wrongly, the Normans were afraid that the Bedan revival might take a nationalist turn.

Meanwhile Reinfrid, the Norman knight who had been so moved by the desolation of Whitby, had returned there from Jarrow. It is likely that he had been in the service of William de Percy, because his son, Fulk fitz Reinfrid, was subsequently steward of Alan de Percy lord of Topcliffe.[26] William de Percy now gave him the site of the monastery at Whitby, and in 1078 he became a monk there. Dangers from pirates and quarrels with William de Percy led, before 1086, to a removal for a few years to Hackness where, according to Bede's *HE* the Abbess Hild had founded a monastery.[27] Subsequently, under a new abbot called Stephen, they moved to Lastingham where, according to Bede, St Chad had been abbot before being consecrated bishop.[28] St Chad's first see had been York – it was later that he was moved to Lichfield – and likewise Stephen and his monks proceeded from Lastingham to York. They could not revive the old monastery of St Peter's, because that was the cathedral, now served by canons, but the abbey which they founded in honour of St Mary was very close by. They seem to have been doing their utmost to relive the glories of the age of Bede.

In this part of the story there is nothing particularly 'national'. The inspiration which Reinfrid and his followers drew from Bede was specifically monastic; this is shown both by the places which they chose for their monasteries, and by the type of monasticism which they were intending to revive. Bede's Jarrow, though more or less Benedictine, had been strongly influenced by Celtic monasticism, Bede himself being unashamedly attracted by the traditions of Saints Aidan and Cuthbert who had preferred the life of hermits to that of conventual monks. This primitive and ascetic monasticism had a great appeal in the eleventh and twelfth centuries when every monastic reformer was striving to recapture the spirit of the primitive ideal; and there was a particular parallel to be drawn between monks like St Cuthbert and the Desert Fathers of the fourth and fifth centuries, whose *Lives* exercised such a powerful influence on the Cistercians. It was therefore to be expected that the Northumbrian reformers and the Cistercians would be attracted to each other, as was in fact the case. Cîteaux had a twelfth-century MS of Bede's *HE* (Dijon, MS 574), and it was from St Mary's York that, in 1132, the prior, sacrist and eleven other monks migrated to found the Cistercian abbey of Fountains. Their first recruit from elsewhere was a monk from Whitby.

---

[24] *Libellum* in *Symeon* i, 112.
[25] *Ibid.*
[26] Sir Charles Travis Clay, *Early Yorkshire Charters*, xi, *The Percy Fee*, Yorkshire Archaeological Soc. 1963, 92–3. He belonged to what was later known as the family of Kyme.
[27] *HE* iv, 21.
[28] *HE* iii, 28.

His name was Robert (later to be St Robert) and he was the Fountains monk who was chosen as first abbot of its first daughter-house.[29] This was Newminster in Northumberland, and it is interesting to find that it had a late-twelfth century copy of Bede's *HE* (BL Add. MS 25014), its text belonging to the 'Durham group', derived from the manuscript given to the first monks of Durham by Bishop William of St Calais, c. 1083 (Durham Cath. MS B.ii.35). It was St Robert also who was responsible for sending a colony of monks from Newminster to found a daughter-house at Sallay on the bank of the Ribble near Clitheroe. The lay founder of that house was William de Percy II, grandson of the founder of Whitby, and himself a benefactor of both Whitby and Fountains. It was Sallay which owned the only known manuscript of the so-called 'Symeon of Durham's' *Historia Regum* which is one of the three most important sources for the history of the Northern revival, together with the History of the Foundation of Fountains Abbey. Possibly, as Mr Baker has suggested, this manuscript may have originated at Fountains itself.[30] But however that may be, it provides us with our only source for the early life of Turgot, the Lincolnshire lawman who became a monk and, with Aldwin, made the unsuccessful attempt to revive monasticism at Melrose. That had been before 1080. In 1136 Melrose was successfully revived by Cistercians, not from Fountains, it is true, but from Rievaulx. The Cistercians seem to have taken a sympathetic interest in the man who had attempted to precede them.

Turgot personifies the English element in the revival. We have seen that he and Aldwin eventually abandoned the venture at Melrose, but that was not the end of their career. They returned to Jarrow and remained there for a few years until, in 1083, Bishop William of St Calais took them to Durham and installed them in the cathedral, so that St Cuthbert's shrine could be served once again by a monastic community instead of secular clergy. Aldwin was the first cathedral prior and was succeeded on his death (1087) by Turgot. But Turgot was not just a cathedral prior. Somehow he had renewed his contact with the Old English royal house by becoming the spiritual adviser of Queen Margaret of Scotland who, on her death (16 Nov. 1093), seems to have committed her children to his care. Mr Baker has shown that he might have been the author of the earliest version of her *Life*, written c. 1093–5,[31] but whether this was so or not, it is certain that one of the first acts of her son, King Alexander I, was to appoint Turgot bishop of St Andrews. That was in 1107. Turgot held the see for eight years, but his tenure was not easy, because Archbishop Anselm insisted that he owed obedience to Canterbury. Turgot insisted that he owed his obedience to

---

[29] *Memorials of the Abbey of St Mary of Fountains*, ed. J. R. Walbran, vol. i, Surtees Soc. xlii, 1862, 9 and 58–61.
[30] Derek Baker, 'Scissors and paste – Corpus Christi Cambridge MS 139 again', *SCH* xi, 1975, 83–123. Cf. Peter Hunter Blair 'Some Observations on the *Historia Regum* attributed to Symeon of Durham' in *Celt and Saxon: Studies in the Early British Border*, ed. Nora K. Chadwick, Cambridge 1963, 63–118. The essential starting point for 'Symeon' is H. S. Offler, *Medieval Historians of Durham*, Durham 1958. I am personally indebted to Professor Offler for much supplementary information.
[31] Derek Baker, '"A Nursery of Saints": St Margaret of Scotland reconsidered' in *Medieval Women*, ed. Derek Baker, *SCH* Subsidia i, 1978, 119–41, esp. 129–32.

York, while Alexander did not wish him to give obedience to either. In these circumstances Turgot's health broke down. He returned to Durham, and it is there that he died and was buried (1115).

The introduction of monks into Durham Cathedral was the climax of the Northern Revival. For Prior Aldwin who had set out from Winchcombe because of the inspiration he had received in reading Bede's *Ecclesiastical History*, it must have been a spiritual homecoming. Now that he was in charge of the shrine which enclosed the earthly remains of St Cuthbert he was literally in touch with things that Bede had known and described. Lindisfarne, the site of St Cuthbert's monastery and see was given to the Durham community so that a dependency could be established there. In Durham cathedral were buried the bones of Bede himself; they had been brought there some forty or fifty years before by Ælfred son of Westou who had spirited them away from Jarrow. As for Bede's *Ecclesiastical History*, Bishop William of St Carilef presented the community with a copy of it (*c.* 1083) which is still (as we have already mentioned) in the cathedral library (MS B.ii.35). To commemorate the fulfilment of the ideal which that book had inspired, the community decided in 1092 to pull down the Anglo-Saxon cathedral, which was then barely a hundred years old and lacked a monastic tradition, and to build in its place the great church we now see. The most magnificent specimen of Norman architecture in England, it celebrates the fact that monasticism had returned to Bede's land of saints, and that St Cuthbert was served once again by a monastic community.

Why was it that this monastic revival had not occurred sooner? Monasticism had been extinguished in Northumbria, not by the Norman Conquest, but by the Danish invasions of the ninth century. Many monasteries south of the Humber had suffered the same fate, but most of them had been revived during the 'Tenth-Century Reformation' by the efforts of Saints Dunstan, Æthelwold and Oswald. Since these three bishops had also ejected clerks from their cathedrals and installed monks in their place, there is an obvious comparison between them and the Norman bishop, William of Saint-Carilef. The difference was that they were a century earlier. Why was Northumbria so far behind? A partial explanation can be offered by the Scandinavian Kingdom of York which did not collapse until 954, but there is still a gap of more than a century before the Evesham monks arrived on their mission. They, as we have seen, were largely inspired by Bede's *Ecclesiastical History*. Was nobody reading that book in Northumbria in the intervening years?

In fact they almost certainly were. Though the twelfth-century historians of Durham, Whitby and St Mary's York would not admit the fact, it is certain that at Durham attempts had been made to replace the clerks with monks in the forty or fifty years before the Norman Conquest. The researches initiated by H. E. Craster[32] have established that the first attempts at reform were made by Bishop Edmund (1020–42). He had been one of the secular clerks serving Durham Cathedral, but desiring to revert to the traditions of St Aidan and St Cuthbert,

[32] H. H. E. Craster, 'The Red Book of Durham', *EHR* xl, 1925, 504–532.

had refused to accept the bishopric until he had become a monk. He travelled south to Winchester and there took the cowl before being consecrated by Archbishop Wulfstan of York. There may have been something symbolic about the choice of place, for Winchester was one of the centres of the Tenth-Century Reformation; it was there that, in 964, Bishop Æthelwold had with the aid of the king ejected the secular clerks and installed Benedictine monks in their place. Following the tradition of the Tenth-Century Reformation Edmund decided to take two monks back to Durham to instruct him in the daily discipline. On his return journey, therefore, he stopped at Peterborough – the first monastic foundation that Bishop Æthelwold had made from Winchester (966) – and recruited two brothers, Æthelric and Æthelwine who were, in the event, to succeed him in turn as bishop. The clerks at Durham opposed them as foreigners and accused them of trying to remove the church's treasures to their own monasteries – and indeed an arm of St Oswald did find its way to Peterborough. But though, after Edmund's death, the clerks succeeded in ejecting Æthelric for a short while after he had become bishop (1042), he did not resign till 1057 when he retired to Peterborough and was succeeded as bishop by his brother Æthelwine (1057–71). Both these men survived the Norman Conquest but both were implicated, or suspected of being involved, in English rebellions. Æthelric was captured at Peterborough and removed to Westminster, while Æthelwine, having attempted to flee the country, was captured with the rebels at Ely and removed to Abingdon.[33]

It might be thought that this earlier attempt at a monastic revival was nothing more than the death agony of the Tenth-Century Reformation. The traditions of St Cuthbert were bound to be strong at Durham, and the monasteries of Winchester and Peterborough were only continuing the tradition of their founder, Bishop Æthelwold. But if we turn to the manuscripts of Bede's *HE*, we find that two of the six known MSS of the Old English Bede, the one early and the other mid-tenth century (BL Cotton MSS Domitian ix and Otho B xi) are thought to have come from Winchester; and that of the three early eleventh-century MSS of the Latin text which can be located, one (Winchester Cathedral MS 1) probably came from Hyde Abbey at Winchester, and another (Oxford, Bodley 163) from Peterborough. In the opinion of Sir Roger Mynors this Peterborough MS was copied from the one at Hyde Abbey. In general both follow the normal *c* (or English) version of the text. But whoever did the transcribing at Peterborough took care to reinstate from a *m* version the text of Book IV chapter 14 which was missing in *c*. This chapter concerned a miracle of St Oswald and would have been important for Peterborough after it had acquired its arm of St Oswald from Durham. How did the transcriber know about the missing chapter at a time when all the *m* texts, which alone contained

---

[33] For Æthelric, the 'Red Book' as printed by Craster, *EHR* xl, 528, *Symeon* ii, 173 (following 'Florence' of Worcester) and *ASC* D and E, *s.a.* 1072. For Æthelwine, the *Libellus* in *Symeon* i, 105, the *Historia Regum* in *Symeon* ii, 177, and *Chronicon Monasterii de Abingdon*, ed. Joseph Stevenson, RS 1858, i; 485–6. Cf. Bernard Meehan, 'Outsiders and Insiders and Property in Durham around 1100' in *SCH* xii, 1975, 45–58 and esp. 50–3.

it, were apparently on the continent? One can only suppose that the information came from Fleury-sur-Loire where there was a *m* text of the early ninth century (Bern, Bürgerbibliothek 49), because Fleury was the place *par excellence* where the English monastic reformers of the tenth century received their training.[34]

Mynors thinks it possible, though he leaves it as an open question, that the Peterborough MS of the *HE* may have been the source of the English vulgate text, which is called C2. It is certainly the text of the eleventh-century MS from Gloucester (BL Royal 13 c.v) and of the early twelfth-century MS from Winchcombe (Bodleian, Douce 368); and the likelihood is that it was the text which Prior Aldwin read at Winchcombe before setting out on his journey. If so, it is virtually certain that he did not take it with him, for the text of *HE* which the monks had at Durham – and the manuscript was given to them by Bishop William of St Calais between 1081 and 1096 – was not C2 but C1 (i.e. without Bk. IV c.14). The most probable explanation is that it was copied from a local manuscript. The memory of Bede was very far from dead at Durham in the half century before the Norman Conquest. It was while Edmund was bishop (1020–42) that one of the priests, Ælfred son of Westou, succeeded in stealing Bede's bones from Jarrow so that they could be buried near St Cuthbert's shrine.[35] Ælfred was an inveterate collector of relics, and some of his lesser acquisitions suggest that he had been reading the *HE* in much the same spirit as Aldwin and Turgot were to do. He collected a relic of King Oswin who was subsequently associated with Tynemouth, which was where Aldwin and Turgot were to plant their first colony from Jarrow; and he collected the relics of St Boisil from Melrose where Aldwin and Turgot were to plant their second colony, though the final establishment of a monastery there was due to the Cistercians of Rievaulx in 1136. By that date Ælfred son of Westou's grandson, Ailred had become a monk of Rievaulx (1134) of which he was later to be abbot (1147–67). Since Ailred had been brought up with Henry son of King David of the Scots, it is very possible that it was because of him that King David sought monks from Rievaulx for his new abbey of Melrose.

The evidence we have been considering suggests that in the eleventh and twelfth centuries, and probably also in the tenth, Bede's *HE* was appreciated primarily as a contribution to monastic history. It may be objected that this is simply because our investigation has been based on the evidence provided by the monastic revival, but in practice it is difficult to find more than a handful of manuscripts of the *HE* which can be demonstrated to have been non-monastic.

---

[34] Monks who trained there included Bishop Æthelwold's pupils, Osgar (subsequently abbot of Abingdon) and Germanus of Winchester. The second St Oswald trained there *c.* 950–8 before he had become bishop of Worcester or had founded Ramsey Abbey. Abbo of Fleury was in England *c.* 970 and was at Ramsey *c.* 986–8 (Knowles, *Monastic Order*, 39–40, 46).

[35] *Libellus* in Symeon i, 87–9. Ælfred son of Westou was one of the hereditary guardians of St Cuthbert's shrine. He travelled round Northumbria collecting relics. In addition to those of Bede, he collected some of King Oswin (most of whose body, however, remained at Tynemouth where Aldwin and Turgot attempted their first colony from Jarrow), and those of St Boisil from Melrose (where Aldwin and Turgot had attempted their second colony). It looks as if he and they had been going to the same places because they had been reading the same book.

In Britain there are only four:- one of the late twelfth century which belonged to Chichester Cathedral (now at the College of Arms in London); two of the fourteenth century (one from Exeter Cathedral – now Edinburgh, Advocates' Library, 18.5.1) and the other from Henry Dispenser bishop of Norwich (now BL MS Arundel 74); and one of the fifteenth century which belonged to a fellow of Lincoln College, Oxford, and Eton (Cambridge, St John's College, 254). History was not a university subject in the Middle Ages, and there is nothing to suggest that Bede's *HE* was popular with the laity.

We can, however, learn something from the way in which the *HE* was used by other historians or chroniclers in the twelfth century. Of these the most important was William of Malmesbury. He was learned – according to R. M. Thomson 'the best-read man of his century'[36] – and he knew Bede's works well; and being half-English by birth he was enthusiastic about English antiquity. But like the Anglo-Saxon Chronicler and Æthelweard before him, he took a West Saxon view of the past and assumed that English history had been predestined to culminate in the hegemony of Wessex. As a result Bede's Northumbria was moved from the mainstream of English history into a backwater. In his *Gesta Regum* he recounts the history of the Anglo-Saxon invasions, using Bede as his principal source. Then, after an account of King Æthelbert of Kent and his immediate successors he turns, not as Bede did to Northumbria, but to Wessex; and within Wessex the main emphasis is placed on Glastonbury, a place unknown to Bede but now given the prominence which he had reserved to Lindisfarne. When William does turn to Northumbria, he sees its main achievement as the learning and culture which made the Carolingian Renaissance possible; he gives a long account of Bede's life and work and a shorter account of Alcuin which serves as an introduction to the Carolingian empire. The serious history of the kings, that is to say its main narrative, concerns the West Saxons from Egbert to the Norman Conquest. In William of Malmesbury's view, all roads led to Wessex. For him the most important fact about St Cuthbert was that he appeared in a vision to King Alfred on the eve of the battle of Edington and promised him victory.[37] We are told that the relics of St Aidan, St Hilda and Abbot Ceolfrid had been removed from Lindisfarne, Whitby and Monkwearmouth to Glastonbury,[38] and that King Oswald's body had been translated by the lady Æthelfleda from Bardney to Gloucester.[39] Everything important seemed to end up in Wessex.

The West Saxon point of view came naturally to William of Malmesbury,

[36] R. M. Thomson, *William of Malmesbury*, Woodbridge 1987, chapter 3 and appx. i, which form a revised version of his article in *Revue bénédictine* lxxxv, 1975, 362–402.

[37] *De gestis regum* i, 125.

[38] *De gestis regum* i, 56.

[39] *De gestis regum* i, 54; cf. the 'refoundation charter' of Gilbert de Gant for Bardney in 1087 (*Monasticon* i, 628): 'And inasmuch as the noble monastery, *as the venerable Bede bears witness in the narrative of his ecclesiastical history*, in reverence of St Oswald the king and martyr, was distinguished by zeal of Christian devotion on account of the frequent miracles which at that time were done in the same place to the honor of God, I have thought meet to restore with my possessions and resources the same place. . . .'.

because Malmesbury was in the centre of Wessex, but one could not expect it to have been welcome in Northumbria. To find an alternative, however, was difficult. Though in the religious sphere a Northumbrian historian might wish to establish the continuity of religious life, as did the monks of Durham, around the shrine of St Cuthbert, in secular history there was the difficulty of finding any inspiration in the spectacle of perpetual decline and inevitable failure. The glory of the seventh-century Northumbria was very great, but the memory of it could only make the subsequent decline more painful. As a result the *Historia Regum* attributed to Symeon of Durham skates over early Northumbrian history by following Bede's Lives of the Abbots of Monkwearmouth and Jarrow.[40] It is preceded by an Introduction which, so far as Northumbria is concerned, is totally irrelevant, since it is devoted to the legend of St Mildred who belonged to the royal house of Kent.[41] For this reason the *Historia Regum* is sometimes known as the *Historia post Bedam*, the presumption being that the author expected his readers to be familiar with Bede's *HE*, but preferred to keep it a work separate from his own. By not attempting to integrate it into his own work, he escaped the difficulty of explaining how Northumbria had declined from its former greatness.

A somewhat similar escape route was used by Henry of Huntingdon. He was neither a West Saxon nor a Northumbrian, and could not see the history of England in the simplistic terms of any one ancient kingdom. In his view the general pattern was that Britain had been afflicted by five scourges; – first the Romans (Bk I), second the Picts and Scots (Bk I), third the Anglo-Saxons (Bk II), fourth the Danes (Bk IV) and fifth the Normans (Bk V). Placed exactly in the middle, like the interval in a play, was the Conversion to Christianity (Bk III). It is longer than the other books and contains most of Bede's good stories, but it is different from the *HE* because it attempts to separate the ecclesiastical from the secular history of the English nation.[42] In thus distinguishing between the spiritual and the secular Henry of Huntingdon was the child of his age, but the separation made it possible for him to insulate the *HE* from his general theme. Whereas 'Symeon' had relegated the *HE* to 'ancient' history, Henry simply pigeon-holed it as ecclesiastical.

It was not essential that the division between secular and spiritual history should lead to this conclusion. William of Malmesbury also had made the separation, but his ecclesiastical history, the *Gesta Pontificum* had been as West Saxon as his *Gesta Regum*. One would have expected the *Gesta Pontificum* to be divided into parts concerning the provinces of Canterbury and York, but in fact William arranged the episcopal sees by kingdoms. Thus Book I concerned Kent (Canterbury and Rochester), Book II Essex, East Anglia and Wessex, Book III Northumbria (the province of York), Book IV 'the province' of the Mercians

---

[40] *Symeon* ii, 13ff.
[41] *Symeon* ii, 3–13. On this history see D. W. Rollason, *The Mildrith Legend: a study in Early Medieval Hagiography in England*, Leicester 1982.
[42] *Huntingdon*. For discussion, see Nancy F. Partner, *Serious Entertainments: the writing of history in twelfth-century England*, Chicago 1977. She points out that Arnold, in the Rolls Series edn., did not print the whole text, but omitted Henry's 'Book VIII' (epilogue to the first edition and the three epistles) and 'Book IX' (*De Miraculis*), printing Henry's 'Book X' as 'Book VIII'.

(Worcester, Hereford, Lichfield, Dorchester-on-Thames (or Lincoln) and Ely), while Book V was devoted to a long account of St Aldhelm and the monastery which he had founded at Malmesbury.[43]

With an arrangement such as this, William of Malmesbury could easily have woven together his *Gesta Regum* and *Gesta Pontificum*, the theme of both being markedly West Saxon. And if he had done this, the general shape of his book would not have been unlike that of Bede's *HE*, with ecclesiastical and secular history pursuing a single course which demonstrated God's will for the West Saxon people. The model for such integrated history lies, as Dr Stephens has pointed out, in the historical books of the Old Testament. But since the second half of the eleventh century this model was no longer in general favour. Whereas in the early Middle Ages no theoretical distinction had been drawn between Church and State, since both were part of the same society, the post-Hildebrandine church encouraged the distinction between spiritual and secular, and devoted much attention to it.

It is interesting therefore to find that in the twelfth century there was one chronicler, an exact contemporary of William of Malmesbury, who was so impressed by the structure of Bede's *HE* that he took it as the model for his own work. This was Orderic Vitalis, the half-English son of a French priest who had been sent by his parents to be a monk in Normandy. We can be certain that he knew Bede's *HE* well, not only because he quoted from it, but because he copied it out in its entirety; the manuscript written in his own distinctive hand is in the municipal library at Rouen (MS 1343), and interestingly enough combines features of the English (or *c*) text with others of the French (or *m*) text.[44] In his own history it has often been observed that the last chapter of the work is modelled on the last chapter of Bede's *HE*, recounting the story of his life and work and ending (as in the English *c* text) with a prayer. More important, however, is his conception of his own work as *The Ecclesiastical History of the Norman* gens. Like Bede he made no attempt to distinguish between the spiritual and secular. Like Bede he was recounting the history of a people in countries which were not, or had not originally been, their own. Since he was not concerned with the history of the English before 1066 he did not have to find a role for Northumbria, but since he was himself a monk, he appreciated the monastic history. He, it seems, was the one person who understood what Bede was intending in his *Ecclesiastical History of the English nation*; and he understood it because he was not concerned with its continuation but rather with a different people at a similar stage of religious and political development.[45]

---

[43] *De gestis pontificum*. 330–443.

[44] Mynors. in *HE* intro., lxi. states that Orderic's transcript 'seems to be the *c* text. but has the *Praeterea . . . inueniam* at the end of the preface'.

[45] In general. see also Antonia Gransden, 'Bede's reputation as a historian in Medieval England'. *JEH* xxxii. 1981. 397–427 which appeared after this paper had been written.

2

East Anglia and the Danelaw

IT has been, and still is, the considered opinion of many scholars that the freemen and sokemen who figure so prominently in the Domesday Survey of the northern and eastern counties of England were the descendants of the rank-and-file of the Danish armies of the ninth century. The theory is not based on any precise knowledge of Scandinavian peasant-society in the ninth century, but on the geographical distribution of the free peasantry in England. It was first propounded by E. W. Robertson in 1862:

> In the Danelage, . . . omitting Yorkshire from the calculation, between a third and a fourth of the entire population were classified either as *liberi homines* or as socmen. . . . Free Socage, the very tenure of which is sometimes supposed to have been peculiarly a relic of Anglo-Saxon liberty, appears to have been absolutely unknown except among the Danes.[1]

Steenstrup was delighted by the theory,[2] Seebohm illustrated it with a map,[3] and Vinogradoff elaborated the details:

> The remarkable congestion of these small freemen in the Danish districts, both in small farms or hamlets and in large

[1] E. W. Robertson, *Scotland under her Early Kings* (1862), ii. 269 ff., and compare ii. 458–9. The figures on which he bases his argument are given on ii. 274, and are:

	Tenentes in capite	Mesne lords	Socmanni	Liberi homines	Villani	Bordarii	Servi
Wessex . . .	948	3,037	44 (Kent)	0	45,860	36,876	14,829
English Mercia .	321	1,335	0	132	18,692	11,458	5,496
Southumbrian Danelage .	764	3,423	22,700	12,233	38,645	39,360	6,497

[2] J. C. Steenstrup, *Normannerne*, iv (Copenhagen 1882), 102 ff.
[3] F. Seebohm, *The English Village Community* (1883), pp. 85ff.

villages, has evidently to be explained by the recent Danish conquest, which introduced large numbers of warriors of the *here*, who had after the settlement to provide for their own subsistence, and who, although very much lowered by their humble condition and scanty outfit, were still proud of their freedom, and able to keep it up.[1]

The theory of this Arcadian demobilization still holds the field. But although detailed research has given it greater clarity and definition in certain districts such as Lincolnshire, the foundation of the theory as a whole is still necessarily geographical. To quote Sir Frank Stenton:

It cannot be an accident that a social organization to which there is no social parallel elsewhere in England occurs in the one part of the country in which regular development of native institutions had been interrupted by a foreign settlement.[2]

The theory has had to face powerful critics. Stubbs, though impressed, considered that 'the differences between the customs of the Danelaga and those of the rest of England . . . might almost with equal certainty be ascribed to the distinction between Angle and Saxon'.[3] Maitland too was sceptical:

But in truth we must be careful how we use our Dane. Yorkshire was a Danish county in a sense that Cambridgeshire was not Danish; it was a land of trithings and wapentakes, a land without hides, where many a village testified by its name to a Scandinavian settlement. And yet to all appearance it was in the Confessor's day a land where manors stood thick. Then we have that wonderful contrast between Yorkshire and Lincolnshire which Ellis summed up in these figures:

	Sochemanni	Villani	Bordarii
Lincolnshire	11,503	7,723	4,024
Yorkshire	447	5,079	1,819[4]

It is, in short, difficult to explain why Yorkshire had so few free peasants, but some reasoned explanation might be found for the anomaly if it were not for a further difficulty—the suspicion that

[1] P. Vinogradoff, *English Society in the Eleventh Century* (1908), p. 417.
[2] F. M. Stenton, *Anglo-Saxon England* (1943), p. 511.
[3] W. Stubbs, *The Constitutional History of England* (6th ed., 1897), i. 216.
[4] F. W. Maitland, *Domesday Book and Beyond* (1897), p. 139.

there was no appreciable settlement of Danish soldiers of the rank and file in East Anglia. This could be a serious matter, for in the counties of Norfolk and Suffolk the free peasantry formed, in 1086, a larger percentage of the population, 41·4% and 45·4% respectively, than in any other county except Lincolnshire, where the proportion was 50·7%. These counties might therefore have been expected to be particularly Danish. If this were not in fact the case, if in addition to the anomaly of Yorkshire (that was Danish but not free) there was to be the anomaly of East Anglia (that was free but not Danish), the whole theory that explained the origin of the free peasantry by reference to Danish soldier-peasants would be severely shaken. It is for this reason that it is proposed in this paper to investigate the problem of whether or not East Anglia was systematically settled by the rank-and-file of the Danish armies of the ninth century.

The arguments that have been put forward by various scholars to show that there was such a settlement in East Anglia can best be summarized *en bloc* as five propositions. First, the evidence of the Anglo-Saxon Chronicle is said to be specific on the point in its statement that in 879 the Danish army went from Cirencester to East Anglia and 'occupied the land and shared it out'. Secondly, evidence derived from thirteenth-century deeds has been held to suggest that the Danish army had, in sharing the land out among its members, divided it into units of $12\frac{1}{2}$ acres which were known as bovates or *manslots*, this last word being of Scandinavian origin and denoting 'a man's share'. Thirdly, the fact that in the late eleventh and early twelfth centuries many free peasants in East Anglia bore names that were of Scandinavian origin would seem to argue that these peasants were themselves Scandinavian by race. Fourthly, the Scandinavian element in East Anglian place-names, though not as strong as in Lincolnshire, and though somewhat puzzling in its details, is thought to support the theory of a peasant settlement, at any rate in Norfolk. Fifthly, it is claimed that since the free peasantry was particularly numerous in the Broadland where the place-names are outstandingly Scandinavian, there is a *prima facie* case that in East Anglia the free peasantry can be explained only in the light of the Scandinavian settlement of the ninth century.

These five propositions are sufficiently important to merit detailed attention.

First there is the evidence of the Chronicle. This leaves no doubt as to the fact that the Danes conquered East Anglia and ruled it for thirty-eight years (879–917). The Dane who first *gesæt* or 'took possession of' it was Guthrum, the northern king who had, after his defeat at Edington (878), received baptism and the baptismal name of Athelstan, with Alfred standing as his god-father.[1] But though the Chronicle is thus far specific, it gives no clue as to the nature of the Danish settlement. It does not say how many Danes were involved, nor whether they settled in East Anglia in such force as to give to that country not only new Danish lords but also a new Danish peasantry. All it states is that in 879:

> *Her for se here of Ciren ceastre on East Engle 7 gesæt þæt lond 7 gedælde.*[2]

In this year the host went from Cirencester into East Anglia and took possession of the land and divided it.

The verb *gedælan* means 'to divide' and in the present context it suggests that the Danes divided the land in the same way as they might have divided an inheritance or divided the spoils. The division might have been into units of any size, smallholdings, large estates, or even administrative districts such as those that 'owed allegiance' (*hyrde*) to fortified towns like the Five Boroughs in the Northern Danelaw, or Huntingdon, Cambridge and Colchester in the Eastern Danelaw. Modern scholars have preferred the suggestion of a minute division, and have translated *gedælan* as 'to share out', thus evoking some primitive system of land-sharing whereby every Danish soldier might have received 'a man's share' of land. In the tenth century, however, the ealdorman Æthelweard understood the passage in a different sense. He put it into Latin as follows:

> *Elevatus est praedictus exercitus, relicto Cyrenceaster, ad Orientalium Anglorum partes, castramentatique sunt ibi, omnesque habitatores illius terrae sub iugo imperii sui duxere.*[3]

The aforesaid army got up and left Cirencester and went to

---

[1] *Two of the Saxon Chronicles Parallel*, ed. C. Plummer (1892), *s.a.* 890.

[2] *Ibid.*, *s.a.* 880. Compare F. M. Stenton, *The Danes in England* (British Academy, 1927), pp. 4–5.

[3] *Monumenta Historica Britannica*, ed. H. Petrie (1848), p. 516.

East Anglia; and they built camps (or fortresses or boroughs) there and put all the inhabitants under the yoke of their empire.

A great advantage of this interpretation is that it does not strain the imagination in regard to the size of Guthrum's army. If the freemen and sokemen of East Anglia had been the descendants of his Danish soldiers, it would have been necessary to explain how it was that the army which in 878 had wintered at Cirencester had so multiplied on its removal to East Anglia that by 1066 its progeny numbered 20,372 households, or more than 40% of the rural population.[1] Could it have been due to the effects of the climate on the Danish soldiers of the rank and file? Or would it be necessary to postulate that Danish armies were normally counted by tens of thousands, with hordes of horses and shoals of ships?

The second proposition has been put forward by Professor Douglas, and is that the peculiar tenemental organization found in East Anglia in the thirteenth century can be explained only by reference to a 'Scandinavian system of land-sharing'.[2] There is, of course, no disputing that the tenemental organization of East Anglia had many peculiar features; all that is questioned is whether these peculiarities really suggest that the Danes had 're-arranged the tenemental organization of the conquered people'.[3] It has been claimed, for example, that the basic units of land held by peasants in East Anglia were all, whether called *tenementa, plenae terrae, eruings, toftlands, landsettagia, tenmanloths* or even *carucates*, 'derived from a single primitive holding, and that this was a Danish bovate whose normal size was $12\frac{1}{2}$ acres' and which 'was itself the *manloth* or "man's share" '.[4] The difficulty is to find the 'normal' bovate in East Anglia. Tenements of twelve acres are not very hard to find, but on Professor Douglas's own showing tenements of exactly $12\frac{1}{2}$ acres are rare, even in the thirteenth century. In earlier periods they are even rarer. In Domesday Book the commonest peasant tenements are of 15 and 30, 20 and 40, or 8 and 16 acres.[5] Before the Norman Conquest, in a will of *c.* 1022–43,

---

[1] The figures are from Barbara Dodwell, 'The Free Peasantry of East Anglia in Domesday', *Norfolk and Norwich Archaeological Soc.*, xxvii. 148.

[2] D. C. Douglas, *The Social Structure of Mediaeval East Anglia* (Oxford Studies in Social and Legal History, vol. ix, 1927), p. 50.

[3] Douglas, p. 49.   [4] Douglas, p. 50.

[5] Dodwell, *art. cit.*, p. 154.

there is mention of a *girde* which is a yardland or virgate, while larger units of land were calculated in hides.[1] In short, the twelve-and-a-half-acre unit does not seem to have been either general or ancient. Even if it had been, it is hard to see how it could have been a bovate. For a bovate was one-eighth of a carucate, and all the evidence goes to show that a carucate contained not 100 acres (which would be 8 × 12½), but 120 (8 × 15).[2] Similarly it is not really possible to equate the East Anglian leet with the 12-carucate-hundreds of Lincolnshire, since the equation rests not only on the belief in a 12½-acre bovate but also on the assumption that every hundred contained 120 carucates, though in Suffolk the actual number varied from 20 to 209, and that the 'typical leet' contributed one-twelfth of the hundred's geld, though the size of the leets varied, in fact, quite considerably.[3] Nor would it be wise to draw elaborate conclusions from the use of the word *tenman-loths* in the Norfolk village of Walpole. The word has not, I believe, been found elsewhere in East Anglia, and the tenement which it described may well have been exceptional, since Walpole was both close to the Lincolnshire border and in the Fenland, where land-reclamation may have created special conditions in the eleventh and twelfth centuries.[4] The only Danish influence to be found at all commonly in the Domesday Survey of East Anglia is the calculation of rents in units of 16*d.* or Danish *orae*; but this

[1] *The Kalendar of Abbot Samson of Bury St. Edmunds*, ed. R. H. C. Davis, (Camden Third Series, vol. lxxxiv, 1954), p. xliii; D. Whitelock, *Anglo-Saxon Wills* (1930), no. xxvii (*c.* 1022–43).

[2] G. J. Turner, *A calendar of the feet of fines relating to the county of Huntingdon* (Cambridge Antiq. Soc., 1913), pp. lxxxiii ff., based an argument in favour of the 100-acre carucate on a passage from Roger of Hoveden (*R.S.*, iv. 46–7) which he seems to have misunderstood. The passage (also printed in Stubbs' *Select Charters* (9th ed.), pp. 249–50) describes the sharp practice whereby, for the aid of 1198, 5*s.* was levied, not from each carucate or hide, but from the 'wainage of a plough' which was declared to be 100 acres.

[3] The carucage of Suffolk hundreds is given by Miss B. A. Lees in the *Victoria County History, Suffolk*, i. 360. For leets (or letes) see C. Johnson in *Victoria County History, Norfolk*, ii. 204–11, and *The Kalendar of Abbot Samson*, pp. xv–xxx.

[4] Douglas, pp. 29–30. Cf. Tait in *E.H.R.*, xliii. 94–7. For land-reclamation in the district, see E. Miller, *The Abbey and Bishopric of Ely* (1951), p. 95. In the Broadland, where (in contrast to the Fenland) Scandinavian place-names are common, the tenement is called by English or Latin names (e.g. *eruing*).

is only what one would have expected in a land where the land-lords or nobility had been Danish.

We proceed therefore to the third proposition, that the personal names of East Anglian peasants in the eleventh and twelfth centuries show them to have been of Scandinavian origin. It is undoubtedly true that about 10% of the personal names recorded in the twelfth-century portion of the Register of St. Benet of Holme are names of Scandinavian origin; similarly, Professor Douglas was certainly not overstating the case when he claimed that of the freemen and sokemen listed in the 'Feudal Book' of Abbot Baldwin of Bury St. Edmunds, 8½% bore Scandinavian names.[1] It is, however, a complete delusion to think that every man with a Scandinavian name was of Scandinavian origin. Professor Ekwall has shown that people of the same family often bore names of different provenance.[2] In East Anglia, for example, Stigand (whose name was Scandinavian) had a brother called Æthelmær. According to the *Liber Eliensis*, there was in the tenth century a priest called Athelstan whose brothers were called Ælfstan (English) and Bondo (Scandinavian).[3] Earlier still, Guthrum, the Danish king who first occupied East Anglia, struck pennies on which he used, not his heathen name, but his Christian name, Athelstan; it did not make him an Englishman. Sure proof that the examples here quoted are not exceptional comes from the records of Bury St. Edmunds. At the end of the eleventh century, less than one-tenth of St. Edmund's freemen and sokemen bore Scandinavian names, and about nine-tenths of them bore English names, such as Ædric, Cenric, Godman, or Æluric Halleman; but by the end of the twelfth century something between one-half and three-quarters of their descendants bore names that had been introduced by the Normans: William, Robert, Henry and the like.[4] Remarkable

---

[1] J. R. West, *St. Benet of Holme, 1020–1210* (Norf. Rec. Soc., nos. ii and iii. 1932), pp. 258–9, and D. C. Douglas, *Feudal Documents from the Abbey of Bury St. Edmunds* (1932), p. cxx. In the case of St. Benet of Holme, 75% of the twelfth-century names were of post-Norman origin or else neither definitely Old English or Scandinavian in origin. Of the remaining 25%, the proportion of Scandinavian to Old English names was 58:81.

[2] E. Ekwall, 'The proportion of Scandinavian settlers in the Danelaw', *Saga Book of the Viking Society*, xii. 22.

[3] *Liber Eliensis*, ed. D. J. Stewart (1848), pp. 128, 149.

[4] Compare the lists in Douglas's *Feudal Documents*, pp. 25–44, with those in *The Kalendar of Abbot Samson*, pp. 1–72. See also the list of religious said

as the Normans were, they had not bred a new race of Suffolk peasantry; they had simply started a new fashion in names.

We may turn, then, to the fourth proposition, which is more serious, the evidence of place-names. This evidence cannot be assessed in detail until the English Place Name Society's surveys of Norfolk and Suffolk are complete, but the more general surveys of Skeat and Ekwall are not likely to need serious revision.[1] The general outline that they have established is that while in Suffolk only about 6% of the village names have Scandinavian elements, in Norfolk the proportion is higher. Even Norfolk, however, has a far smaller and weaker Scandinavian element in its place-names than counties such as Lincolnshire and Yorkshire; for the total number of Scandinavian names is smaller in Norfolk than in those two counties, and most of them are not of pure Scandinavian type, but are *thorpes* or Anglo-Danish hybrids. Both the addition of *thorpe* to an English place-name (e.g. *Shouldham Thorpe*) and the creation of hybrid place-names (e.g. *Grimston*) are characteristic of districts where Scandinavian settlement was not intense.

> They point (writes Sir Frank Stenton) to a state of society in which the immigrants from the North formed a minority of the population, dominant, but too small to impress a purely Scandinavian character on the names given to estates.[2]

But in one district, the Broadland, the situation is different. There, especially in the two hundreds of Flegg, there is a concentration of villages with names of the purest Scandinavian type— Ashby, Oby, Billockby, Clippesby, Stokesby, Herringby, Thrigby, Filby, Ormesby, Hemsby and Rollesby—and a considerable number of Scandinavian field-names. In this district, therefore, there would seem to have been a Scandinavian settlement of some intensity. But that settlement need not necessarily

by Hermann to have been attendant on St. Edmund's shrine *c.* 925–39: Leofric the deacon, Leofric the priest, Alfric the priest, Bomfild the priest, Kenelm the deacon, Eilmund the priest, and Adulf, later bishop of Elmham (*Memorials of St. Edmund's Abbey*, ed. T. Arnold, Rolls Series, i. 30).

[1] W. W. Skeat, *The place-names of Suffolk* (Camb. Antiq. Soc. 1913); E. Ekwall in *Introduction to the Survey of English Place Names* (Place Name Soc., vol. i, pt. i, pp. 81–2), and in H. C. Darby, *An Historical Geography of England before 1800 A.D.* (1948), p. 151.

[2] F. M. Stenton, 'The Scandinavian Colonies in England and Normandy', *Trans. Roy. Hist. Soc.*, 4th series, xxvii (1945), 10.

have been made in the ninth century or by the Danish soldiers of the rank and file. Indeed the Broadland, with its great extent of marsh, is not a district in which we would have expected the Danish army to settle when it first took possession of East Anglia, for, as Professor Ekwall put it, 'the victorious army', coming as it did from Cirencester, 'would not march right through Norfolk and settle on the lower Waveney'.[1] An even greater difficulty is that the Chronicle would give us to understand that the main Danish bases in East Anglia were not in Norfolk but at Cambridge and somewhere in the region of Colchester. Danish ships were to be found at the mouth of the Stour,[2] Harwich (though a name of English formation) means 'army-dwelling' and may have been a Danish camp,[3] and Guthrum, according to the Annals of St. Neots, was buried at Hadleigh in Suffolk, ten miles from Ipswich and twelve from Colchester.[4] Just as the fall of Huntingdon led to the submission of the Danish army at Cambridge, so the fall of Colchester led to the submission of the Danish army in East Anglia—a natural occurrence if the Danish base was in that region, but most unnatural and inexplicable if it was more than fifty miles away in the Broadland.

In consequence, Professor Ekwall has suggested two alternative theories to explain the place-names of the Broadland. The first is that though the place-names denote a Scandinavian settlement, the settlement was not made by the Danish army but by 'a later influx of Scandinavian settlers who might have been induced to come over after the conquest had been made by the army'. The second, not necessarily incompatible with the first, is based on the theory, confirmed by the archaeology of the area, that the low-lying parts of the Broadland were 'probably not much inhabited before Scandinavian times'.[5] Elsewhere in Norfolk, if Danes became lords of

---

[1] *Introduction to the Survey of English Place Names* (Place Name Soc., 1924), p. 82.   [2] *Chronicle, s.a.* 885.

[3] P. H. Reaney, *The Place Names of Essex* (P.N.S., 1935), p. 339.

[4] *Asser's Life of King Alfred*, ed. W. H. Stevenson (1904), p. 140.

[5] Ekwall in *Introduction to the Survey of English Place Names*, pp. 81–2. The villages with the highest land in two hundreds of Flegg have English names, Caister, Winterton, Somerton and Martham. Except at Caister and Yarmouth, there is no evidence of pre-Scandinavian settlements in these two hundreds. See *Victoria County History, Norfolk*, vol. i, and Rainbird Clarke, 'Norfolk in the Dark Ages, 400–800 A.D.', *Norfolk and Norwich Archaeological Soc.*, xxvii (1939–40), 163–249.

existing villages, the English villagers would not change the name of their village; but if a Scandinavian lord reclaimed land and made a village where previously there was none, it might well have become known as his *by*. The *by* names of this region (with the single exception of Stokesby) are compounded with Scandinavian personal names which would seem to refer, not to peasants, but to the lords or owners of the villages. There is no reason why the villagers themselves should not have been English. But whatever be the explanation of these place-names, it must be remembered that according to their evidence the Broadland is the part of East Anglia where Scandinavian influence is strongest.

It is this fact that the fifth of our propositions attempts to explain, for Miss Barbara Dodwell has pointed out that it is in this very area, and especially in the two hundreds of Flegg, that one of the greatest concentrations of free peasantry is to be found. She has therefore concluded that

> the exceptionally large number of free peasants, *liberi homines* and sokemen, recorded in the Domesday Surveys of Norfolk and Suffolk, and the peculiarities of their distribution, . . . are most easily understood when regarded as the result of Scandinavian influence.[1]

It is not altogether certain, however, that her statistics and distribution-map of the Domesday free peasantry do really support such a conclusion. They show that while the proportion of free peasantry varied immensely from hundred to hundred (from 87% of the population in Parham half-hundred to 12·9% in Lackford Hundred), the free peasantry was mainly concentrated in two districts. If the hundreds in which half or more than half of the peasantry was free are plotted on a map, it will be seen that they form two compact blocks, one in east Norfolk, based on the Broadland, and the other stretching diagonally across Suffolk from Sutton Hoo to Thetford. Unfortunately Scandinavian influence cannot explain the preponderance of free peasantry in both these areas at once. For if Scandinavian place-names are prominent in the Broadland, they are very far from being prominent in Suffolk. To make matters worse, it cannot even be claimed that just as Suffolk is less Scandinavian, so its free peasantry is less numerous, for it is the contrary that is true; in Suffolk the free peasantry

[1] Dodwell, *art. cit.*, p. 155.

formed a higher proportion of the population than in Norfolk (45·4% as against 41·4%), and the only two East Anglian hundreds in which the proportion of free peasantry was over 80% were both in Suffolk (Parham and Wilford hundreds).

An even more serious difficulty is that there is documentary evidence to show that there was already an English free peasantry in East Anglia before the year 890. In Alfred and Guthrum's treaty (which is assumed to be genuine) it is stated (clause 2), that the 'ceorl who sits on *gafolland*' is to have the same wergeld of two hundred shillings as the Danes' freedman (*liesing*).[1] The context makes it clear that this ceorl was both English and to be found in Guthrum's East Anglian kingdom, and all scholars are now agreed that the ceorl was a freeman. The difficulty lies in the meaning of *gafolland*, whether it meant (as Vinogradoff claimed) land that the ceorl held in his own right but under tribute to the king, or whether it meant (as Liebermann and Stenton have claimed) land which had been 'taken at rent from a lord'.[2]

Fortunately, the evidence derived from the Kalendar of Abbot Samson of Bury St. Edmunds enables us to see how both interpretations could be right. For the Kalendar sets out in detail the financial dues paid by the tenants of socage land and shows how they look like rents and are paid as rents, although they are in origin regalian rights or the tribute due to the king. Moreover, the details of the payments reveal the surprising fact that tenure by socage in Suffolk had its nearest parallel with tenure by gavelkind in Kent. In both cases the tenure was free and the inheritance partible; in both cases the most prominent money-payment, whether called *hidage* or *gafol*, was paid, not to the lord of a manor, but to the lord of the hundred or lathe, and was calculated at the rate of a penny an acre; and in both cases carriage-service and an occasional boon-work were due at the central estate of the lord of the hundred or lathe. With a parallel so close between tenure by socage and gavelkind, it is surely legitimate to argue that socage land and *gafolland* might be parallel terms also, and that the 'ceorl who sits on *gafolland*' was the equivalent of the free peasant who in the Domesday Survey is known as a freeman or sokeman.[3]

[1] F. Liebermann, *Die Gesetze der Angelsachsen* (Halle, 1916), i. 126.
[2] Stenton, *Anglo-Saxon England*, p. 259, n. 1, and Vinogradoff, *The Growth of the Manor* (1905), pp. 132 and 240–1, and Liebermann, iii. 83.
[3] *The Kalendar of Abbot Samson*, pp. xli–xlvii.

The whole tenor of Alfred and Guthrum's treaty supports such a conclusion, for it divides the society of East Anglia into two main classes. The lower class, with a wergeld of 200 shillings, consisted, as we have already stated, of the ceorl who sits on *gafolland* and the Danes' freedman (*liesing*). The upper class is not described in detail; the treaty simply states that 'if a man is slain, whether he is an Englishman or a Dane, all of us shall place the same value on his life—namely 8 half-marks of pure gold'. Sir Frank Stenton considers that this class 'included not only Danish and English nobles but also Danish settlers of peasant rank and English ceorls farming their own land',[1] but it is hard to see why in the case of the English, no less than in that of the Danes, the peasant-farmer should of a sudden have been given the same wergeld as a nobleman; and it is still harder to see why an East Anglian ceorl should have been rated six times as high as his equal in Wessex. It is surely better to accept the more straightforward interpretation that the two classes of society mentioned in the treaty were what would have been known as the *twihynde* and the *twelfhynde*. The West Saxon ceorl was *twihynde* or worth 200 shillings, like the ceorl who sits on *gafolland* or the Danes' freedman of the treaty. The West Saxon 'nobleman' was *twelfhynde* or worth 1,200 shillings, which was (in Chadwick's opinion) the sum which the eight half-marks of pure gold of the treaty represented.[2] The only ground on which this simple explanation has hitherto been rejected has been that it conflicts with the belief that the great mass of Danes who settled in East Anglia were of peasant status. If that belief is set aside as unproven, it is easy to see why the ceorl who sits on *gafolland* was equated with the Danes' freedman (*liesing*).[3] For if all the Danes were given the status of nobility, it is reasonable to suppose that they had nobles' estates, as large as five hides, for example, in which case their freedmen (*liesing*) would have represented the only class on the Danish side that looked like peasants.

Alfred and Guthrum's treaty, therefore, shows not only that there was an English free peasantry in East Anglia before 890, but

---

[1] Stenton, *Anglo-Saxon England*, p. 259.

[2] H. M. Chadwick, *Studies on Anglo-Saxon Institutions* (1905), p. 50.

[3] 'By the northern law the touch of oar or sail conferred freedom so that every *thrall* who crossed the sea into England by so doing became a *leysing*' (or freedman), (E. W. Robertson, *Scotland under her Early Kings*, ii. 281).

also that the only peasants of equivalent standing that the Danes possessed were their freedmen. It would follow that, so far as East Anglia was concerned, the theory of the Danish soldiers of the rank and file humbly taking a peasant holding in the years of peace is incorrect. This conclusion need not surprise us. It is not out of harmony with the evidence of the Anglo-Saxon Chronicle, the tenemental system, the personal names or the place-names. It is not even out of harmony with the peculiar geographical distribution of the free peasantry in 1086, which is not really so puzzling as it might at first sight have seemed. For the districts in which the freemen and sokemen formed the largest section of the population were the districts that were, in 1086, the richest.[1] This fact emerges clearly from Professor Darby's Domesday maps. For the 'free' districts of East Anglia were those in which the recorded population per square mile was highest, and in which the recorded number of plough-teams per square mile was greatest.[2] If further confirmation be needed, it can be demonstrated that even from the tax-surveyor's point of view these districts were the richest, since in them the hundreds were small in area and the incidence of geld per square mile was correspondingly heavy.[3] What has to be explained, therefore, is why it was in the richest areas that the free peasantry congregated so densely; and the explanation lies ready to hand if only it is remembered that what Domesday Book shows is not the total number of free peasants that had ever existed in East Anglia, but the number that was still left in 1086. 'Manorialization' was progressing rapidly in the eleventh century. On almost every page of Domesday there is mention of some lord who had 'added' freemen or sokemen to his manor, or who had made a manor where none existed before. This process of manorialization had made the greatest progress in the poorer districts of East Anglia—the fact can be ascertained by counting, as Miss Lees did, the number of Domesday manors with five carucates of land or more[4]—and the reason for this rapid progress need have been

[1] Could this be true not only of East Anglia, but also of England as a whole? See Maitland, *Domesday Book and Beyond*, pp. 21–2.

[2] H. C. Darby, *The Domesday Geography of Eastern England* (1952), figs. 100, 101, 102.

[3] Darby, figs. 20 and 36. In East Anglia the geld was levied in a manner that assumed that every hundred contained 100 hides, every double-hundred 200 hides, and so on.

[4] B. A. Lees in *Victoria County History, Suffolk*, i. 371–2.

nothing more involved than economic pressure; the poorer the freeman, the more likely he was to betake himself to a lord. In the richer districts the free peasants retained their freedom longer because their powers of resistance were greater.

There is therefore nothing inherently Danish about the free peasantry of East Anglia, and there is no reason to suppose that there was a systematic settlement of the Danish soldiers of the rank and file in East Anglia. Such a conclusion, though it runs counter to the belief that the peasant's freedom was necessarily imported from Scandinavia, helps to explain many general features of East Anglian history that would otherwise be inexplicable.

It explains the sharp contrast that can be drawn in many respects between East Anglia and the Northern Danelaw. In Domesday Book the contrast is so marked that it led J. H. Round to declare out of hand that while the Danes had conquered many districts, it was in the district of the five boroughs that they had settled.[1] East Anglia did not have Danish trithings or wapentakes but English hundreds; its towns did not have the twelve Danish law-men; and 'the peace given by the hand or seal of the King' was protected in East Anglia, not by a fine of 'eighteen hundreds' as in the Danish districts, but by a smaller fine of 'ten-and-a-half hundreds' as in the English districts.[2] In religion the contrast is equally striking. For Miss Whitelock has shown that East Anglia had been largely reconverted to Christianity by the end of the ninth century, a remarkable piece of anonymous missionary work if the Danish population was large, and that by the middle of the tenth century it was certainly not 'behind the rest of England in piety and zeal for the work of the Church'. But in the Northern Danelaw, even at the beginning of the eleventh century, Wulfstan still thought it necessary to legislate against heathen practices.[3]

The absence of any systematic Danish settlement in East Anglia also helps to explain its history in the tenth century. Though most of the districts that had been reconquered from the Danes seem to have been ruled, especially in Athelstan's reign, by Danish governors, East Anglia was governed by Englishmen. From 932 to 992 the ealdormanry of East Anglia was held by Athelstan

---

[1] J. H. Round, *Feudal England* (1895), pp. 71–2.

[2] *Leges Edwardi Confessoris*, c. 33 (Liebermann, i. 660).

[3] D. Whitelock, 'The Conversion of the Eastern Danelaw', *Saga Book of the Viking Society*, xii. 159–76.

'half-king' and his sons, a family that had close links with the royal house of Wessex.[1] Their East Anglian ealdormanry included Cambridgeshire, and accounts of several of the lawsuits that they heard in that county are preserved in the *Liber Eliensis*. There is no suggestion in these accounts that the courts, or the law used in them, were Danish; and the suitors are called the nobles (*proceres*) of East Anglia, or 'all the men of high birth of East Anglia' (*omnes majores natu Orientalis Angliae*).[2]

It may even be that too much significance has been attached to the statements of late-eleventh and twelfth century writers that not only East Anglia but fifteen or sixteen counties north of Watling Street and the Thames (including even Middlesex and Buckinghamshire) were in the *Denalagu* or under Danish law.[3] Sir Frank Stenton has pointed out that the statement does not necessarily imply that the majority of the population was Danish in these counties, since

> the establishment of a Danish aristocracy which controlled the course of business in the local courts would be hardly less effective than the settlement of an army in imprinting a Danish character on the law of a shire.[4]

But quite apart from this, it is by no means certain how early this district of *Denalagu* was formed. The word itself is not to be found earlier than the eleventh century, its first recorded use being in *vi Æthelred* 37 (1008),[5] and the actual district accords more closely with the area overrun by Sweyn and his Danes in 1013 than with the extent of Guthrum's kingdom in the tenth century.[6] Still more

---

[1] Stenton, *Anglo-Saxon England*, pp. 345–7.

[2] *Liber Eliensis*, pp. 123, 129.

[3] Stenton, *Anglo-Saxon England*, pp. 498–9; Steenstrup, *Normannerne*, iv. 35–39; and *Symeon Dunelmensis Opera et Collectanea* (ed. H. Hinde, Surtees Soc., vol. li, 1868), i. 221.

[4] Stenton, *Anglo-Saxon England*, p. 499.

[5] D. Whitelock, 'Wulfstan and the so-called laws of Edward and Guthrum', *E.H.R.*, lvi. 19. In this article she shows that the so-called laws of Edward and Guthrum refer, not to East Anglia in the tenth century, but to Northumbria in the eleventh. Liebermann was consequently mistaken in quoting these laws as evidence that East Anglia formed part of the Danelaw in the ninth century.

[6] William of Malmesbury, *Gesta Regum* (Rolls Series), i. 188: 'cum numerentur in Anglia triginta duo pagi, illi jam sedecim invaserant'. Cf.

important are the facts that in King Cnut's second legal code (*c.*
1018–23) East Anglia is specifically distinguished from the Danish
districts (*mid Denum*), and that even in 1086 the *maior emendatio
forisfacture* was not the same in East Anglia as in the Northern
Danelaw.[1] It would consequently seem possible that the extension
of the *Denalagu* to fifteen counties was, as Chadwick suggested,
part of 'some artificial redistribution of the country' made in the
eleventh century.[2] Such an administrative reform could most easily
be understood if it had taken place in the reign of King Cnut.
Indeed it would seem that many misconceptions about the Danelaw could be due to the difficulty of distinguishing between
Danish innovations of the ninth and eleventh centuries. Sir Frank
Stenton has shown that it was in the eleventh century, and probably in Cnut's reign, that the Northern Danelaw was first assessed
for taxation by the division of the land into (Danish) carucates
grouped in duodecimal units;[3] and an administrative reform that
brought East Anglia into a district known as *Denalagu* might well
have been made at the same time, especially since it was a period
during which the earl of East Anglia was himself Danish, Thorkell
the Tall.

It is clear, however, that no matter when East Anglia may first
have been considered as part of the Danelaw, its law was not influenced by Danish custom to anything like the same extent as
that of the Northern Danelaw. Indeed the two areas stand in contrast to each other not only in law, but also in religion, administration and the extent of Danish place-names; and the only rational
explanation of the contrast is that the Danish settlement of East
Anglia was less intense than that of the Northern Danelaw. That
it had some sort of a Danish aristocracy we know, for quite apart
from the evidence of place-names it is categorically stated that

Anglo-Saxon Chronicle (E), *s.a.* 1013. According to Alfred and Guthrum's
treaty, on the other hand, Middlesex would not have been in Guthrum's
kingdom.

[1] ii Cnut, 71, 2 and 3 (for the date of which, see Whitelock in *E.H.R.*,
lxiii. 433–52). For the *major emendatio forisfacture*, see, besides Domesday
Book, the so-called *Leges Edwardi Confessoris*, c. 33.

[2] Chadwick, *Anglo-Saxon Institutions*, pp. 198–201.

[3] Stenton, *Types of Manorial Structure in the Northern Danelaw* (Oxford
Studies in Social and Legal History, ii, 1910), pp. 87–90. A similar conclusion is reached by Reginald Lennard in 'The Origin of the Fiscal Carucate', *Economic Hist. Rev.*, xiv (1944–5), 51–63.

Archbishop Oda was the son of one of the Danes who came over with Hinguar and Hubba.[1] But that it had a Danish peasantry, from which were descended the freemen and sokemen who in 1086 formed more than 40% of the rural population, we cannot believe. For if these freemen and sokemen were Danish, East Anglia should, in law, religion, administration and place-names, have been not less Danish but more Danish than any other county except Lincolnshire.

The weight of the evidence is therefore against the theory of a settlement of East Anglia by the Danish soldiers of the rank and file. The evidence of the Alderman Æthelweard, Cnut's second legal code, Domesday Book, and the *Liber Eliensis* all militate against it, while the evidence of Alfred and Guthrum's treaty would seem to be decisive. That treaty provides the only direct evidence extant for the state of East Anglian society during the Danish occupation. If, as is here claimed, it shows that the free peasantry of East Anglia had its origin, not in, but before the Danish invasions of the ninth century, it will be necessary to re-open the whole question of the origins of free socage. For the free peasantry of East Anglia—that is to say of the two counties of Norfolk and Suffolk alone—formed approximately one half of the total number of freemen and sokemen recorded for the whole of Domesday England. What in fact their origin was, we cannot yet pretend to say, but we must at least, as Maitland put it, 'be careful how we use our Dane'.

[1] *Vita Sancti Oswaldi* (written at Ramsey, *c.* 995–1005) in *Historians of the Church of York*, ed. J. Raine, Rolls Series, i. 404. Hinguar and Hubba were, according to Abbo of Fleury, the Danes who attacked East Anglia in 869 (*Memorials of St. Edmund's Abbey*, ed. Arnold, i. 8).

Postscript

This article, published in 1955 was followed rapidly by P.H. Sawyer 'The density of Danish settlement in England', *University of Birmingham Historical Journal* vi, 1958, 1-17, who argued forcefully that the size of the Danish armies was small and that consequently the density of Danish settlement must have been much smaller than had been imagined. He maintained this position also in *The Age of the Vikings* (London, 1962), but in its second edition (1970) suggested that a greater degree of Danish settlement occurred after the military victory which enabled further Danes to come to England and buy land. Articles which have in one form or another shown scepticism about the extent or depth of Danish influence in England are J.M. Kaye 'The Sacrabar', *EHR* 83 (1968) 744-58, Barrie Cox, 'Rutland and the Scandinavian settlements: the place-name evidence' and R.A. Hall, 'The Five Boroughs of the English Danelaw' in *Anglo-Saxon England* 18 (Cambridge, 1989) 135-48 and 149-206. The fact that the Norfolk Broads have now been shown to be the result of peat-workings which were not flooded till the second half of the thirteenth century (J.M. Lambert *et al*, *The Making of the Norfolk Broads: a Reconsideration of their origins in the light of new evidence* (London, 1960) does nothing to make it look more probable that the Scandinavian place-names surrounding them could have formed a ninth-century base of the Danish army or fleet.

Though general opinion has been slow to move on this subject, I believe that the negative argument against the extravagant claims made for Danish influence in East Anglia is unanswerable, but unfortunately I did not pursue its positive implications. In the Introduction to *The Kalendar of Abbot Samson of Bury St Edmunds* (Camden third series cxxxiv, London, 1954) pp. xlv-xlvi I had pointed out that the East Anglian socage dues were very similar to 'the services due to the "shires" of Northumberland, the principalities of Wales and the lathes of Kent', so that they might be 'general for at least a half of pre-Danish England', but in my ignorance I did not pursue the matter further. Fortunately there were others working independently on the matter. In Wales Glanville R. Jones in a series of articles including 'The pattern of settlement on the Welsh border' (*Agricultural Hist Rev* viii (1960) 66-81), 'Settlement patterns in Anglo-Saxon England' (*Antiquity* xxxv (1961) 174-81) and 'The portrayal of land settlement in Domesday Book' (*Domesday Studies*, ed J.C. Holt (Royal Hist Soc 1987), 183-200) has shown that 'multiple' or 'discrete' estates are found in southern England as well as in Wales and date 'from at least Celtic times'. G.W.S. Barrow in a series of articles including 'Northern English Society in the Middle Ages' (*Northern History* iv (1969) 1-28) and 'Pre-Feudal Scotland: shires and thanes' in his *The Kingdom of the Scots* (London, 1973) 7-68, has made new discoveries which have enabled him to draw all the threads together: 'On the one hand, the shires of Northumbria are the counterparts of the cantreds or commotes of Wales. On the other hand, they are also the counterpart of the lathes of Kent, the sokes and half-vanished "shires" of West Wessex, East Anglia and the Five Boroughs' (p. 57). He believes that their origin goes back to the sixth century at least, and that since they are to be found among the British Celts as well as the Anglo-Saxons, it is at least possible that they were taken over from the former by the latter.

Anne K.G. Kristensen, in 'Danelaw Institutions and Danish Institutions in the Viking Age: *Sochemanni, Liberi Homines* and *Königsfreie*' (*Medieval Scandinavia* 8 (1975), 27-85) goes one further by pointing out that in the early medieval period institutions comparable to those of East Anglia, Kent, Wales and Northumbria can be found in most parts of Western Europe, where the *centena* can be equated with the hundred, soke or Northumbrian 'shire', and the *Königsfreie* with *liberi homines* or sokemen. *Königsfreie* are 'soldier colonists whose freedom has been conferred upon them or their forbears at some particular moment and who in return were obliged to provide special services and pay special dues'. They were similar to the late Roman *laeti* and were much used by Longobard and Frankish kings who recruited them from prisoners of war or conquered peoples. The point is fairly made but must not be pressed too far. Britain was not unique, but it would be a mistake to insist that because its institutions could be paralleled in most parts of Western Europe, they were therefore identical.

3

Alfred the Great: Propaganda and Truth

IN CELEBRATING the eleventh centenary of King Alfred's accession in 871, it is perhaps best to start from the point which everyone knows, the story of the cakes. It is no more than a legend, and there is no secure evidence for its existence before the Norman Conquest, but as found in the Annals of St. Neot's, which probably date from early in the twelfth century, it reads as follows:

> It happened one day that a certain peasant woman, wife of a certain cowherd was making loaves (*panes*), and this king [Alfred] was sitting by the fire, preparing his bow and arrows and other instruments of war. But when the wretched woman saw that the loaves which she had put on the fire were burning, she ran up and took them off, scolding the invincible king and saying: 'Look man, you see the loaves burning but you are not turning them, though I'm sure you'd be charmed to eat them warm!' The miserable woman little thought that he was King Alfred who had waged so many wars against the pagans and won so many victories over them.[1]

The point of the story was not that Alfred was preoccupied with military affairs, but to demonstrate the straits to which the great king had been reduced, for St. Neot was said to have foretold that Alfred would suffer a great disaster as divine retribution for his refusal to relieve his subjects of oppressive burdens at the beginning of his reign. It falls into a general class of tales found in saints' lives, and would doubtless have remained nothing more than a hagiographical curiosity, if it had not been for the fact that in 1574 Archbishop Parker interpolated it into his edition of Asser's Life of King Alfred. From then on the picture of the fugitive king has dominated the historical imagination to such an extent that we may not be free of it yet.

Putting legend on one side and turning to fact, King Alfred's reign presents the historian with an interesting problem, since he is confronted with the possibility that almost all the sources may have originated with either Alfred himself or his immediate entourage. Those explicitly stated to have been written by him are the preface to his laws, the laws themselves, and the autobiographical comments and reminiscences inserted in his translations of

---

[1] W. H. Stevenson, *Asser's Life of King Alfred* (Oxford, 1904), pp. 41–2 and 256–61. The Annals are in Latin and make the woman speak in verse:

> Heus homo
> Urere, quos cernis, panes gyrare morare
> Cum nimium gaudes hos manducare calentes

This may be an indication that the story developed out of an Anglo-Saxon saga, but that does not necessarily give it any great antiquity. See C. E. Wright, *The Cultivation of Saga in Anglo-Saxon England* (Edinburgh, 1939), pp. 34–6.

Orosius, Pope Gregory the Great and others. More problematical is the Anglo-Saxon Chronicle's account of the reign, which some scholars claim, and others disclaim, as the king's own work. As for Asser's Life of King Alfred, it is still an open question whether it is genuine or not;[2] but if genuine it was written by the king's own mass-priest, who took the Anglo-Saxon Chronicle as the basis of his narrative and dedicated it to none other than his lord King Alfred. In these circumstances it is perhaps not surprising that we find no criticism of the king but only adulation. The composite picture given by the sources, if accepted at face value, is of a man who overcame the most frightful physical disabilities to become an outstanding war-leader, a sincere christian, an upholder of the Church, a naval architect, an inspired educationalist and an earnest and painstaking scholar. It reads almost like the school report which every schoolboy would like to write about himself, and challenges us to re-examine where our information about Alfred really comes from.

We must therefore turn to the Anglo-Saxon Chronicle and examine it critically in order to test its objectivity. In this connection one of the most dramatic annals for Alfred's reign is particularly revealing. It is for the year 878, and in Professor Whitelock's translation starts as follows:

> In this year in midwinter after twelfth night the enemy army came stealthily to Chippenham, and occupied the land of the West Saxons, and settled there and drove a great part of the people across the sea, and conquered most of the others; and the people submitted to them, except King Alfred. He journeyed in difficulties through the woods and fen-fastnesses with a small force.[3]

Most recent authorities have understood this passage to mean that the Danes had (in Sir Frank Stenton's words) 'received the submission of a large part of the West Saxon people',[4] but all have found it difficult to determine exactly how large that part was. Wessex consisted, if we exclude its more recent extensions, of the six shires of Devon, Somerset, Dorset, Hampshire, Wiltshire and Berkshire. Of these we know that Devon was not occupied since the Chronicle in its very next sentence tells us:

> And the same winter the brother of Ivar and Healfdene was in the kingdom of the West Saxons in Devon with 23 ships. And he was killed there and 840 of his men with him. And there was captured the banner which they called 'Raven'.

It would be simplest then to assume that the Danes had occupied all, or most of the other five shires, having started their campaign from Gloucester in Mercia and having passed through Chippenham to the south coast, thus driving 'a great part of the people over the sea'. But though this inter-

---

[2] See V. H. Galbraith, 'Who wrote Asser's Life of Alfred?' in his *Introduction to the Study of History* (London, 1964), pp. 88–128, and Dorothy Whitelock, *The Genuine Asser* (University of Reading, 1968).

[3] This and subsequent quotations from the Chronicle are from *The Anglo-Saxon Chronicle: a revised translation*, ed. Dorothy Whitelock with David C. Douglas and Susie I. Tucker (London, 1961). (This translation by Professor Whitelock was originally published in the first two volumes of *English Historical Documents* (1955 and 1954).)

[4] F. M. Stenton, *Anglo-Saxon England* (3rd ed., Oxford, 1971), p. 255.

pretation may at first seem obvious, it has difficulties which emerge as the story continues:

And afterwards at Easter, King Alfred with a small force made a stronghold at Athelney, and he and the section of the people of Somerset which was nearest to it proceeded to fight against the enemy. Then in the seventh week after Easter he rode to 'Egbert's stone' east of Selwood, and there came to meet him all the people of Somerset and of Wiltshire and of that part of Hampshire which was on this side of the sea, and they rejoiced to see him. And then after one night he went from that encampment to Iley, and after another night to Edington, and there fought against the whole army and put it to flight. . . .

So far as the place-names are concerned, 'Egbert's stone' is unidentified but is generally thought to have been near Penselwood or Stourton on the borders of Wiltshire, Dorset and Somerset. Iley has been identified as Iley Oak in Warminster some thirteen miles from Stourton, and only eight miles from Edington in Wiltshire.[5] But the real problem is how the military manœuvre was executed. The term 'all the men' of a shire is used in the Chronicle as a technical term to denote the army or shire-levy under the command of its ealdorman, but it would be fanciful to suggest that the armies of three shires just happened to be exercising themselves at 'Egbert's stone' when Alfred arrived there. They must surely have received orders in advance; that, presumably is why the date ('the seventh week after Easter') is recalled as well as the meeting place. But in that case it is difficult to see what there can have been in the way of an enemy occupation, since nothing was done to prevent the ealdormen of these shires from receiving orders from the king, levying their armies, and converging from three different directions on a spot near the centre of the kingdom. The impression given by the Chronicle is that the dangerous time, when speed was essential, was *after* the armies had united at 'Egbert's stone', since we are expressly told that they reached Iley in one day and Edington on the next, there joining battle with the whole Danish army (*alna pone here*) as if in a surprise attack; and it was surely because they understood this that both 'Asser' and Æthelweard said that the Danes had been wintering at Chippenham.[6]

We therefore turn back to the beginning of the Chronicle's annal to see if we could have mistaken its meaning. There is a certain amount of difficulty in the translation, particularly of the verb *geridan*. In its simplest sense it means 'to ride', as when in this very annal Alfred *gerad* to 'Egbert's stone', but it can also mean to 'ride over', 'obtain by riding' or 'take possession of', and unfortunately there is no sure way of determining which sense is intended when the Chronicle says that the Danes *geridon Wesseaxna lond* . . . and drove a great part of the people across the sea and *geridon* most of the others; the meaning could be either that the Danes harried the land and its people or that they took possession of them. By a curious coincidence there is a further ambiguity in the word *gesæton* since it could mean 'settled' either in the sense of staying there or in the sense of taking possession of a place

[5] The best discussion of the place-names is in Stevenson's *Asser*, pp. 267–78.
[6] *Asser*, p. 40 (ch. 52); *The Chronicle of Æthelweard*, ed. A. Campbell (Nelson's Medieval Texts) (London, 1962), p. 42.

which had been conquered, while the syntax leaves it an open question whether the place which was settled was 'land of the West Saxons' (there is no definite article) or just Chippenham.

To some extent all modern historians have recognized these difficulties and have shown themselves both puzzled and cautious in their accounts of the Danish offensive. Though their individual standpoints vary considerably in detail, they can be divided into those who lean more to the minimum interpretation of an occupation of Chippenham followed by raids farther afield, and those who lean more to the maximum of an occupation of a large part of the kingdom.[7] But perhaps more attention should be paid to the fact that the Chronicle is ambiguous throughout this passage, for when it tells us that 'a great part of the people was driven across the sea' it does not say which sea. Historians have assumed it was the English Channel[8]—though the winter seas or the danger of encountering Viking fleets might have made them hesitate—but if the sea in question had really been the Bristol Channel all the main difficulties about the campaign would disappear. If the Danes had advanced westward from Chippenham to the Bristol Channel, it would have been natural for Alfred to retreat, as he did, into Somerset, but it would also have been possible for the ealdormen to raise their shire-levies east of Selwood, since the occupied part of Wessex would have been no more than west Wiltshire and north Somerset, and an attack from east of Selwood would have taken the Danes in the rear.

In one sense the very simplicity of this explanation raises a problem, for it is necessary to explain how it could be that the words of the Chronicle have been so generally misunderstood. A partial explanation may be afforded by the story of the cakes which was interpolated into the account of this particular campaign and which has, as Plummer pointed out, subconsciously influenced the historical imagination more powerfully than is sometimes realized.[9] But it may also be that the words of the Chronicle are genuinely misleading. Everyone knows that the easiest way of enhancing the significance of a victory is to exaggerate the perils and dangers endured before it was won; it is a very common and natural thing to do when overcome by emotion at one's own success. But if that is what the author of the Chronicle has done, he has done it with great literary skill, for his words do not contain a single untruth but merely an invitation to wishful thinking. It is as if he had

[7] Towards the minimum, B. Thorpe in his translation of *The Anglo-Saxon Chronicle* (Rolls Series) (London, 1861), vol. ii, p. 64; C. Plummer, *The Life and Times of Alfred the Great* (Oxford, 1902), pp. 58–9 and 102; T. Hodgkin, *The Political History of England;* vol. i (1906), p. 283; B. A. Lees, *Alfred the Great* (Heroes of the Nations) (New York and London, 1919), p. 158. Towards the maximum, R. H. Hodgkin, *A History of the Anglo-Saxons* (2nd ed., Oxford, 1939) vol. ii, pp. 559–68; F. M. Stenton, *Anglo-Saxon England* (Oxford, 1943), and the translations of the Chronicle by G. N. Garmonsway (Everyman's Library) (London, 1953) and D. Whitelock (*op. cit.*). In a midway position Eleanor Duckett, *Alfred the Great* (London, 1957), pp. 70–1; H. R. Loyn, *Alfred the Great* (Clarendon Biographies) (Oxford, 1967), pp. 23–4.

[8] Æthelweard was the first to make this assumption (ed. Campbell, p. 42) but he was apparently embroidering on the Chronicle—about a century after the event. R. H. Hodgkin (*op. cit.* vol. ii, p. 565) has cited a passage from the Life of John of Gorze (d. 974) in support of a migration across the English Channel, but it is far from clear that this is the occasion to which it refers.

[9] C. Plummer, *The Life and Times of Alfred the Great*, pp. 58–9.

wanted us to understand more than he had actually said, and it is consequently a matter of some moment to discover who he could possibly have been.

The opinion which is most generally accepted about the authorship of the Chronicle is that of Sir Frank Stenton who argued that it was written not at Winchester, nor under the patronage of the king, but for an ealdorman or thegn of one of the south-western shires, preferably Somerset.[10] So far as Winchester was concerned, Stenton was surely right in insisting that the Chronicle was not written there. But, as he himself pointed out, Winchester was not the 'capital' of Wessex (the notion of any 'capital' city at that date being an anachronism) so that the fact that the Chronicle did not originate there does not necessarily mean that it could not have been written for the king. Stenton was greatly impressed by the detailed knowledge which the annalist seemed to show of the south-western shires, particularly Somerset. He recognized that an equally detailed knowledge of Berkshire and Hampshire was shown in the account of the campaign of 871, but considered that this was because the annalist 'certainly drew his information' about this campaign 'from someone who had been intimately concerned in it'. The knowledge of Somerset shown in the annal for 878 was, in his opinion, different because 'Athelney, Aller, and Wedmore, Ecgbryhtes stan and Iglea, were not, like Ashdown and Basing, the sites of battles'.[11] It is difficult to accept this reasoning, for the places concerned, though not the sites of battles, were of such moment that everyone who had taken part in the campaign would surely have remembered them. Athelney was the fortress from which Alfred had started his offensive, Ecgbryhtes stan ('Egbert's stone') was where the army assembled in circumstances of some danger, Iglea (Iley) was where it spent the night immediately before the battle of Edington, and Aller and Wedmore were the places where the victory was celebrated by the baptism and chrism-loosing of the Danish King Guthrum.

To identify the place where a chronicle was written it is not enough to search out the obscure places which it names, because famous events can easily make obscure places well known. It is more important to concentrate on the places or areas in which unimportant or trivial events are recorded. It is difficult to find any such events in the Chronicle itself, though Stenton showed that in Æthelweard's translation of it there were some additional details of campaigns in the South-West together with the names, and sometimes the burial-places, of several bishops, ealdormen or reeves.[12] What Stenton could not show was that these details were merely of local interest. Details of campaigns would be of interest to all who took part in them, while the names and even the burial places of bishops, ealdormen and reeves would

[10] F. M. Stenton, 'The South-Western Element in the Old English Chronicle' in *Essays in Medieval History presented to T. F. Tout*, ed. A. G. Little and F. M. Powicke (Manchester, 1925), pp. 15–24; reprinted in F. M. Stenton, *Preparatory to Anglo-Saxon England*, ed. D. M. Stenton (Oxford, 1970), pp. 106–115. A reply to Stenton's views is in R. H. Hodgkin, *op. cit.* vol. ii, pp. 624–8 and 706–8, but on the whole he is covering rather different ground from that covered in this article.
[11] Stenton, in *Essays to Tout*, p. 18.
[12] Stenton, *op. cit.* p. 19.

surely have been of interest both to the king who was their lord and to their fellow officials. There is no more local significance in Æthelweard's statement that Bishop Heahmund of Dorchester was buried at Keynsham than in his statement that the ealdorman Athulf was killed at Reading in 871 and buried secretly in Mercia at 'the place called *Northworthige*, but in the Danish language Derby'.[13]

For these reasons it would be a mistake to ignore the opinion of the Chronicle's most distinguished editor, Charles Plummer, who considered that the Chronicle was basically the work of Alfred himself.

> I do not mean that the actual task of compiling the Chronicle from earlier materials was necessarily performed by Alfred, though I can well fancy that he may have dictated some of the later annals which describe his own wars. But that the idea of a national Chronicle as opposed to merely local annals was his, that the idea was carried out under his direction and supervision, this I do most firmly believe.[14]

Stenton, on the other hand, refused even to accept the conception of a 'national chronicle', claiming that 'when compared with the Frankish annals of the ninth century, which seem to have descended from an official record, the Chronicle has definitely the character of a private work'.[15] It is hard to see why the comparison led him to this conclusion, which many scholars must have found surprising. With no detailed case to rebut, one can only record dissent and urge two general reasons for thinking that the Chronicle was not a private work but composed in the king's court.

First it is remarkable how the Chronicle follows the movements of the Danish armies not only in England but also on the continent, giving an overall picture which is unrivalled in the chronicles of Europe. For example:

880 ... And the same year the host which had occupied Fulham went oversea to Ghent in the land of the Franks, and remained there one year.

881 In this year the host went deeper into the land of the Franks, and the Franks fought against them, and there the host were supplied with horses after this fight.

882 In this year the host went along the Meuse far into the land of the Franks and there remained one year. ...

883 In this year the host went up the Scheldt to Condé and there remained one year.

884 In this year the host went up the Somme to Amiens and there remained one year.

885 In this year the above-mentioned host separated into two, one part east and the other to Rochester and besieged the city. ...[16]

The terse but precise statements read almost like Intelligence Reports, and it is hard to believe that they were written or compiled merely for some ealdorman or thegn of Somerset, rather than for the military headquarters of the king.

---

[13] *Æthelweard*, p. 37.
[14] C. Plummer, *Two of the Saxon Chronicles Parallel* (Oxford, 1892), vol. ii, p. civ.
[15] Stenton, *Anglo-Saxon England*, 692. For a different view see J. M. Wallace-Hadrill, 'The Franks and the English in the ninth century', in *History* vol. xxxv (1950), pp. 212–14.
[16] *The Anglo-Saxon Chronicle*, trans. G. N. Garmonsway (London, 1953), pp. 76–8.

A similar conclusion may be reached by a consideration of the extant manuscripts of the Chronicle. There are seven of them, but textually speaking they fall into four groups, all virtually identical down to 891 but then divergent. The accepted explanation of this fact is that the annals down to 891 must have been circulated to various churches such as Winchester and Abingdon,[17] where they were copied and subsequently kept up-to-date, sometimes by copying further material which was circulated, and sometimes from alternative sources of information. It is not easy to imagine this form of publication (for that is what it amounts to) being successfully organized by a South-Western ealdorman or thegn; but it is known that it was employed by King Alfred for the distribution of his translation of Gregory the Great's *Pastoral Care*. In the preface to that work he states specifically that he intended to send one copy to every see in his kingdom. (The copy sent to Worcester has survived, as also have fragments of what are apparently the master-copy, the copy sent to London, and a transcript of the one sent to Sherborne.)[18]

The preface to the *Pastoral Care* is famous for its statement of Alfred's intention of translating into English 'some books which may be most necessary for all men'. The reason for this educational drive was that the standard of learning had declined dramatically during the previous century; and Alfred claimed that whereas previously it was foreigners who came to England in search of knowledge and instruction, it was now the English who had to seek them abroad.

> So completely had learning decayed that there were very few men on this side of the Humber who could apprehend their services in English or even translate a letter from Latin into English, and I think that there were not many beyond the Humber. There were so few of them that I cannot recollect a single one south of the Thames when I succeeded to the Kingdom.[19]

For us perhaps the most interesting fact about this statement is that all modern scholars are agreed that it is an exaggeration and that it gives a misleading impression. Provided that we interpret the word 'few' loosely, it need not contain any specific untruth, but it hardly prepares us for the fact that of the seven of Alfred's literary advisers whose names are known, four came from Mercia.[20] There is every reason to believe that in that part of England a vigorous literary tradition had survived, but in this statement Alfred ignored it, with the result that the magnitude of the educational achievement of his own reign was enhanced.

The way in which the reader is misled by subtle implications in this passage, which is undoubtedly the work of King Alfred himself, is of course the same as was employed in the Chronicle account of the campaign of 878, and it is

---

[17] It is thought that the 'D' version is a Worcester transcript of a manuscript sent to a northern monastery (York or Ripon) soon after 892, but how it could have got there at that date remains a mystery.

[18] Dorothy Whitelock (ed.), *English Historical Documents, i. c. 500–1042* (London, 1955), p. 817.

[19] Trans. Whitelock, *Engl. Hist. Docs.*, vol. i, p. 819.

[20] Stenton, *Anglo-Saxon England*, pp. 270–1.

not difficult to regard it as the hallmark of a single author. But perhaps the most significant indication of Alfred's authorship of the Chronicle comes with its very first mention of him, in the annal for 853.

> And that same year King Æthelwulf sent his son Alfred to Rome. At that time lord Leo was pope in Rome and he consecrated him as King and adopted him as his spiritual son.

It is very difficult not to think that the writer wanted us to imagine that King Æthelwulf had already recognized Alfred's quality and intended him to be his heir. We are not reminded that at that date Alfred was only four years old, that he was only the fourth son, or that his three elder brothers did succeed to the throne in turn before him. On the contrary, the main effect is gained by one positive error of fact. We know from a letter of Pope Leo IV himself that he did not consecrate Alfred king but 'decorated him as a spiritual son with the dignity of the belt and the vestments of the consulate'.[21] Both Sir Frank Stenton and Professor Whitelock have considered this error to be evidence that Alfred could not have been the author of the Chronicle, believing it to be 'impossible that he himself should have mistaken the ceremony that took place at Rome when he was a child'.[22] But quite apart from the fact that a four-year-old could easily have been baffled by a ceremony which took place in a foreign land and a strange language, it is surely obvious that Alfred stood to gain by the mis-statement. It is fatally easy to imagine that his accession to the throne of Wessex was inevitable, and to forget that one of his elder brothers had a son who, when Alfred died, was prepared to ally even with the Danes in an attempt to win the kingdom which he thought was his rightful inheritance. The notion that Alfred was predestined to rule Wessex because he had been consecrated by the pope must surely have been convenient to Alfred, and it would have been only human if, over the course of the years, he had come to believe it as true.

It is perhaps significant that the Chronicle tells us very little about Alfred's elder brothers. After the third of them, Ethelred, had succeeded to the throne the information becomes somewhat less sparse, but we are not told anything about King Ethelred alone; it is always 'King Ethelred and his brother Alfred'. After Alfred himself had become king (871) we hear little of anyone else. Till near the end of 893 we are allowed to imagine that Alfred commanded the English in every engagement against the Danes whether on land or sea. It is only from Æthelweard that we discover that at the beginning of 893 one army was commanded by his son Edward or—and this is really surprising—that in 878 Alfred was not the only commander to remain in the field after the loss of Chippenham, since 'Æthelnoth the ealdorman of Somerset also lurked in a certain wood with a small force' and was responsible with Alfred for the fortification of Athelney.[23]

---

[21] Whitelock, *Engl. Hist. Docs.*, vol. i, p. 810; Stevenson's *Asser*, pp. 180–5.
[22] Stenton, *Anglo-Saxon England*, p. 692; Whitelock, *Engl. Hist. Docs.* vol. i, p. 125.
[23] *Æthelweard*, pp. 49, 42.

In face of all this evidence it seems impossible to deny that the Chronicle was most intimately connected with King Alfred; and since Anglo-Saxon scholars have repeatedly commented on the strong resemblance between its phraseology and that of King Alfred's translation of Orosius,[24] there seems to be no difficulty in believing that in a general sense he wrote it. This was the general opinion of all scholars before 1925, and we will do well to accept it now. But if we do so we have to admit an important consequence. If the Chronicle's account of Alfred's reign was written under the direction of the king, it follows that almost all our direct sources of information about the reign come from Alfred or his immediate entourage. Those that were not written by him were written for him. It is pointless to try and control the Chronicle's bias by reference to Asser, for while the Chronicle tells us what Alfred wanted us to know, Asser (if genuine) merely tells us what Alfred wanted to hear. Somehow or other we must try to liberate ourselves from the Alfredian sources, so that we can see him, not as he wanted us to see him, but as he really was.

Perhaps the most objective point of departure is the nature of the Danish military threat, for this was seen and described not only by King Alfred but also by several chroniclers in Europe. From them it is clear that the main reason for the success of the Danes was the speed with which their armies could move and switch the direction of their attack not only from one part of the country to another but also (as we have seen) from England to the continent and back again. Their fleets could move faster than any land-army, and when their warriors disembarked they seized horses and rode over the country without the encumbrance of infantry or baggage-train, looting wherever possible, and riding away whenever threatened by superior forces. It was almost impossible to bring them to battle. If an army was raised against them in the east they turned west, and if in the north, south. If the whole country seemed to be in arms against them they would take their ships to some other land until the troops had returned home and left the country defenceless again. It was therefore evident that unless the Vikings could be deprived of their mobility, the defence would always be in a hopeless position. It was generally recognized that in theory the best way of impeding their movement would be to build a fleet capable of defeating them at sea, while an alternative or additional method would be to obstruct the navigation of rivers with fortified bridges and towns. But for most rulers both methods proved too difficult in practice. Even if a king had the means to build a fleet, he would have great difficulty in protecting it from the Danish fleets before it was ready for battle; and though one Frankish King gave orders for the construction of suitable fortresses and fortified towns, he had not got the resources to make the system complete. It was not just a question of intelligence and skill, but of willpower and manpower. There was a limit to the amount that any king could persuade or force his subjects to do, and

---

[24] A list of parallels is given in Plummer's edition of the Chronicle, vol. ii, pp. cvi-cvii. For a more cautious view, see D. Whitelock, 'The Prose of Alfred's reign', in *Continuations and Beginnings*, ed. E. G. Stanley (London, 1966), pp. 96-7.

most kings found that they simply could not construct and co-ordinate defences on the scale required against the Danes.

But Alfred did it. That is the astounding fact about him. The Chronicle has references to his naval force from 875, and though it may have tried to exaggerate the personal contribution of the king, who is said to have designed an entirely new type of warship 'swifter, steadier and also higher than the others', it seems indisputable that a fleet of some sort was in existence.[25] We have no indication of how the manpower and finance were found for the building and manning of the ships, and we can only guess that there may have been some such system as existed a century later whereby groups of three 'hundreds' (subdivisions of a shire bearing a notional tax-assessment of 100 hides each) were reckoned as 'ship sokes' responsible for one ship each.[26]

We have better information about the building and manning of the fortresses or *burhs*, since in addition to the incidental reference in the Chronicle for 892 and 893, we have the 'Burghal Hidage' which dates from within twenty years of Alfred's death. It consists of a list of 29 *burhs* (several of them towns of some importance) with the number of hides belonging to them—a hide being a taxable unit of land, often about 120 acres in size. It goes on to say that 'for the maintenance and defence of an acre's breadth (22 yds) of wall, 16 hides are required', and explains that 'if every hide is represented by one man, then every pole (5½ yds) of wall can be manned by four men'.[27] From the figures which it gives it is possible to calculate the length of the walls surrounding particular *burhs*, and wherever these can be checked with the sites which survive the results prove reasonably accurate; at Winchester, for example, the calculation gives 3280 yds as against 3300 yds for the existing line of the medieval walls. What is truly astounding is the scale on which the whole venture was planned, for the sum total of all the garrisons required was 27,671 men, and this at a time when most historians would guess that the total population of Wessex could not have been much more than half a million. When one has made allowance for women and children, one wonders how there can have been any men left for the mobile army, let alone the fleet, and one would be tempted to discredit the figures as wishful thinking, were it not for the fact that the measurements of the surviving *burhs* confirm them. The burghal ramparts still surround the towns of Cricklade, Wallingford and Wareham, and anyone who sees them cannot but be astonished at the scale on which they were laid out. At Crick-

---

[25] *Anglo-Saxon Chronicle*, s.a. 896. *Cf.* 875, 877, 882 and 885.
[26] F. E. Harmer, *Anglo-Saxon Writs* (Manchester, 1952), pp. 266–7; C. Warren Hollister, *Anglo-Saxon Military Institutions* (Oxford, 1962), pp. 108–15.
[27] Printed with a translation and discussion in A. J. Robertson, *Anglo-Saxon Charters* (2nd ed., Cambridge, 1956), 246–9 and 494–6. Three further *burhs* are identified by N. Brooks in *Medieval Archaeology*, vol. viii (1964), pp. 74–90. There are two opinions about whether the number of men required referred to the building or garrisoning of the *burhs*. To me the latter is the more natural interpretation, and it is supported by the Chronicle's annal for 893 where it describes how the army was divided into two 'so that there was always half at home and half on active service, *with the exception of those men whose duty it was to man the fortresses*'. See also (1971) David Hill, 'The Burghal Hidage: the Establishment of a Text' in *Medieval Archaeology*, vol. xiii (1969), pp. 84–92.

lade it even seems that the Thames was diverted in order to improve the fortifications.[28]

A further problem of logistics arises when the mobile army is considered. If we accept the bare facts recorded by the Chronicle, the Danes were pursued in 893 from Essex to Buttington-on-Severn, and from East Anglia across the midlands to Chester, and in 895 from the River Lea to Bridgnorth. It has long been recognized that these pursuits show that by these dates the English must have had a mounted force,[29] and indeed in 895 we are specifically told that the army rode (*rad*) after the Danes. But the fact that must not be forgotten is that the organization required for such a force must have been considerable. It presumably had to be kept at the ready so as to be able to start a pursuit without delay, and it had to have enough horses, food and fodder for an expedition which might last many weeks. It is hard to believe that it could have been manned by the ordinary shire-levies, and we therefore have no alternative but to consider it as either a mercenary force or a 'select fyrd'. Whichever type of force it was, it would have cost money—we may recall the customs of Berkshire recorded in Domesday Book: 'If the King sent an army anywhere, only one soldier went from five hides, and four shillings were given him from each hide as subsistence and wages for two months.' We do not know that this was the system in Alfred's day, but it seems probable that something like it may have existed.[30]

Besides the mounted pursuit-force there was the main body of the army. At the beginning of the reign this consisted, as we have already seen, of the shire-levies under the command of their ealdormen. At the end of the reign this basic organization was probably the same, though in 893 the Chronicle informs us that 'the King had divided his army into two, so that always half its men were at home, half on service, apart from the men who guarded the boroughs'. Nowadays an arrangement such as this seems little more than common sense, but for a people who had had nothing like it before, it may well have seemed very complicated. It implied long periods of service, and since some men would have been away at harvest time, it would have been necessary to make special arrangements for getting the crops in. Considerable organization must also have been required to ensure that the system worked efficiently, so that the second half of the army was really ready to relieve the first at the correct time.

There can be no doubt that King Alfred was making very heavy demands on his subjects. Either by taxation or by personal services they had to provide a fleet, a whole system of fortified *burhs* with garrisons totalling 27,671 men, a mounted pursuit-force, and an army which mobilized in two shifts. But as if these obligations were not enough, Alfred added one more. In his preface to the *Pastoral Care* he explained his intention of having English

---

[28] The best visual impression of one of the large *burhs* is that of Wallingford, in M. W. Beresford and J. K. S. St. Joseph, *Medieval England, An Aerial Survey* (Cambridge, (1958), pp. 179–81. For Wareham, see *Medieval Archaeology*, vol. iii (1959), pp. 120–38, and for Cricklade, *Wilts. Arch. and N. H. Magazine*, vol. vi (1955), pp. 162–6.

[29] J. H. Clapham 'The Horsing of the Danes' in *E.H.R.*, vol. xxv (1910), pp. 287–93.

[30] C. Warren Hollister, *op. cit.* chs. iii and iv; Domesday Book, vol. i, f. 56v.

translations made of all those books 'which may be most necessary for all men to know', and enjoined:

> That all the youth now in England, born of free men who have the means that they can apply to it, may be devoted to learning as long as they cannot be of use in any other employment, until such time as they can read and write well what is written in English.[31]

Not a soul in the kingdom was to be idle. Those who could not serve the king in any other way had to be put to their letters.

It is, of course, because of this fact that we know as much as we do about King Alfred, but it is difficult not to speculate on his motives for devoting so much of his attention to his literary work. His own explanation is to be found in his preface to the *Pastoral Care*:

> It has very often come into my mind what wise men there were in former times throughout England, both of spiritual and lay orders; and how happy times there were throughout England; and how kings who had rule over people were obedient to God and His messengers; and how they both upheld peace and morals at home, and also extended their territory abroad; and how they prospered both in warfare and wisdom.[32]

In one sense therefore he desired the revival of learning for its own sake, and in another for the sake of victory over the Danes. But historians have not been slow to point out that most of the books which he translated had a very immediate relevance to his own times. Bede's *Ecclesiastical History of the English Nation*, for example, was about the conversion of the English to Christianity—a timely reminder for Alfred's subjects at a time when they were threatened by the heathen Danes. Pope Gregory the Great's *Pastoral Care* was a handbook for bishops, explaining their duties and how they should be fulfilled. If Alfred wanted his people to regain God's favour and be rewarded with victory, it was obviously important that the Church should be above reproach; and by circulating copies of the *Pastoral Care* to every see in the kingdom, Alfred did his best to provide his bishops with the necessary instructions. Orosius's *History against the Pagans*, on the other hand, had been written to comfort the christians after the fall of Rome in 410. Attempting to explain how it was that God had allowed the city to fall even though it had become christian, he insisted that though the present age might seem full of disasters, previous ages had been very much worse. Small comfort, perhaps, for a people beleaguered by the Danes, but none the less comfort of some sort.

What was really needed was some assurance that things might get better, for no people can survive defeat after defeat and continue fighting unless it believes that in the end it will be victorious. At a time when the East Anglians, Northumbrians and Mercians had all submitted to the Danes, and even one of King Alfred's own ealdormen deserted him,[33] it must have been a matter of life and death to persuade the West Saxons that their fate could be dif-

---

[31] *Engl. Hist. Docs.*, vol. i, p. 819.
[32] *Ibid.* p. 818.
[33] Birch, *Cartularium Saxonicum*, no. 595; trans, in *Engl. Hist. Docs.*, vol. i, p. 499.

ferent since they had reason to hope for victory. That seems to have been the purpose of the Anglo-Saxon Chronicle. It is not a survey of all Anglo-Saxon history but an account of King Alfred's ancestors, the kings of Wessex; and since it gives a minimum of information about the more unfortunate periods of West Saxon history, it is able to convey the impression that in spite of occasional reverses the house of Cerdic always emerged victorious. It was just what was needed to encourage the faint-hearted in times of defeat; and when the Battle of Edington showed that Alfred was indeed worthy of his ancestors, the fact had to be shouted from the roof-tops. It was the first genuine victory over the Danes for eighteen years, and there could surely have been no better way of spreading the news of it than by putting it in the Chronicle, which would then have been circulated to churches where, at the King's command, those youths who could not be of use in any other employment were learning to 'read and write well what was written in English'.

It would be a mistake, however, to think that the propaganda of the Chronicle was aimed solely at the glorification of King Alfred. A further and very practical purpose is suggested by some passages which read like cautionary tales for those of the King's subjects who were lax or inefficient in their duty. The least important of them is the account of a sea-battle in 896, narrated in such a way as to drive home the point that when fighting in shallow waters sailors should watch the tide. More significant, and perhaps more ominous, are two which point to the very real difficulties experienced in the organization of defence. At the beginning of 892 there is the dry comment about the fortress in the Weald which the Danes took by storm —'inside that fortification there were a few peasants (*cirlisce men*) and it was only half made'—which perhaps may be linked with Asser's account of the difficulty Alfred experienced in getting his fortresses completed on time.[34] In the following year there is a bitter passage about the English forces (those whom Æthelweard tells us were commanded by the King's son Edward) who surrounded the Danes on an island in the Colne but abandoned the siege because they had 'completed their service and used up their provisions'; it is pointed out twice that as they went home the king was actually on his way to relieve them.

If read with care, the Chronicle tells us not only of the triumphs of King Alfred but also of his difficulties. We tend to assume that in the ninth century, just because there were no democratic institutions, every king could command what he willed and be instantly obeyed; and we sometimes forget that in an age which lacked all modern forms of communication, the king would never know how strictly his orders were being followed, unless he was able to go and see for himself. Even in a kingdom as small as Wessex it was impossible for the king to oversee everything that concerned him, because he could not be everywhere at once; he had to rely on his ealdormen, bishops, reeves and thegns. The difficulty was that he could not be sure of their strict obedience—we have already mentioned that one of his ealdormen deserted

[34] *Asser*, p. 78 (ch. 91).

him—unless he could indoctrinate them with loyalty to himself and enthusiasm for his cause. That was why he needed propaganda. Alfred needed it so badly that he had much of it put into writing and circulated to the more important churches of his kingdom in a literary campaign which, though not unprecedented (for something similar had been achieved on the continent by Charlemagne) was none the less remarkable. If we are right in our contention that Alfred's greatness lay in his ability to persuade his subjects of the necessity of accepting new and burdensome institutions, then the whole secret of his success lies in how he managed to convince them. His literary and historical works tell us a great deal about that, because they were themselves a means of persuasion. If we regard them frankly as propaganda we will find them far more revealing than if accepted at face value, for they allow us to guess the immensity of the difficulties he was facing, and show him in the act of surmounting them.[35]

[35] I wish to thank Professors H. R. Loyn and G. T. Shepherd and Dr. W. Davies for much help and criticism.

Postscript

See p. 49 n. 1, below.

4

Alfred and Guthrum's Frontier

NEARLY every textbook of Anglo-Saxon history has a map showing the areas of Scandinavian settlement, featuring particularly the boundary drawn by the treaty between Kings Alfred and Guthrum. The boundary runs up the Thames; then up the Lea and along the Lea to its source; then straight to Bedford and from there up the Ouse to Watling Street.[1] On the one side was the territory of the English (*ealles Angelcynnes*), and on the other that of the people (*ðeod*) which dwelt in East Anglia. King Guthrum, as is well known from the *Anglo-Saxon Chronicle*, had had to accept baptism after his defeat by King Alfred at Edington in 878 and had settled his army in East Anglia in 880. Since the treaty places London firmly on the English side of the border, it cannot be earlier than 886, the year in which King Alfred occupied that city.[2] Nor can it be later than King Guthrum's death in 890.

It is sometimes assumed that the boundaries fixed by the treaty lasted for a considerable time, but this cannot have been the case. According to the treaty, Hertford and Bedford would have been frontier towns, the one being on the south bank of the Lea, just in English territory, and the other on the north bank of the Ouse, just in Danish territory, while Buckingham would have been safely in English territory, seven miles from the nearest point of Watling Street which is also where it crosses the Ouse. According to the *Chronicle*, these three towns were taken from the Danes only in the reign of King Alfred's successor, Edward the Elder: Hertford in 912, Buckingham in 914 and Bedford in 915. In the interim there must have been a large Danish advance, but the *Chronicle* does not record any such thing.

Though the *Chronicle* is silent, some confirmation of a change of frontier is given by a charter of King Athelstan dated 926. In it he grants Chalgrave and Tebworth (Beds.) to his faithful servant Ealdred who, according to the charter, had purchased the land from

1. The treaty is printed in F. Liebermann, *Die Gesetze der Angelsachsen* (3 vols., Halle, 1898–1916) i. 126–8 and notes iii. 82–86; and (with English translation) in F. L. Attenborough, *The Laws of the Earliest English Kings* (Cambridge, 1922, repr. New York, 1963), 98–101. There is also a translation and commentary by Dorothy Whitelock in *English Historical Documents*, i (London, 1955), no. 34.

2. Sir Frank Stenton, *Anglo-Saxon England* (3rd edn. 1971), p. 260. References to the *Chronicle* throughout this article are by annals and refer to the translation by Dorothy Whitelock in *English Historical Documents*, i (London, 1955) and (with revisions) in *The Anglo-Saxon Chronicle: a revised translation*, ed. Dorothy Whitelock with David C. Douglas and Susie I. Tucker (London, 1961).

the pagans 'at the command of King Edward [899–925] and the ealdorman Ethelred of Mercia [d. 911]'.[1] According to the Treaty, Chalgrave and Tebworth should have been in English territory, being about two miles west of a line drawn from the source of the Lea (at Sundon Park near Luton) and Bedford, but the charter implies that at some date between 899 and 911 they were Danish. An almost identical charter concerning land purchased from the Danes in Derbyshire reveals, as Sir Frank Stenton put it, 'a policy of compelling thegns under his [King Edward's] own allegiance to settle in districts still in the occupation of the Northern *here*',[2] and in the Derbyshire case the land cannot have been reconquered until King Edward advanced to the Peak District and Bakewell in 920.

There is no escaping the fact that places which, according to Alfred and Guthrum's treaty, were already English in 886/90 were, according to the *Chronicle*, being recovered from the Danes by King Edward the Elder in 912–14. Unless it can be shown that the treaty is a forgery, it must follow that the Chronicle's information is seriously deficient, since it fails to explain either how Buckingham was in English hands in 886/90, or how it had fallen to the Danes between then and 914.

The authenticity of the treaty has never been called in question. Though the original document is lost, the earliest copies occur in a manuscript of *c.*1100 (Cambridge, Corpus Christi College, MS 383) which is of good repute and apparently emanates from St Paul's Cathedral, the place where one would have expected a copy to be kept by the bishop of London, through whose diocese much of the frontier ran.[3] The language of the treaty and the styles of the two kings and their *witan* or people seem authentic, and there is nothing anachronistic in any of the clauses of the treaty. It is therefore necessary to accept its evidence and to conclude that the frontier which it established in

---

1. Translation and commentary by Dorothy Whitelock in *English Historical Documents*, i. no. 103. Full text (which is in Latin) in *Chronicon Monasterii de Abingdon*, ed. Joseph Stevenson, 2 vols. (Rolls series, 1858), i: 83–85. *Cf.* P. H. Sawyer, *Anglo-Saxon Charters: an annotated list and bibliography* (London, 1968), no. 396, and most recently, Margaret Gelling, *The early Charters of the Thames Valley* (Leicester, 1979), no. 1.

2. F. M. Stenton, *Types of Manorial Structure in the Northern Danelaw* (Oxford Studies in Social and Legal History, ed. Paul Vinogradoff, vol. ii, Oxford, 1910), p. 74. The charter itself is printed in *The Charters of Burton Abbey*, ed. P. H. Sawyer (London, 1979), no. 3. *Cf.* C. R. Hart, *The Early Charters of Northern England and the North Midlands* (Leicester, 1975), no. 101. The lands were at Hope (near Hathersage) and Ashford (near Bakewell).

3. *Corpus Christi Coll. Cambridge, MS 383.* N. R. Ker, *Catalogue of Manuscripts containing Anglo-Saxon* (Oxford, 1957), no. 65, shows that it probably belonged to St Paul's Cathedral. The bishop of London would naturally have had an interest in the treaty since it drew a frontier through part of his diocese. Bishop Theodred of London (909 × 921–955) would have had a further interest in it since he was also bishop of Suffolk. (Dorothy Whitelock, *Anglo-Saxon Wills* (Cambridge, 1930), pp. 4, 99, 102.)

886/90 had disintegrated at any rate by 911, the last possible date for Ealdred's purchase of Chalgrave and Tebworth from the pagans.

To some it may seem inconceivable that events so important as the establishment and the collapse of a frontier should not have been mentioned in the *Anglo-Saxon Chronicle*, but it seems to me, as I have argued elsewhere, that the *Chronicle* was produced under the direction of King Alfred for the specific purpose of persuading his subjects that, if they made sufficient effort, they were capable of winning victories which they had previously considered impossible.[1] Like all good propaganda, the *Chronicle* refrained from making statements which were obviously untrue, but it was prepared to pass over unwelcome facts in silence. In the present instance reticence would have been easy, because the Alfredian *Chronicle* was concerned primarily with the history of Wessex, while the frontier outlined in Alfred and Guthrum's treaty was in Mercia and could therefore belong to a different story.

Although the *Chronicle* is silent, historians have accepted Stenton's view that Alfred and Guthrum's frontier must have been 'superseded by an advance of the Danes into southern Bedfordshire and northern Buckinghamshire'.[2] Stenton placed this advance 'soon after Alfred's death', presumably because of the *Chronicle*'s statement that in 903 the army in East Anglia broke the peace and 'harried all over Mercia till they reached Cricklade' and crossed the Thames to Braydon (Wilts).

1. R. H. C. Davis, 'Alfred the Great: Propaganda and Truth', above, chapter 3, 33-46. The general theme of my argument has been questioned by Professor Dorothy Whitelock in *The Importance of the Battle of Edington, AD 878* (Edington, 1978 for 1977). She points out (p. 2) that the *Chronicle* 'did not begin to be circulated until about 890, and it gives no impression that it was compiled in haste for immediate use'. It is true that the existing manuscripts suggest a first circulation *c*.890, and that the general thrust of my argument demands an earlier circulation soon after 878. But the earlier circulation need not have been one of the complete chronicle. The version which we now have would, in my view, be what Alfred had been saying, and circulating, for years and which was now put in its final form. It is interesting to find that M. B. Parkes in 'The Paleography of the Parker manuscript of the *Chronicle*, Laws and Sedulus, and history at Winchester in the late ninth and tenth centuries' (*Anglo-Saxon England*, 5, ed. P. Clemoes (Cambridge, 1976), pp. 149–72) gives palaeographical reasons for thinking that the Parker MS was written at Winchester, and copied from exemplars which were booklets, and that two individual folios (one of them covering the period from 871 to the beginning of 878) are 'cancels' showing that the text had been revised or rewritten. Some suggestion of an early edition ending in 878 or 879 is given by Janet Bately in 'The Compilation of the Anglo-Saxon Chronicle, 66 BC to AD 890: vocabulary as evidence' (*Proc. Brit. Acad.* lxiv (1980 for 1978), 93–129) since she shows that in some respects the vocabulary for the 870s is different from that for the 880s (pp. 110, 115). She also shows (and this is her main purpose) that the vocabulary of the *Chronicle* is in some significant ways different from that found in Alfred's known works, or the *Orosius*. Naturally I accept this conclusion, but I do not think that it demolishes or weakens my argument. I had never imagined, and was careful not to suggest, that Alfred had written the *Chronicle* with his own hand or dictated it word by word. On the contrary, my assumption was, and remains, that he told his scholars what to say and left them to write it down 'sometimes word for word and sometimes meaning for meaning' in the same flexible way that he advocated in his translations.

2. Sir Frank Stenton, *Anglo-Saxon England* (3rd edn. 1971), p. 261.

But it seems likely that the frontier had already collapsed ten years previously, in the campaigns of 893, 894 and 895. In 893 we are told in general terms that the East Angles, in spite of the oaths and six preliminary hostages which they had given to King Alfred, broke their pledge and, 'as often as the other [Danish] armies went out in full force, they went either with them or on their behalf'. Certainly the main Danish armies gave them every opportunity. In 893, starting from Shoebury (Essex) they went up the Thames till they reached the Severn, returned from Buttington-on-Severn to Essex, placed their women and ships in safety in East Anglia, and then rode 'by day and by night' across to Chester. In 894 they returned, by way of Northumbria and East Anglia, to Mersea, in order to row up the Thames and then up the Lea. In 895 they built a fortress by the Lea; since it was '20 miles above London' it was presumably at Hertford. When Alfred threatened to beseige them there, they 'went overland till they reached Bridgnorth on the Severn' – the shortest route would have been along Watling Street – and then returned, some to East Anglia and others to Northumbria.[1] It is surely reasonable to suppose that it was during these campaigns that the Danes moved into south Bedfordshire and north Buckinghamshire. In that case the frontier drawn by Alfred and Guthrum can have lasted no more than seven years at the very most. Even if it had survived (as Stenton thought) till 903, it would not have been in existence for more than seventeen years. Any attempt to see it as an important factor in defining the limits of Danish settlement in England is therefore bound to be misconceived.

The real importance of the treaty is that it demonstrates that King Alfred, West Saxon though he was, was able to negotiate a frontier with the East Anglian Danes, even though it ran for the whole of its length through territory which once had been Mercian. In the treaty there is no mention of the ealdorman Ethelred or the Mercians, but only of King Alfred, King Guthrum, the councillors of all the English nation (*Angelcynnes*) and the people (ðeod) who dwelt in East Anglia. It therefore follows that the territory on the English side would have been under the control of the West Saxon king. That conclusion also explains why the description of the frontier ends so abruptly with 'up the Ouse to Watling Street'. Modern scholars have often asked why the treaty gave no indication as to how far along Watling Street the frontier was meant to continue, but if our reasoning has been correct, the answer is simple: the further extension

---

1. D. P. Kirby, 'Asser and his Life of King Alfred', *Studia Celtica*, vi (1971), 12–35, elucidates the background to these campaigns. In his opinion the grant of London to the ealdorman Ethelred was a reward for his submission to King Alfred. This submission, which produced a united front between Wessex and Mercia, alarmed Amarawd of Gwynedd to such an extent that he entered into an alliance with the Danes. Hence their persistent attempts to reach N. Wales.

of the frontier was no concern of the West Saxons, but only of the Mercians.

One of the most interesting silences in the Alfredian *Chronicle* concerns the part played by free Mercia in the struggle against the Danes. We have sufficient evidence from other sources to be sure that West Mercia was ruled by the ealdorman Ethelred who, at some date before 889, had married Alfred's eldest daughter, the lady Æthelflaed, and played a vigorous part in the war.[1] In the reign of Edward the Elder the *Chronicle* gives information about his and his widow's campaigns, but in Alfred's reign the silence is almost total. The only mentions of Mercia (874 and 877) suggest that that part of the country which was not actually occupied by the Danes, was controlled by their puppet-King Ceolwulf, whom the *Chronicle* dismisses as a 'foolish King's thegn'. The ealdorman Ethelred is mentioned once, when in 886 King Alfred 'entrusted the borough [of London] to his control', but there is no suggestion that he was a Mercian. On the contrary, the bald statement could easily lead the unwary to believe that he was simply a West Saxon ealdorman who was being given a new shire.

Alfred and Guthrum's treaty shows that for a short period between 886/90 and 893 (but not necessarily the whole of it), King Alfred was ignoring Mercia's claim to the territory north of the lower and middle Thames. In particular it shows that he considered Buckingham, which was on the Ouse but seven miles upstream of Watling Street, to be under his control, almost as if it was in Wessex. This is important, because the dating of the document known as the *Burghal Hidage* depends very largely on the status of Buckingham, which figures in it as the one *burh* north of the Thames.[2] Scholars have hitherto held, albeit reluctantly, that since the *Chronicle* records the advance of the English to Buckingham only in 914, that must be the earliest possible date of the *Burghal Hidage*. But if we treat the evidence of Alfred and Guthrum's frontier seriously, we can postulate an earlier date in the region of 886/90.

It is instructive to compare the frontier suggested by the *Burghal Hidage* with that of Alfred and Guthrum's treaty. (See map.) The big difference between them is that whereas Alfred and Guthrum put London on the English side of the frontier, the *Burghal Hidage* apparently leaves London to the Danes. The final *burhs* in the list are Cricklade, Oxford, Wallingford (all three of them on the Thames), Buckingham (well to the north of it), *Sceafesige* (which is Sashes, an island in the Thames just below Cookham Bridge), Eashing (on the

---

1. Stenton, *op. cit.* pp. 259–60.
2. The text of the burghal hidage in A. J. Robertson, *Anglo-Saxon Charters* (2nd edn. Cambridge, 1956), pp. 246–9 should now be compared with that by David Hill in 'The Burghal Hidage, the establishment of a text', *Medieval Archaeology*, xiii (1969), 84–92.

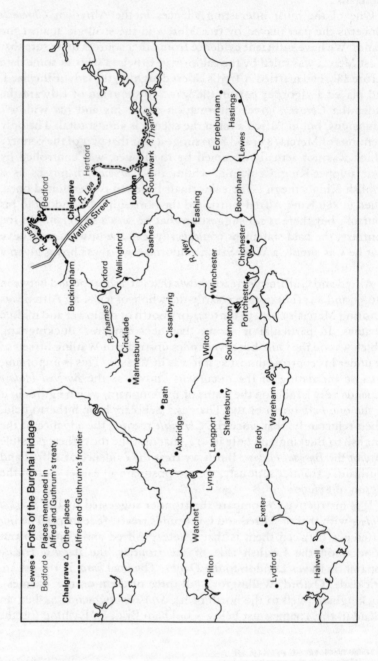

Forts of the Burghal Hidage

Lewes ● Forts of the Burghal Hidage

Bedford ○ Places mentioned in
Alfred and Guthrum's treaty

Chalgrave △ Other places

------- Alfred and Guthrum's frontier

River Wey just above Godalming) and Southwark.[1] In other words, the frontier zone ran north of the Thames between Wallingford and Sashes, but south of the Thames between Sashes and Southwark. Sashes would have been an island-fortress blocking navigation up the Thames in the same way as at Paris the *île de la cité* could block navigation up the Seine. Eashing could similarly block navigation up the Wey, the one sizeable tributary on the south side of the Thames and an obvious route for any advance on Winchester. Southwark, on the other hand, suggests that the Danes in London were themselves being threatened, with the south end of London Bridge blockaded by the English. The suggestion would therefore be that the date of the Burghal Hidage must be very shortly before Alfred's occupation of London in 886. We have no information as to how Alfred captured it, but in similar circumstances 180 years later, William the Conqueror made no attempt to cross the river from Southwark, but went upstream as far as Wallingford before making a crossing so as to advance on London from the north-west via Berkhamstead. It is therefore significant that in the *Burghal Hidage* the *burh* listed after Wallingford is Buckingham.[2] Could it be that it was from there the English advanced on London by way of Watling Street? In Alfred and Guthrum's treaty, Watling Street is placed firmly on the English side of the frontier, all the way from Stony Stratford to London.

Though the *Chronicle* does not tell us about the campaign of 886, it is precise about the sequence of events which followed Alfred's occupation of London. First 'all the English people (*all Angelcyn*) that were not under subjection to the Danes submitted to him', and then 'he entrusted the borough to the control of the Ealdorman Ethelred'.[3] There is no mention of anything Mercian, and one is left wondering whether, in practice, *all Angelcyn* did not refer, as in the Treaty, to the people of what we might describe as 'West Saxon Mercia'. It is probable also that the district with which Alfred entrusted Ethelred consisted not only of London, but also of all the land between the Thames and his frontier with Guthrum, *viz.* Hertfordshire, Bedfordshire, Buckinghamshire and Oxfordshire. We cannot be certain of the first three because they were soon reconquered by the Danes, but the *Chronicle* does state that in 911

1. For the identification of the forts, see Nicholas Brooks, 'The Unidentified forts of the Burghal Hidage', *ibid.* viii (1964), 74–90.

2. It must be appreciated that the *burhs* listed in the *Burghal Hidage* would not all have been constructed at the same date. Some would already have been relatively old while others – and in particular Buckingham – could have been very new. If the burh at Buckingham had only just been constructed, it would be easy to explain the confusion about the number of *burhs* and hides in the *Burghal Hidage* which has been pointed out by David Hill, *op. cit.* p. 88.

3. For Alfred's occupation of London, see also Tony Dyson, 'Two Saxon Land Grants for Queenhithe', in *Collectanea Londoniensia: studies . . . presented to Ralph Merrifield*, ed. J. Bird, H. Chapman and J. Clark (London and Middlesex Archaeol. Soc. Special Paper no. 2 (1978), pp. 200–15.

'Ethelred ealdorman of the Mercians died, and King Edward succeeded to London and Oxford and all the lands which belonged to them'.

The implications of the succinct statements of the *Chronicle* might easily be missed if they were not seen in the context of Alfred and Guthrum's treaty and the *Burghal Hidage*. The statement that 'all the English people that were not under subjection to the Danes submitted to him' is precise but does not encourage the mind to dwell on the fact that in practice this meant that the King of the West Saxons was ruling not only Wessex but also territory which had formerly been Mercian. No doubt the Mercians would have been relieved to be rid of the Danes, but they might also have been critical when they found that the West Saxon King was not able to defend the frontier which was supposed to protect them from the Danes. That, presumably, is why the *Chronicle* is silent about Alfred and Guthrum's treaty and the frontier which it outlined but failed to establish.[1]

1. In writing this paper I have benefited from the helpful suggestions and criticisms of Mr S. R. Bassett, Dr C. C. Dyer and Mr P. R. Kitson, to whom I am duly grateful.

5

The Norman Conquest

THE MOST INTERESTING PROBLEM about the Norman Conquest is what made it so complete. If it were not such a familiar fact, we would have thought it incredible that England, or any other state, could have been completely overwhelmed after a single battle. But this was what happened after the Battle of Hastings. Apparently as the result of one day's fighting (14 October 1066), England received a new royal dynasty, a new aristocracy, a virtually new Church, a new art, a new architecture and a new language. By 1086, when Domesday Book was made, less than half-a-dozen of the 180 greater land-lords or tenants-in-chief were English. By 1090 only one of the 16 English bishoprics was held by an Englishman, and six of the sees had been moved from their historic centres to large towns.[1] By the end of the twelfth century almost every Anglo-Saxon cathedral and abbey had been pulled down and rebuilt in the Norman style. Nothing was allowed to stand which might remind the English of the glories of their past. The Normans put it out that the Anglo-Saxons had been used to wooden palaces and wooden churches, that they had lived by a 'natural' economy, and that since they had no money they had been forced to pay their taxes in kind. They claimed that their military prowess had been ineffectual and their culture non-existent, and they relegated the English language to the underworld of the lower classes. For almost two centuries the language of polite society—the aristocracy and the court—was French, and the reality of the English past was smothered with romantic stories about King Arthur and the ancient Britons.

To some extent the explanation of these facts must be sought in the larger European background. The third quarter of the eleventh century was a period of rapid development throughout Western Europe, and it was possible for countries which suffered no Norman conquest to be transformed in some of the same ways as England. The reform of the Church, for example, was a general movement which swept across Europe in the 1050s and 1060s, and would presumably have reached England in any case by the time of Pope Gregory VII (1073-85). Economic prosperity was increasing everywhere, as evidenced particularly by the spectacular expansion of the Flemish cloth industry, for which England supplied most of the raw wool. Churches and palaces

---

[1] Dorchester (Oxon.) to Lincoln (1072), Elmham to Thetford (1072) and subsequently to Norwich (c. 1095), Lichfield to Chester (1075), Selsey to Chichester (1075), Sherborne to Salisbury (1078), and Wells to Bath (1090).

were being built or enlarged in the new Romanesque style throughout
Latin Christendom. What was particular to the Normans was the skill
with which they exploited these movements. They reformed the English
Church in such a way that it became less English and more Norman,
and they developed an advanced type of Romanesque architecture
because the conquest of England had made them so rich that there was
almost no limit to the number or size of their buildings.[2] Above all they
succeeded in expropriating all the greater English landlords, so that
they could step into their shoes as a new Norman aristocracy. In sharp
contrast to the English plantations of Ireland or the more recent efforts
of colonial powers in Africa and Asia, the Norman settlement of England
was completed in less than twenty years and has been accepted as a
'natural' fact of English history for nine centuries. By what means was
it accomplished?

Perhaps the most obvious reason for the success of the Norman
settlement was that William had a legitimate claim to the English crown.
After the death of Harold, the only possible alternative was the aetheling
Edgar, and since he was too young and too much of a simpleton to
inspire confidence, the English had no option but to accept William as
their king. But his accession would have had little practical effect if it
had not been for the fact that the English kingdom had an efficient
system of government. Countries which are well governed should be
able to resist invading armies more easily than countries which are not,
but if by any chance they fail they are easier for a conqueror to control.
They do not lend themselves to guerrilla resistance, because efficient
governments remove the opportunities for such activities.

It was therefore important that the English administrative machine
was probably the most efficient in the whole of Western Europe. Its
strength lay in the fact that it had trained officials in charge of both
central and local administration. There was a royal exchequer which
received taxes, a chancery (or writing office) which produced standard-
ized letters (writs) to convey instructions to the provinces, and local
officials who had been trained to obey them. The most important of
these officials were the shire-reeves or sheriffs who, as their name implied, controlled the shires. In contrast to the local divisions of France,
Normandy, or most other parts of Europe, the English shires covered
the whole kingdom and had boundaries which were well-known and
precisely defined. There was no vagueness about what belonged to
where, and as a result it was difficult, if not impossible, for any person
or place to evade the control of the sheriff. Every village belonged to a
'hundred' which had a court every four weeks, and every 'hundred'
belonged to a shire which twice a year held a court which all the principal men were compelled to attend. Their meetings provided an

---

[2] It is sometimes forgotten that most of the Romanesque churches of Normandy were
built *after* the conquest of England. The only notable exceptions are Bernay (*c.* 1017–50),
the nave of Mont Saint-Michel (*c.* 1040) and Jumièges (1040–67), and the chancel of the
Abbaye aux Dames at Caen (1062–6).

occasion not only for giving judgements in lawsuits, but also for receiving the orders of the king.

Two examples may be given to show the enormous power which these institutions gave to an English King. First they enabled him to levy a land-tax on the whole kingdom at regular intervals. The tax was called *geld*, and it was levied at the rate of so many shillings (usually two) on the 'hide'. The whole of England was divided into hides or carucates—taxable units of a notional value and usually something like 120 acres in size—and the central government knew how many hides there were deemed to be in every shire. The demand for the tax was sent to the shire court which divided it among its component 'hundreds'; in the hundred courts it was subdivided among the component tithings; and within each tithing each landholder knew what proportion he had to pay.[3] When, in the tenth century, Anglo-Saxon kings had declared that every man had to be in a hundred and tithing, they were ensuring not only that all men could be brought to justice but also that they could be taxed. As a system it was unique in Western Europe, and we can well imagine that William the Conqueror was both amazed and delighted, when he discovered that by merely declaring a geld year he would receive cartloads of money with no further effort of his own.

The second example of governmental power concerns the coinage in which the tax was collected. Not only were all moneyers appointed by the crown, but (in the words of a recent authority) 'they were dependent for their dies on a strictly-controlled die-cutting agency, and each man's name was stamped on his work'.[4] From 973 to 1066, and even later, the coin-types were apparently changed at six-yearly intervals, when all money had to be brought in and re-minted. So as to facilitate this re-minting there were at least 40, and perhaps as many as 70 minting-places in England, so distributed that hardly a village south of the Trent would have been more than 15 miles from one of them. The succeeding types of coin could, and did, vary in weight, and it has been claimed that these variations amounted to a systematic monetary policy. To quote the numismatists again, 'such elaborate control of the coinage was almost unprecedented in a medieval state; one would probably have to look as far as the Byzantine empire to find a more complex monetary policy',[5] a fine contrast to the Norman stories about the Anglo-Saxons having to pay their taxes in kind!

The government which fell into the hands of the Conqueror was efficient and centralized, and William realized its potentialities at once. Though it had been devised to provide England with an army for its defence, it could now be used as an instrument of expropriation, so that the lands of the English could be transferred to Norman ownership.

---

[3] *The Kalendar of Abbot Samson of Bury St. Edmunds*, ed. R. H. C. Davis (Camden Society. Third Series, lxxxiv (1954)), pp. xv–xxv.
[4] R. H. M. Dolley and D. M. Metcalf in *Anglo-Saxon Coins*, ed. R. H. M. Dolley (London, 1961), 155.
[5] *Ibid.*

It was for this reason that William was anxious to stress his rights
as the lawful heir of Edward the Confessor; he had to preserve the
continuity of the Anglo-Saxon administrative system in order to make
his conquest complete. He welcomed the continued service of Anglo-
Saxon scribes in his chancery, Anglo-Saxon sheriffs and portreeves in
shires and boroughs, an Anglo-Saxon justiciar in the six West Midland
shires, three Anglo-Saxon earls, and the Anglo-Saxon archbishop of
Canterbury. He might not need their services for long, but he needed
them urgently until sufficient Normans or other foreigners had been
trained to replace them.

In order to secure the collaboration of these men, William would
have had to make them believe that what he wanted was a 'genuine
Anglo-Norman state', in which equal protection would be given to all
men, whether English or Norman. To Englishmen of the time the notion
would not have seemed implausible, because the last conquest which
they had experienced, only 50 years before, had been that of King
Cnut who had pursued just such a policy and had become almost more
English than the English. For William, however, such an Anglophile
policy can never have been more than wishful-thinking, if as much as
that.[6] He had recruited his army not only from Normandy, but also
from northern France, Brittany and Flanders, and (as has often been
observed) it was something like a joint-stock enterprise. Those who took
part in it not only expected to be rewarded with land in England, but
required it; and it was obviously impossible to satisfy them without
expropriating large numbers of Englishmen.

We have very little information about the way in which the land
was allotted to the leading Normans, but the subject is an important
one and deserves investigation. We know that William had made
some grants of land before he returned to Normandy in February 1067,[7]
but by then he could have known little more of England than what he
had been able to see on his march from Hastings to London by way of
Wallingford and Berkhamsted. It must therefore have been difficult
for him to know what land he had at his disposal. English collaborators,
such as the earls Edwin, Morcar and Waltheof, may have given him
information about the men who had fought against him at Senlac, so
that a start could be made with the distribution of their lands; but
even so, William can hardly have known the exact location or extent
of the estates concerned. That, presumably, was why he had to extem-
porize by granting to individual Normans the lands which had been
held by particular Anglo-Saxons in specified shires. It would not have
mattered if he did not know precisely what those lands were, provided
he had a rough idea of their value; but sometimes he seems to have
made mistakes, rewarding some men more lavishly and others more

---

[6] For a contrary view, see F. M. Stenton, *Anglo-Saxon England* (Oxford, 1943), 617.
[7] When Eustace of Boulogne revolted in 1067, he forfeited the lands which he had already
been given (*Guillaume de Poitiers: Histoire de Guillaume le Conquérant*, ed. R. Foreville (Paris,
1952), 266–8).

meagrely than he had intended. Orderic Vitalis tells us that while some Normans found themselves endowed with lands which were rich beyond expectation, others complained that they had been given 'barren farms and domains depopulated by war'.[8]

It therefore looks as if a Norman who was granted the lands of a particular Anglo-Saxon was expected to discover for himself exactly what and where those lands were. The task must have seemed formidable. A Norman could not very well ride round an English shire 'alone and palely loitering' asking in every village if Ulf or Tovi had held any land there; even if the villagers had been able to understand him, they would probably have done their best to cheat him, if not to murder him. To the Normans, therefore, it must have seemed a godsend that the Anglo-Saxon administrative machine provided an easy way of getting the necessary information. The procedure was that anyone who was granted land by the king was given a sealed writ which stated the fact and had to be taken to the relevant shire court to be inspected and read out aloud.[9] The theory was that the whole shire was thus made witness of the king's grant, and would be held responsible for its execution; in this case it would have to inform the Norman what the lands of his predecessor were, and help him gain possession of them.

In the circumstances of the Conquest, it might well have been feared that the theory would not be strictly observed, and that King William's writ would be received with less respect than that of King Edward the Confessor. Even so, it must have been a great help for the Normans to know that all the landholders of a shire would be assembled at the shire-court at six-monthly intervals. The meeting-place would be known —it was usually in the open air and away from towns—and it would not have been difficult for a body of Normans to arrive with a strong force of soldiers and surround the place completely. With no escape possible, the members (or 'suitors') of the court could soon have been reduced to a state of terror, so that the Normans could present their writs and demand the necessary information and assistance. Since William the Conqueror was careful not to expropriate all the English at once, there would probably have been some who were willing to be coerced, in the hope that they would be able to save their own property by giving information about that of their neighbours. Failing such collaboration it would have been necessary to use violence, but if the Normans were in sufficient force, and the court effectively surrounded, any attempt to refuse the information would have been suicidal, unless it took the form of planned rebellion. Rebellions did in fact occur in some shires in 1067, but they were not concerted, because William had removed all the natural leaders and taken them with him to Normandy. When he returned to England at the end of the year, he

---

[8] Orderic Vitalis, Bk. iv, ch. 14.
[9] T. A. M. Bishop and P. Chaplais, *Facsimiles of English Royal Writs to A.D. 1100* (Oxford, 1957), p. xi.

suppressed the revolts with ease, and made them the excuse for further
expropriations.

Even in shires where there were no rebellions, it would have been
some time before it was safe for the Normans to split up and reside
on their new estates, for if they had dispersed immediately, it would
have been easy for the English to murder them in their beds. For some
years the Normans would have had no option but to behave in the
manner of all armies of occupation, living, eating and sleeping together
in operational units. We know that they built castles in the chief towns
of nearly all shires, and we may assume that they lived in them as the
'household knights' of their overlords, exploiting their estates as absen-
tee landlords for the time being.[10] How they managed it we do not
know, but if we may make a guess, it would be that they toured the
whole shire in force, and interrogated the men of each village with
brutality, until they had been told what dues their predecessors had
received from their respective estates. If they did not think their
predecessors had received enough, they could doubtless have demanded
more; and they would probably have threatened to burn the village
or kill its inhabitants, if the full amount were not brought to the castle
by the stipulated date. The Normans proved themselves capable of
such conduct in the Harrying of the North.

Castles were by far the most important instrument which the Normans
used for the subjugation of the country. Before the Conquest they had
been almost unknown in England, for they were basically different
from the fortified towns or boroughs of the Anglo-Saxons. The boroughs
were large because they had been designed as places where all men could
take refuge against external invaders. The castle, on the other hand,
was small and was designed as a place from which a few men could
dominate a subject population. Basically it was a wooden tower erected
on a mound of earth (or *motte*), the purpose of which was to defend the
base of the tower from incendiaries, while also being steep enough to
make a cavalry-charge impossible. Though small in comparison to
a borough, the building of a *motte* must have been a major undertaking.
The one at Oxford was 64 ft. high with a diameter of 81 ft. at the top
and 250 ft. at the base; it consisted of more than a million-and-a-half
cubic feet of earth, all of which would have been piled up by the forced
labour of the townsmen, working with spades, baskets and wheel-
barrows. The site of Oxford's *motte* was typical, since it was not in the
centre of the old borough where the townsmen could have surrounded
it, but at one extremity where the Norman garrison could keep in
touch with the outside world if the town was in revolt. It had been

---

[10] Sir Frank Stenton, *The First Century of English Feudalism* (2nd ed., Oxford, 1961), 140–5
discusses household knights. The date at which it would have been safe for them to be enfeoffed
and live on their own estates would have varied greatly from district to district. A rough conclusion to be drawn from W. E. Wightman, *The Lacy Family in England and Normandy, 1066–1194*
(Oxford, 1966), would be that in Herefordshire it took place in the 1070s, and in the West
Riding of Yorkshire in the 1080s. *Cf.* C. Warren Hollister, *The Military Organization of Norman
England* (Oxford, 1965), 54–5.

designed as an instrument of oppression and was undoubtedly effective; in the opinion of Orderic Vitalis the English would never have been conquered if they had possessed castles of their own.[11]

In the general confusion and terror of the Conquest, there must have been many opportunities for individual Normans to seize more lands than they had been granted, and the *clamores* of Domesday Book show that it was by no means uncommon for one Norman to take possession of a manor which should have gone to another. In some cases this seems to have been done with no attempt to conceal the use of naked force in a cloak of legality, but in others the Normans concerned attempted to secure their position by forcing the shire court to give false evidence. In many cases they may have succeeded in covering their traces completely, but we know of some in which they failed. Rochester cathedral has preserved a full account of the way in which a Norman sheriff, Picot, attempted to rob it of its manor at Freckenham (Suff.) by claiming it as royal demesne and keeping the profits himself. So long as the bishop was only an Anglo-Saxon, the sheriff experienced no difficulty, but after 1076 there was a Norman bishop of Rochester, and he immediately complained to the king.

> The king ordered all the men of the county to be assembled, so that it might be proved by their judgment whose the land ought to be. The men were assembled, and from fear of the sheriff affirmed, that the land was not St. Andrew's [of Rochester] but the king's. Since the bishop of Bayeux, who was presiding over the plea, did not put much faith in them, he ordered them, if they knew that what they said was true, to choose twelve of their number to confirm on oath what they had all said. But they, when they had withdrawn for consultation, were terrified by a message from the sheriff, and swore that what they had said was true.[12]

There the matter might have rested, if the Norman bishop of Rochester had not at last discovered the Anglo-Saxon monk who had previously managed the estate for the cathedral. In the face of his evidence one of the jurors was forced to admit that he had committed perjury. Rochester recovered its land, and the twelve jurors were fined £300, an enormous sum for a time when £20 a year was considered a suitable income for a Norman knight. It was necessary to be severe 'pour encourager les autres', for the only way in which the king could prevent his followers from helping themselves to all the lands they wished, was by ensuring that the shire courts did not turn a blind eye to their activities.

Eventually the Conqueror extended his inquiries to the whole kingdom, in order to produce the Domesday Survey (1086). Commissioners went round all the shire courts and inquired into all the possessions of the king, the churches and all the magnates, enumerating the number of hides or carucates, the amount of plough-land, wood, meadow, sokemen, villeins, serfs and cattle, and estimating the value

[11] Orderic Vitalis, Bk. iv, ch. 4.
[12] *Registrum Roffense*, ed. J. Thorpe (London, 1769), 31.

of each estate at three different dates—when King Edward was alive (1065), when its present holder first took possession, and as it actually was in 1086.[13] In this way William used the basic machinery of the Anglo-Saxon government, in order to discover the exact location, extent, and value of the lands which he had given his followers. He was also able to detect if they had seized more lands than they had been granted, for the first question asked about each manor was 'Who held it in King Edward's time?', and if the answer was not the present holder's official *antecessor*, there would be trouble in store. At Wilksby in the South Riding of Lindsey the commissioners reported on a claim by the bishop of Durham against Gilbert de Gant, declaring that 'the men of the Riding say they never saw the bishop's *antecessor* given seisin either by writ or by envoy (*legatum*), and they give their testimony in favour of Gilbert' (i. 375). In cases where the royal demesne had suffered, their language became more threatening:—'Berengar the vassal of St. Edmund's (Abbey) "invaded" this, and is in the king's mercy. He was ill and could not come to the hearing.' (ii. 449).

The Domesday Survey brought the Norman Conquest to a conclusion by examining all the details of the ruthless spoliation, and approving them only when they had been done by authority. That was how it got its name; it was the survey and book of Judgement Day. Every Norman had been forced to account for the way in which he had acquired his English lands; and if it was approved, his name was inscribed and his claim upheld for ever by the hundred, the shire, the king's justices and the king. It brought the tenurial revolution to an end and made the Norman settlement permanent.

It is a commonplace of history that the difficulties of getting a revolution started are nothing like so great as those of getting it to stop. The men who first put it in motion are usually swept away by those who follow, and the passage from one change to the next becomes increasingly rapid as the revolution gathers momentum. That something of this sort nearly happened after the Norman Conquest, is suggested by the fact that some lands had changed hands two or three times between 1066 and 1086,[14] but William the Conqueror did not lose control of the situation. His grip was firm, because he recognized the potentiality of the Anglo-Saxon machinery of government and exploited it to the full. He used it to expropriate the English and to make the Domesday Survey, to start his revolution and to bring it to a halt. And in so doing he demonstrated to the English what a formidable weapon their kings had devised for their undoing.

[13] For a full discussion of the administration behind the survey, see V. H. Galbraith, *The Making of Domesday Book* (Oxford, 1961).

[14] E.g. *D.B.* ii. 449. 'In Cavendish (Suff.) Ralph de Limesi holds the land of one freeman which Edric the deacon held. He was killed with him (the freeman) in the battle (of Hastings), and his holding was given as land to Bainard. Etgar added it to Cavendish after Bainard lost it. Now Ralph de Limesi hold it in the demesne of the hall.' For examples on a larger scale, see W. E. Wightman, *The Lacy Family in England and Normandy, 1066–1194*, 20–1, 28, 123–4.

6

The Warhorses of the Normans

The question to which this paper is addressed is whether the pre-eminence of the Normans in war in the eleventh century was due in any significant measure to their possession of more and better warhorses than any of their neighbours. The suggestion that this might have been the case occurs in one of the stories told by the continuator of William of Jumièges who was writing soon after 1087, with reference to Duke Robert the Magnificent (1027–35).

> Duke Robert was generous not only with words but also with gifts, and if he made anyone a gift in the morning, he would keep on sending him everything that came to hand. One day a smith came from Beauvais [which was outside Normandy] and offered him two knives. The Duke, not wishing to spurn a little gift from a poor man, accepted it gratefully and told his chamberlains to give the man one hundred pounds Rouennais. The smith had hardly received the full sum when behold! two horses of outstanding strength appear; they had just been presented to the duke by two nobles, and the duke had ordered them to be given to the smith. The smith, afraid that he was being laughed at, was heartbroken and fell with his face to the ground, fearful that the magnificent gifts which the duke had given him would be taken back. At last, recovering his breath, he looked quickly to left and right, jumped on the back of one horse, grabbed the other with his right hand and returned to his city as fast as he could ... A year later the smith returned to Normandy, bringing with him his two sons well instructed in arms, and coming to the Duke he said 'Do you recognize me, your servant, o lord?' The Duke said 'No'. And the smith replied, 'I am the man on whom you conferred magnificent presents last year, and I have come with my two sons to offer you faithful service, if your Excellency will not refuse it'.[1]

The story itself is folkloric, but it suggests that Duke Robert was able to recruit warriors from outside Normandy because of the quality of the horses which he could offer them. If good horses were an essential feature of a victorious army, any ambitious warrior who, like a modern footballer, wanted to serve where fame and fortune could most easily be found, would seek out the lord with the best horses.

[1] Jumièges, 106–8.

The Bayeux Tapestry certainly makes a great feature of horses.[2] In some scenes they are so crowded that it is impossible to count them with confidence, but there are at least 179 in the main tapestry and perhaps as many as 186, while in the lower margin there are two dead warhorses, one farm horse pulling a harrow and one mule hauling a plough. The artist has made it his business to show William's army as an army of cavalry. He shows 5 archers (4 on foot and one mounted) in the main sequence and 23 in the lower margin of the Battle of Hastings, but although he thus admits their importance, it is easy to overlook them because of the enormous emphasis placed on the horses. These are often shown as equine personalities, enjoying the sea-trip, combative in the battle, and furious when they find themselves tumbling down a hill. Their colouring is imaginative, 20 of them being some sort of green, 44 some sort of blue, 46 terracotta red and 60 of them buff or gold. What is more (perhaps as a substitute for perspective) the legs on the far side of a horse are in a colour different from those on the near side, so that the far legs of a buff-coloured horse might be dark blue or green. The horses' manes are also varied in colour; a buff-coloured horse could have a green or red mane, and a blue horse a golden mane. It might be suggested that the terracotta reds are intended to suggest chestnut or dark bay horses, and the buffs light chestnuts or light bays. The dark blues and greens would then be blacks and the light blues grays. The bodies of one or two horses are shown in two colours, but this seems to be due to some technical fault or repair, and cannot be seen as an attempt to portray a piebald or skewbald.

All the horses are stallions, some of them with a very prominent feature. Their facial expressions often suggest, quite wittily, the emotions of their riders, and when Guy of Ponthieu is forced to hand Harold over to Duke William, his humiliation is suggested by the fact that his horse is given donkey-like ears. The horses' manes are treated in five different ways:

(a) with longish hair hanging down on both sides of the neck; this is much the most common type shown
(b) with longish hair which does not hang down but is blown backwards as if by the wind (pls. 20, 66)
(c) with longish hair not hanging down but brushed upwards and forwards, so as to look almost barbed (pls. 15, 45, 54, 59, 69), suggesting anger or ferocity
(d) short, upstanding and crestlike (pls. 1, 2, 9, 21, 58, 73). All the horses which are certainly English have manes like this, but so also does Guy of Ponthieu's horse in pl. 15, and several Norman horses
(e) short and crestlike but apparently plaited, pls. 42–3, 55–6. It is not always easy to distinguish this type from (d), especially when allowance is made for artistic licence

It may be that different types of mane are intended for different types of horse, but it is equally possible that the artist's intention was to indicate

---

[2] All subsequent references are to the plates as numbered in *BT*.

the changing moods of the horses. Those shown on ships during the crossing all have manes of types (d) and (e) which make them look rather smug. As soon as they disembark their manes have changed to types (a) and (c). (pls. 42–5).

It is not easy to be sure of the size of the horses. None of them wears any protective armour and there does not seem to be any difference of size in the horses ridden by Harold in England (pl. 2), Count Guy of Ponthieu (pl. 9) or the Normans in general. Sometimes, however, the artist has made particular horses look very large, as in the case of those held by Turoldus (pl. 12) or the destrier which is led up to Duke William before the Battle of Hastings (pl. 53), but in general the 'standard' size of horse may not have been more than fourteen hands tall. If one looks at the legs and stirrups of the knights one is reminded of the story of Richard son of Ascletin, the Norman count of Aversa, who (according to Amatus of Monte Cassino) liked to ride horses so small that his feet almost touched the ground.[3] Nevertheless the Bayeux Tapestry leaves one in no doubt that in 1066 the Normans' horses were thought marvellous in both quantity and quality. Later generations might think them too small, but at the time they were thought to be both magnificent and enormous.

How did the Normans get such horses? The question is important because the indigenous horse of NW Europe was probably no bigger than a Shetland pony, standing only about ten hands; anything larger would have had to be produced by selective breeding. We know that this had been done in antiquity, particularly by the Persians who introduced a Bactrian strain which they took with their armies to Greece, and from which both the Greeks and the Macedonians eventually benefitted. The Romans also had been keen horse-breeeders, as can be seen both in the mosaics found at their stud farms (e.g. Oued Athménia near Constantine in N. Africa) and in the equestrian statues of their emperors. But it should not be thought that because the Romans had developed fine breeds of horses, a supply of good horses would remain in Europe for ever. On the contrary, it is a notorious fact that breeds can be 'lost' much more quickly than they can be established. To establish a breed one has to select a stallion of exceptional promise and get him to cover mares which also have the qualities desired (speed, size, strength, ferocity or docility), and then select those of their offspring who display those qualities to the greatest extent and mate them, breeding 'in' and 'in', so as to breed 'out' the qualities that are not desired. In this way it is possible to produce a new 'design' of horse, whether it be a warhorse or English Thoroughbred, but the whole business takes a very long time, and can be maintained only if the mating of the horses remains strictly controlled. If the mares follow their natural desires and allow themselves to be covered by common males, it will be very few generations before the breed is lost.

The most notorious example of this happening concerned the horses taken to America by the conquistadores in the sixteenth century. The likelihood is that they were Andalusians, Barbs or Asturións, but we do not know

---

[3] *Storia dei Normanni di Amato di Montecassino*, ed. V. de Bartholomeis (Fonti per la Storia d'Italia, Roma 1935), 110.

which, because the breed was soon lost. Some of the horses escaped or were captured by the Indians, who had never seen horses before and allowed them to breed as they wished. As a result their genes 'separated out', and in a very few generations their descendants were 'mustangs' with little to distinguish them from the wild horses from which the original Andalusians, Barbs or Asturións had been bred.

The only way in which one can prevent such a regression is by segregating the mares, so that they can be covered only by those stallions which have been specially selected for them. The segregation is not accomplished easily because male equids scent females from a great distance, and show great ingenuity and persistence in reaching them; even in modern stud farms it has been known to happen that the selected stallion has been anticipated by an inferior male, so that the resulting foal has been both a surprise and a disappointment to its owner. What is needed for the security of the mares is a park surrounded by a stallion-proof fence, which is always kept in first-class repair. If in times of economic crisis the fences are not properly maintained, male horses or ponies will break in and cover the mares. In times of civil disorder or war the fences may well be broken down by mobs, armies, deserters or thieves, so that the mares, whether they escape or are stolen, are scattered widely. There can be little doubt that this was what happened at the end of the Roman Empire. The Germanic invaders would seize the Roman horses, keep them with their own and allow them to breed at will. Even though allowance must be made for some exceptions, the quality of horses would have declined rapidly, resulting in many places in feral herds.

'Feral' horses are the descendants of domesticated horses which have gone wild. Breeding freely with each other, their offspring are smaller in each generation until after four or five generations they become pony-sized and acquire zebra-like stripes on their legs. Several herds of such horses are to be found in the USA, particularly on the Granite Range of Nevada and on islands off the East Coast. They have recently been the object of considerable scientific study, much of which is relevant to our present purpose, since it shows the basic characteristics of the 'woodland' or 'untamed' horses which formed such a feature of the early medieval landscape.[4]

In general feral horses move about in herds, each herd consisting of a stallion and his harem of anything up to 10 or 15 mares and their foals. Broadly speaking the mares are fertile from the age of three to seventeen, the maximum fertility being achieved at the age of seven. They can be expected to have nine or ten offspring in a lifetime. Gestation lasts eleven months, and

[4] For what follows I am greatly indebted to Professor Daniel I. Rubenstein, professor of Biology at the University of Princeton. See also his paper on 'Ecology and Sociality in Horses and Zebras' in Daniel I. Rubenstein and Richard W. Wrangham (eds.) *Ecological Aspects of Social Evolution: Birds and Mammals* (Princeton, NJ 1986) 282–302; Joel Berger, *Wild Horses of the Great Basin: Social Competition and Population Size* ('Wild Life Behaviour and Ecology' series, ed. George B. Schiller), (Chicago and London 1986); Ronald Keiper and Katherine Houpt, 'Reproduction in Feral Horses: an eight-year study' [on Assateague Island], *American Journal of Veterinary Research* 45, 1984, 991; S. R. Speelman, W. M. Dawson and R. W. Phillips, 'Some Aspects of the Fertility of Horses raised under Western Range conditions', *Journal of Animal Science* 3, 1944, 233–41, and 'Growth of Horses under Western Range conditions' (*ibid.* 4, 1945, 47–54).

the foals are generally born in April, May or June (more than half of them in May itself) when there is plenty of grass in the fields. The foals will have been weaned after six months, but will run with their dams for about two years. Though the number of male and female births are about equal, the stallion does not tolerate other adult males in his herd. Consequently the young males will break away from, or be driven out of, the herd when they are about two years old, and will roam singly or in pairs hoping to acquire some females of their own by successfully challenging a stallion. The majority of these 'bachelors' have no success in this respect, and die early, either as a result of injuries incurred in a stallion fight, or from malnutrition caused by the fact that, lacking the protection of a herd they are continually interrupted in their grazing.

The strongest and most successful stallions not only acquire the largest 'harems' but also establish a specific territory for their herds and keep all other horses off it. In its grazing the herd moves round this territory systematically, led by its leading mare, while the stallion keeps guard in the rear. The adult horses take little sleep, and when they do so, they do not lie down but remain standing. They are awake for 20–22 hours of the day, and in the summer spend 70 per cent of their time (42 minutes in every hour) grazing. In winter, when the grass is sparser, their grazing time increases to 80 per cent (or 48 minutes of every hour). If the herd is harassed by stray males, other animals or humans, feeding time tends to be lost while the leading mare conducts the others out of harm's way, and the stallion prepares to do battle. In the case of weak herds which have not established a territory of their own, the amount of grazing-time lost in this way may be as much as 9 per cent, or 2 hours a day; it is probably because of this, that the fertility-rate of mares in non-territorial herds is lower than that of mares in territorial herds.

Feral horses have difficulty in finding sufficient grazing in winter. They are often close to starvation during the coldest season of the year. The importance of this fact has been demonstrated on Assateague Island where the herds on the northern half of the island are completely unmanaged, while those in the south are 'managed' to the extent that all foals are removed from their dams at the end of July, when they are one, two or three months old. The results of this management are beneficial to both mares and foals. The fertility rate of the mares is increased by 17.3 per cent (from 57.1 per cent to 74.4 per cent) because, no longer having to nurse their foals, they retain all the nourishment of their grazing for themselves. The foals which have been removed are also better nourished because they are given a daily ration of 1 lb of grain for every 100 lb of bodyweight, and as much hay as they desire. In consequence they do not lose weight in winter, and grow markedly taller and heavier than those foals which remain with their herds in the other part of the island.

From this brief survey of feral horses we can immediately see some ways in which even the most elementary forms of management could improve both the quality and the quantity of the horses. First, in order to avoid the wastage of surplus male horses which are driven out of the herd and die early, all foals should be removed from the herd before they reach the age of two. Secondly, each herd should be provided with a territory of its own, fenced off so as to exclude intruders. Thirdly, in order to maintain their growth and condition, the whole herd (particularly the mares) should be provided with winter feed.

There is evidence to suggest that the first two of these forms of management had been adopted in the Medieval West by the time of Charlemagne, and that the third may have been adopted also. In the *Capitulare de Villis*, which dates most probably from the last years of the eighth century, it is stated that the stewards of the royal vills or estates should:

(13) take good care of the stallions, and under no circumstances allow them to stay in one pasture (*loco*), lest it be spoiled. And if any of them is no good (*quod non bonus sit*), too old or dead, the stewards are to see to it that we [Charlemagne] are informed at the proper time, before the season comes for sending them in among the mares.

(14) look after our mares well and separate them from the colts (*poledros*) at the proper time. And if the fillies (*pultrellae*) increase in number, let them be separated so that they can form a new herd by themselves.

(15) have our foals at the winter palace at Martinmas (11 Nov).[5]

It is not stated whether the foals are to be sent to the winter palace at the age of five months or seventeen, and it is therefore unclear from this text whether they were to be removed from their dams before the onset of the first winter. But we do know from Carolingian capitularies that great emphasis was laid on feeding riding horses with grain, specified allowances of it being supplied to bishops, abbots and royal vassals when travelling on the King's business. (See below p. 75)

The passage quoted from the *Capitulare de Villis* shows also that Charlemagne had advanced one step further and was taking considerable pains over the management of his stallions. Instead of letting them run with their own 'harems' throughout the year, he kept the stallions apart and put them in with the mares only during the mating season. As a result he would have been able to put them in with several groups of mares, one after the other. In this way each stallion could service more mares than before; and since the number of stallions at stud could be reduced, there would have been no need to use any which were not of the highest quality. It is impossible to overemphasize the importance of this development, even though it subsequently became commonplace among horsebreeders. As Robert Blakewell put it:

even one superior male may change considerably the breed of a country. But in a year or two, his offspring are employed in forwarding the improvement. Such of his sons as prove of a superior quality are let out in a similar way; consequently the blood, in a very short time, circulates through every part, and every man of spirit partakes in the advantage.[6]

[5] *Cap. Reg. Franc.* i. 84, following in the main the translation in H. R. Loyn and John Percival, *The Reign of Charlemagne*, London 1975, 66–7.
[6] Quoted from Keith Chivers, *The Shire Horse: A History of the Breed, the Society and the Men*, London 1976, 51.

It was one thing to recognize the advantage of using stallions in this way, another to find stallions of the necessary quality. Those that were to be found in NW Europe were not nearly so good as those in Spain, where, since the Moslem conquest in the first quarter of the eighth century Arabian horses and Barbs from N. Africa were to be found. When Charles Martel defeated the Spanish Moslems at Poitiers in 732 he must have seen many of these horses and probably captured some. The earliest reference to a Spanish horse comes in the *Life* of St Corbinianus, written soon after 769. It relates how the saint rode around Lombardy on a horse called *Iberus*, a stallion so beautiful that the king coveted him and contrived to steal him.[7] In 778 when Charlemagne himself was campaigning in Spain he would have seen horses of this sort himself, and in 795 his son Louis, writing to tell his father of a victory he had won at Barcelona, mentioned that one of the most valuable spoils was a fine horse.[8] By the end of the ninth century a regular trade may have developed, since various abbeys in the Cantabrian Mountains made a business of breeding horses. In 876 Pope John VIII wrote to the Christian King of Galicia, asking him for some of the 'excellent Moorish horses which the Spanish call *al faraces*', *faras* being the Arabic word for 'horse'.[9]

Not only do we know that the organization of studs and introduction of new bloodstock *should* have improved the standard of horsebreeding, but we also know that Charlemagne and his successors were convinced that they had succeeded, because they put a prohibition on the export of stallions, so that they should not be acquired by their enemies. The first such prohibition was in the Capitulary of Mantua, c. 781, but with the arrival of the Northmen the prohibitions became increasingly urgent. Horses and armour were not to be sold to the Northmen on any account, not even when they were demanded as ransom. In the Edict of Pîtres (864) Charles the Bald decreed it treason to pay such ransoms:

> when these things [arms, armour or horses] are given for the ransom of one man or sold for a small price, the result is that aid is given to those who are against us, very great damage is done to our Kingdom, many of God's churches are destroyed, many Christians are robbed, and the resources of the Church and Kingdom are destroyed.[10]

Ernoul le Noir, in his adulatory poem on Louis the Pious (written c. 826–28) had praised Datus, the founder of the abbey of Conques, for his refusal to ransom his mother for a warhorse, even though the refusal resulted in his mother being killed before his own eyes.[11] Yet in spite of all the Franks' efforts to keep their warhorses to themselves, the Northmen succeeded in

---

[7] Arbeo Frisingensis, 'Vita Corbiniani episcopi Baiuvariorum', ed. B. Krusch, *Scriptores Rerum Merovingiarum* vi, *MGH* 1913, 573, 578–9.

[8] Loyn and Percival, *Reign of Charlemagne*, 148.

[9] Anne-Marie and Robert-Henri Bautier, 'Contribution à l'histoire du cheval au Moyen Age', *Bulletin Philologique et Historique du Comité des Travaux Historiques et Scientifiques*, Paris BN *Année 1976*, 209–49 and *Année 1978*, 9–75 (esp. 16–20).

[10] *Cap. Reg. Franc.* ii. 321, para 25.

[11] Ernoul le Noir, *Poème sur Louis le Pieux et épître au Roi Pépin*, ed. E. Faral, Paris 1932, 22–4. I owe this reference to Mr James Campbell.

winning enough for themselves. How did they do it?

To answer this question we must first consider where the Carolingian studs are most likely to have been. Because of the *Capitulare de Villis*, we must assume that many of them would have been on royal estates. From subsequent references to *equae silvaticae* or forest mares, we could look for an area with plenty of woodland. And if we were consulting a modern horsebreeder, he would suggest a terrain of limestone or chalk, since if horses feed on grass containing calcium, their bones will be strengthened. All these conditions – royal estate, forestland and limestone – are to be found to a most unusual extent, in the valley of the Seine as it passes through Normandy.

There were Frankish palaces, each with its own forest, at Le Vaudreuil in the 'forêt du Bord' and *Aurelanum* in the Forêt de Brotonne. Both above and below Rouen both banks of the river are lined with forests; on the right bank those of Lillebonne, Maulévrier, Jumièges, Roumare, Selvoissin (now la Forêt Verte), Longboël (which extends northeast to the forest of Lyons), Les Andelys and Vernon; on the left bank, those of Brotonne, Vatteville, Mauny, Rouvray, Londe, Bord and Bizy. Nor was this all, for the tributaries of the Seine, particularly the Risle and the Eure, led to many more forests. Especially tempting for the Northmen were the abbeys and churches many of which were situated, like Saint-Wandrille, Jumièges and the churches of Rouen, almost on the water's edge. The general tactic of the raiders was to seize a church and threaten to burn it down unless a specific ransom was paid, or alternatively to capture a bishop or abbot and hold him hostage, threatening to kill him if his ransom was not paid. Most of the details which we have about these ransoms refer to Paris and its district; the abbey of Saint Denis, for example, ransomed its church in 857 and its abbot in 858 but in 859, presumably because it refused to pay a third time, it had its church burnt down. Ferdinand Lot, when he demonstrated that the monks of Saint Wandrille did not abandon their abbey until 858, was surely right in saying that it must have paid ransom not only in 841, when it paid six pounds, but also in 845, 851–2, and 852–3. The Annals of St Bertin sometimes tell us the sums of money involved in these ransoms (seven thousand pounds for Paris in 845) and sometimes they tell us that in addition to money there were payments of animals. It is very likely that the animals included horses.

One way or another the Northmen certainly did obtain horses in France, adding further to the confusion of the Franks by riding across country so as to extend the range of the raids from their ripuarian bases. They rode so swiftly that no ordinary army could catch them, and when they sailed away, if they had no room for the horses on their ships, they could leave them behind or kill them. The way in which they operated is widely known. What is not generally appreciated is the fact that in their raids they must have disrupted the horse-breeding establishments of France very badly. Quite apart from capturing horses for themselves, they would have broken down park fences and caused such panic in the civilian population that the keepers of the studs and their servants would have fled. For a period of seventy years (841–911) at least they disrupted normal life in, and between, all the river-valleys of Northern France, Belgium and Holland. In that region the studs must have been so pillaged and disorganized that all breeds would have deteriorated and many would have been lost completely. In consequence, though the Northmen had been successful in securing horses for the time being, they would soon have discovered that there were no more horses of quality to be found.

Once they had taken Normandy for themselves, they would have needed, like the Franks before them, to organize parks for studs. Duke Rollo and his successors took over the Carolingian fisc, or royal demesne as their own, and would therefore have had plenty of suitable wooded land in the Seine valley, but they would have had to repair or remake the fences, reconstitute suitable herds of mares and organize an adequate staff to manage them. The staff's duties would have been the same as under the Carolingians, to ensure that the mares were visited by a suitable stallion in the breeding season, to remove the foals from their dams before they reached the age of two, and if over the years the number of mares increased markedly, to form some of them into new herds with separate enclosures of their own. This separation of the animals was not always easy; in the case of the foals, they were usually trapped in nets.

It was also important to supply the foals with winter feed in order to ensure that their growth was not stunted. As we have already mentioned, veterinarians now consider that an adequate daily diet for foals or horses would be 1 lb of grain for every 100 lb of bodyweight and as much hay as is desired. These figures may not have been quite the same in the eleventh and twelfth centuries but at any rate the need for oats or some sort of grain was generally understood. Writing in the 1130s Orderic Vitalis, who shows no special expertise on equine matters, made a passing remark to the effect that in western climes a horse could barely be maintained without its daily sester of oats.[12] It is not surprising that he knew this because there had been regulations since the time of the Franks about the rations that could be claimed for horses used in the public service. A capitulary of 819 stated that the allowances of grain for the horses of bishops, abbots or royal vassals when acting as royal *missi* were 4, 3 and 2 *modii* respectively, the differences referring (presumably) not to the differing appetites of horses but to the number of horses allowed in each retinue.[13] In 845–50 the allowance for a bishop going round his diocese in N. Italy was 6 *modii*.[14]

If the King was to supply his servants with fodder for their horses, he needed large supplies of it. Hence the importance of the tax which the Franks called *fodrum* and the Normans *bernagium*. The duty of supervising this fodder was placed on officers who were called marshals by both Franks and Normans. In the capitulary of 853 Charles the Bald decreed:

13. That *missi* should take care in their districts that neither our vassals nor anyone else should despoil or oppress their neighbours, whether great or small, when they put their horses out to graze in summer, or when the marshals (*marescales*) are directing them to the fodder (*fodrum*).[15]

---

[12] Orderic, v. 242.
[13] *Cap. Reg. Franc.* i. 219.
[14] *Cap. Reg. Franc.* ii. 83.
[15] *Cap. Reg. Franc.* ii. 274.

Lucien Musset has recently explained the importance of these marshalls and demonstrated, that in the years immediately preceding the conquest of England there were some marshals in Normandy who had not yet become great officers of the court but were still engaged in the relatively lowly task of supervising the provision of fodder. In particular he has shown that at Caen the hay from the meadow or *prairie* was managed by Milo the marshal whose descendants, known as the 'marshals of Venoix', subsequently climbed a little way up the social ladder before being toppled by rivals.[16]

The proper management of parks and pasture, however, would not in themselves be sufficient to breed horses of the standard required. As always, it would have been necessary to procure some first-class stallions. The most valuable of these would have been Arabians or Barbs. It is possible that Duke Robert the Magnificent, who died at Nicaea in 1035 on his way back from Jerusalem, might have procured some Arabian horses, and possible also that his companions might have brought them home. But the solid information which we have all points not to the East but to Spain where, as we have already seen, horses of Arabian and Barb stock were to be found. William of Poitiers, writing c. 1077, states that in the 1040s the great men of Gascony and Auvergne, and even the Kings of Spain sought Duke William's friendship with gifts of horses.[17] In the *Roman de Rou*, written a hundred years later, it is said that the horse which William the Conqueror rode at Hastings had been bought from Spain by Walter Giffart.[18] Before that there had been Norman adventurers campaigning in Spain. Roger de Tosny 'the Spaniard' had assisted in the defence of Barcelona in 1023, and his son Ralph was in Spain at some date between 1065 and 1072.[19] Robert Crespin was there about 1064 and returned with a lot of plunder.[20] Spanish horses were said by Gerald of Wales (who was writing c. 1214) to have been the foundation of the stock of the fine horses of Powys, having been brought there (c. 1098–1102) by Robert of Bellême, the eldest son of Roger de Montgomery.[21] Robert had presumably kept his Spanish horses in Normandy before bringing them to England. His Norman lands bestrode the southeast border of the duchy, one of his nearest neighbours who was also a relative and bitter enemy, was Rotrou Count of Mortagne and Perche whose first cousin was Alfonso the Battler King of Aragon (1104–34). Rotrou took part in several campaigns in Spain (probably in 1108, 1118 and 1124–5), giving assistance in the reconquest and resettlement of the Ebro valley, but returning home after each campaign.[22] Another near neighbour in Normandy was Robert Bordel of Cullei who went to Spain and became Count of Tarragona c. 1125.[23]

---

[16] Lucien Musset, 'Une institution peu connue de la Normandie ducale: Les prés et le foin du Seigneur Roi', in *Autour du Pouvoir ducal normand, X^e–XIIe* par Lucien Musset, J-M. Bouvres and J-M. Maillefer (Cahiers des Annales de Normandie, n° 17, Caen 1985), 77–93.

[17] *Gesta Guillelmi*, 26.

[18] Wace, ii. 64.

[19] Orderic, iii. 124 and n.

[20] D. W. Lomax, *The Reconquest of Spain*, London 1978, 58.

[21] Gerald of Wales, *The Journey through Wales and the Description of Wales*, trans. Lewis Thorpe (Harmondsworth, 1978), 20.

[22] Orderic, vi. 394–404.

[23] Orderic, vi. 402–4.

The reason why we know these facts is that they were recorded by Orderic Vitalis who took a particular interest in the men concerned because they lived close to his abbey of Saint-Evroul. This was a long way from the Seine, but it was in a forest region which is still noted for horsebreeding, Merlerault being the centre for Percheron horses and Le Haras au Pin a national stud since the seventeenth century. Saint-Evroul may have been engaged in horse-breeding itself – it certainly received tithes of mares at Beaunai in the North of Normandy (21 km south of Dieppe)[24] and from various places in England. But to judge from the information given by Orderic, the abbey's speciality lay in buying and selling horses. The earliest instance dates from c. 1059–60 when Engelnulf de l'Aigle, having lost his eldest son, gave the monks a valuable horse in return for their prayers. The monks promptly gave the horse to Arnold of Echaffour, from whom they received in return a much-coveted estate at Bocquencé.[25] About 1107 the monks, in return for a confirmation of land and tithes, gave to Ansold of Maule 'as a free gift' a horse which had formerly belonged to Grimoald of Saulx-Marchais and was worth 100 shillings.[26] About the same time Ansold bequeathed his best palfrey to the monks, and they gave it to the dead man's son in return for land at Mortmarcien.[27] The language used is always that of free gifts, but it is impossible to conceal the fact that what was being recorded was sales and purchases. The same is true of transactions recorded by many other abbeys, but what distinguished Saint-Evroul is that the sales seem always to have been balanced by purchases.

Jumièges and Fécamp seem to have had an unending supply of horses to 'give away' or sell, and it must be assumed that they bred them. Between 1020 and 1030 the Abbey of Jumièges paid Hugh Bishop of Bayeux a horse 'of great price' for land and privileges at Rouvray.[28] In 1030 it paid Drogo Count of Amiens and the Vexin six horses 'of very great price' for land at Genainville.[29] In 1045–48 it paid Roger de Montgomery a horse worth 30 pounds, together with a cuirass worth seven, for the land of one of his vassals who had become a monk.[30] About 1054 Gilbert Crispin was paid 200 pounds in money, 2 ounces of gold and a horse worth 20 pounds for the fief (*beneficium*) of Hauville on the edge of the forest of Brotonne.[31] This forest, part of which had been bought by the abbey from William of Arques c. 1040 was notable horse-breeding country, immediately across the Seine from Jumièges itself.[32]

Fécamp, just outside the estuary of the Seine was famous both for its close relations with the dukes and for its reforming zeal, but our knowledge of its horsebreeding comes almost exclusively from documents concerning the

[24] F. Lot, *Etudes critiques sur l'abbaye de Saint-Wandrille*, Bibl. de l'Ecole des Hautes Etudes, 204 (Paris 1913), charter no. 43, disposing of the remainder in 1071.
[25] Orderic, ii. 82.
[26] Orderic, iii. 186.
[27] Orderic, iii. 200.
[28] J-J. Vernier (ed.) *Chartes de l'Abbaye de Jumièges*, 2 vols., SHN 1916, no. viii.
[29] Vernier, no. xiv.
[30] Vernier, no. xxii.
[31] Vernier, no. xxv.
[32] Vernier, no. xx.

foundation of its priory at Saint Gabriel near Caen (1059/66).[33] From them
we learn that the lands involved were purchased for 312 pounds 2 shillings,
seven horses and the loan of two more. Of these horses two, worth 10 pounds
each, were given to the duke who also received a third valued at 50 shillings.
Another two, worth 7 pounds each, went to Robert le Gai, one worth 40
shillings to Richard de Rocqueville, and another worth 14 shillings and 6
pence to Brother Osmund. The two horses on loan went to Turstin, the lord
of one of the benefactors, but their value was not stated. The implications of
the transaction are that Fécamp must have had a large number of horses, that
they were of several types and that the abbey had no difficulty in pricing
them accurately. There is some evidence that the Abbey of Saint Ouen at
Rouen may have been similarly involved, because Robert the Magnificent
(1027–35) is said to have granted it the right to cut wood in the Forêt de Bord
in return for 20 pounds in money 'or two horses worth no less'.[34]

It may seem strange that monasteries, especially those that were reformed
and highly respected for their religious life, should make a business of
horsebreeding, but since monks wanted to live their lives in the remoteness
of forests, as also did untamed horses, it was only natural for the one to look
after the other. Nearly all monasteries received gifts of tithes, and it is likely
that they often included tithes of animals, even where the fact is not
specifically stated. But we do know that c. 1050 William fitz Osbern gave the
Abbey of Lyre half the tithes of his mares at Glos-la-Ferrière, not far from
Saint-Evroul,[35] and that at about the same time Raoul Tancarville gave the
tithes of his mares at Roumare to Saint-Georges-de-Boscherville,[36] on the
Seine below Rouen, while in 1067 a knight called Gerold gave the tithes of
his mares in Roumare to the nuns of Saint-Amand in Rouen.[37] Hugh Earl of
Chester (1077–1101) gave the tithes of all his animals, including mares, to the
abbey of Saint-Sever in Lower Normandy.[38]

We have no reason to think that this combination of monasteries and
horsebreeding was confined to the eleventh century. At Saint-Wandrille it
can be traced back to the pre-Norman period because in 854, very shortly
before the monks abandoned the abbey, they received a grant from Charles
the Bald of *Noviomum cum paraveredis viii* – a place called Nojon-sur-Andelle
(now Charleval) and eight *paraveredi*.[39] The word *paraveredus*, though it
subsequently developed into *palefridus* or palfrey, at this date still preserved
its original meaning of post-horse, a horse provided by the *cursus publicus* of
the late Roman Empire. In other words, the estate at Nojon was burdened
with the duty of providing eight posthorses, a duty which becomes very
credible when it is realized that Nojon is situated on the Roman road (now

[33] Lucien Musset, 'Actes inédits du xie siècle: i Les plus anciennes chartes du prieuré de Saint-Gabriel (Calvados), *Bul. de la Soc. de Antiquaires de Normandie* lii, années 1952 à 1954, Caen/Rouen 1955, 117–41, esp. 133–6.

[34] Fauroux no. 78.

[35] Fauroux 285, no. 120.

[36] Fauroux 382, no. 197.

[37] Léopold Delisle, *Etudes sur la condition de la classe agricole et l'état de l'agriculture en Normandie au Moyen Age*, Paris 1903, 226.

[38] Delisle, 227.

[39] Lot, *St-Wandrille*, 34, no. 5. He notes that the name of Nojon-sur-Andelle was changed to Charleval in 1571, when it was acquired by Charles IX.

Route Nationale no. 14) from Troyes to Rouen, Lillebonne and Harfleur, at the point where it crosses the River Andelle. What is more, it had been held by the abbey long before 854, for the *Gesta Sanctorum Patrum Fontanellensis Coenobii* tells us that Abbot Wando was deposed because a prominent rebel had made good his escape from the battle of Vinchy (718) by taking one of his horses which was grazing on the abbey's estate at Nojon.[40] The accusation must have been that the abbot had committed treason by allowing a horse reserved for the public (or royal) service to be used by a rebel.

It should not be thought that horsebreeding in eleventh-century Normandy was practised only by religious houses. On the contrary the very fact that many nobles and barons gave the tithe of their mares to religious houses indicates that they kept herds and retained nine-tenths of them themselves. There may also have been an ulterior motive in directing the tithes of mares to an abbey rather than to a number of parish churches; when great men gave the tithe of mares from all their Norman estates to one particular abbey, as did the Taissons to Fontenay, Robert du Hommet to Saint-Fromond, and Goscelin de Pommeraie to Le Val, they were in fact ensuring that their payment of tithes did not result in their foals being spread all over the country.[41]

The duke himself must have had many studs. Those that he retained in his own hand were presumably near his favourite residences. His park at Rouen was across the river at Quevilly, but he also spent a lot of time hunting in the nearby forest of Lyons, at Bonneville on the edge of the forest of Saint-Gacien, at Caen where he had the large meadow or *prairie*, or Falaise which was close to the forest of Gouffern. We have already mentioned that he was happy to receive horses both from his abbey of Fécamp and from foreign princes and kings. He was also happy to receive them from his own nobles. When, in 1035, Humphrey de Vieilles, was founding the abbey of Saint-Pierre-de-Préaux, he persuaded Duke Robert the Magnificent to give it his demesne manor of Toutainville (Eure), the price he paid for this 'gift' being 12 pounds of gold, 2 textiles and 'two horses of very great price'. The transaction was duly recorded in a charter, and in view of the story of the smith of Beauvais, with which this paper began, it is amusing to find that one of the witnesses was a certain Turoldus 'who received one of the above-mentioned horses from Duke Robert as a gift'.[42]

It must be stressed that our prime concern is not with all horses but with warhorses or destriers. They were far more costly than other horses and were always stallions, the mares of equivalent quality being employed wholetime at the studs. But in addition to a warhorse, every knight would require three lesser horses: one to ride so that the war-horse was not tired before the battle had begun, one for his squire (who would also lead the war-horse (*dextrarius*) on his right (*dexter*) hand, and one for his baggage which would include his armour; armour is both heavy and hot, and no knight would wear it on an ordinary journey. At the approach of battle the knights would stop and change both their clothes and their horses, strapping on their armour and mounting

---

[40] *Gesta Sanctorum Patrum Fontanellensis Coenobii*, eds. F. Lohier and R. P. J. Laporte, SHN 1936, 23–4. Cf. *The Fourth Book of the Chronicle of Fredegar*, ed. J. M. Wallace-Hadrill, Nelson's Medieval Classics, London 1960, 88–9.
[41] Delisle, 226–7.
[42] Fauroux, 231, no. 89.

their destriers as described in *La Chanson de Roland*.[43] Similarly in the Bayeux Tapestry we see Duke William's squire leading his destrier up to him at the onset of battle (pl. 53), though in this case he leads him by the *left* hand.

Those who attended the eighth Battle Conference (1985) will undoubtedly recall the paper by Professor Bernard S. Bachrach on the military administration of the Norman Conquest.[44] He was particularly concerned with the supplies which William's army would have required during the month which it spent at Dives in August-September 1066. On the assumption that the army would have included 2,000–3,000 warhorses weighing no less that 1,300 lbs each, and that each would have received a daily diet of 12 lbs grain (either oats or good barley) and 13 lbs of hay, he reckoned that the daily requirement would have been 14 tons of both grain and hay for 2,000 horses, or 20 tons for 3,000. Even if one acccepts these daily totals (which I do not) they do not produce a monthly total of 1,500 tons of both grain and hay, but 434 tons for 2,000 horses and 620 tons for 3,000. But in any case such a statistical exercise cannot be taken seriously, because no-one knows the number or weight of the horses involved. Judging by the enormous range of prices paid for horses, I would *guess* that only a handful of horses (those costing 20 or 30 pounds) would have approached the weight of 13,000 lbs or the height of 14 hands. The remainder would have varied greatly; my *guess* would be that a horse of 12 hands would have been thought fairly good and one of 10–12 hands small but passable. I would also be surprised if the army needed more than 300 tons of grain and 300 tons of hay during its month-long stay at Dives, but I would be the first to admit that even this amount could not have been produced without a first-class administration. Providing for the army during the fortnight which it spent at Hastings would have been even more of a problem. The Bayeux Tapestry shows that food for the men was seized locally, but it does not show what was done for the horses.

Finally we may ask how the horses of the Normans would have compared with those of the Anglo-Saxons. Strictly speaking it is impossible to answer this question, but we can compare our knowledge of the two. If we restrict ourselves to record evidence in the period before 1066, we have to say that at first sight far more is known about the Anglo-Saxons' horses which are mentioned in fourteen wills and at least four marriage-agreements or wills, the totals involved being 95 horses, 6 stallions, 3 studs, three groups of wild horses and two groups of mares and colts (16 in all). Particularly noticeable are the heriots consisting 2, 4 or 8 horses, which occur in thirteen of the relevant documents extending right through the period 946–1045.[45] In contrast we have so far found in Normandy no more than ten charters referring to 20 horses and 2 studs.

These totals are misleading. In the first place the eighteen Anglo-Saxon documents range over a hundred years (946–1045), while the ten Norman

---

[43] *The Song of Roland*, trans. Howard S. Robinson, London 1972, lines 994–1004.
[44] Bernard S. Bachrach, 'Some Observations on the Military Administration of the Norman Conquest', *ANS* viii, 1985, 1–26. If his figures for both the horses' food and their excreta are correct, they must have been losing weight at an alarming rate. In spite of these criticisms it has to be said that Professor Bachrach has done us a real service in revealing the extent of the problems involved in the organization of the army.
[45] See Appendix.

documents belong to only forty-six (1020–66), seven of them falling in the twenty-one years between 1045 and 1066 during which there are no relevant English documents at all. Evidently horses were far more important in England than in Normandy during the period 946–1020, but after that the balance began to change and by 1045 had been reversed completely; Duke William's Normandy was far more horse-minded than Edward the Confessor's England. What could have been the reason for the sudden decline in English horses? Those who have followed the argument of this paper will consider, I hope, that the most likely cause would have been the disruption of the English studs during the disastrous wars of the reign of King Æthelred II (978–1016). It is true that King Cnut (1016–35) restored peace to the land, but since his organization of the army was by ships and 'shipfulls' there would not have been much incentive for him or his subjects to invest large sums of money in the production of larger and heavier horses.

One final contrast should be noted. In the English records all horses are treated as equal. There is never any mention of the value of the horses concerned, and it is only in the will of the Ætheling Æthelstan (1014/15) that an attempt is made to identify individual horses by reference to colour or previous owner. The Norman sources, on the other hand, always mention value. At first, in the 1020s and 1030s, a vague phrase is used – a horse is said to be of 'great' or 'very great' price – but subsequently the price is nearly always stated in terms of pounds, shillings and pence. We have seen that those mentioned in charters (which would exclude cheap work horses) range from 14 shillings and 6 pence to 30 pounds, the most expensive costing forty times as much as the cheapest. There could be no clearer indication of the emphasis which the Normans put on improving the quality of their horse, and there can be no doubt that they succeeded.

APPENDIX

Horses in Anglo-Saxon Wills and Agreements

In the following list of relevant Anglo-Saxon wills, the Roman numerals without prefix refer to those in *Anglo-Saxon Wills*, ed. Dorothy Whitelock, Cambridge 1930. The prefix C refers to *The Crawford Collection of Early Charters and Documents*, ed. A. S. Napier and W. H. Stevenson, Oxford 1895; the prefix H to *Select English Historical Documents of the ninth and tenth centuries*, ed. F. E. Harmer, Cambridge 1914.

H xx	Earl ÆTHELWOLD	946–7	4 horses (*heriot*).
i	Bishop Theodred	c. 951	4 horses, the best that he has (*heriot*).
ii	Earl Ælfgar	946–51	3 stallions (*heriot*).
iii	Wynflaed	c. 950?	(1) a horse (2) wild horses (unspec.) (3) tame horses (unspec.)
x	Ealdorman Æthelmaer	971/83	8 horses (4 with trappings) (*heriot*).
xi	Brihtric and Ælfswith	973/87	4 horses (2 with harness) & a stallion (*heriot*).
xii	Æthelwold	after 987	2 horses (*heriot*) (+ 2 swords, shields, and spears).
xiii	Ælfhelm	975/1016	4 horses (2 harnessed) as *heriot*, and the stud at Troston, (Suff.).
xvii	Wulfric	1002/4	4 horses (2 saddled) as *heriot*, and 100 wild horses & 16 tame geldings (*hencgestan*).
xix	Wulfgeat	?? 1006	2 horses as *heriot* (+ 2 swords) and (1) 10 mares with 10 colts and (2) 6 mares with 6 colts.
C x	Alfwold Bp Crediton	1008/12	4 horses (*heriot*) + (1) *wildra worfa* at Ashburn (2) a horse to each of 9 named people and (3) to each retainer (*hired men*) his steed which he had lent him.
xx	Ætheling Æthelstan	c. 1014/15	(1) The horse which Thurbrand gave me (2) The white horse which Leofwine gave me (?these 2 as *heriot*, to the King) (3) a black stallion (4) my horse (with harness) (5) a pied stallion, (6) the stud which is in *Colungahrycg*.
xxvii	Wulfsige	c. 1022–3	2 horses with harness (*heriot*).
xxi	Thurstan	1043/5	2 horses with trappings (*heriot*) and the stud at Ongar (Essex).

Four agreements referring to horses are found in
A. J. Robertson (ed.) *Anglo-Saxon Charters* (Cambridge 1939; rept. 1956):

(vii)	Agreement of Abbot Ceolred of Peterborough with Wulfred	'852, but necessarily after 965	a horse as part of an annual rent.
(lxv)	Oswald Abp of York and Bp Worcester to Æthelmaer	972–92	a horse as part of the purchase price of a lease.
(lxxvi)	Wulfric's marriage agreement	1014/16	30 horses as part of a marriage agreement.
(lxxvii)	Kentish marriage agreement	1016/20	10 horses (with 30 oxen and 20 cows) as part of a marriage agreement.

7

The Carmen de Hastingae Proelio

THE *Carmen de Hastingae Proelio* is a Latin poem of 835 lines, which was discovered in 1826 by Georg Heinrich Pertz and subsequently published by Henry Petrie in England and F. X. Michel in France.[1] The title by which it is now known has no manuscript authority and is in some ways misleading, since the battle of Hastings occupies no more than a third of the poem which is really concerned with Duke William's Conquest of England. It starts, after a conventional introduction, with an account of Duke William's fleet port-bound at Saint-Valery, and proceeds to relate how the wind changed, how the crossing was accomplished and how the landing was effected without opposition. It then carries the story forward with a series of speeches: by the rustic who reports the landing to Harold; by Harold; by the monk whom he sends to demand William's withdrawal; by William; and by the monk whom he sent to Harold to remind him that he (William) had been designated by Edward the Confessor. The battle is described at length with some striking set-pieces; the first blow is struck by a Norman mummer called *Incisor-ferri* (Taillefer); a feigned flight by the Normans almost becomes a reality but is checked with a fighting speech by William; William has two horses killed under him, one by Gyrth and the other by the son of Helloc; and Harold is eventually slain by four named Normans, each of whom pierces, or cuts off, a separate part of his body. William refuses to hand the body over to Harold's mother, but buries it on a cliff-top by the sea. He advances to Dover and Canterbury, receives the surrender of Winchester from a distance, and finally arrives before London. When the city resists him, he besieges it in force, but eventually secures its surrender through skilful negotiations with a wounded leader called Ansgard. The Londoners accept William as king, the crown jewels are described at length, and the poem ends with a description of the coronation at Westminster.

The tone of the poem suggests a literary exercise. It has flowery references to the Muses, Hades, Cynthia, Vulcan, Mars and Hercules, likens the Conqueror's battles to those of Pompey and Julius

1. Henry Petrie, 'De Bello Hastingensi Carmen, Auctore W' in *Monumenta Historica Britannica* (London, 1848), pp. 856–72; (though not published till 1848 this was in fact printed before 1833); Francisque Xavier Michel, 'Widonis Carmen de Hastingae Proelio' in *Chroniques Anglo-Normandes*, i (Rouen, 1840), 1–38.

Caesar, and describes the duke himself as the equal of King David, 'more beautiful than the sun, wiser than King Solomon, more bountiful and valiant than Charlemagne'. One gets the impression that the author was, above all, determined to show that he knew what was expected of a poet. He is more intent on how he sings than on what he sings about; and just as in an opera the action is suspended for a conventional aria, so in the *Carmen* the poet pauses at the opening of the battle for an invocation to Mars, the God of War (ll. 345–62) and at the first mention of a coronation bursts into song about the crown jewels (ll. 755–86).

Though a first impression of this poem suggests a literary contrivance, several scholars have produced reasons for believing that it was written very soon after the battle and that it has value as a historical source. When Pertz discovered it, he immediately realized that it could be the lost poem of Guy Bishop of Amiens which Orderic Vitalis had described and used in his *Ecclesiastical History*. This identification was generally accepted – though with some reserve in the case of Henry Petrie and Thomas Duff Hardy – until 1944 when G. H. White produced arguments to show that, so far from being an original source, it was really a derivative work of the twelfth century.[1] Though this view was for a time accepted, recent critics have rejected it. Sten Körner[2] and Frank Barlow[3] have argued that the poem was both early and used as a source by William of Poitiers, while Catherine Morton and Hope Muntz, the poem's most recent editors, claim that it is both the earliest source and the best, being 'at once fuller than the *Gesta Normannorum Ducum* [of William at Jumièges], more honest and reliable than the *Gesta Guillelmi* [of William of Poitiers] and more explicit than the Bayeux Tapestry'.[4] They accept its story in every detail and use its evidence to revise accepted views on the use of crossbows, on oaths and claims to the English crown in 1066, on the form of the English coronation *ordo*, and on the attitude of Pope Alexander II to Duke William's invasion.[5] But is the poem really as early or as reliable as they claim?

The case in favour of an early date for the *Carmen* rests on three propositions: first that it is evidently the poem described by Orderic Vitalis as having been written by Guy Bishop of Amiens; second,

1. G. H. White, 'Companions of the Conqueror', *Genealogists' Magazine*, ix (1944), 418–24, and 'The Battle of Hastings and the Death of Harold', *Complete Peerage*, xii, pt. i (London, 1953), Appendix L.
2. Sten Körner, *The Battle of Hastings: England and Europe, 1035–66* (Lund, 1964).
3. Frank Barlow, 'The Carmen de Hastingae Proelio' in *Studies in International History presented to W. Norton Medlicott*, ed. K. Bourne and D. C. Watt (London, 1967), pp. 35–67.
4. Catherine Morton and Hope Muntz (eds.), *The Carmen de Hastingae Proelio of Guy Bishop of Amiens* (Oxford Medieval Texts: Oxford, 1972) (henceforth cited as MM), xxxv.
5. *Ibid.* Appendices C, A, and pp. liv–lix; Catherine Morton, 'Pope Alexander II and the Norman Conquest', *Latomus*, xxxiv (1975), 362–82.

that it was used as a source by William of Poitiers who was himself writing *c.* 1077; and thirdly that the text of the poem, already somewhat corrupt, is found in a manuscript which has been dated as early as *c.* 1100. Though to a certain extent these propositions interlock – and perhaps even because of that – it is important to discuss them in turn.

First there is the identification with the poem which Orderic knew. He refers to it twice, once in his third book (written *c.* 1114–25) and once in his fourth (written *c.* 1125):

(*a*) Guy (Guido), Bishop of Amiens also wrote a poem describing the battle of Senlac in imitation of the epics of Virgil and Statius, abusing and condemning Harold but praising and exalting William.[1]

(*b*) In the year of Our Lord 1068 King William sent ambassadors to Normandy to summon his wife to join him. At once she gladly obeyed her husband's commands and crossed with a great company of vassals and noble women. Among the clergy who ministered to her spiritual needs was Guy Bishop of Amiens, who had already celebrated (*iam . . . ediderat*) the battle between Harold and William in verse. Ealdred Archbishop of York, who had anointed her husband, now anointed Matilda as queen consort on Whit Sunday in the second year of King William's reign [11 May 1068].[2]

The *Carmen* is the only poem about the battle which we possess and its opening lines consist of a dedication which might seem to put the identification beyond doubt.

> Quem probitas celebrat, sapientia munit et ornat,
> Erigit et decorat, L . . . W . . . salutat.

If the initials in the second line stood for 'Lanfrancum' and 'Wido', the verse would scan and the dedication would be by Guy (Wido) Bishop of Amiens to Lanfranc Abbot of St Stephen's Caen (1066–70) and Archbishop of Canterbury (1070–89).

Attractive though this solution may seem, it is not free of difficulties. It has often been pointed out that in the eleventh century Guido is usually spelt (as also by Orderic) with an initial Gu rather than a W – and of course there are plenty of other names which would fit the initials and the verse.[3] But what is really difficult to understand is why a secular poem of this nature should have been dedicated to an ecclesiastic such as Lanfranc. Poets usually dedicated their works to those whom they expected to reward them most highly. In the present case the most obvious choice would have

1. *The Ecclesiastical History of Orderic Vitalis*, ed. Marjorie Chibnall (Oxford Medieval Texts: Oxford, 1969–) (henceforth cited as *OV*), ii. 185–7.

2. *OV*, ii. 215.

3. MM (p. xxvi n) cite a charter in which 'Guy of Amiens calls himself W', but it is a cartulary copy. Other possibilities for L and W are: Lambertum, Lanzonem, Letoldum, Ludolfum, Leofricum, Leofgarum, Leopoldum, Lietardum, Wado, Walo, Wazo, Warra, Wigo, Wine and Wulfra.

been King William or his queen. Indeed, Orderic's statement about
Guy having been in the queen's entourage (a fact otherwise unknown) reads as if it had been taken from the prologue or dedication
of the poem which he knew. But when we turn to the *Carmen* we
find, not only that the poem was dedicated to someone else, but
that in all its 835 lines it does not once refer to the queen. Frank
Barlow, who obviously found this situation puzzling, lays great
stress on the fact that the *Carmen* is incomplete as we have it – it
ends with a hexameter instead of a pentameter – and suggests that
there might have been references to the queen in the final passages
which are lost. This is, of course, possible but it is hardly evidence.[1]

A further objection, which has often been raised, is that Orderic,
who made no comment on the bias of William of Poitiers, criticized
Guy of Amiens for 'abusing and condemning Harold but praising
and exalting William'. though in fact the *Carmen*'s tone is relatively
cool. Barlow rejects the criticism on the ground that the *Carmen*
does oppose Harold and 'several times describes him as a perjurer
and faithless vassal', but he has to admit that when compared with
'the almost hysterical vituperation' of William of Poitiers, the
Carmen is 'much fairer'.[2] Similarly Morton and Muntz, though they
support Barlow's conclusion, cannot help glossing his reference to
the poem's 'rather detached tone' towards Duke William, with the
comment that to their mind it verges 'into acidity at times'.[3]

Attention must also be paid to the fact that Orderic claims to
have used Guy's poem as one of his sources, for if Guy's poem was
in fact the *Carmen* we ought to have no difficulty in seeing what he
has taken from it. Normally it is easy to see how Orderic has used
his sources; in the case of William of Poitiers it has even proved
possible to reconstruct from Orderic's borrowings the chapters
which have been lost. But in the case of the *Carmen* it is different;
Orderic's most recent editor states that she has found no clear
evidence that he was borrowing from it. 'If the *Carmen* was the work
of Guy,' she writes, 'Orderic took nothing from it that he could not
also have found in William of Poitiers.'[4] This is strange because the
Carmen has some striking scenes which are not in William of
Poitiers – the opening of the battle by the mummer Taillefer, the
slaying of Harold, or the part played by Ansgard in the seige of
London – and it is hard to believe that Orderic would not have
enjoyed the retelling of them, if only he had known them.

But if Orderic was unaware of the stories which were peculiar to
the *Carmen*, the *Carmen* is unaware of the one fact which Orderic

1. Barlow, *op. cit.* pp. 41–42.
2. Barlow, p. 42.
3. MM, xxvii, *Cf.* Barlow, 62: ' "de-bunking" was not an art much practised in the
eleventh century'.
4. *OV*, ii. 186 n. But she has to make a similar remark about Orderic's reference to
Foucher of Chartres, *OV*, v. 6n.

might have taken from the poem written by Bishop Guy. As is well known, Orderic is the only authority to call the battle of Hastings 'Senlac', and he seems, as Freeman observed to have taken 'a kind of pleasure in repeating it'.[1] It is the one fact in his account which cannot be traced to any authority which we know; and it is tempting to believe that it came from Bishop Guy's poem because, when describing that poem, he specifically states that it was about the battle of 'Senlac'.

The situation is that there is nothing in Orderic which must have come from the *Carmen*, and that the only facts which he tells us about Bishop Guy's poem are not in the *Carmen*. It begins to look as if there might have been two poems written about the Norman Conquest, one of them known to Orderic and the other to us.

One way of advancing the question is by attempting to establish the relationship between the *Carmen* and the *Gesta Guillelmi* of William of Poitiers. This latter work was probably written *c.* 1077,[2] and has some passages which are undoubtedly reminiscent of the *Carmen*. If these resemblances indicate that the *Carmen* was borrowing from William of Poitiers, as was believed by G. H. White, then the *Carmen* must have been written after *c.* 1077 and could not be the work of Guy of Amiens who died in 1074 or 1075.[3] If, on the other hand, it was William of Poitiers who was borrowing from the *Carmen*, as is believed by Raymonde Foreville, Sten Körner, Frank Barlow and Morton and Muntz, it would follow that the *Carmen* was written before *c.* 1077, and the likelihood of its being the work of Bishop Guy increased.

Of those who took this latter view, the simplest position was that of Raymonde Foreville who, since she did not question the belief that the *Carmen* was the poem described by Orderic, found it self-evident that a poem written by Bishop Guy before 11 May 1068 was earlier than a work written by William of Poitiers in the 1070s.[4] But unless the identification of the *Carmen* with Bishop Guy's poem can be proved, her argument is, at best, circular.

1. E. A. Freeman, *The History of the Norman Conquest of England* (2nd ed., Oxford, 1875), iii. 758.

2. Raymonde Foreville whose edition, *Guillaume de Poitiers: Histoire de Guillaume le Conquérant* (Paris, 1953), we cite throughout as *GG* considered the date of the work to be 1073–4 (pp. xvii–xx), placing the *terminus a quo* in 1073 because she believed that it was in that year that St Stephen's, Caen, was dedicated. We now know that that dedication was on 13 Sept. 1077 (Lucien Musset, *Les Actes de Guillaume le Conquérant et de la reine Mathilde pour les abbayes Caennaises* (Mems. de la Soc. des Antiquaires de Normandie, xxxvii (1967), 14–15). It is true that William of Poitiers seems also to be writing before the death of Hugh Bishop of Lisieux, who died on 17 July 1077, but the composition of his work must have occupied him several months, and '*c.* 1077' is the closest we can get to the date. Nothing can be deduced from the fact that he does not mention Norman defeats in the Byzantine Empire, because he is interested only in victories.

3. The date of Bishop Guy's death is usually given as 21 Nov. 1075, but Barlow (*op. cit.* p. 64) points out that it could equally well have been 21 Nov. 1074.

4. Foreville in *GG*, pp. xxxv–xxxviii.

Sten Körner, in his study of the Battle of Hastings, argued for the priority of the *Carmen* because he considered that at various points the *Gesta Guillelmi* (*GG*) 'enlarged upon and heightened the account in the *Carmen*'.[1] The three main examples which he adduced were: (1) in the *Carmen* William is told that Harold has 500 ships, in *GG* 700; (2) in the *Carmen* there is one feigned flight, in *GG* three; (3) in the *Carmen* William has one horse killed under him, in *GG* three. But though at first sight these examples seem to illustrate the growth of legend, they do not bear close examination. The change from 500 ships (*Carmen*, l. 319) to 700 (*GG*, p. 180) is hardly significant because both numbers are the sort which medieval writers used in the vague sense of 'very many'. The number of feigned flights would be important if it could be established with certainty how many there really were in each narrative; but different commentators have come to different conclusions, and it is at least possible that both the *Carmen* (ll. 424–6 and 444–7) and *GG* (p. 194) were attempting to describe two.[2] As for the number of horses killed under William, though *GG* states boldly that there were three, the *Carmen* goes into far greater detail, and though it refers only to two horses, it describes how the first was killed by Gyrth, how William acquired the second by upturning a knight of Maine, and how this second horse was killed by 'the son of Helloc' (ll. 470–506). If we are witnessing the growth of legend, it is surely in the *Carmen* rather than in *GG*. 'The son of Helloc' is particularly suggestive because, as Morton and Muntz point out 'the name is not English and may be an attempt at Havelock';[3] if they are right, the name provides an interesting link with a famous twelfth-century legend.

Both Barlow and Morton and Muntz concede that Körner has not established his point beyond question,[4] and attempt to clinch the argument by studying the extent of the flattery contained in the two works. After making a detailed comparison of their accounts of the battle, Barlow concludes:

This comparison between the stories told by the poet and the historian does not prove conclusively who was indebted to the other. Either could have adapted the other's account. Yet the nature of the modifications points unmistakeably in one direction. Each author was writing to please the Conqueror and directing his work to the king's ear. If the poet used the history, he excised or cut down William of Poitiers's more extravagant praise of the Normans and their leader, deleted the moralizing, cut out episodes which did honour to individual Normans, especially the duke, and introduced persons and scenes which, although producing a more balanced picture, could easily have caused offence.[5]

1. Körner, *op. cit.* p. 98.
2. 'Bis eo dolo simili eventu usu' (*GG*, p. 194).
3. MM, p. 33 n.
4. Barlow, pp. 53 n. and 61–62; MM, p. xix.
5. Barlow, pp. 61–62.

It is faultless logic provided that the poet really was 'writing to please the Conqueror'; if he was writing after the Conqueror's death he might well have thought it both safe and desirable to tone down the flattery which William of Poitiers had provided in such copious supply.

Both Barlow and Morton and Muntz had independent reasons for thinking that the *Carmen* had been written before the Conqueror's death. So far as Barlow was concerned, the decisive argument was based on the early date of the manuscript, to which we will presently turn,[1] but Morton and Muntz believed that they could also show that the *Carmen* was necessarily written before the deposition of Archbishop Stigand (11 April 1070).[2] Their starting point was the *Carmen*'s statement (ll. 803-4) that two metropolitans (*honore pari*) assisted at William's coronation, and they assumed, reasonably enough, that they would have been the archbishops of Canterbury and York. The presence of these two archbishops would have been a natural assumption for a later writer who was uncertain of the facts, because it was normal for the archbishops of Canterbury and York to assist at English coronations. In the case of William I, however, we are told by William of Poitiers, the Anglo-Saxon Chronicle (D and E), Orderic Vitalis, William of Malmesbury and Florence of Worcester that the coronation was performed by Ealdred Archbishop of York, the reason (either stated or implied) being the uncanonical position of Archbishop Stigand.[3] Morton and Muntz, believing that the *Carmen* is the earliest and most trustworthy source, insist that Stigand must have assisted at the coronation, but that after his deposition in 1070 everyone denied it.[4] They also consider that 'no work composed after the accord (of Winchester in 1072), and furthermore addressed to Lanfranc, could have spoken of two archbishops of equal dignity'.[5] It is true that Lanfranc would have objected to such a description, but we do not know that he was the 'L' to whom the poem was dedicated, and we do know that the archbishops of York, most popes of the time and

---

1. Below, pp. 90-94.   2. MM, pp. xxi–xxii.

3. *GG*, p. 220; *Anglo-Saxon Chronicle* (D and E), *s.a.*; *OV*, ii. 183; William of Malmesbury, *Gesta Regum* (Rolls Series), ii. 307; Florence of Worcester, ed. Thorpe, i. 228–9.

4. Catherine Morton has elaborated the argument in 'Pope Alexander II and the Norman Conquest', *Latomus*, xxxiv (1975), 362–82. She believes that the pope did not approve the conquest until 1070, and then in return for (i) the Normans agreeing to do penance for the conquest; (ii) William agreeing to be recrowned by papal legates; and (iii) the deposition of Stigand. It would then follow that the *Carmen*, if it was completed by 1068, could not possibly have known about these events. But the evidence for the irregularity of Stigand's position being well-known (he was an intruder who had received the pallium from an anti-pope), and Miss Morton does not succeed in explaining away the statements in Pope Gregory VII's letter of 24 Apr. 1080. The redating of the Penitentiary of Ermenfrid does not affect the issue, since the implication of the penitentiary is that offences incurred in the cause of the conquest were less serious than others; (*e.g.* involving a penance of one year instead of three).

5. MM, p. xxi.

the great majority of continental churchmen would have insisted that all metropolitans were equal. As so often happens in the case of the *Carmen*, we are caught in a circular argument, 'proving' its early date by reasons based on assumptions which are themselves based on the supposedly early date of the poem.

It has to be admitted that close textual comparison of the *Carmen* and *Gesta Guillelmi* has proved unrewarding, because in the last resort it has been impossible to determine by textual arguments which author was copying from which. We will therefore attempt a different approach by concentrating on those scenes which are unique to the *Carmen*, not being found in the *Gesta Guillelmi* or any of the other early sources – the Bayeux Tapestry (which probably dates from the 1070s), the *Gesta Normannorum Ducum* of William of Jumièges (*GND*) (*c.* 1070–1), or the Anglo-Saxon Chronicle (D) whose annal for 1066 may have been written as early as 1071 but cannot be later than 1093. There are five such scenes, and we will discuss them in turn.

1. The story of Taillefer (*Incisor-ferri*), a player (*histrio*) or mummer (*mimus*) who juggled with his sword in front of the Norman army, inciting the English to attack him, killing the first man to do so, and cutting off his head so as to display it to the Normans as a good augury for the battle (ll. 391–402). As Morton and Muntz note 'the *Carmen* is the only eleventh-century source to name him,' and they give a solemn 'appraisal of his role in the battle',[1] but they do not stop to ask whether 'Taillefer' was his real name or why the Bayeux Tapestry missed the opportunity of illustrating his feats. It is an interesting fact that, though the *Carmen* is the only supposedly eleventh-century source to include this story, it does come into currency in the twelfth century. Still unknown to Orderic Vitalis (*c.* 1114–21) and William of Malmesbury (*c.* 1125) it makes its appearance in the first edition of Henry of Huntingdon's history (1129). Since in this case the details are slightly different, Taillefer being made to kill two Englishmen before being killed himself by a third, it is clear that Henry had not learnt the story from the *Carmen*, and since we know of no other written source for it, it is natural to assume that he had picked it up as a legend. As G. H. White pointed out,[2] it is in harmony with the story (which first appears in William of Malmesbury, *c.* 1125) that the Normans advanced into battle singing the Song of Roland, and it is natural to suggest that the legend or epic which both writers were following would have been coming into circulation in the 1120s.

2. The story of the slaying of Harold by four named men who respectively pierce his breast, cut off his head, disembowel him and cut off his loin. This is the most improbable scene in the whole

1. MM, pp. 27 n. 1 and 81–3.
2. *Complete Peerage*, xii, pt. i, Appendix L.

poem, and it is perhaps typical that though the four slayers are named, it has proved extremely difficult to identify them. Before the appearance of the edition by Morton and Muntz it was thought that they were (i) Eustace Count of Boulogne, (ii) the (unnamed) 'noble heir of Ponthieu', (iii) 'Hugh' (presumed to be Hugh de Montfort) and (iv) 'Gilfard' (presumed to be Walter Giffard). G. H. White, the leading genealogist of his time, was quick to point out that if the poem was by Guy of Amiens, it was strange that he did not know who the heir of Ponthieu was, since he was himself the uncle of the reigning count and quite possibly his heir.[1] The genealogy of the counts of Ponthieu has since been revised both by Barlow and by Morton and Muntz, though with slightly different results,[2] the most radical conclusion being that of Morton and Muntz who considered that in 1066 the heir of Ponthieu would have been Hugh, a son of Count Guy whom White and Barlow had apparently overlooked. This enabled them to repunctuate the *Carmen* so as to make 'the noble heir of Ponthieu' and 'Hugh' the same person, and since this left them with only three named slayers, they deduced that the fourth must have been Duke William himself.[3] We thus have two possible lists:

A	*B*
(i) Eustace of Boulogne	(i) Duke William
(ii) the noble heir of Ponthieu	(ii) Eustace of Boulogne
(iii) Hugh [de Montfort]	(iii) Hugh, the noble heir of Ponthieu
(iv) [Walter] Gilfard	(iv) [Walter] Gilfard

The absurdity of list *B* is self-evident, because it is impossible to imagine why, if Duke William really killed Harold with his own hand, all the other sources and narratives suppressed the fact. The difficulty is particularly acute for those who believe that William of Poitiers took material from the *Carmen* but heightened and enlarged it in order to flatter the Conqueror, because in this case the natural expectation would have been for William of Poitiers to glory in the Conqueror's part in the affair. Are we to believe that the Conqueror wanted the story to be suppressed?

Barlow accepts list *A*, but with caution, considering that the phrase 'the noble heir of Ponthieu' has 'probably been viewed with exaggerated suspicion', and that 'the historicity of these episodes does not concern us here';[4] but if the poem really were written for the Conqueror's court, the truth of this central assertion would have been important. Could anyone invent a claim to King William's favour by asserting that he personally had killed Harold, or even

1. *Genealogists' Magazine*, ix (1944), 418–24.
2. Barlow, p. 67; MM, pp. 130–1.
3. MM, pp. 116–20.
4. Barlow, pp. 42, 57.

had a fourth part in his killing? Alternatively, if the claim was true, is it conceivable that it should have been unknown to any other chronicler and forgotten by the descendants of the slayers? As G. H. White most pertinently asked, if the noble heir of Ponthieu really was involved, why is there no trace, in Domesday Book or elsewhere, of his being rewarded with lands in England?

The simplest explanation is surely to admit that the poet was not attempting to record events for Duke William's court, but simply composing a literary exercise in the twelfth century. Though there is nothing like this story in any eleventh-century account of the battle, William of Malmesbury (*c.* 1125)[1] has one which, though different, is reminiscent of it. He says that Harold was killed by an arrow, but that after he had fallen, a knight (*miles*) cut off his thigh with his sword, and that when William heard of the dastardly act he expelled the man from his service (*militia*). As in the case of the story of Taillefer, it looks as if we have two variations on a legendary theme, one in William of Malmesbury and the other in the *Carmen*, and it is natural to suggest that they arose at about the same time.

3. The story of the siege of London (ll. 673–8, *cf.* 697–706) is less picturesque, but nonetheless unique to the *Carmen*. William of Jumièges mentions a skirmish in the main square (*in platea urbis*) when the Norman advance-guard entered the city, and William of Poitiers says that the chief men (*principes*) of the city went out to parley as soon as William's army came in sight.[2] So also the Anglo-Saxon Chronicle speaks only of submission. But the *Carmen* has a real siege in which Duke William raises a high mound on which he mounts a siege engine so as to bombard the walls of the city (ll. 674–5). If this really were the case, it is hard to guess why the Conqueror might have wanted to suppress the fact after 1068. On the other hand, it would have been natural for a twelfth-century poet to wind up his story with a siege, if only to exploit the necessary vocabulary and show that his poem was in a Trojan tradition.

4. The story of Ansgard, a wounded warrior who had to be borne in a litter, who was in command of London and negotiated with the Conqueror in the hope of tricking him, but 'because the fox can hardly be held by open snares' was himself deceived (ll. 679–752), is rather less implausible, since Ansgard may be identified as Esgar the staller, a known official of King Edward the Confessor who could conceivably have been in charge of London. But the story has picturesque elements – the Normans were very fond of stories which made them out to be cunning and wily – and it is strange that there is no mention of the Earls Edwin and Morcar or Archbishops Ealdred and Stigand who, according to William of Poitiers and the

---

1. William of Malmesbury, *Gesta Regum*, ed. W. Stubbs (Rolls Series, 1887–9), ii. 303.
2. *Guillaume de Jumièges: Gesta Normannorum Ducum*, ed. Jean Marx (Soc. de l'histoire de Normandie, 1914) (henceforth cited as *GND*), p. 136; *GG*, p. 216.

Anglo-Saxon Chronicle (D) played the leading part at this stage.[1] The general effect of the *Carmen*'s account is to change the story from the last despairing effort of the English ruling class to a brave defiance of the Conqueror by the Londoners. It is the rulers of the city who are made to elect the Ætheling Edgar as King, and when that happened:

> Sparsit fama volans quod habet Londonia regem
> Gaudet et Anglorum qui superest populus (ll. 653-4)

One cannot say that it could not possibly have been like that, but one cannot help feeling wary.

5. The story of the coronation, complete with its description of the crown jewels and its mention of the two metropolitans (which we have already discussed) reads as a very conventional 'coronation piece' (ll. 753-835). Barlow has pointed out that the account of the ceremony is 'not in agreement with the surviving Anglo-Saxon and Anglo-Norman *ordines*'.[2] Morton and Muntz insist that it is 'a coronation recognizably made up of elements drawn from the Romano–German tradition (which has affinities with the earlier Frankish rites) and the English tradition, together with some common to both',[3] but this is surely the sort of hotch-potch that one would have expected of a poet if he had no special knowledge and was not even a native of the country.

A final comparison between the sources which purport to date from the eleventh century can be made by listing all the people whom they mention (see Table 1). It is immediately apparent that William of Poitiers is the best informed, naming thirty-seven people, fourteen of whom are not mentioned by any of the other narratives, though they can be identified as living at the time. The *Carmen*, rather surprisingly in view of its length, names fewer people than either the Anglo-Saxon Chronicle (D) or the Bayeux Tapestry, amongst its most unexpected omissions being Archbishop Stigand and the Conqueror's half-brothers, Odo of Bayeux and Robert Count of Mortain. The most significant comparison, however, is of those names which occur in one work only. The fourteen from William of Poitiers are all known members of the Conqueror's court or army. The four from the Anglo-Saxon Chronicle are English or Norse, mainly concerned with the battle of Stamford Bridge. The three from the Bayeux Tapestry are two tenants of the Bishop of Bayeux and the mysterious Ælfgiva of Rouen. But of the four from the *Carmen* only one, Ansgard, can be firmly identified as a real person; the 'noble heir of Ponthieu' is uncomfortably vague, and Taillefer (*Incisor-fevri*) and the son of Helloc are probably

---

1. *GG*, pp. 214–16; *Anglo-Saxon Chronicle* (D), *s.a.* For the place of Asgard/Esgar in London, see C. N. L. Brooke and Gillian Keir, *London, 800–1216: the shaping of a city* (London, 1975), p. 192. 2. Barlow, p. 66. 3. MM, p. lix.

TABLE I

	Carmen	Bayeux T	Wm. Jum.	Wm. Pict.	A.S.C.(D)
1. William	✓	✓	✓	✓	✓
2. Edward the Confessor	✓	✓	✓	✓	✓
3. Harold	✓	✓	✓	✓	✓
4. Eustace Count of Boulogne (ASC in 1051 only)	✓	✓		✓	✓
5. Odo Bishop of Bayeux		✓		✓	✓
6. Archbishop Stigand		✓		✓	✓
7. Guy Count of Ponthieu		✓	✓	✓	
8. Gyrth (*Carmen*, Gernt)	✓	✓			✓
9. Leofwin		✓			
10. Tostig				✓	✓
11. Earl Edwin				✓	✓
12. Earl Morcar				✓	✓
13. Earl Waltheof				✓	✓
14. Harold Hardrada King of Norway				✓	✓
15. Aldred Archbishop of York				✓	✓
16. Edgar Ætheling				✓	✓
17. William fitz Osbern				✓	
18. Hugh de Montfort (*Carmen*, Hugo)	✓		✓	✓	
19. Robert (of Jumièges) Archbishop of Canterbury			✓	✓	
20. Alfred brother of King Edward			✓	✓	
21. Conan (duke of Brittany)			✓	✓	
22. Robert Count of Mortain (*BT*, Robert)			✓	✓	
23. Walter Giffard (*Carmen*, Gilfardus)	✓			✓	
24. A monk (Harold's envoy)	✓			✓	
25. Harold's mother (unnamed)	✓				
26. Incisor-Ferri (Taillefer)	✓				
27. Filius Hellocis	✓				
28. The noble heir of Ponthieu	✓				
29. Ansgardus (Esgar, Æsgarus)	✓				
30. Ælfgiva		✓			
31. Wadard		✓			
32. Vital		✓			
33. Robert Count of Eu				✓	
34. Richard Count of Evereux				✓	
35. William son of Richard Count of Evereux				✓	
36. Roger de Beaumont				✓	
37. Robert son of Roger de Beaumont				✓	
38. Robert fitz Wimarc				✓	
39. A monk of Fécamp				✓	
40. Geoffrey Bishop of Coutances				✓	
41. Geoffrey son of Count Rotrou of Mortagne				✓	
42. Aimeri de Thouars				✓	
43. Raoul de Tosny				✓	
44. Hugh de Grandmesnil				✓	
45. William de Warenne				✓	
46. William Malet				✓	
47. Æthelnoth Abbot of Glastonbury					✓
48. Olaf sone of the Norse King					✓
49. Their (Norse) bishop					✓
50. The earl of Orkney					✓

legendary. In view of these facts it is hard to give much credence to the *Carmen*, and even harder to see how it could have been used by William of Poitiers as a source, rather than vice-versa. Whenever it provides information which is not to be found in the other sources, that information looks implausible and has the appearance of literary (or legendary) embellishment.

In our discussion we have repeatedly come across features of the *Carmen* which suggest that it should really be dated to the twelfth century, and one might well ask why this conclusion has not been accepted as self-evident. The crux of the matter, and the reason for all the difficulties, has been the manuscript, because (to quote Morton and Muntz) 'Professor Francis Wormald of London University, Mr. N. R. Ker of Oxford University, and Dr. R. Laufner, Direktor, Stadtbibliothek, Trier, have all independently dated the manuscript to *c.* 1100'.[1] As a result, when Frank Barlow concluded that the *Carmen* could not have been derived from the *Gesta Guillelmi* unless it was 'a twelfth century romance',[2] he assumed that this latter eventuality was impossible, because the manuscript showed that the poem had been copied and recopied before 1100.

Its anonymous appearance in a collection, the probable incompleteness of even the fuller text, and much textual corruption suggest a lengthier *stemma codicum*. Indeed, solely on textual grounds, it would seem safe to hold that the poem could hardly have been composed later than the death of William I [1087].[3]

In consequence, though he considered that the *Carmen*'s narrative was sometimes 'larded with improbable detail' and contained 'some incredible episodes, legendary in tone', he concluded that none of these features was evidence as to date, and declared that 'the earliest account of an event is not necessarily the most circumstantial, the soundest or the most truthful'.[4]

But were the palaeographers right about the manuscript? Strictly speaking there are two manuscripts, both in the Bibliothèque Royale de Belgique where they are numbered MS 10615–792 and MS 9799–809, but the latter contains only the first sixty-six lines of the poem. Since both manuscripts emanated from the scriptorium of the abbey of St Eucharius-Matthias at Trier, and since the fragment in MS 9799–809 was copied direct from the fuller version in MS 10615–792, we need only concern ourselves with the latter. It passed in the fifteenth century (as also did MS 9799–809) to the hospital founded by Nicholas of Cusa at Kues on the Moselle, and from there to the Bollandists, whence it eventually reached the Belgian royal library.[5]

1. MM, p. lix n.   2. Barlow, p. 62.   3. Barlow, p. 37.
4. Barlow, pp. 56 and 44.
5. MM, pp. lix–lxvi. For a fuller account of the contents, see Baron de Reiffenberg, 'Manuscrit de Kues', *Annuaire de la Bibliothèque Royale de Belgique*, iv (1843), 51–79.

On palaeographical grounds it has been dated '*c.* 1100', but this date cannot be considered absolute. It is never wise to give a precise date to a handwriting without considering what it was that the hand had written, if only to avoid the hazards of the 'generation gap' which, at any given moment, causes the old and the young to have different styles of handwriting, the one being more old-fashioned and the other more 'modern'. In the present case such caution is particularly necessary because, although Morton and Muntz accepted the findings of K. Manitius and K. Schlechte that our manuscript was one of a group written at the abbey of St Eucharius-Matthias in Trier, they did not mention, or comment upon, the fact that these scholars dated the group to 'the middle or second half of the twelfth century'.[1]

Though Manitius and Schlechte identified the group by its hand-writing and general style, they did not date it purely on stylistic grounds, but also considered the contents of a number of the manuscripts, and we will do well to follow their example with regard to our particular volume. It is a book of 231 folios, about 27 × 19 cm, written in a very small hand which permits two columns of seventy lines on each side of a folio.[2] The contents include works by Augustine, Gregory Nazianzen, Frontinus, Notker, Isidore of Seville and Berengar of Tours. The *Carmen* is the only item which concerns English or Norman history, but it obviously owed its inclusion to the fact that it was in verse, since the volume contains a large number of poems. Amongst those of a relatively late date are: (i) *Astiensis Novus Avianus*, a collection of fables composed by a poet from Asti in Piedmont, which has been dated on stylistic grounds as 'no earlier than the beginning of the twelfth century'[3]; (ii) a lengthy narrative poem on the First Crusade by Gilo de Toucy, which ends with the fall of Jerusalem (1099) and is thought to have been written shortly before 1120[4]; (iii) a short poem, *Nullus salus aut pax veniat tibi, gens tenebrosa*, which refers to events which took place in Metz in 1097-1103[5]; (iv) two poems, *De anulo et baculo pontificis* and *Certamen regis cum papa* which are pleas for terminating the Investitures Contest and seem to date from *c.* 1119, the *Certamen* having a specific reference to Paschal II's decree of 1111 and implying that that pope, who died in 1118, was dead already.[6]

1. Karl Manitius, 'Eine Gruppe von Handschriften des 12 Jahrhunderts aus dem Trierer Kloster St Eucharius-Matthias', *Forschungen and Fortschritte*, xxix (1955), 317-19.

2. The facsimile in MM shows part of one column on fo. 229ᵛ and is about actual size

3. Léopold Herviaux, *Les Fabulistes Latins* (Paris, 1893-9), iii. 182-3.

4. *Recueil des Historiens des Croisades: Historiens Occidentaux*, v. 727-800; for the life of Gilo, see *The Letters of Peter the Venerable*, ed Giles Constable (2 vols., Cambridge, Mass., 1967), ii. 293.

5. *Libelli de Lite*, ed. H. Boehmer (M.G.H., 1891-7). iii. 619.

6. *Ibid.* iii. 720-1 and iii. 711 ff.

It is true that the volume as a whole may well have been written over a period of years; though it is obviously the product of a single scriptorium, one can by no means be sure that it is the work of a single scribe. But the gathering or quire which contains the *Carmen* consists of eight folios (224–31) which are certainly in one hand and contain: (i) *Astiensis Novus Avianus* (fos. 224ff.) which, as we have just mentioned, is thought to date from the twelfth century; (ii) *Nulla salus aut pax*, (fos. 227ᵛ), the poem referring to the events of 1097–1103 in Metz; (iii) the *Carmen* (fos. 227ᵛ–230ᵛ); and (iv) the opening of Gellius's *Attic Nights*, xiv. 5 (second century A.D.), (fo. 230ᵛ). Only the first of these works is given a title (and that one wrong), and a careless reader could easily miss the end of one work and the beginning of the next, since the divisions are marked by a gap of a single line and an insignificant marginal sign.

Folio 227ᵛ is particularly interesting, because it contains eighteen lines of the *Novus Avianus*, the whole of the *Nulla Salus aut Pax* (100 lines) and the first twenty-one lines of the *Carmen*, all written by the same hand as part of a single project. But the eighteen lines of the *Novus Avianus* are not the last eighteen lines of that work. This is obvious because the eighteenth line is a hexameter and an incomplete sentence, the sentence being in fact completed with a pentameter which is found, with the remaining 140 lines of the poem, on folio 231. It therefore looks as if the scribe was copying all three poems from a manuscript in which there was a binding error, so that he ran on from the middle of the *Novus Avianus* to *Nullus Salus aut Pax* and the *Carmen*, only discovering his mistake after he had embarked on the *Attic Nights* at the foot of folio 230ᵛ. He would then have corrected his mistake by devoting the whole of folio 231 to the remainder of the *Novus Avianus*, though he does not seem to have reverted to the *Attic Nights* which remain a fragment in this manuscript, even though folio 231ᵛ (the last in the volume) is blank.

There are therefore many reasons for thinking that the manuscript is later than 1100. It contains poems which were not composed till *c.* 1119, and the beginning of the *Carmen* is found on the same folio as part of one poem 'no earlier than the beginning of the twelfth century' and the whole of another which refers to the events of 1097–1103. Since, as Barlow pointed out, one must allow for a considerable passage of years between the composition of a poem and its inclusion in an anthology which has itself been copied from another anthology,[1] there are no real grounds for doubting that Manitius and Schlechte were correct in attributing the manuscript to 'the middle or second half of the twelfth century'.[2]

In short there is no palaeographical reason for thinking that the

1. Quoted above, p. 91.
2. *Supra*, p. 92, n. 1.

Carmen could not have been a twelfth-century romance, and therefore no reason for rejecting the obvious reading of the poem as such. In the prologue the poet does not suggest that he has been working in haste in order to celebrate the latest news; on the contrary he states that he has *re*-told (*reponi*) the Norman campaign in verse in order to 'avoid the wastefulness of an indolent mind and spirit'[1] or, as we would now put it, for want of anything better to do. He then goes on to say that he has 'chosen to sing in light measures rather than subject the genius of his mind to vain cares' which, putting aside the scholastic formulae, means (as Curtius has explained) 'I have written a secular poem'.[2] In the same vein he opens his poem with a metaphor of a 'very safe ship' (*tutissima navis*). Barlow took this as a figure for Lanfranc taking the poem across the sea to England,[3] but it is really a 'topos' or poetical commonplace. As Curtius has explained, the Romans often compared the composition of a work to a nautical voyage:

'To compose' is to 'set the sails, to sail'. . . . The poet becomes the sailor, his mind or his work the boat. Sailing the sea is dangerous, especially when undertaken by an 'unpracticed sailor' . . . or in a leaky boat.[4]

The *Carmen* is above all a literary piece written by a man who had no special information, who knew the names of very few of the individuals involved in his story, and of equally few places. His narrative shows a deliberate attempt to recapture the glories of the ancients and is constructed according to a literary plan, the various episodes being balanced against each other with care. The narrative of the army's sea crossing is followed by pairs of speeches, those of Harold and the monk being balanced by those of William and his monk; the description of the battle is followed by a pair of sequences, one recounting the personal exploits of William and the other the death and burial of Harold; and the siege of London provides the opportunity for more paired speeches by William and Ansgard. It is hard to believe that anyone would ever have thought of this literary exercise as a serious historical source, if it had not been for the chance that made it the only surviving poem on the battle of

1. The correct translation, here quoted, is that of Barlow, p. 47. MM render it wrongly as 'Idly wishing to avoid undue taxing of intellect and talent', thus giving the impression of a busy man seeking recreation rather than a poet looking for something to write about.

2. E. R. Curtius, *European Literature and the Latin Middle Ages*, trans. W. R. Trask (London, 1953), p. 430. The Latin (ll. 18–19) reads:

Elegi potius leuibus cantare camenis
Ingenium mentis uanis quam subdere curis.

MM translate the second line as 'rather than to constrain the bent of my mind to profitless toil'; they were convinced that the author was a bishop.

3. Barlow, pp. 45–46, used it in this sense as an argument for date, but MM (pp. xxvii–xxviii) recognized it as a commonplace.

4. Curtius, *op. cit.* pp. 128–9.

Hastings, and tempted everyone to believe that it was therefore the poem which Orderic had known.

We must now turn from negative arguments about what the *Carmen* was not, and attempt a more positive approach. First as to date. If William of Poitiers did not use the *Carmen* as a source for his *Gesta Guillelmi*, it necessarily follows (such are the similarities between the two texts) that the *Carmen* borrowed from the *Gesta Guillelmi*; and since this latter work was not written till *c.* 1077, the *Carmen* must be later. On the other hand, the appearance of the poem in a manuscript dating from 'the middle or second half of the twelfth century' implies that it must have been in circulation by about 1150. These are outside limits of date for the composition of the *Carmen*. Can we narrow them down?

One clue is offered by line 259, *Apulus et Calaber, Siculus, quibus iacula feruunt*, which implies that Duke William's army included Apulians, Calabrians and Sicilians. In 1066 Normans were in control of Apulia and Calabria, but not of Sicily. Count Roger had secured a foothold on the island at Messina and Troina in 1061, but his further expedition of 1064 had been a fiasco, and it was not until the battle of Misilmeri in 1068 and the capture of Palermo in 1072 that the Normans were seen to be getting the upper hand. The source of the *Carmen*'s mistake can almost certainly be found in William of Poitiers who, in a final apostrophe, explains to the English how lucky they are to have been conquered by the Normans, and in the course of his explanation writes: 'Norman knights are in possession of Apulia, have conquered Sicily.'[1] This statement would have been more or less justified in 1077 (even though the conquest of Sicily was not completed till 1090), but the author of the *Carmen* has allowed it to fire his imagination into producing Sicilian forces at Hastings, thus suggesting that he was aware of the Norman myth of themselves as world conquerors. We get the first hint of this myth in William of Malmesbury's story (*c.* 1125) of William the Conqueror stimulating and inciting his own valour 'by recalling the memory of Robert Guiscard',[2] but it only comes into full view with the battle speeches composed by Henry of Huntingdon for the second edition of his *Historia Anglorum* (1139).[3] Similarly, as we have already noted, the story of Taillefer is not found outside the *Carmen* before 1129, but William of Malmesbury's stories about the Normans singing the Song of Roland and the knight who cut off Harold's thigh, while not being the same as anything in the *Carmen*, show that stories of a similar *genre* were in circulation by 1125.

1. *GG*, p. 228.
2. William of Malmesbury, *Gesta Regum*, ed. W. Stubbs (Rolls Series, London, 1887–9), ii. 320.
3. R. H. C. Davis, *The Normans and their Myth* (London, 1976), p. 66.

Another indication seems to be given at the end of the speech of the monk who brings news of the English army to Duke William (ll. 329–32).

Remember your ancestors great duke, and may you achieve what your grandfather and father achieved. Your forefather (*proavus*) overcame the Normans, your grandfather the Bretons, your sire (*genitor*) laid the neck of the English under the yoke.

If this is really part of the monk's speech it is puzzling, because (i) the duke who conquered the English was not William's father but (*pace* Morton and Muntz) William himself[1]; (ii) the duke who overcame the Bretons was not William's grandfather, who maintained an alliance with them, but his father[2]; (iii) his forefather, Rollo, did not conquer the Normans but led the Normans in the conquest of the land which was subsequently called Normandy. This last is a typical twelfth-century mistake,[3] but the first two can only be explained on the assumption that the passage is not a continuation of the monk's speech, but an apostrophe by the poet to the duke who was reigning in his own time. If that duke was one of the Conqueror's sons the passage would make sense and the limits of date would be reduced to 1087–1135.

It is also significant that while the poet gives some personal names in an unusual or antiquarian form (*Hetguardus*, *Heraldus*, *Gernt*, and *Ansgardus*) and others are left almost deliberately vague, like 'the noble heir of Ponthieu', 'Hugh' and 'Gilfard', Eustace Count of Boulogne is named correctly (twice) and given great prominence in the poem. This prominence would have been very puzzling if the poem had been written in 1067–8, since at that date Eustace had forfeited his English lands as a result of his rebellion against King William. Barlow and Morton and Muntz have tried to explain it by reference to a supposed relationship or friendly connection between the count and Guy Bishop of Amiens,[4] but a more plausible reason for this special interest would have been the marriage, in 1125, of Eustace's granddaughter and heiress to Stephen Count of Mortain. A poet living in or near the County of Boulogne might well have thought this marriage a suitable pretext for a poem on the Conquest of England, even if he did not know that in 1135 Stephen was to become England's king.

1. MM, pp. 60–61, postulate an invasion of England by Duke Robert in 1035, but they cannot make it a conquest.
2. For Duke Robert's victory over the Bretons, see *GND*, p. 110. Duke Richard II (William's grandfather) is shown in alliance with the Bretons in *GND*, pp. 77–78, 84.
3. R. H. C. Davis, *The Normans and their Myth*, pp. 58 ff.
4. Barlow, p. 67 finds a relationship; MM, p. 131 do not. Barlow, p. 46, thinks that Guy wrote the poem in order to plead Eustace's cause after his rebellion, but MM, pp. xxii, xxviii, think that the poem must have been written before it. Eustace's rebellion took place in 1067 while William was in Normandy (*c.* 21 Feb.–7 Dec.). He had been restored to favour by *c.* 1077 (*GG*, p. 268).

It may be that a similar significance can be seen in the prominence which the *Carmen* gives to the Londoners and Ansgard whom it represents as kingmakers. The idea of townsmen electing their king would not have seemed strange to anyone who had witnessed events in Flanders after the murder of Count Charles the Good (1127), and in 1135 the Londoners did in fact follow the Flemish example and 'elect' Stephen as their king. As for Ansgard, since he was the *antecessor* of the Mandevilles, it is possible to see his story as a reminder of the claims of that family to the shrievalty of London and Middlesex and the custody of the Tower of London, for these were offices which William de Mandeville lost when he forfeited in 1103, and which his son, Geoffrey de Mandeville II, did not regain until 1141.[1]

It must be admitted that these indications of date are neither uncontrovertible nor free of ambiguities, but taken together they have a cumulative effect and suggest that the *terminus a quo* for the composition of the poem should be *c.* 1125. Whether the *terminus ad quem* should be 1135 (when one of the Conqueror's sons was still duke), or *c.* 1140 (after Stephen had become king) is more doubtful. We will probably do best to keep both alternatives before us, and date the poem *c.* 1125–35, or *c.* 1125–40 so as to remind ourselves of the uncertainties involved in either.

If we turn from the date to the place where the *Carmen* was written, the first observation must be that while there is nothing in the poem to suggest that its author was specifically at Amiens, there are several indications that he belonged to that general area of northern France or southern Flanders. He names two places in that area which are not named in any eleventh-century source, Vimeu and the River Somme; he describes the port of Saint Valery; he mentions a 'noble heir of Ponthieu' who (whoever he may be) is not found in any other narrative; and he gives a very special, and favourable, prominence to Eustace Count of Boulogne.

He says nothing to suggest he was a Norman or Englishman – as we have already stated he was more familiar with the West Frankish than the English coronation *ordines* – but he must (in our view) have had access to a manuscript of William of Poitiers's *Gesta Guillelmi* – an unusual circumstance, because the circulation of that work seems to have been very restricted.[2] In addition he must have been working in a milieu which would account for the fact that, while there is no known manuscript of his poem emanating from

1. C. Warren Hollister, 'The Misfortunes of the Mandevilles', *History*, lviii (1973), 18–28. *Cf.* C. N. L. Brooke and Gillian Keir, *London, 800–1216*, p. 192, and J. H. Round, *Geoffrey de Mandeville* (London, 1892), *passim*.

2. There are now no manuscripts of it extant. Orderic Vitalis had used one at Saint-Evroult *c.* 1114–25, and the text printed by André Duchesne in 1619 was from a manuscript which he had borrowed from Sir Robert Cotton, but which can no longer be traced.

England or Normandy, there was one (and the beginning of another) in the abbey of St Eucharius-Matthias at Trier in Lotharingia.

It is not very difficult to explain how a text could have travelled from southern Flanders or northern France to Trier, since there was a natural route between them and, as noted by Morton and Muntz, particular connections linking St Eucharius-Mathias to the abbeys of Saint Bavon at Ghent and Saint Jacques at Liège.[1] At first sight it is more difficult to explain the presence of a manuscript of William of Poitiers's work in this same district. But while the subject matter of the *Gesta Guillelmi* was of interest primarily to Normans or Englishmen, its style might well have been the object of wider admiration and study. William of Poitiers wrote history in a very literary manner and obviously took pride in his Latinity. He used many models for the composition of his work, choosing whichever was relevant to the particular occasion, 'the *Aeneid* for the sea crossing, Sallust for the battle speeches, Cicero for the apostrophes, Virgil or Sallust for the fighting, Cicero or Augustine for the moral or philosophical dissertations', with references also to the *Thebaïs* of Statius, the *Satires* of Juvenal, the *Agricola* of Tacitus, and the *Lives* of Suetonius and Plutarch.[2] It is just the sort of piece which would have been valued in schools, and it is not difficult to envisage it being used as a model for literary exercises such as the *Carmen* must have been.

There were several schools in northern France and southern Flanders, and it might seem imprudent to name any one of them as more likely than the others as the place where the *Carmen* could have been written. Nonetheless it is hard not to comment on the special connection between England and Laon. Amongst those who had taught or studied there were Adelard of Bath, William de Corbeil Archbishop of Canterbury (1123–36), Alexander Bishop of Lincoln (1123–48), Nigel Bishop of Ely (1133–69) and Robert de Béthune Bishop of Hereford (1131–48). Waldric Bishop of Laon (1106–12) had previously been chancellor to King Henry I, and when Laon cathedral was burnt down in 1112, the canons went on a tour of southern England to collect money for its rebuilding.[3] It was a place where there might well have been a special interest in English history; indeed it was there that André Duchesne found the manuscript of the *Gesta Stephani* which (like that of the *Gesta Guillelmi*) disappeared as soon as he had published it.[4]

1. MM, p. lxii.   2. Foreville in *GG*, p. xxxix.

3. Hermann of Tournai 'De Miraculis S. Mariae Laudunensis', Migne, *Patrologia Latina*, clvi. Guibert de Nogent (*De Vita Sua*, bk. iii) tells us a lot about Bishop Waldric but never suggests that he was a poet, historian or man of letters.

4. André Duchesne took his text of the *Gesta Stephani* from a manuscript which is now lost but was then (1619) in the episcopal library at Laon. A second, and later, manuscript comes from the abbey of Vicoigne, a daughter-house of the abbey of Saint Martin de Laon. (*Gesta Stephani*, ed. K. R. Potter and R. H. C. Davis (Oxford, 1976), pp. xi-xii.)

But in the last resort the claims of Laon, attractive though they may be, are purely hypothetical. What we can say with confidence is that the *Carmen* is neither an original source nor the poem by Guy of Amiens which was used by Orderic Vitalis. Written by someone whose name began with 'W' and dedicated to L . . . ,[1] it seems to have been composed as a literary exercise in one of the schools of northern France or southern Flanders between 1125 and 1135 or 1125 and 1140. As a literary curiosity it was worth the attention of an anthologist at Trier, but as a source for the history of the Norman Conquest it is simply ridiculous.[2]

1. Though unable to identify W or L, I suggest that the following names may be worth investigation: Wido II who administered the County of Ponthieu for his father, William I Talvas, from 1126 to 1147. (*Letters of Peter the Venerable*, ed. Constable, ii. 289); Wido de Montreuil, who witnessed a charter in favour of the abbey of Arrouaise for Queen Matilda, wife of King Stephen, in 1141 (*Regesta Regum Anglo-Norm.*, iii. 24); Guibert de Nogent (*c.* 1066–*c.* 1125), who, amongst other things, was well-acquainted with Laon and wrote a history of the First Crusade which he dedicated to Lisiard Bishop of Soissons (1108–26) – he also has a good deal to say about Guy (*Guido*) who was archdeacon and treasurer of Laon cathedral *c.* 1110–12 and perhaps later. The most common name beginning with L in northern France at this time was Lambert. I have been unable to find any echo of the *Carmen* in the *Liber Floridus* of Lambert of Saint-Omer (d. 1125), but there were also Lambert of Ardres who wrote a history of the Counts of Guines and lords of Ardres down to 1201, Lambert prior of Saint Vaast d'Arras (d. *c.* 1200), poet and *scholasticus*, and Lambert le Court author of the Romance of Alexander. I might add that when Pope Eugenius III consecrated the church of Saint Eucharius-Mathias at Trier in 1148, four of the sixteen cardinals present were called Wido, (*M.G.H. Scriptores*, xv. 1278–9), but none of them seem likely as author of this poem. I have been unable to discover anything useful about the household of Faramus of Boulogne, but he had lands in the county of Boulogne, where he was known as Faramus de Tingry, and in Essex and London, and was related both to the counts of Boulogne and to the Mandeville earls of Essex.

2. I wish to thank Dr J. W. Binns who has given me much help on the literary aspects of the poem. Thanks are also due to those who, over the years, have listened to me patiently and (whether they agreed with me or not) have offered valuable criticisms and suggestions – Professor Frank Barlow, Miss B. F. Harvey, Dr H. M. R. Mayr-Harting and Dr D. S. H. Abulafia.

Postscript

For subsequent discussion see L.J. Engels *et al* in *Proceedings of the Battle Conference 1979*, ed R.A. Brown and Elisabeth M.C. van Houts, 'Latin Poetry and the Anglo-Norman court, 1066-1135: the *Carmen de Hastingae Proelio*', *Journal of Medieval History* 15 (1989) 39-62. These all argue in favour of the *Carmen* being the work of Guy of Amiens and written before 1068 because: (1) If it is not the poem described by Orderic, it is strange that there is no other possibility extant; (2) that where verbal parallels can be made with William of Poitiers it may be thought that William is borrowing from the poem rather than vice-versa; (3) the poet apostrophizes William as if he were alive. Elisabeth van Houts also shows that Bishop Guy of Amiens had the opportunity to gain first-hand information about the Conquest when he was attending the court of Philip I of France in the spring and early summer of 1067.

What the critics do not try to explain is how a contemporary with access to good information could have written for King William a poem which included episodes both incredible and legendary in tone without being flattering to William. The crux here is the death of Harold. Apparently the critics agree with Professor Barlow's claim that this would have been acceptable poetic licence, but D.D.R. Owen, 'The Epic and History: *Chanson de Roland* and *Carmen de Hastingae Proelio*', *Medium Aevum* li (1982) 18-34 has argued persuasively that the structure of the *Carmen* (the story and the way in which it is told) suggests that the poet was familiar with *La Chanson de Roland* and consequently writing after c. 1100.

8

William of Poitiers and his History of
William the Conqueror

THE WORK

AS we have it, the *History of William the Conqueror* by William of
Poitiers is incomplete. The manuscript which André Duchesne used
for his edition in 1619 has been lost, but he stated that it was already
lacking at both the beginning and the end.[1] No other manuscript
has yet been found, and consequently all subsequent editions have
been based on Duchesne's printed text.[2] What we have, therefore,
is a torso; it has no account of William's parentage, birth, or
accession, but starts in mid-sentence with an account of English
affairs on the death of King Cnut (1035); and it breaks off in mid-
sentence among the events of 1067-8, though there are good reasons
for thinking that it originally extended to 1071-2.[3] None the less
it is an essential source for the Conqueror's career.

The surviving text is impressive. It is impossible to read it without
appreciating that its author was a classical scholar and stylist of
distinction, intent on producing a work of great literature. Though

---

[1] André Duchesne, *Historiae Normannorum scriptores antiqui* (Paris, 1619),
pp. 178–213. For a discussion of the manuscript, see below pp. 124-28.

[2] By Francis Maseres (London, 1783 and 1807), J. A. Giles (London, 1845),
and J. P. Migne in *PL*, 149 (Paris, 1853). The standard edition is Raymonde
Foreville, *Guillaume de Poitiers: Histoire de Guillaume le Conquérant* (Paris,
1952), henceforth cited as WP, which has a full scholarly apparatus and a
French translation. Like Duchesne she divides the text into two 'books', but
chooses a different (and better) point of division. This is important, since it
means that references to the *chapters* of Book II are different in the various
editions. For this reason the references in this paper are to the *pages* in WP.

[3] For the lost beginning, see Appendix, pp. 128-29.

Orderic stated that his style was modelled on that of Sallust, WP himself demonstrates that he was capable of imitating the style of quite a number of ancient authors, choosing for each of his themes the model which seemed most suitable, and often interrupting his narrative for a passage of pure rhetoric. Sometimes it even happens that the rhetorical interludes are piled on top of each other, or strung together like a series of exercises on given themes—on obedience in the manner of Cicero, on victory in the manner of Caesar or Sallust, or on the sailing of a fleet in the manner of Virgil. One of his pieces, on the temperance and prudence of William's government, pleased him so much that he used it twice over.[1] He was not a plagiarist, nor was he merely a purveyor of apt quotations. He thought himself into the relevant style and used it boldly; in his comparison between the invasions of Julius Caesar and William the Conqueror, which naturally favours the latter, he moves about Caesar's *Gallic Wars* with the ease of a master, using its facts solely as they are relevant to his purpose.

This classical view is important and sets the tone of the whole work. Some commentators have emphasized that WP's prime aim was to flatter the Conqueror, but this is only half the truth; he was also flattering himself, demonstrating to his readers that he was a real man of letters, capable of extolling a monarch who could be likened to the heroes of old. The conquest of England was by any standard a major event—a whole country conquered as the result of one day's battle—and it merited not just a history but a panegyric. Just as Einhard had modelled his *Life of Charlemagne* on the lives of earlier emperors, as written by Suetonius, so WP also sought classical models for the history of a conquest. Naturally his thoughts turned to the Trojan War as the most famous of sea-borne invasions, but he made considerable use also of Caesar's *Gallic* and *Civil Wars*, Sallust's *Conspiracy of Catiline*, Lucan's *Pharsalia*, Statius's *Thebaid* and Virgil's *Aeneid*. We can only guess the extent to which these models may have taken hold of his

[1] WP, pp. 152 and 262.

imagination. It may be, and probably was, that the Conqueror's fleet was becalmed at Saint Valéry as Agamemnon's had been at Aulis, and that in each case a divinity had to be placated.[1] But had there also been shipwrecks, and had the Conqueror attempted, like Xerxes, to conceal the extent of the disaster by burying the dead secretly?[2] When we are told that the Conqueror, realizing that his ship had lost contact with the rest of his fleet, subdued the crew's alarm by settling down to a banquet, we cannot help wondering whether WP was not too conscious that that was what Aeneas had done when he was shipwrecked on the coast of Africa.[3] Similarly when the Conqueror is made to refuse Harold's mother permission to bury her son, even though she offered his weight in gold, one cannot help feeling that the reality was WP's memory of Achilles and the body of Hector.[4]

If the literary *topos* offers one caution against accepting everything in WP as historically true, another is offered by the formal structure of the work. It is no mere chronicle relating events in the order in which they happened. It collects information about particular topics, so that here we have rebellions, there Angevin wars, and in yet another place all the virtues of the Norman Church. It is a sensible arrangement, but there is no denying that it endows the narrative with a plot, particularly since the early part is punctuated with 'advance notices' of English affairs. The surviving text opens with an account of England at the death of Cnut (pp. 2–12), and reverts to England for the accession of Edward the Confessor (pp. 28–32),

[1] WP, p. 160. The story of Troy was known in various Latin versions, and WP specifically refers to Agamemnon in this context (WP, p. 162) and again later (WP, p. 208). Most of these classical allusions were noted by E. A. Freeman in his *History of the Norman Conquest* (2nd ed., Oxford, 1875), iii. pp. 390, 394, 397, 400, 407, 437, 439, 473, 476, 483, 484, 491, 493, 498, 512, etc., though it is often hard to tell whether he regarded them as literary *topoi* or as examples of history repeating itself.
[2] WP, p. 160, Herodotus, vii. 146.
[3] WP, p. 16 and *Aeneid*, i. 195–222. As in many other cases, I owe the reference to Foreville's footnote. Aeneas's banquet was in fact on land, like that shown in the Bayeux Tapestry.
[4] *Iliad*, xxiii. 351–4.

Harold's embassy and oath to Duke William (pp. 100–4 and 114), and his final seizure of the English throne (p. 146), while the history of the conquest itself occupies most of the last half of the book. WP may have been composing a literary work worthy of the ancients, but he was also writing propaganda to show that the conquest of England was just and inevitable.

How much trust, then, can we put in his history? The question is difficult because there is very little means of controlling it from the English side, and such control as can be exercised depends on the other Norman sources, which are equally problematic. But we can start by attempting to fix the date at which WP was writing. It cannot have been earlier than 1071 because, according to Orderic Vitalis whose text of the work was fuller than ours, WP's narrative extended to the death of Earl Edwin in that year.[1] It also refers to the dedication of St. Stephen's abbey in Caen, which is now accepted as having taken place on 13 September 1077,[2] but it is possible that this reference is due to a late revision, since WP's panegyric of Hugh bishop of Lisieux suggests that he was still alive, though he died on 17 July 1077.[3] We cannot be very far out, however, if we date the completion of WP *c.* 1077.

The alternative Norman sources, if we exclude the controversial *Carmen de Hastingae proelio*,[4] are the Bayeux Tapestry (BT) and the

[1] Below, p. 115.

[2] Foreville (pp. xix and 128 n. 2) noted that Orderic had given this date for the dedication, but followed Lemarignier in thinking he was mistaken. Subsequently Lucien Musset has confirmed Orderic's date from the cartulary of St. Stephen's, Caen. (Lucien Musset, *Les Actes de Guillaume le Conquérant et de la reine Mathilde pour les abbayes caennaises* (Méms. de la Soc. des antiquaires de Normandie, xxxvii (1967), pp. 14–15, n. 15) and OV, ii. p. 148 n. 3.) It should perhaps be added that Foreville's attempt to date WP by reference to the career of Roussel de Bailleul in the Byzantine Empire (1073–4) has been invalidated by the criticism of Marguerite Mathieu in her edition of *Guillaume de Pouille: La Geste de Robert Guiscard* (Palermo, 1961), p. 339.

[3] WP, pp. 136–42.

[4] I have explained why I think the *Carmen de Hastingae Proelio* a twelfth-century composition, in *EHR*, xciii (1978), pp. 241–61. Catherine Morton and Hope Muntz, who edited the work (Oxford, 1972), consider it to have been composed before 11 May 1068 as a reliable narrative. Others, like Frank

Gesta Normannorum Ducum of William of Jumièges (WJ).[1] Of these the more difficult to date is the Bayeux Tapestry. Since it glorifies the part played by Bishop Odo of Bayeux, it is generally thought to have been made before his fall (1082) and perhaps also before the consecration of his new cathedral (1077), but Dr N. P. Brooks[2] has recently pointed out that later dates are possible, even if they are less likely.

WJ extends to the first months of 1070. Louis Halphen considered the composition later than, and in some places an abbreviation of, WP, but most commentators have held the opposite view, believing that WP used, and enlarged upon, WJ. In support of this latter view I have argued elsewhere that WJ's treatment of Robert Curthose gives added weight to the view favoured by most scholars that it dates from 1070–1.[3]

Halphen's view, though originally based on a mistaken view of the lordship of Domfront, opened up a lengthy and fruitful controversy about the chronology of Duke William's campaigns between 1047 and 1054.[4] We need not rehearse the various arguments in detail, but it is important to realize that the root cause of

---

Barlow (in *Studies in International History presented to W. Norton Medlicott*, ed. K. Bourne and D. C. Watt (London, 1967), pp. 35–67, and L. J. Engels (in *Proceedings of the Battle Conference 1979*), consider it early but so full of poetic licence as to make its account of such major incidents as the death of Harold incredible.

[1] The editions cited are: *The Bayeux Tapestry*, ed. Sir Frank Stenton (London, 1957) and *Guillaume de Jumièges: Gesta Normannorum Ducum*, ed. Jean Marx (SHN, 1914).

[2] N. P. Brooks and the late H. E. Walker, 'The authority and interpretation of the Bayeux Tapestry', *Proceedings of the Battle Conference on Anglo-Norman Studies*, i (1978), pp. 1–34, particularly 9–10.

[3] Louis Halphen, *Le Comté d'Anjou au xi siècle* (Paris, 1906), pp. xii–xiii and 72 n. 4. See also his review of Marx's edition in *Revue historique*, cxxi (1916), pp. 317–20. Marx's reply is in *Mélanges d'histoire du moyen âge offerts à Ferdinand Lot* (Paris, 1925), pp. 543–8. I have outlined my own views in 'William of Jumièges, Robert Curthose and the Norman Succession', below, pp. 131–40.

[4] Halphen, *Comté d'Anjou*, pp. 70–80; R. Latouche, *Histoire du Comté du Maine pendant les xe et xie siècles* (Paris, 1910), pp. 27–32; Henri Prentout, *Histoire de Guillaume le Conquérant—Le duc de Normandie* (*Méms. acad. nat. de*

WP's subject-matter and its order in WJ compared

WP (refs. to pages)		WJ (refs. to pages)
2–12	England 1035–40	120–1
12–20	Revolt of Guy of Brionne and Battle of Val-és-dunes (1047)	122–4
20–8	William's glory; Henry I's growing jealousy	
28–32	England: accession of Edward the Confessor (1042)	**122**
32–44	War against Anjou: campaign of Domfront and Alençon	124–7
44–50	William's marriage	127–8
50–64	Revolt of William of Arques	**119–20**
64–74	Henry I's invasion: battle of Mortemer (1054)	129–30
74–8	Angevin war: building of the castle of Ambrières	**127**
80–2	Invasion of Normandy and battle of Varaville	131–2
82–4	Death of Henry I (1060) and Geoffrey Martel (1060)	132
86–98	Submission of Le Mans and revolt of Geoffrey of Mayenne	**130–1**
100–6	Harold Godwinson's embassy to Normandy: oath of Bonneville	132–3
106–12	War against Brittany	
114	Harold's return	
114–46	Panegyric of Duke William, Normandy, the Norman Church, and the Duke's alliances	
146–242	Story of the conquest of England from the death of Edward the Confessor to William's coronation (1066)	133–6
242–62	William's return to Normandy Panegyrics of the Conqueror and of his government	137
262–70	Revolts in England (1067): Eustace of Boulogne and Copsi	138–40

Note: figures in heavy type show where the order of events in WJ is different from that in WP.

the controversy was that though WJ and WP narrate many of the
same events, they place them in a different order. Since WJ's
narrative reads like a series of annals and WP's is highly literary, it
would be natural to assume that it was WP who had tampered with
the true sequence of events. But this does not seem to have been
the case. Modern scholars, in spite of their disagreements on other
points, are unanimous in thinking that the main fault lies with WJ,
since it is he who has misplaced the revolts of William of Arques
and Geoffrey of Mayenne. It is hard to believe that WJ was abbreviating WP's material and reorganizing it in order to fit a theme,
because it is impossible to see what that theme could have been. But
there is no difficulty in supposing that WP had sufficient independent
knowledge to correct WJ's chronology.

So far as information is concerned, WP and WJ have a great
deal in common for the period before 1066, but if one reads them
side by side to see which is deriving his knowledge from the other,
one is constantly baffled by the way in which it is first one, then the
other, who seems the better informed. Thus in his account of the
rebellion of Guy of Burgundy, WP gives more facts than WJ,
mentioning that Guy held the castle of Vernon in addition to
Brionne, and that amongst his accomplices were Ranulf the vicomte
of Bayeux and Hamo Dentatus.[1] But WJ is rather better than WP
on the battles of Val-és-dunes[2] and Varaville,[3] in each case mentioning that the French King's approach was through the county of

---

Caen, viii (1936), pp. 136–52; J. D. Dhondt, 'Les Relations entre la France et
la Normandie sous Henri I' (*Normannia*, xii (1939), pp. 465–86) and 'Henri I,
l'empire et l'anjou' (*Rev. belge*, xxv (1946), pp. 87–109); finally, David C.
Douglas, *William the Conqueror* (London, 1964), pp. 383–90, who is generally
in agreement with Prentout, should be compared with Olivier Guillot, *Le
Comté d'Anjou et son entourage au xi siècle* (Paris, 1972), i. pp. 69–79 and 82–6, who
on many points makes a very effective counter-case.

[1] WP, p. 16, WJ, pp. 122–3.
[2] WP, pp. 14–18, WJ, pp. 123–4.
[3] WP, pp. 80–2, WJ, p. 131. It should be added, however that WP did
appreciate that it was the tide which prevented Duke William from pursuing
the defeated French. There may also be a verbal similarity in the use of
alacriter superveniens, sub regis oculis by the two authors.

Exmes, and in each case making the course of the battle more intelligible, stating, for example, that the reason why half the French army was caught on the wrong side of the ford at Varaville was that the tide had risen. When it comes to the conquest of England the two works diverge completely, WP being full and detailed while WJ is perfunctory and (so far as he gives any details at all) at variance with WP, considering that Harold fell in the *first* Norman attack at Hastings, and that London did not surrender peacefully but was captured after a skirmish in the main square.[1] But just as one is concluding that the two works must have lost contact with each other completely, one finds striking similarities in their accounts of the revolt of Eustace of Boulogne at Dover (1067).[2]

The verbal parallels between the two texts have been carefully studied by Foreville.[3] She points out that they are confined to six episodes, mostly in the early part of WP, and that, except in the account of the English expedition of the athelings Edward and Alfred, they are not particularly striking. She argues that if one author was borrowing from the other, the borrower was probably WP, since words and phrases which are grouped in WJ have been tastefully dispersed through longer passages in WP. This is a fair observation, but a similar result could also have been obtained if

---

[1] WJ, pp. 135, 136.

[2] WJ, p. 138, WP, p. 266. There are many verbal similarities in the two passages, but while WJ latinizes Dover as *Dorobernia*, WP uses the more usual *Dovera*. *Dorobernia* normally indicates Canterbury, but William of Malmesbury (*GR*, i. pp. 155, 279) and *Flor. Wig.*, i. p. 201 use it, like WJ, for Dover. But elsewhere *GR*, i. p. 241, and Eadmer's *HN*, 7, use *Dovera* and *Dofris*.

[3] WP, pp. xxv–xxxv. The principal passages, which she discusses in detail, are:

(i) The English expedition of the athelings Alfred and Edward (WP, pp. 4–10; WJ, pp. 120–2).

(ii) The battle of Val-és-dunes (WP, pp. 14–18; WJ, pp. 122–4).

(iii) The building of the castle of Arques (WP, p. 54; WJ, p. 119).

(iv) The submission of Le Mans and Mayenne (WP, pp. 88–92, and 96–100; WJ, pp. 130–1).

(v) The capture of Harold by Guy of Ponthieu (WP, p. 100; WJ, p. 132).

(vi) The revolt of Eustace of Boulogne at Dover (WP, pp. 264–8; WJ p. 138).

both authors had been using a common source which is now lost.

Such a hypothesis was indeed propounded by Gustav Körting as long ago as 1875,[1] but he weakened his case by insisting that the lost source must have been a national epic (*Volkspoesie*), thus enabling Marx to reply that 'If there had been such a source, Orderic would have known it and cited it.'[2] In fact there is no reason why the lost source should have been a national epic, and it is clear that Orderic does not name all the sources which he used; he mentions those which he found particularly important, especially if they were by well-known writers, but he obviously thought that the general run of monastic annals and saints' lives could be taken for granted.[3]

It seems clear that WJ was using written sources of some sort. In his account of the capture of Alençon (1048 × 51), he says that the Conqueror 'ordered all the jokers [*illusores*] to have their hands and feet cut off in full view of all the inhabitants of Alençon',[4] but he does not explain who these 'jokers' were or what they had done wrong. To find the explanation we have to turn to Orderic's edition of WJ where he continues as follows: 'without delay 32 men were maimed at his command, for they had beaten on pells and hides to insult the duke, disrespectfully calling him a tanner because his mother's relatives were tanners [*polinctores*]'.[5] Since WJ was dedicating his history to the Conqueror, it is understandable that he should have censored remarks about his illegitimate birth, but it is hard to see why he had included even part of the story, unless he had begun copying it before he realized how unsuitable was its end. For Orderic, writing in the early years of the twelfth century, the joke was no longer dangerous. But how had he known it?

It is clear that WP also was following some earlier work or

---

[1] Gustav Körting, *Willhelms von Poitiers Gesta Guillelmi Ducis Normannorum et Regis Anglorum: Ein Beitrag zur anglo-normannischen Historiographie* (Separatabdrück aus dem Programm der Kreuzschule zu Dresden vom Jahre 1875) (Dresden, 1875).

[2] WJ, pp. xvii–xviii.

[3] Cf. Chibnall in OV, ii. p. xxii.

[4] WJ, p. 126.

[5] WJ, p. 171.

works. In one of his references to Arques he refers to 'the whole part of Normandy next to it which is situated on this side of the River Seine [*citra flumen Sequanam*]',[1] though one would have expected him to describe it as 'on the other side' (*ultra*) of the river, since he lived to the south of it and Arques was a long way north of it. In his account of the accession of Edward the Confessor he seems to follow two different sources. At first he implies what WJ explicitly states, that Harthacnut, being a son of Emma's facilitated his half-brother's succession by inviting him back to England to reside at his court.[2] But when it comes to Harthacnut's death, WP states that Edward was not in England but in Normandy, that it was because of representations by the Duke of Normandy that he was elected King, and that when he did cross the channel he was provided with a Norman escort.[3] The first story suggests that the Norman claim to England would stem from the marriage of Emma, daughter of Duke Richard I, to Kings Ethelred and Cnut; the second that it would stem simply from military might; and it looks as if, in constructing his narrative, WP had borrowed from two sources, one of which had also been used by WJ, and the other not.

As they approach the conquest of England, the narratives of WJ and WP become much less similar, and the comparison which has to be made is between WP and the Bayeux Tapestry. For example, WJ's account of Duke Harold's visit to Normandy is very brief; it says that Harold was sent to Normandy by Edward the Confessor, that he was blown on to the coast of Ponthieu and imprisoned by Count Guy, and that he was eventually rescued by Duke William, to whom he did 'fealty concerning the Kingdom', and by whom he was rewarded before returning to England.[4] BT and WP enlarge

[1] WP, p. 52. It is true that Nithard (*Histoire des fils de Louis le Pieux*, ed. Ph. Lauer, Paris, 1926, pp. 18, 44) uses *citra* to indicate 'the other side of', but WP's own use of it is both consistent and correct (e.g. WP, pp. 82, 216, 262).

[2] WP, p. 12, WJ, p. 122. This is also the story given in *The Anglo-Saxon Chronicle*, C and D, s.a. 1041, and in *Encomium Emmae Reginae*, ed. Alistair Campbell (Camden 3rd series, lxxii, 1949), p. 52.

[3] WP, pp. 28–30.

[4] WJ, pp. 132–3.

the story considerably. First, on a point of detail, they both name the place where Harold's oath was taken, but whereas BT says it was Bayeux, WP says it was Bonneville.[1] Secondly they both add that Harold accompanied Duke William on an expedition against Brittany, though once again the details are significantly different. BT shows that when the army was passing Mont-Saint-Michel, Harold rescued two men from the quicksands, dragging one of them by the hand while he carried the other on his back.[2] It then shows how Duke Conan was attacked in Dol but escaped from the castle by sliding down a rope, after which the Normans advanced past Rennes to Dinan , which surrendered to them.[3] It may be un-important that WP tells nothing of the march past Mont-Saint-Michel or the incident of the quicksands, but when it comes to Dol he is quite specific that Conan was not inside the castle but besieging it. The castle was held, he says, by an ally of Duke William's called Ruallus, and when William approached, Conan raised the siege and retreated. He is also specific in stating that William did not advance beyond Dol because of the unknown and inhospitable country, and because he learnt that Geoffrey of Anjou had joined forces with Conan. He stayed near Dol in order to confront his enemies, but this upset Ruallus because Duke William, though his ally, was living off his land. William therefore promised compensation, for-bad further foraging, and awaited battle against Conan and Geoffrey, though in the event they did not dare to confront him.[4]

A further difference of detail, this time about the battle of Hastings may have some bearing on the dates of the two works, for in the Tapestry Eustace of Boulogne is shown as something of a hero and in WP as rather a coward.[5] The reason for WP's unfavourable

[1] BT, pls 28–9; WP, pp. 102–4.

[2] BT, pl. 22.

[3] BT, pls 23–6. In an interesting passage Brooks and Walker (*op. cit.*, p. 3) claim that the Tapestry's inscription, *Venerunt ad Dol et Conan fuga vertit*, is correct but has been misunderstood by the artist. None the less,the continuation of the inscription, telling how the duke marched past Rennes to Dinan , which surrendered to him, is unambiguously in opposition to WP's account.

[4] WP, pp. 110–12.

[5] BT, pls 68–9; WP, pp. 202–4.

view is almost certainly connected with Eustace's revolt against King William in 1067, as a result of which Eustace was condemned to forfeit his fiefs.[1] WP adds that Eustace was subsequently restored to favour (as is confirmed by the Domesday Survey), but his tone suggests that this was only recently, since his misdeeds were still fresh in the memory. In this case the Bayeux Tapestry, unless it was completed in the first months of 1067, would have to be later than WP's account of *c.* 1077.

The real difficulty, however, is that neither BT nor WP is wholly convincing. BT, which was probably made for Bayeux Cathedral, places Harold's oath at Bayeux, while WP, who was an archdeacon of Lisieux and a native of Préaux, places it at Bonneville, the ducal palace nearest to him. BT's description of Harold's rescue of two men from the quicksands looks like a piece of Herculean folklore, while Conan's escape down a rope from the castle at Dol suggests a standard medieval joke which was subsequently to be repeated, for example, with regard to the *funambuli* or 'rope-trick men' who escaped from the siege of Antioch.[2] WP, on the other hand, has (as befits a Norman from Poitiers) a fixation about Geoffrey of Anjou as the chief enemy of Duke William, while his account of the Duke's measures to protect the crops of his allies is surely a classical *topos*. As for his story of Conan announcing the precise day of his invasion, it is one of the commonplaces of chivalric literature, which WP himself had already employed twice with regard to Duke William in his wars against Anjou.[3]

Fabulous stories are by no means uncommon in WP. Some of them are little more than the literary conventions of the panegyric, as when Duke William with four companions is said to have routed 15, 300, or 500 of Count Thibaud's cavalry, or with a group of 50 knights to have defeated an Angevin force of 300 cavalry and

[1] WP, pp. 266–8.
[2] OV, v. p. 98.
[3] WP, p. 108, cf. pp. 40 and 74–6. But Eric John in 'Edward the Confessor and the Norman succession', *EHR*, xciv (1979), p. 260 n. 2, is disposed to accept WP more literally.

700 infantry.[1] These events were supposed to have occurred some twenty-five years before. But others which seem equally legendary or folkloric concern the conquest of England and could only have had ten or eleven years to develop before WP wrote them down. They include the banquet at sea which, as we have already remarked, may have been inspired by the *Aeneid*; the story of Duke William carrying fitz Osbern's cuirass when they both returned on foot from an exhausting reconnoitre;[2] William putting his armour on back to front;[3] and probably the story of Harold's burial.[4]

Raymonde Foreville was rightly struck by the fact that such fabulous tales could have been told so soon after the actual conquest. Considering that there could not have been sufficient time for popular imagination to work up a 'spontaneous collective poetry', she argued that the epic legends could not have contributed to WP, but on the contrary must have been derived from him. 'Born in court chapels and addressed to an educated world ... the *Gesta Guillelmi* show that propaganda organized by clerks round recent events was able to give birth to an epic legend.'[5] Expressed in this way, Foreville's view has not won general favour. Quite apart from a general reluctance to believe that the medieval epics originated in Latin prose, it has been pointed out that the circulation of WP was extremely limited, and that there is nothing to suggest it was sufficiently well known to inspire a popular literature. Foreville was unwilling to believe that popular imagination could create new legends within ten years of the historical event to which they referred, but the truth of the matter is surely that the legends were not new, but old ones adapted to new circumstances. WP would have accepted them as cheerfully as he accepted the legends of classical

[1] WP, pp. 24–6, 36.
[2] WP, p. 168.
[3] WP, p. 182. Cf. 'le bon roi Dagobert portait ses pantalons à l'envers'.
[4] WP, p. 204.
[5] Raymonde Foreville, 'Aux Origines de la légende épique: les *Gesta Guillelmi ducis Normannorum et Regis Anglorum* de Guillaume de Poitiers', *Moyen Age*, 56 (1950), pp. 195–219 (esp. 218). It should be added, however, that she then believed that WP was writing in 1073–4 rather than *c.* 1077.

antiquity, and used them in a very similar way, as a natural part of his literary apparatus.[1]

For this reason any editor of WP has to be an expert not only on the classics but also on the vernacular literature of the period, so as to identify the *topoi* and the stock-in-trade of contemporary poets. In this respect Kurt-Ulrich Jäschke has performed a useful service in his analysis of the burial of Harold and accession of William the Conqueror.[2] But the question remains whether men acted as they did because they modelled their lives on the legends which they had learnt in infancy, or whether an author asserted that they had behaved in a particular way because that was what his literary models demanded.

THE AUTHOR

In his *Ecclesiastical History* Orderic Vitalis has three passages bearing on the career of WP, the first two probably written in 1114–15 and the third in 1125:

(i) William of Poitiers, an archdeacon of Lisieux, who has published a book wonderfully polished in style and mature in judgement. He was for many years the King's chaplain, and he set out to describe authentically, in detail, the events which he had seen with his own eyes, and in which he had taken part, although he was unable to continue the book to the King's death because he was prevented by unfavourable circumstances (*adversis casibus impeditus*)[3]

---

[1] It is interesting to see which of WP's stories reappear in Wace and which in Benoît. Neither has the banquet at sea or Duke William carrying fitz Osbern's cuirass. Wace (iii. 7500–7520) has William putting on his armour back to front, but the story is not in Benoît. On the other hand Benoît has William striking Eustace of Boulogne (396949 ff.) and the same Eustace's revolt (40449–40558). The fact that Benoît places Harold's oath at Bonneville, while Wace places it at Bayeux (of which he was a canon), suggests that Benoît must have known WP, because we know of no other source from which he could of got this information. See *Le Roman de Rou de Wace*, ed. A. J. Holden (3 vols, Soc. des anciens textes de France, Paris, 1970–3); and *Chronique des ducs de Normandie par Benoît*, ed. C. Fahlin (3 vols, Uppsala, 1951–67).

[2] Kurt-Ulrich Jäschke, *Willhelm der Eroberer; sein doppelter Herrschaftsantritt im Jahre 1066* (Vorträge und Forschunger, Sonderband 24) (Sigmaringen, 1977).

[3] OV, ii. p. 184.

(ii) William of Poitiers has brought his history up to this point [1071], eloquently describing the deeds of King William in a clever imitation of the style of Sallust. He was by birth a Norman from the village of Préaux where he had a sister who was the superior of the nuns in the monastery of St. Léger. He was called 'of Poitiers' because he had drunk deeply of the fountain of philosophy at Poitiers. When he came back to his own people he was distinguished by being more learned than all his friends and neighbours, and in ecclesiastical affairs he helped bishops Hugh [1049–77] and Gilbert [1077–1101] in the office of archdeacon. Before he became a cleric he lived a rough life in the affairs of war and put on knightly arms to fight for his earthly prince, so that he was all the better able to describe the battles he had seen, through having himself some experience of the dire perils of war. In his old age he gave himself up to silence and prayer, and spent more time composing prose and poetry than in dicosurse. He published many subtly linked verses intended for declamation, and was so free from jealousy that he invited his juniors to criticize and improve them.[1]

(iii) The books of William called Calculus of Jumièges and William of Poitiers archdeacon of Lisieux, who carefully recorded the deeds of the Normans and, after William became King of England, dedicated (*praesentauerunt*) their books to him to gain his favour.[2]

In these accounts there are three datable points. First, WP himself remarks that he was away in Poitiers (*dum Pictavis exularem*) around the time of the siege of Mouliherne, the date of which, though much disputed, must have been somewhere between 1048 and 1051.[3] Second, WP's history extended, according to Orderic, to 1071. And third, WP must have been an archdeacon both before and after 1077, the year in which Bishop Hugh died and Gilbert Maminot was consecrated. In another passage Orderic gives a list of the dignitaries of Lisieux Cathedral at about this same time, naming William of Glanville dean and archdeacon; Richard of Angerville and William of Poitiers, archdeacons; Geoffrey of Triqueville, treasurer; Turgis, precentor and Ralph his son.[4]

[1] OV, ii. p. 258.
[2] OV, ii. p. 78.
[3] WP, p. 22. For the date of the siege of Mouliherne, see p. 105 n. 4 above. Halphen proposed 1048, Guillot 1049, Prentout and Douglas 1051.
[4] OV, iii. pp. 20–1. Geoffrey de Triqueville was the son of William de Triqueville, and while still only a canon of Lisieux was a benefactor of the abbey of Grestain (ex. inf. Dr David R. Bates).

If Orderic is right in saying that WP served as a knight before he became a clerk, we would assume that his military career had been completed before he began his studies at Poitiers, (i.e. before 1048 × 51). At such an early date it is hardly surprising that we cannot trace him, particularly since we do not know his family name; he cannot have been called 'of Poitiers' before he resided there. All that we know of his birthplace, Préaux, is that it contained two abbeys, Saint-Pierre for monks and Saint-Léger for nuns, the one refounded (*c.* 1034), and the other founded (*c.* 1040) by Humphrey de Vieilles, the ancestor of the Beaumonts.[1] WP shows himself well-informed about this family, stating that Roger de Beaumont 'son of the illustrious Humphrey', assisted the Duchess Matilda in governing Normandy during her husband's absence for the invasion in which (as WP states twice over) Roger's son, Robert, played a prominent part.[2] It is plausible, therefore, to believe that WP's father could have been a tenant of the Beaumonts; and if his sister was Emma the first abbess of Saint-Léger, it is possible that his family also had assisted in the foundation of that house.[3] But unfortunately we have no solid information.

WP's studies at Poitiers, which must have lasted four or five years at least,[4] included (as we have seen) some date between 1048 and 1051. It may be presumed that he studied at the school of Saint-Hilaire-le-Grand, [5]which had been made famous under the direction

---

[1] For the nunnery of Saint-Léger (now is the commune of Saint-Michel-des-Préaux) and theabbey of Saint-Pierre (now in the commune of Notre-Dame-des-Préaux) see A. Le Prévost, *Mémoires ... et notes pour servir à l'histoire du département de l'Eure* (3 vols, Evreux, 1862-9), iii. pp. 162-3 and ii. pp. 495-8.

[2] WP, pp. 260, 192.

[3] The statement in *Gallia Christiana*, xi. p. 853, that Emma was WP's sister is no more than an intelligent guess based on Orderic's statement (above, p. 85).

[4] For the length of studies, see A. Cobban, *The Medieval Universities: their development and organization* (London, 1975), p. 208.

[5] There were other schools, at the cathedral and perhaps at the abbey of Saint-Cyprien (*Letters of archbishop Lanfranc*, ed. Margaret Gibson (OMT, 1979), p. 142) but those of Saint-Hilaire were by far the most famous. See Robert Favreau, 'Les Écoles et la culture à Saint-Hiliare-le-Grand de Poitiers, des

of Hildegar (1024–8), the pupil and personal representative of
Fulbert of Chartres. We know that Hildegar had connections with
Normandy, because two of his letters (*c.* 1022–3) are addressed to
Siegfried chaplain of Duke Richard II.[1] We are also told that the
abbey of Saint-Hilaire-le-Grand, dedicated on 1 November 1049,
had been built largely at the expense of Queen Emma, daughter of
Duke Richard I of Normandy and wife successively of Kings
Ethelred and Cnut of England.[2] What exactly had formed the connection between Queen Emma and Saint-Hilaire-le-Grand we do
not know, but Normandy and Poitou were both enemies of Anjou
and therefore likely to be in alliance with each other.

In two passages WP shows that he retained a special interest in
Poitou. The first is in his account of the revolt of Guy of Brionne
who (as WJ also points out) was the nephew of both Robert Duke
of Normandy and William Count of Poitou. WP informs us
(which WJ does not) that when he had been defeated in Normandy
he went south to the county of Burgundy, where he plagued his
brother, William 'tête hardie', for another ten years.[3] The second
passage makes a special feature of Aimeri vicomte of Thouars—
Thouars being the most important castle on the border between
Poitou and Anjou—and states not only that he took part in the
conquest of England, but also that it was he who solemnly urged
the Conqueror to be crowned King.[4] Neither of these events, if

---

origines au début du XIIe siècle', *Cahiers de civilisation médiévale*, iii (1960),
pp. 473–8.

[1] *The Letters and Poems of Fulbert of Chartres*, ed. Frederick Behrends (OMT,
1976), nos 67–8.

[2] '*Istud monasterium magna ex parte construxerat regina Anglorum per manus
Gaufredi Coorlandi*', chronicle of Maillezais in *Chroniques des églises d'Anjou*,
ed. Paul Marchegay et Emile Mabille (SHF, 1869), pp. 349–433.

[3] WP, p. 14; WJ, pp. 122–4. William 'tête hardie' did not succeed to
the county of Burgundy till 1057. This would probably have been about ten
years after the siege of Brionne—a possible confirmation of WP's chronology.

[4] WP, pp. 196, 218. For Aimeri, see A. Richard, *Histoire des comtes de
Poitou, 778–1204* (2 vols, Paris, 1903), i. p. 298. There may be an attestation by
Aimeri (as Aymeri) in the Conqueror's charter granting Steyning to the
abbey of Fécamp in 1066. (*Reg.*, i, no. 1.)

events they were, is mentioned by any other source, and it must therefore be concluded that WP had a special interest in Aimeri de Thouars or his family.

We have already pointed out that WP was a man of considerable learning, and it is natural to ask whether he may not have held some official position in Saint-Hilaire-le-Grand or its schools. Lists of treasurers and deans (the Counts of Poitou being titular abbot) have been compiled, and the names of several masters of the schools are known,[1] but we are hampered by our ignorance of the surname which WP may have borne at this date. By itself 'William' is too common a name for the purposes of identification, but there was a William who was *grammaticus* in 1080, and master of the schools in 1090 and 1092. It is tempting to think that this might have been WP because, if he had held his archdeaconry in plurality with these posts, it might be possible to explain why he is so hard to find as a witness of charters in Normandy, and why he did not continue his history to the Conqueror's death. But unfortunately we must reject the identification. Orderic clearly implies that WP returned to Normandy for good, at any rate by the time he became an arch-deacon; and the same impression is given by WP's own reference to *dum Pictavis exularem* (1048 × 51). Moreover, the William who was *grammaticus* and master of the schools at Saint-Hilaire-le-Grand had a brother, Thibaud, who had been chancellor to the Duke of Aquitaine in 1068;[2] and though such a chancellor could have been a Norman, it does not seem likely.

If Orderic is right in his statement that WP was 'for many years the king's chaplain', this would presumably have been after his studies at Poitiers (1048 at the earliest) and before he became an archdeacon (1077 at the latest); and since chaplains were normally members of the chancery, one would expect to find WP witnessing ducal or royal charters. But though we have the texts of about 450

---

[1] M. De Longuemar, *Essai historique sur l'église collégiale de Saint Hiliare-le-Grand de Poitiers* (Méms. de la Soc. des antiquaires de l'Ouest, xxiii, 1856), pp. 326–51, and cf. Favreau, art. cit. p. 86 n. 4.

[2] Favreau, p. 476.

of the Conqueror's charters (144 of them before 1066 and the rest after) it is not possible to identify WP in any of them. One might be tempted by 'William the duke's tutor' (*Willelmun magister comitis*), but his only attestations are *c.* 1035–43 and *c.* 1037–45, which would have been before WP's own studies.[1] After the conquest there are said to have been four Williams who served the Conqueror as chaplain, but one of them was probably fictitious since he appears only in forged charters, and another turns out, on closer inspection, to have been no chaplain at all.[2] Of the remaining two, one was William of Beaufai (*Bellofago*) who was promoted bishop of Thetford in 1085, and the other William fitz Suein who was still styling himself *canonicus* in 1082, by which date WP had been an archdeacon for five years at least.[3] If one adds that in the surviving text WP offers no hint that he was a chaplain of the Conqueror, one is bound to wonder whether Orderic could not have been mistaken, though there is an unidentified *Willelmus capellanus* who attested with the Conqueror's whole chancery in a charter of 1068 for St. Martin-le-Grand of London

Orderic was consistent in describing WP as an archdeacon of Lisieux. Otherwise we might have doubted that statement also, since it has proved impossible to trace him in other sources, perhaps because of the sparsity of early cartularies for religious houses in that diocese. But it is surprising to find that when we abandon the search for a royal chaplain or archdeacon and look simply for someone called William of Poitiers, we are rewarded, not just with one reference but two.

[1] Marie Fauroux, *Recueil des actes des Ducs de Normandie de 911 à 1066* (Méms. de la Soc. des antiquaires de Normandie, xxxvi, 1961), nos 100, 103.

[2] *Reg.*, i, p. xxi, where it is noted that William the chaplain occurs only in Durham forgeries. The full text of *Reg.*, i. no. 193 is printed in J. J. Vernier, *Chartes de l'Abbaye de Jumièges* (SHN, 1916), i. p. 107, and shows that William brother of Rainald was almost certainly not a chaplain, though his brother Rainald was.

[3] *Reg.*, i. no. 168, and Lucien Musset, *Les Actes de Guillaume le Conquérant et de la reine Mathilde pour les abbayes caennaises* (Méms. de la Soc. des antiquaires de Normandie, xxxvii, 1967), no. 7, a charter of William fitz Suein, datable

The first comes as an attestation of a charter by Serlo of Lingèvres granting the church of Bucéels to Saint Stephen's abbey in Caen; it is recited in two *pancartes* and can be dated 1079–82.[1] In this case there is nothing to suggest that *Willelmus Pictavensis* was a cleric, let alone an archdeacon. In the second case, however, *Willelmus Pictavensis* must have been both a cleric and a priest, since he figures as a canon of St. Martin's, Dover. In Domesday Book (vol. i, fo. 1ᵛ), it is stated that the prebends of that church, formerly held in common, had been divided among the canons by the Bishop of Bayeux. As a result:

In Sibertesuuald [Sibertswold, Shepherd's Well] tenet Willelmus Pict (avensis) dimidium solinum et xii acras, et in Addelam [Deal] dimidium solinum xii acras minus, et ibi habet ii villanos et iii bordarios cum i caruca et dimidia. Totum hoc valet lv solidos. TRE iiii libras.

Could this *Willelmus Pictavensis* have been our man? The identification is made attractive by the connection between St. Martin's, Dover, and the English royal chapel, since this would help to justify Orderic's description of WP as a chaplain of the king.[2] It also postulates a connection with Odo of Bayeux, which is made plausible by WP's eulogy of him in Book II, comparable only to the equally fulsome eulogy of Hugh Bishop of Lisieux in Book I. He tells us that Odo was outstanding in both ecclesiastical and secular affairs; that he governed the church of Bayeux wisely and adorned it magnificently; that he was intelligent and eloquent; that his munificence was unequalled in Gaul; that he never took up arms and never wanted to, but was greatly feared by those who did

---

1079–82, is recited (p. 76) in a *pancarte* of 1080–2 which itself has the *signum* of *Willelmi canonici filii Sueini*.

[1] Musset, *Actes . . . caennaises*, nos 7 and 18. Serlo's charter cannot be earlier than 1079 because it refers to abbot Gilbert, nor later than 1082 since that is the latest possible date for the earlier of the two *pancartes* (no. 7).

[2] Domesday Book, i, fo. 1ᵛ notes that one of the pre-conquest canons, Esmellt, was a chaplain of King Edward's. Cf. C. R. Haines, *Dover Priory* (Cambridge, 1930), p. 35; 'Lyons states, but I do not see on what authority, that not only Esmellt, but also Lewin, Edwine, Alwi, Alric, Spirites and Baldwin were chaplains of the King.'

because in cases of necessity 'he gave aid in battle through his most excellent advice'; and finally that he was 'uniquely and constantly loyal' to his half-brother the king.[1]

If we are right in thinking that WP was writing *c.* 1077, this last statement about Odo's unique and constant loyalty is interesting, because 1077 was the first year of the first rebellion of the Conqueror's eldest son, Robert Curthose. So far as we know, Odo was not implicated in this rebellion, which lasted till 1080, but his subsequent association with Robert was close, and it is likely that his arrest in 1082 did have some connection with Robert's second rebellion (1083–7). Could it be that WP was trying to defend Odo from the king's suspicion? Could it also be that the 'unfavourable circumstances' which (according to Orderic) prevented him from finishing his history were connected with these rebellions? In 1077 Robert's party was particularly strong in the diocese of Lisieux, because it included William de Breteuil, Yves and Aubrey de Grandmesnil, and Roger son of Richard fitz Gilbert de Clare, while on its southern borders were the lands of Ralph de Toeny and Roger de Bellême.[2]

According to Orderic, Odo of Bayeux 'sent promising clerks to Liège and other cities where he knew that philosophic studies flourished, and supported them generously there, so that they might drink long and deeply from the springs of knowledge'.[3] He does not name WP as one of these protégés, but there are indications of a connection between Odo and WP. Odo's father was Herluin de Conteville, and Conteville was only 15km from Préaux, where WP was born. When Herluin founded an abbey at Grestain, some of the first monks were brought from Saint-Pierre-des-Préaux.[4] At a later stage in WP's life, after 1077, his bishop at Lisieux was Gilbert Maminot who, besides being a chaplain and physician of

---

[1] WP, pp. 240–2. Cf. pp. 262–6, 134–6, and 182. For Odo's advice in battle of BT, pp. 67–8, 'Hic Odo episcopus, baculum tenens, confortat pueros.'
[2] C. W. David, *Robert Curthose: Duke of Normandy* (Cambridge, Mass., 1920), p. 22, with refs. to OV, ii. p. 358 and iii. pp. 100–2.
[3] OV, iv. pp. 118–19.
[4] Charles Bréard, *L'Abbaye de Notre-Dame de Grestain* (Paris, 1904).

the king,[1] was a tenant of Odo's in England, holding three estates of him in Kent and two in Buckinghamshire,[2] just as Roger de Beaumont, in whom WP displayed a special interest, was a tenant of Odo's in Buckinghamshire.[3] We might add that the Conteville lands stretched into the diocese of Bayeux and included Tilly-sur-Seulles,[4] which is adjacent to Bucéels where the church was granted to St. Stephen's, Caen, in a charter witnessed (as we have seen) by a 'William of Poitiers'. On the other side of Bucéels was Juaye, a 'peculiar' of the diocese of Lisieux,[5] and 5km to the south there was a Beaumont estate at Saint-Vaast.[6] Taken singly these facts might have been considered coincidences, but there are enough of them to make one suspect that there could be a genuine link between them.

A connection with Odo of Bayeux might also help to explain one of the most puzzling facts about WP's work—that it was apparently a failure. One would have expected that such a fulsome eulogy would, when presented to the Conqueror (as Orderic says it was), have given great pleasure and satisfaction, and that royal and ducal monasteries would have been encouraged to make copies of it. But this does not seem to have been the case. At present we do not know of a single manuscript of the work although—to make the obvious comparison—we know of more than 43 of WJ. It could conceivably be that the style was thought too involved and the Latin too difficult, but other works which were often transcribed were equally difficult, as in the case of Dudo's history of the early dukes,

[1] OV, iii. pp. 18–20.

[2] DB, i. fos. 6ᵛ, 7, 144, 144ᵛ.

[3] I am grateful to Dr David Bates for the information that the Roger who in 1086 held nine estates of Odo of Bayeux in Buckinghamshire was Roger de Beaumont, as has been shown by David Crouch in his Ph.D. thesis for the University of Wales.

[4] David R. Bates 'Notes sur l'aristocratie normande', *Annales de Normandie* 23 (1973), pp. 7–38, esp. p. 23.

[5] H. de Formeville, *Histoire de l'ancien évêché-comté de Lisieux* (2 vols, Lisieux 1873), p. clxxxiv, cf. pp. x–xi.

[6] In 1133 Robert de Neufbourg, who had inherited part of the Beumon lands in Normandy held two fiefs of the Bishop of Bayeux, at Saint-Vaast anc Boulon. *Complete Peerage*, new ed. by Vicary Gibbs et al. (13 vols, London 1910–59), xii, Appendix A, p.5.

of which at least seven manuscripts have survived. Perhaps, then, the reason for the failure was that WP or his patron was in political disgrace. WP does not seem to have received any promotion as a reward for his work, for he was archdeacon of Lisieux already in 1077, and seems to have risen no higher. Orderic's statement that in his old age he gave himself up to silence and prayer and spent more time in the composition of prose and poetry than in discourse suggests rather that he had retired to the obscurity of a religious house. To someone who was too closely associated with the rebellions of Robert Curthose or with Odo of Bayeux, such retirement might have been in the best interests of all. Perhaps that was what Orderic meant when he said that WP was unable to carry his history through to the king's death 'because he was prevented by unfavourable circumstances'.[1]

Unfortunately, none of this can be proven; it must remain speculation. But if the connection with Odo can be established beyond doubt, we may find that we have solved some of the problems of WP's sources. As we have already explained, WP is connected in some way with WJ, except in the account of the conquest of England. At that point the two narratives diverge sharply, WJ taking his own rather uninformative course, while WP expands, following a course similar to, but not identical with, the Bayeux Tapestry. If WP was a protégé of Odo of Bayeux, we would have to assume that the story he told was not so much the 'Norman' story as the 'Bayeux' story at a slightly different stage of development from that to be found in the Tapestry. Perhaps WP was not so much an eye-witness, as the protégé of an eye-witness or participant who was lucky enough to have his story told twice over, once in prose and once in pictorial form.

THE MANUSCRIPTS

Some of the questions posed in this paper might be capable of more definite answers if we could discover a complete text of WP, because it is likely that a dedicatory preface or epilogue would give

---

[1] See p. 114 above.

more information about his career. What chance have we of finding
such a manuscript?

We have already commented that the work seems to have
lacked success at the time, with the result that there were few
manuscripts of it. Orderic must have seen a copy at Saint-Evroul
by *c.* 1114–15 when he began Book III of his *Ecclesiastical History,*
but there is nothing to suggest that he knew it when he made his
additions to WJ (no earlier than 1113).[2] The MS seen by Orderic
could have been the only one in Normandy; Robert de Torigni
refers to WP but seems to have derived his knowledge of it at
second-hand through Orderic; and Benoît de Sainte-Maure has one
or two stories which seem to be derived from WP directly or
indirectly.[3] In England also there must have been a manuscript of
WP, because the work was known both to William of Malmesbury
and the author of the *Liber Eliensis*.[4] One manuscript might have
been sufficient for both authors, because in 1075–82 the abbey of
Ely was put in charge of a monk of Jumièges called Godfrey, and
he subsequently became abbot of Malmesbury (1087/9–1106).[5]

Duchesne's edition of 1619 was based on a MS from the library
of Sir Robert Cotton, which could well have been the one from
Ely/Malmesbury. Because it cannot be traced in any of the early
Cottonian catalogues or lists of loans, its fate has puzzled editors.[6]

---

[1] Chibnall in OV, ii, p. xv.

[2] WJ, p. 151. Orderic's interpolations used to be dated no later than 1109
(Marx, in WJ, p. xxv), but in 'Quelques observations sur les interpolations
attribuées à Orderic Vitalis dans les *Gesta Normannorum Ducum* de Guillaume
de Jumièges' (*Revue d'histoire des textes*, viii, 1978, pp. 213–22) Elisabeth van
Houts has shown that they cannot be earlier than 1113.

[3] See p. 114 n. 1 above and postscript, p. 130 above.

[4] See Appendix, pp. 128–29 below.

[5] David Knowles, C. N. L. Brooke, and Vera London, *The Heads of Religious
Houses in England and Wales, 940–1216* (Cambridge, 1972), p. 55. For the use
of WP by William of Malmesbury and *Liber Eliensis*, see Appendix.

[6] Foreville in WP, pp. l–li. As she points out, 212 of the 958 Cottonian MS.
were destroyed in whole or in part in the fire of 1731, but there is no trace of
WP in the catalogue made by Sir Henry Savile, in the seventeenth-century
catalogue at Trinity College, Cambridge (MS 1243) or in the printed catalogue
by Thomas Smith (1696). I have also failed to find it in Cotton's own catalogue

But insufficient attention has been paid to Duchesne's statement that the MS had been borrowed from Cotton's library, not by himself, but by William Camden who, in his turn, had dispatched it across the channel on loan to Nicholas Fabri de Peiresc. Both these men were prolific letter-writers, and their correspondence refers specifically to this loan.[1] In a letter to Camden dated 5 March 1618 Peiresc acknowledges receipt of a transcript of Cotton's WP, but alleges that it was so full of mistakes that it could not be printed. As an alternative, he says: 'Feu Mons. Pithou en avoit un exemplaire tout entier, lequel on m'a promis. . . . Si nous n'avons l'exemplaire de Monsieur Pithou, possible prieray-je Monsieur Cotton de nous envoyer son original.'[2] Evidently the Pithou MS could not be found, because on 29 April 1618 Peiresc wrote to Camden acknowledging receipt of 'l'autographe du fragment de *Guillelmus Pictavensis* bien conditionné'.[3] Though we cannot prove that Peiresc returned it, it is most probable that it was included in the consignment of books which he dispatched back to London in the autumn of 1618,[4] in which case we may presume that it perished in the Cottonian fire of 1731.

Its fate, however, is less important than that of the Pithou MS,

---

of 1621 (British Library, Harley MS 6018) or in the list of MSS lent by Sir Thomas Cotton between 1637 and 1661 (British Library, Cotton MS Appendix xlv. 13) or in the further list of cartularies and loans made in 1638 (British Library, Add. MS 5161). Cf. Kevin Sharpe, *Sir Robert Cotton, 1586–1631: history and politics in Early Modern England* (Oxford, 1979), ch. ii.

[1] For Peiresc, see G. Cahen-Salvador, *Un grand humaniste, Peiresc, 1580–1637* (Paris, 1951), and P. Tamizey de Larroque (ed.), *Lettres de Peiresc aux frères Dupuy* (7 vols, Collection de documents inédits, Paris, 1888–98). For Camden, G. *Camdeni, et illustrorum virorum ad Camdenun epistolae; praemittitur Camdeni Vita*, scriptore T(homa) Smitho (London, 1691), henceforth cited as *GC*. Cf. Sharpe, pp. 95–8.

[2] *GC*, no. clxxvi (p. 222).

[3] *GC*, no. clxxxv (p. 231).

[4] *GC*, no. ccx (p. 269), cf. pp. 261, 266. The Cotton *Genesis* did not get back to England till April 1622 (no. cclix, p. 326). There had been many complaints about the failure to return that book, but none about WP. Duchesne, whom Peiresc treats as a very subsidiary figure, was able to send his printed volume of *Rerum Normannicarum* to Camden by 15 July 1619 (*GC*, no. ccxxi, p. 282).

since this latter (which could well have been the one used by Orderic Vitalis at Saint-Evroult) was said to have contained the text of WP in its entirety. Pierre Pithou (1539–96), editor of two volumes which became the prototype of Bouquet's *Recueil des historiens des Gaules et de la France*, had a famous library, collected by his father and himself at a time when the monastic libraries of France were being dispersed by the Wars of Religion. Acutely aware of its scholarly value, he made a will with elaborate arrangements to ensure that it was preserved entire, but after his death it was none the less divided and dispersed. What exactly happened is uncertain— as early as 1716 Jean Boivin found two contradictory accounts in circulation[1]—but part found its way to the French royal library, part remained with the family, part was kept in the college founded by Pithou at Troyes,[2] and individual volumes somehow got to the library of the Faculty of Medicine at Montpellier (H137 and H151), the Arsénale in Paris (MSS 483, 2590, 4818), the British Library (Add. MS 11506), and the Burgerbibliothek at Bern (MS 163). Other volumes are believed to be in the private library of the Marquis de Rosambo, a descendant of Pithou's in the female line,[3] and others are doubtless elsewhere.

In these circumstances it might seem unduly optimistic to search for the missing WP, but since the prize would be the full text of the lost portions at the beginning and end, an attempt must surely

---

[1] *Claudi Peleterii Regni Administri vita, Petri Pithoei ejus proavi vita adjuncta accurante Joanne Boivin* (Paris, 1716) is the earliest account. Claude Le Peletier was Pierre Pithou's great-grandson and his share of the library still belongs to his descendant, the Marquis de Rosanbo. See also Louis de Rosanbo, 'Pierre Pithou: Biographie', *Rev. du seizième siècle*, xv (1928), pp. 279–305; and 'Pierre Pithou érudit', ibid. xvi (1929), pp. 301–30.

[2] A catalogue of those still at Troyes was published by Pierre Jean Grosley in *Vie de Pierre Pithou avec quelques mémoires de son père et ses frères* (2 vols, Paris, 1756), ii. pp. 275–86.

[3] The Marquis de Rosanbo is descended from Claude Le Peletier who was Pierre Pithou's greatgrandson. Some Pithou MSS are cited, as being in the Château de Rosanbo, by Louis de Rosanbo, in 'Pierre Pithou: biographie' (*Rev. du seizième siècle*, xv (1928), pp. 279–305) and 'Pierre Pithou érudit' (ibid., xvi (1929), pp. 301–33).

be made. It is unlikely that even the complete text would fill a whole volume, and it is quite possible that it has been bound up with works of a different nature. As Jean Grosley commented, when reporting (1756) on the sad state of Pithou's library at Troyes:

This confusion is the effect of the care and vigilance which the reverend fathers devoted to this precious deposit. One of their superiors, seeing manuscripts mutilated, degraded and without bindings, scattered around the library, had them bound in divers volumes, without regard to their contents, but only to their sizes.[1]

Such heterogeneous volumes, by no means rare in other libraries, are always difficult to catalogue. A hasty cataloguer may miss the end of one work and the beginning of the next; and though the perfect cataloguer will efficiently record the *incipit* and *explicit* of every work, even his pains may be wasted in the case of WP, since without the manuscript we have no idea of what the *incipit* and *explicit* are.

It seems that there are three ways of conducting the search for the lost manuscript. The first is to search in large and imperfectly catalogued libraries where there are known to be manuscripts collected in France at the time of the Wars of Religion, but where it is not to be expected that most librarians had been experts in the history of Normandy. Following this principle I have started my search among the MSS of Queen Christina of Sweden in the Vatican Library at Rome, but without success. The second is to assume that the reason why the full WP has not been discovered is because it is bound up with a very similar work, in the same way as the Valenciennes MS of the *Gesta Stephani* was bound up with the *Gesta Regum* of William of Malmesbury.[2] It has therefore seemed desirable to inspect all known MSS of WJ, the work which would offer the most perfect camouflage for WP. A drawback to this course is that most of the MSS of WJ, being in the Bibliothèque nationale at Paris, would inevitably have been well known to

[1] Grosley, ii. p. 272.
[2] *Gesta Stephani*, ed. K. R. Potter and R. H. C. Davis (Oxford, 1976), p. xiv.

Léopold Delisle who, as the greatest expert on Norman history of this period, could not have failed to recognize WP if he saw it. None the less, since he did not know *all* the MSS there may be some hope in this course, though so far it has proved fruitless. The third, and probably the most promising, method is to hunt down every manuscript which ever belonged to Pithou. Many of them can be identified from the editions which he published.[1] Others can be traced through the history of his family or, since he usually wrote his name in his books, through library catalogues. As a result the number of his known manuscripts is growing. If we can make it grow faster, we may succeed in finding the full text of the *History of William the Conqueror* and then we should be able to discover a great deal more about the life of its author and the reliability of his narrative.

APPENDIX

Reconstruction of the beginning and the end of WP

The end of WP has to be deduced from the use of it made by OV. See Chibnall in OV, ii. pp. xviii–xxi. For the beginning it is necessary to turn to William of Malmesbury's *Gesta Regum* (ed. William Stubbs, 2 vols, RS 1887–9 and henceforth cited as *GR*). In his preface Stubbs (vol. ii, pp. cxi–cxiii) showed that *GR* had used WP as one of his sources. In confirmation of his argument it may be added that *GR* follows WP rather than WJ in placing the revolt of William of Arques after (rather than before) that of Guy of Burgundy; in the additional details he gives about Guy (above, pp. 77, 87); and in stating that Domfront belonged to Anjou rather than Normandy (*GR*, 288, WP 36). *GR* 288 also has the story of William's challenge to Geoffrey of Anjou (WP 38–40). Compare also *GR* 290 and WP 70 (note the use of *Celtigallus*), the acquisition

---

[1] See particularly *Annalium et Historiae Francorum ab anno Christi DCCVIII ad annum DCCCCXC scriptores coaetani xii, nunc primum in lucem editi ex bibliotheca P. Pithoei* (Paris, 1588) and *Historiae Francorum ab anno Christi DCCCC ad annum MCCLXXXV scriptores veteres xi ... ex bibliotheca P. Pithoei* (Frankfurt, 1596).

of Maine (*GR* 294, WP 86–92), and the deposition of Archbishop Mauger of Rouen (*GR* 327, WP 130–2).

It may also be noted that the *Liber Eliensis* (ed. E. O. Blake, Camden 3rd Series xcii, London, 1962) reproduces almost verbatim (ii. 90) WP's account of the capture and murder of the atheling Alfred (WP 8–10), and in its account of the Hastings campaign uses many of WP's words and phrases, as pointed out by Blake in the footnotes and in his Introduction, p. xxviii.

Using the clues offered by these three works, the following suggestions can be made about the contents of the lost beginning and end of WP.

(i) *Beginning*

1. William's birth (*GR* 285).
2. Duke Robert's decision to go on crusade; the nobles' oath to William; Count Gilbert [of Brionne] as William's guardian (*GR* 285).
3. Duke Robert's death at Nicaea (*GR* 286).
4. Revolts during William's minority (*ut supra docuimus*, WP 14). Murder of Count Gilbert (*GR* 286).
5. Marriage of Emma to Ethelred and Canute (*GR* 191, 218–19). This would lead well into the section on England with which the surviving text of WP opens, and would also explain the relatively favourable attitude to Harthacnut (WP 12) as a son of Emma's.

(ii) *End*

1. Murder of Copsi (*Coxo*) WP 268–70, cf. OV, ii. 206–8.
2. Loyalty of Ealdred archbishop of York WP 270, cf. OV, ii. 208.
3. William's return from Normandy. He rallies the waverers (OV, ii. 210).
4. His capture of Exeter; his great mercy (OV, ii. 212–14).
5. Coronation of Queen Matilda, Whitsun 1068 (OV, ii. 214).
6. Revolt of Edwin and Morcar; including William's castle-building, the war-weariness of the Normans and the exhaustion

of the country. (OV, ii. 220 (cf. OV, ii. 236) and *Liber Eliensis*, 185–93.)

7. Swein's invasion; William hears of it in the Forest of Dean. Troubles overcome at York, Montacute, Exeter, Stafford, and Shrewsbury (OV, ii. 226–34; *Liber Eliensis*, 187, 190–1, and GR 312).

8. William and the English Church. Council of Winchester; deposition of Stigand; eulogy of Lanfranc; ecclesiastical appointments, including that of Gilbert fitz Osbern, canon and archdeacon of Lisieux, to the bishopric of Evreux (OV, ii. 248–54; *Vita Lanfranci*, chs v, vi.

9. Peace over England—eulogy of the Conqueror's just rule (OV, ii. 256).

10. The arrest of Earl Morcar and the death of the Earl Edwin (OV, ii. 256–8).

POSTSCRIPT

Since this article was written, Dr Elizabeth van Houts has pointed out to me (re p. 94) that the text of WP was also known to Ralph de Diceto, who used it in his *Abbreviationes Chronicorum* (*Radulfi de Diceto . . . opera omnia*, ed. William Stubbs (R.S., 2 vols, 1876), ii. pp. 263-4). She points out that Ralph was a friend of Arnulf Bishop of Lisieux (1141-82) and might have got the MS. of WP from him (cf. G. A. Zinn in *Speculum* lii (1977), 59-60), in which case it could have been the same MS. that Orderic Vitalis had used.

More recently, in 'The origins of Herleva, mother of William the Conqueror' (*E.H.R.* ci (1986), 399-404) Dr van Houts has shown that Orderic's reference to *polinctores*, quoted p. 109 above, is more obscure than I had thought, since a *polinctor* was not a tanner but a superior sort of undertaker.

9

William of Jumièges, Robert Curthose and the Norman Succession

IN his *Gesta Normannorum Ducum* William of Jumièges (henceforth *WJ*) makes three references to Robert Curthose, the eldest son of William the Conqueror, and in all three cases he makes him out to be duke of Normandy.[1] One of them, in the Epilogue, is well known, and we therefore print it first, but the other two are equally important.

(*a*) (Epilogue) . . . our pen is directed to Robert, the same king's son, in whom at present we rejoice as duke and advocate (*quo in presentiarum duce et advocato gaudemus*). While distinguished by a most handsome body and pleasing age, he is blossoming into the flower of youth . . . (*cum enim pulcherrimo tam decentissimi corporis quam gratissimae aetatis flore vernans in juventutem enitescat*) . . . (pp. 143–4).

(*β*) (Bk. vii, ch. ix) . . . by whom [Matilda] in the course of succeeding years he [William I] begat sons and daughters, one of whom Robert subsequently succeeded to his parents' duchy, performing his father's office – long may he do so! (*ex quibus postmodum in ducatu genitori Rodbertus successit, functus honore paterna, et utinam tempore longo*). If life is spared us, we will dictate more fully about him in the appropriate places (p. 128).

(*γ*) (Bk. vii, ch. xix). Now [1067] that he had satisfactorily completed all the tasks which he had come [to Normandy] to do, the king handed over the lordship of the duchy of Normandy to his son Robert who was in the flower of his youth (*Roberto filio suo juvenili flore vernanti, Normannici ducatus dominium tradidit*) (p. 139).

The obvious meaning of these passages is that King William made Robert duke in 1067, and that Robert was still duke when *WJ* was writing, which is usually thought to have been *c*. 1070–1. But this interpretation is not generally accepted. It is commonly assumed that Robert did not become duke until his father's death (1087), and that *WJ* must then have updated his work, adding to the original Epilogue, which was addressed to William the Conqueror, the passage quoted in *a* addressed to his successor.[2]

1. Jean Marx (ed.), *Guillaume de Jumieges: Gesta Normannorum Ducis: édition critique* (Soc. de l'histoire de Normandie, Paris and Rouen, 1914), pp. 143–4. 128, 139,

2. Marx has misled subsequent writers by stating (p. xvi) that *WJ*'s addition to his original epilogues was addressed to William Rufus. This is a mistake. The only William mentioned is William I – *WJ* specifically states that he has narrated his deeds as duke and subsequently as king.

This belief has been encouraged by the fact that in five of the extant manuscripts of *WJ* our passage α does not appear, the Epilogue in them being addressed to William the Conqueror alone. In consequence, *WJ*'s editor, Jean Marx considered – and here he was following the great Delisle[1] – that these five manuscripts (A1, A2, A3, B1, B2) must represent the 'primitive text' written *c.* 1070-1. Plausible as was this explanation for α, it took no account of β and γ which occur in *all* known manuscripts. Nonetheless Marx printed a 'primitive text' which omitted the reference to Robert in β, explaining that though this version was 'not to be found in any manuscript', it was 'easily reconstituted'.[2] As for γ, it is impossible to say what Marx made of it, since he printed it without proposing any emendation or explanation.[3]

A further difficulty which Marx did not notice is that the five manuscripts (A1, A2, A3, B1, B2), which in his opinion represented the 'primitive text' of 1070-1, are the only ones to record the career, death and burial of Nicholas son of Duke Richard III.[4] Since the passage occurs only in these five manuscripts he dutifully labelled it 'Première rédaction', without apparently realizing the significance of the fact, which he recorded in a footnote, that Nicholas did not die until February 1092.[5] Clearly these five manuscripts cannot possibly represent a text earlier than that date. If we want to find such a text, we must look for it in those manuscripts which do *not* contain this passage, in other words, in the C group, even though its text contains all three references to Duke Robert (α, β and γ) entire. In this case the address to Duke Robert in the Epilogue would have been part of the original work, but would have been omitted from later editions when it became politically embarrassing, as it would have done when Robert was in revolt against his father (1077-9 and 1083-7), or when he had lost the duchy to his brother Henry I and was being held prisoner by him (1106-34).

This seems to be the only satisfactory interpretation of the manuscript tradition, but it raises the historical question whether *WJ* was right in thinking that Robert Curthose was made duke in his father's

---

1. Léopold Delisle in his 'Notice' attached to Auguste Le Prévost's edition of the *Historia Ecclesiastica of Orderic Vitalis* (Soc. de l'histoire de France, 5 vols., Paris, 1838-55), v. lxxiii-lxxvi.
2. *WJ*, p. 128.
3. *WJ*, p. 139.
4. *WJ*, p. 99.
5. The date comes from an interpolation by Orderic (*WJ*, p. 153). Since Orderic's language is different, and since he also differs on a point of fact, saying that Nicholas was originally a monk of Saint Ouen (while *WJ*, p. 99 says that he was originally a monk of Fécamp but subsequently became abbot of Saint Ouen), the two passages seem independent.
It should be noted that since B1 and B2 reproduce the text found in the 'A' group of manuscripts but with interpolations by 'the monk of Caen' which are found in these two manuscripts only, it must follow that these interpolations also are later than 1092. *Cf.* L. J. Engels, *art. cit.* in p. 600, n. 2 below.

lifetime. If he was not, it will be hard to believe that he was a contemporary historian writing as early as *c.* 1070–1; but if *WJ* can be proved correct, our confidence in him will be greatly increased. Unfortunately the question does not admit a simple answer because, quite apart from any conflict of evidence, it is not easy to understand the language or thought of the time. When *WJ* says that the Conqueror 'gave the lordship of the duchy to his son', did he mean that he was designating him as his heir, making him regent during his absence abroad, making him co-duke, or resigning in his favour? So far as we can see, the father meant one thing and the son another, so that the question we have to ask is how contemporaries interpreted them at various dates.[1]

To discover this, it will be simplest if we start with the fullest account, that of Orderic Vitalis, even though it was not written till *c.* 1127–30. Orderic was not born till 1075, but he was at the abbey of Saint Evroul from 1085, where one of the other monks, (who lived till *c.* 1105) was a Breton called Samson who had served Queen Matilda as a messenger to plead the cause of the young Robert with his father, William the Conqueror.[2] As a result Orderic's story, though it may be partial, should not be ill-informed. The basic facts which it alleges come in three distinct places:

(*a*) In the speech which he puts into Robert's mouth at the beginning of his revolt of 1077–9: 'My lord king, give me (*da michi*) Normandy, which you recently granted me (*michi concessisti*) before sailing to England to fight King Harold'.[3]

(*b*) In the reconciliation at the end of this same revolt William, according to Orderic, 'again granted Robert the duchy of Normandy after his death (*post obitum suum . . . concessit*), as he had once granted it to him (*concesserat ei*) when he lay sick at Bonneville'.[4]

(*c*) In the deathbed speech which he put into William's mouth (1087): 'I granted (*concessi*) my son Robert the duchy of Normandy before I fought against Harold on the heath of Senlac; because he is my first-born son and has received the homage of almost all the barons of the country (*patriae baronum*), the honor then granted cannot be taken away (*concessus honor nequit abstrahi*).[5]

In (*a*) and (*c*) Orderic says that William *granted* Normandy to Robert before his invasion of England, but in (*b*) he seems to be saying that William *designated* Robert as his heir in 1079, as he had done once before 'when he lay sick at Bonneville', whenever that may have been.

William of Malmesbury, writing in England *c.* 1125, gives little

---

1. C. W. David, *Robert Curthose Duke of Normandy* (Cambridge, Mass., 1920), pp. 3–16, has an admirable survey of the material, though his conclusions are different from those expressed here.

2. Marjorie Chibnall (ed.), *The Ecclesiastical History of Orderic Vitalis* (Oxford, 1969–78), henceforth cited as *OV*, iii. 104–5.

3. *OV*, iii. 98–99; *cf.* ii. 356–7.   4. *OV*, iii. 112–13; *cf.* ii. 356–7.   5. *OV*, iv. 92–93.

help, though what he says could be reconciled with either of Orderic's stories. He says that Robert revolted against his father because he 'took it ill that he was denied Normandy', and that eventually 'he was disappointed of his heritage, since he did not have (*caruit*) England after his death and barely retained the county of Normandy (*comitatu vix retento*).[1] Strictly speaking Robert could not have 'retained' Normandy unless he had had it before, but it is possible that William of Malmesbury was using the word loosely.

Slightly earlier is the *De Obitu Willelmi* printed by Marx in his edition of *WJ* (pp. 145–9). Though this was formerly thought to be near-contemporary, it is found only in the B group of manuscripts which, as we have seen, must be later than 1092, and Professor Engels has shown that it most probably belongs to the first decades of the twelfth century.[2] It describes how, on his deathbed, the Conqueror had his treasures brought before him, 'and allowed his son William', though he was not present, 'to have the crown, the sword and the sceptre studded with gold and jewels'. When this proposal caused dismay, the archbishop of Rouen persuaded the Conqueror to change his mind, and as a result he said that though he would do what he liked with his own (which presumably meant England), he would confirm Robert in 'the whole duchy of Normandy which he had already previously granted to him (*illi jamdudum ante largitus fuerat*)' (p. 147). Various interpretations have been put on this narrative, but Professor Engels has now shown that it has almost all been taken from the Astronomer's Life of Louis the Pious (*Vita Hludovici Imperatoris*). He prints the relevant passages in parallel columns and shows that the only statement about the Conqueror's death which has not been lifted from the Astronomer, and which must therefore be taken seriously, is the confirmation of Normandy to Robert since 'he had already previously granted it to him'.[3]

More positive is the confirmation given to Orderic's story by the *Anglo-Saxon Chronicle* (D) which seems at this stage to have been written more or less from year to year.[4] It says that the reason for Robert's revolt of 1078–9 (which it places under 1079) was that 'his father would not let him govern his earldom (*earl domes*) in Normandy, which he himself and also King Philip with his consent had given him; and the leading men in the country (*on þam lande*) had sworn him oaths and accepted him as lord (*hlaforde*)'.[5] This statement, which

1. William Stubbs (ed.), *Willelmi Malmesbiriensis Monachi De Gestis Regum Anglorum* (London, Rolls Series, 1887–9), ii. 332.
2. L. J. Engels, 'De obitu Willelmi ducis Normannorum regisque Anglorum: Texte, modèles, valeur, origine' in *Mélanges Christine Mohrmann* (Utrecht/Antwerp, 1973), pp. 209–55. I am grateful to Dr Chibnall for drawing my attention to this important study.
3. *Ibid.* pp. 226, 235.
4. N. R. Ker, *Catalogue of Manuscripts containing Anglo-Saxon* (Oxford, 1957), p. 254.
5. *The Anglo-Saxon Chronicle*, trans. G. N. Garmonsway (London, 1957), 213–14. *Cf.* Charles Plummer, *Two Saxon Chronicles Parallel* (Oxford, 1892–9), i. 213–14.

is repeated by Florence of Worcester (*s.a.* 1078) with the addition that the grant in the presence of the king of France had been before the invasion of England, suggests a formal investiture by the duke's overlord.

William of Poitiers is silent on this subject. If, as is commonly supposed, he was writing *c.* 1077 his silence might be due to the fact that Robert's rebellion was already in progress. It is striking that he does not name Robert once; when he wishes to refer to his betrothal to the heiress of Maine, he calls him simply the Conqueror's son (*nato suo*).[1] He says nothing about designation or investiture either before or after the conquest of England, though he does state that during the Hastings campaign Normandy was governed by the Conqueror's wife, Matilda, with the assistance of councillors who included Roger de Beaumont.[2] This might imply that at that date Robert Curthose was still considered a minor.

If we put all these statements together we have allegations that Robert was granted the duchy in 1066 or before (Orderic (*a*) and (*c*) and Florence of Worcester); that he was still a minor in 1066 (*WP*); that he was granted the duchy in 1067 (*WJ*); that the grant was made with the consent of King Philip of France (*ASC* (D) and Florence); that Robert was duke when *WJ* was writing (supposedly 1070–1); and that he was designated William's heir when the king 'lay sick at Bonneville' and again in 1079 (Orderic, (*b*)). These statements are not all inconsistent with each other, but they do not immediately suggest a single and coherent story.

We turn therefore to the evidence of charters. Those of the Conqueror are at first sight disappointing because they are often ambiguous. In them Robert is styled twelve times as 'the King's son',[3] eleven times as 'Count Robert'[4] and another eleven times as 'Count Robert the King's son',[5] but unfortunately it is impossible to determine the significance of the term 'count'. The dukes of Normandy often styled themselves *comes* as if that title was synonymous with *dux*, and Duke William styled himself thus as late as 1066.[6] But Robert was also count of Maine and *Robertus comes* could, at any rate sometimes, have signified no more than that. In four charters he is styled specifically count of Maine,[7] but on the other hand there are four in

---

1. Raymonde Foreville (ed.), *Guillaume de Poitiers: Histoire de Guillaume le Conquérant* (Paris, 1952), henceforth cited as *WP*, pp. 94–95.

2. *WP*, pp. 260–1.

3. H. W. C. Davis (ed.), *Regesta Regum Anglo-Normannorum*, i (Oxford, 1913), henceforth cited as *Reg.* i, nos. 2, 73, 92a, 123, 126, 137, 144, 165, 168, 171, 218, 255.

4. *Reg.* i. nos. 2, 96, 114, 127, 135, 173, 175, 182, 183a, 199 and W. H. Hart (ed.), *Historia et Cartularium Monasterii Sancti Petri Gloucestriae* (London, Rolls Series, 1863–7), no. 411.

5. *Reg.* i, nos. 30, 74–75, 105, 125, 147, 149, 150, 158, 169–70.

6. Marie Fauroux, *Recueil des Actes des ducs de Normandie de 911 à 1066* (Méms. de la Soc. des Antiquaires de Normandie, xxxvi, Caen, 1961), nos. 229–30. *Cf.* 220–1 and 225–6.   7. C. W. David, *Robert Curthose*, p. 10, n. 34.

which he is styled count of the Normans.[1] These can be dated to April 1067 at Vaudreuil, 22 June 1082 at Oissel (two), and 1079–82 – dates which are consistent with a grant of the duchy in 1067 or before, and a renewed grant made in the reconciliation which ended the revolt of 1077–9.

Attention must also be paid to two later charters which have a direct bearing on our problem. One of them is a grant by Odo bishop of Bayeux and the other a confirmation of it by duke Robert, his nephew. Both are dated 24 May 1096 and both state that this was in the nineteenth year of Robert's *principatus*.[2] If the years of Robert's *principatus* were calculated in the same way as regnal years, they would run from the day of his investiture; and since we do not know what that day was, the first year of his *principatus* could, according to these two charters, have started as early as 25 May 1077 or ended as late as 23 May 1079, which certainly suggests that Robert considered his *principatus* to have begun during his revolt of 1077–9.

In this revolt, Orderic tells us that Robert, having left his father's court in disgust, went to the king of France who installed him in the castle of Gerberoy from which he could harass the Norman border. As a result, William laid siege to Gerberoy in the early months of 1079, but after three weeks abandoned the siege and returned to Rouen. There intermediaries eventually reconciled him to his son, persuading him (as we have already seen) to grant the duchy of Normandy after his death to Robert again, as he had previously granted it to him 'when he lay sick at Bonneville'.[3] Since it is clear that the king of France was supporting Robert and that William was worsted at Gerberoy, it has always proved difficult to explain a charter which King Philip of France issued in the presence of King William 'in the siege of the aforesaid kings around Gerberoy (*in obsidione predictorum regum . . . circa Gerborredum*)'.[4] It has generally been taken as evidence that King Philip must have suddenly changed sides and joined in the campaign against Robert, but the language is so curious that one is tempted to think that it must be deliberately ambiguous. In this case the charter might represent the first step in peace-making. There was no real reason why the king of England should attest a charter for St Quentin de Beauvais which had nothing to do with Normandy; and it has been noticed as extraordinary that a charter of the king of France should, even in the manner in which it displayed their *signa*, go out of its way to stress the equality of the

---

1. *Reg.* i. 6a, 145–6, 172. *Cf.* David, *op. cit.* 13.
2. Charles Homer Haskins, *Norman Institutions* (Cambridge, Mass., 1918; repr. 1969), p. 67, n. 19.
3. *OV*, iii. 112–13.
4. M. Prou, *Recueil des Actes de Philippe I Roi de France (1059–1108)* (Paris, 1908), no. xciv.

:ings of France and England.[1] This must have flattered William
onsiderably, but it was probably no more than the sugar-coating on
. pill, for the fact is that the charter does not at any point describe
William as duke of Normandy. The only obvious explanation of this,
.nd it is wholly in accord with Orderic's story, would be that King
Philip had already recognized Robert as duke and was unwilling to
.dmit that William could retain the title for himself also.

We can therefore claim that after his revolt of 1077-9 Robert did
;ain some sort of recognition in Normandy. Though the Conqueror
obviously did not agree that he himself had resigned the duchy, he
did let his son attest charters as 'Count Robert' or 'Robert Count of
he Normans'. Doubtless he consoled himself with the fact that the
itle *comes* could be ambiguous, signifying either the duke or a sub-
ordinate of the duke, but in the opinion of Robert himself, his uncle
Odo and his overlord the king of France, it was thought that
Robert's *principatus* should be dated from this time.

We are still faced with the fact that both Orderic and the Anglo-
Saxon Chronicle (D) stated that a similar grant had been made once
before, and indeed that it was the Conqueror's refusal to implement
t which had led to Robert's revolt. This earlier grant might have
been made before the English campaign of 1066 (Orderic (*a*) and (*c*)),
or in 1067 (*W.J.* (*γ*)) or 'when the king lay sick at Bonneville' (Orderic
b)); and Robert might have received the grant either when he had
attained his majority (which would probably have been when he was
6) or when he was still a minor.

This latter possibility must be emphasized, because we know that
n the winter of 1034-5 William's father, Robert the Magnificent,
.ad, on announcing his intention to go to Jerusalem, had his son
made duke although he was only seven years old. According to *WJ*,
Robert summoned his nobles, displayed his son, arranged for him to
e his successor 'and bade his men choose him as lord in his place
nd set him over their army' (*ut hunc sibi sui loco dominum eligerent,
militiaeque suae preficerent, ab eis exigebat*)', and then appointed guar-
.ians for the child until he came of age.[2] If a similar ceremony had
been arranged for William's own son, Robert, before the conquest
f England, there would be no difficulty in explaining why (as *WP*
alleges) Normandy was nonetheless governed by Matilda and her
ouncil; they would have been the boy-duke's guardians.

In that case, when did the boy come of his age? Unfortunately we
o not know when he was born: he was the eldest child, but we do
ot know when his parents were married. All we do know is that
he marriage had been projected before October 1049, since at the
Council of Rheims Pope Leo IX forbade it. We also know that

---

1. This is the comment of J.-F. Lemarignier, *Le Gouvernement royal aux premiers temps
capétiens (987-1108)* (Paris, 1965), p. 118.
2. *WJ*, pp. 111-12.

William and Matilda ignored the prohibition, and that the firs
dated appearance of Matilda as the duke's consort is in a charter o
1053.[1] As a result, we can suppose that Robert was born betweer
1050 and 1054. William of Poitiers tells us that when betrothed to the
heiress of Maine (at some point between 1055 and 1062) Robert wa
still a boy and too young to marry,[2] but in a charter of 29 June 1063
Stigand of Mézidon states that his gifts to the abbey were made 'witł
the consent of count William his lord and Matilda his wife anc
Robert their son, whom they had chosen for the governance of the
kingdom after their death (*quem elegerant ad gubernandum regnum pos.
obitum suum*)'.[3] If this is correct it means that Robert was designatec
William's heir by 1063, when he was between the ages of 9 and 13
In 1066 a further advance is recorded; when Duke William was abou
to invade England, the monks of Marmoutier persuaded him to have
his gifts to the abbey confirmed by his son Robert, since he was ther
of an age to do so (*quia scilicet maioris iam ille aetatis ad praebendum
spontaneum auctoramentum idoneus esset*); it does not quite say that he
had attained his majority (we may notice that one of the witnesse
was his tutor Ilger – *Ilgerio pedagogo ipsius Roberti filius comitis*) but i
does suggest that he was very close to it.[4] If he had been born ir
1051, he would have been 16 in 1067, the year in which *WJ* says that
his father gave him the duchy, and the year in which he witnessed one
of his father's charters at Vaudreuil, as Robert count of the Normans

The various dates offered by Orderic and *WJ*, therefore, are no
so incoherent as was at first feared. Though the evidence is not con
clusive, it suggests that William the Conqueror had designatec
Robert as heir to the duchy by 1063, and had had a further ceremony
'making' him duke in 1067 before leaving Normandy for what turnec
out to be an interval of four years during which Robert was regardec
as 'duke' in Normandy. After 1071 the Conqueror visited Normandy
at least once a year and resumed his ducal authority to the full. As a
result Robert thought that he was being cheated of what he hac
already been granted, revolted and forced his father to give him a yet
more formal grant. In the event the only result of this second gran
would seem to have been that Robert was given a more formal title
in his father's charters, 'Count Robert' or 'Robert Count of the
Normans'. Eventually, therefore, he revolted again in 1083, anc
remained in revolt until his father's death.[5]

If this reconstruction is correct, we have to decide whether i
throws any light on when *WJ* was writing his *Gesta Normannorun*

1. David C. Douglas, *William the Conqueror* (London, 1964), appendix C.
2. *WP*, pp. 94–95.
3. Fauroux, no. 158. Dr Chibnall has pointed out to me that its use of the word
regnum with reference to Normandy suggests that the charter was not actually writter
till after 1066.
4. Fauroux, no. 228.
5. *Supra*, p. 132.

Ducum. If we are right in thinking that the earliest version of the Epilogue is that which is addressed to both king William the Conqueror and Duke Robert, the possible dates would be limited to 1067–71, after Robert had been 'made' duke and while he was governing Normandy in his father's absence, unaware that his father was treating him merely as a temporary regent. Since *WJ*'s narrative ends in 1069–70 and reads as if it were contemporary, historians have generally suggested, albeit cautiously, that the most likely date for its composition would have been 1070–1. Our study of its treatment of Duke Robert confirms this.

Further confirmation comes from the wording used by *WJ* in his references to the young duke. When William granted him the duchy in 1067, Robert was *juvenili flore vernanti*; and when *WJ* addresses Robert in the Epilogue he is again *flore vernans in juventutem*.[1] Although it is always difficult to know precisely what ages are covered by a man's 'youth', it is hard to believe, as Delisle and Marx would have us do, that Robert could have been 'blossoming into the flower of youth' both in 1067, when he would have been about sixteen, and after 1087 when he would have been over thirty-six. It is surely simpler to believe that the full Epilogue was written in 1070–1, when Robert would have been about twenty and when, thanks to his father's absence in England, his subjects could believe that he really was their duke.

If these conclusions are correct, they raise a general point of some importance. Recent discussions of the development of the hereditary principle in Normandy[2] have made no allowance for the possibility that the real difficulty experienced by the Conqueror in relation to his eldest son, was not that he had 'designated' or 'recognized' him as his heir to Normandy, but that he had in fact made him duke. This was not an unusual way of ensuring the succession of a chosen son in the eleventh and twelfth centuries. The Capetian kings of France practised it normally, and so did the dukes of Normandy who, though they sometimes left it till the last moment, nearly all made their sons duke in their lifetime.[3] Constitutional historians call the process 'association' and tend to call the son 'co-king' or 'co-duke', but the

---

1. *WJ*, pp. 139, 144. The phrase was a favourite of *WJ*'s; he applied it to the Conqueror, *jam flore vernans gratissimae juventutis* when he was about 19 (*WJ*, p. 122) and to Duke Richard I, *flore juventutis vernanti*, before his marriage (*WJ*, p. 60). I have been unable to trace the source of the phrase.

2. John Le Patourel, 'The Norman succession, 996–1135', *ante*, lxxxvi (1971), 225–50, and *The Norman Empire* (Oxford, 1976), pp. 179–84; J. C. Holt, 'Politics and Property in Early Medieval England', *Past and Present*, lvii (1972), 3–52.

3. In France Henry I (d. 1060) had his son Philip I crowned in 1059. Louis VI (d. 1137) had his son Louis VII crowned and anointed by Pope Innocent II at Reims in 1131. Louis VII (d. 1180) had his son, Philip II, crowned in 1179. In Normandy according to *WJ* (who for the earlier dukes follows Dudo) only one of Rollo's successors was not made duke by his father; this was Robert the Magnificent, who acquired the duchy by overthrowing his brother. For the others, see *WJ*, pp. 31, 40, 71, 97, 111, 139.

reality of the matter is best illustrated by a charter of 1025–6 to which Duke Richard II and his son appended their joint approval, *jubentibus piissimis principibus RICHARDO scilicet secundo et tertio*.[1]

The traditional, and common-sense, explanation of 'association' is that it was the best way of ensuring the succession of one's chosen son at a time when there was no assurance that the hereditary principle would be followed. It was dangerous because, as Kings William and Henry II found to their cost, it could easily encourage a son and 'colleague' to revolt, but it had the advantage of facing the barons with a *fait accompli*. If one relied on 'designation' there was always the danger that the barons would break their word, as king Henry I's barons did when he forced them to recognize Matilda as heir. The two methods therefore had alternative drawbacks, so that at any particular moment there might be special reasons for the adoption of one instead of the other. But in very general terms the progression is clearly from 'association' to 'designation', and from 'designation' to the acceptance of the hereditary system as a rule of law.[2] Our study of Robert Curthose's succession should serve as a reminder that for most of the eleventh century the Normans were still only in the first of these three stages.

1. Fauroux, no. 55. *Cf.* her remarks on pp. 57–58.
2. For France in the twelfth century, see p. 603, n. 3 above. In England, King Henry I 'designated' his son William as heir to England and Normandy when he was 12 (*c.* 1115) (William of Malmesbury, ii. 495). But in 1120, when he was 17, William did homage to King Louis VI and received the lordship of Normandy from him (*Normanniae sub illo suscepit dominium*) (Symeon of Durham, ed. T. Arnold (Rolls Series, 1885), ii. 258. *Cf.* Florence of Worcester, ed. Thorpe (2 vols., London, 1848–9), ii. 72–73). It was very soon after this that the young William was drowned in the White Ship (25 Nov. 1120). Subsequently, as is well known, Henry I 'designated' his daughter Matilda (1126), but as the barons broke their word, the 'designation' was unavailing; the story that Henry changed his mind on his deathbed, though probably untrue, was supposed to suggest a 'designation' of Stephen. Stephen, the most insecure of kings, tried but failed to get his son crowned in his lifetime. Eventually in the 'Treaty of Westminster' he had to designate Henry II as his heir (*Reg.* iii. 272). Henry II had his son, Henry, crowned in 1170, but he revolted in 1173 and died before his father. Subsequently, Henry II would neither crown nor designate anyone as his successor, and neither did Richard I, though in both cases the succession was not without its difficulties.

10

Domesday Book: Continental Parallels

THE CONTINENTAL PARALLELS of Domesday Book can be divided into two classes, those which were made before 1086 and those which were made after. The first could have influenced the making of Domesday Book, the second could have been influenced by it. Both enable us to see more clearly those features of Domesday Book which are unique.

To start with the first class, we must observe that most of Domesday's predecessors, like Domesday Book itself, were known as *descriptiones*. The English word 'description' does not do justice to them, and we would do better to translate *descriptio* as an assessment or survey, which is the sense in which it was used from the first century AD to the eleventh. One reason why it retained this technical use is probably to be found in the Vulgate's version of Luke 2: 1, 'there went out a decree from Caesar Augustus that all the world should be taxed', *ut describeretur universus orbis.*[1]

If Domesday Book is in some sense a tax register, it is even more obviously a land register, recording ownership. Both aspects are discussed by Professor John Percival in the important paper on 'The Precursors of Domesday Book', which he has contributed to Peter Sawyer's *Domesday Book: a reassessment.*[2] It should be noticed that in writing of Roman and Carolingian land registers, Professor Percival deliberately avoids two misleading terms which have hitherto been in common use – Roman 'census rolls' and Carolingian 'polyptychs'. It is always unsatisfactory when records are classified simply by their physical appearance, but it is particularly misleading when it is found that physical appearance is not always correct. A 'polyptych' means literally a book ('many leaves'), but some of the so-called Carolingian 'polyptychs' were not written in books but on scrolls; while outside Egypt (where everything was different) the only census 'rolls' that have survived are neither scrolls nor books but inscriptions in stone. Walter Goffart cites nine of them, five from the Greek islands and four from Asia Minor, commenting that stone seemed an unsuitable material on which to

---

[1] Cf. Numbers, 33: 1-2: 'Hae sunt mansiones filiorum Israel . . . quas descripsit Moyses juxta castrorum loca. . . .'
[2] Percival (1985), 5–27.

record facts which would be 'bound to change from year to year'.[3] The Romans did not see matters in this way. They often preserved and publicised important records by displaying them as inscriptions in public places. Many cities followed the example of Rome itself which maintained a *tabularium publicum* with a curator in charge of it; examples in Southern Gaul were at Aix-en-Provence, Vienne, Vaison and Orange. At Orange (*Arausio*) there were also three separate stone *cadasters* or land surveys; archaeologists have discovered 269 fragments of them and have made considerable progress in fitting them together again. There now seems no doubt that the earliest of the three was erected for the Emperor Vespasian in AD 77, in order to record in perpetuity the recovery of public lands from the hands of private usurpers. Though it could well have had some use for taxation, it was primarily a public title-deed. It was erected in a prominent place in the town and covered quite a large wall; when complete it would have measured about 4.35 m by a little more than 4 m.[4] Though it was concerned only with the territory of *Arausio* it can be compared with Domesday Book because of the way in which it attempted to establish titles to land in perpetuity, particularly when they were lands which had only recently been recovered by the state. Though archaeologists have been unable to date the period at which the wall and its inscription collapsed, it seems probable that this monumental *cadaster* did not in fact survive quite as long as Domesday Book has done. Walls cannot be protected quite as easily as books.

It has been established that the Roman *census* records originally covered two sorts of tax, a poll or head tax (*tributum capitis*) and a tax on land (*tributum soli*), but by the time of Diocletian (284–305) the two seem to have been combined and to have become a fixed customary payment, bearing little or no relation to changing monetary values. Diocletian introduced the assessment of land by *jugera*, a *jugum* (pl. *jugera*) being, like the later *mansus* or hide, not a fixed area but a notional value. If vines were cultivated, the area of a *jugum* would be much smaller than in the case of arable land, which in its turn would be less extensive than land which could hardly be cultivated at all. According to the law codes, the assessments were made by an official called a *censitor*, who had to enter on the register the names of the farms concerned and the *civitas* and *pagus* to which they belonged, together with the amount of arable, vines, olive-trees, meadowland and pasture.[5] The ideal tax register would therefore have borne some resemblance to Domesday Book. The same general sort of questions were being asked, and they were being asked by a government official who recorded the answers and kept the record as public property. On the other hand, the information was arranged not by the holdings of particular landowners but according to the geographical lie of the land. This was presumably because the imperial govern-

---

[3] Goffart, *Caput and Colonate*, 121. The inscriptions are from Lesbos, Mylasa, Hypaepa, Thera, Cos, Chios, Astypalaea, Magnesia-on-the-Meander, and Tralles. Goffart thought that the use of stone for them might have been 'a momentary fad'.
[4] For both the surveys at Orange and for *tabularia publica* in general, see André Piganiol, 'Les Documents cadastraux de la colonie romaine d'Orange' (xvi supplement to *Gallia*, Paris, 1962).
[5] Percival (1985), 12.

ment did not levy its taxes on individual landowners but on the land itself, imposing a lump sum on each district such as a *colonia* or *civitas*, and requiring its *curiales* to collect it in detail.[6]

There is nothing to suggest that the Roman tax registers came to an end with the collapse of the Roman Empire in the West. No ruler likes to forgo an opportunity of receiving taxes, and the barbarian kings who took over the government of the various parts of the Empire would have found it in their interest to take over the tax registers. There is some evidence that they did so in Italy, and even more in Gaul.

In Italy the continued existence of the tax registers under the Ostrogothic kings is attested by Cassiodorus in the first quarter of the sixth century.[7] We know also that the papacy maintained land registers, either in its own name or in that of the empire, till the time of Pope Gregory the Great (590–604).[8] As public authority declined, many landowners may have usurped the rights of government and deliberately confused taxes with rent. The Land Register of the Church of Ravenna may well be a case in point. Part of it has survived on a papyrus fragment known as 'P. Ital. 3'. It dates from some time in the sixth century and is concerned with estates in the region of Padua; it gives the name of each estate, the names of the *coloni* on it, their dues payable in money or kind, and the number of day-works owed in each.[9] In South Italy the authority of the Empire lingered on through the Byzantine period to the eleventh century. Though it is impossible to prove complete continuity, it is known that the Normans who occupied S. Italy and Sicily made use of survey records called *dafâtir* which were written in Arabic but probably originated from διφθέρα (rolls or pells), which would have been the *cadasters* of the Byzantine Empire.[10] As a result there has been a temptation for historians to jump to the conclusion that the idea of making a Domesday Survey could have come to the Normans in England from their relatives in Italy, but Miss Dione Clementi, the leading English authority on Norman Italy, has explained why this is improbable. Indeed it is much easier to demonstrate how the Normans could have found prototypes of Domesday earlier and more directly in Normandy and the adjacent parts of France.

The Roman tax registers continued to be used or renewed in Merovingian Gaul. Gregory of Tours (d. 594) has several references to them, one being an account of how (*c*. 587–9) King Childebert II was asked to revise those of Poitiers, since many of those named on the lists had died, 'and the weight of the tribute pressed heavily upon their widows and the orphans and the infirm'.[11] The oft-quoted reference to an official land register (*tabula fiscorum*)

---

[6] Ibid., 7.

[7] *Cassiodorii Senatoris Variae*, ed. Th. Mommsen (MGH, *Auct. Antiq.*, xii, 1894), v. 14 (pp. 150–1), *tabularius*; v. 39 (pp. 164–6), *polypticis publicis* and vii. 45 (p. 225).

[8] *Gregorii I Papae Registrum Epistolarum*, ed. P. Ewald and L. M. Hartmann (2 vols. MGH, *Epistolarum*, ii, Berlin, 1883–93) ii, 188 (ix. 199), 433–4 (xiv. 14). Cf. the *Life* of Gregory the Great by John the Deacon, Book ii, Chs. 24 and 30, *MPL*, 75, cols. 96–8.

[9] J.-O. Tjäder, *Die nichtliterarischen lateinische Papyri aus der Zeit 445–700* (Lund, 1955), 184–9.

[10] Dione Clementi, in Galbraith (1961), 55–8.

[11] Gregory of Tours, *History of the Franks*, Bk ix, Ch. 30, trans. O. M. Dalton (Oxford, 1927), ii. 40.

under King Dagobert (629–39) is of less value because it occurs in the book of *The Miracles of St Martin of Vertou* which was not written till near the end of the ninth century.[12] But we do know that Bishop Rauracius of Nevers had a *descriptio mancipiorum* made on his lands in the bishopric of Cahors, *c.* 630–50.[13] Better still, fragments of an original seventh-century *census* list have been found in the binding of a medieval manuscript. It names some 900 *coloni* and the amount of *agrarium* and *lignaticum* which they paid on estates belonging to Saint Martin de Tours, an abbey whose estates were to be surveyed again in 856.[14]

In the eighth and ninth centuries, references to, and texts of, surveys become frequent. When Pepin III was raised to the throne in 751, he immediately ordered the property of the Church to be described and divided (*res ecclesiarum descriptas atque divisas*). This command must have been received by the churches with mixed feelings. On the one hand the mention of dividing their lands could only suggest that the king intended to take a portion of them as benefices for his vassals. On the other hand, those estates which were left to the churches would have their titles re-enforced.

To take the first point first, we know that in 787 Charlemagne ordered Landric Abbot of Jumièges and Count Richard to enumerate the property of the abbey of Fontanelle (Saint-Wandrille), and we are also told that immediately afterwards some of the abbey's lands were given to the king's men. The actual survey has not survived, but a summary of it was included in the *Gesta Abbatum Fontanellensium* some fifty years later, indicating that on the demesne there were 1569 manses occupied (and 158 unoccupied) with 39 mills, and also 2395 occupied manses (and 156 unoccupied) with 24 mills given out as benefices. But we are also told that there were other (unspecified) manses which had been handed over to royal vassals, or given to others on lease, by Wido, a layman who had been put in charge of the abbey for two years;[15] as in the case of the Emperor Vespasian's *cadaster* of the territory of *Arausio*, the effect of this survey was to confirm a partial redistribution of the land by the state. It is important for our present purpose, because the abbey of Fontanelle was situated on the lower Seine in what was later to become the heartland of Normandy. Under the name of Saint-Wandrille, it was to become one of the most venerable abbeys of the duchy, and its traditions would have been well known to the Normans.

Once a survey had been made by public authority, the advantage to those left in possession would soon be apparent, because the effect of it would be to validate their title. In 780, for example, the bishop of Marseilles won a lawsuit at Digne because he was able to produce in court the survey (referred

---

[12] MGH, *Scriptores Rerum Merovingicarum*, ed. B. Krusch (Hannover, 1896), iii. 571–2.
[13] MGH, *Epistolae Merowingici et Karolini Aevi*, i, 206–7 (letter of Bishop Rauracius to Desiderius Bishop of Cahors).
[14] Ed. P. Gasnault, *Documents comptables de Saint Martin de Tours a l'époque merovingienne* (*Documents inédits*, Paris, 1975).
[15] *Gesta Abbatum Fontanellensium*, ed. S. Loewenfeld (Scriptores Rerum Germanicarum, Hannover, 1886), 45.

to as both *descriptio* and *poleticum*) of the estate in question.[16] Similarly, in 828 the abbot of Cormery discomfited his *coloni* of Chasseneuil (Vienne) by producing in court a survey (*descriptio*) of 801–2, which had been drawn up in accordance with the evidence of these same *coloni* or their predecessors.[17] The public nature of such surveys gave them an authority far greater than that of any private document. In the same way, one of the greatest values of Domesday Book was that it confirmed titles to land, because they had been recognised by the sworn testimony of the hundred and shire in the presence of the commissioners of the king.

There is evidence to suggest that Charlemagne may have contemplated the idea of having the whole of his kingdom surveyed. In 807 he ordered his *missi* to send him inventories of the benefices (i.e. fiefs) and allods of the churches in every county.[18] In 811–13 he ordered his *missi* diligently to hold inquests and describe (*diligenter inquirere et describere faciant*) what everyone had in the way of a benefice and how many tenants (*homines casatos*) were in it; how these benefices had been agreed upon (*condicta*), and who had bought or constructed an allod out of his benefice. The benefices to be described were those not only of the bishops, abbots, abbesses, counts or vassals of the king, but also of the fisc (or royal demesne), so that the king could know how much he had delegated to everyone (*quantum etiam de nostra in uniusquisque delegatione habeamus*).[19] Such a survey embracing the whole kingdom or empire would have been far larger than Domesday Book, if ever it had been executed. In the event it proved little more than wishful thinking – Robert Fossier, for one, believes that it was never more than a pious exhortation – and it is difficult to know what, if anything, resulted from it. Some scholars have thought that the well-known *Brevium Exempla* may have been produced as models for this exercise, others that they were a result of it, but there is nothing like agreement on this point.[20] A large fragment of a roll (now 25 cm × 216 cm) from S. Victor-de-Marseille contains part of a survey of about the right date; it records the abbey's *colonica* estate by estate, naming the *coloni*, their wives and children, and stating the ages of those under sixteen.[21] Also of approximately the right date (811 × 29) is the well-known *Polyptych of Abbot Irmino of Saint-Germain-des-Prés*, outside Paris. It is probably the fullest of all Carolingian surveys, and it also is careful to name the *coloni* and their wives and children.

The period with the greatest number of these surveys was undoubtedly the forty years from 830 to 870, in which we know of at least twenty-two. The most important reason for this concentration is probably the fact that one of the main preoccupations of this period was the partition of the

---

[16] *Cartulaire de l'abbaye de Saint-Victor-de-Marseille*, ed. B. Guérard, 2 vols. (vols. viii and ix of *Collection des Cartulaires de France*, in *Documents inédits*, Paris, 1858), i. 45 (no. 31).

[17] *Polyptyche de l'Abbé Irminon*, ed. Guérard, ii. 344–5.

[18] *Capitularia Regum Francorum*, ed. A. Boretius (MGH, Hannover, 1883), i. 136.

[19] Ibid., i. 177, 'capitulare de justiciis faciendis', Chs. 5–7.

[20] Ibid., i. no. 128. Translation and commentary in H. R. Loyn and J. Percival, *The Reign of Charlemagne* (London, 1975), pp. 98–105.

[21] Guérard, *Cartulaire de Saint-Victor-de-Marseille*, i. pp. xi–xiii; ii. 633–54. The probable date is c. 814–18.

Empire amongst the sons and grandsons of Louis the Pious, particularly in 843 (the Partition of Verdun) and 870 (the Partition of Meersen). The *Annals of Saint Bertin* relate how in 842, the three brothers, Lothar I, Louis the German and Charles the Bald, eventually agreed to send *missi* throughout the kingdom, to make a survey (*descriptio*) which would make it possible for the land to be divided equally between them.[22] In the event these *missi* did not succeed in their task because, as Nithard would have it, they were impeded by Lothar.[23] It is possible, however, that some of the extant surveys are the result of their activities; O. P. Clavadetscher and F. L. Ganshof certainly made a strong case for the survey of the estates of the see of Chur being made in this context, and it is possible that the Freising fragment may also be connected with it.[24]

None the less, if these surveys were the result of deliberate royal policy, it has to be admitted that they are a very heterogeneous lot. Whereas the Domesday commissioners were given a detailed set of questions to ask about every manor, those who made the Carolingian surveys can have received only the most general instructions from their superiors. Some include the churches' treasures (chalices, vestments, books, etc.), others do not. Some include the land given out as benefices, others not. Some enumerate only the units of land, *mansus*, *huben* or *modia*, the equivalents of our English hides or carucates; others give also the numbers of *coloni* or cultivators, others give also their names, and yet others give also the names of their wives and children. The variety is enormous, but not surprising when it is appreciated what disparate lands the surveys come from – North France, South France, Belgium, different parts of Germany, Switzerland and Italy.

The distinctions which can most often be made are four in number. The first is between those surveys which we can call 'public' because they were drawn up by order of the king or emperor, as opposed to the private surveys which were drawn up by the landlords on their own initiative. In the case of a public survey, commissioners (*missi*) would come from the king or emperor and (as in the Domesday Survey) either collect their information from inquests held on the spot, or alternatively use local inquests to verify the information which had already been provided by the landlord. We have an instructive example of this latter method in a letter from Archbishop Hincmar of Reims to the monk Anselm at the abbey of Hautvillers (Marne), instructing him to make an inventory of his monastery, including all its possessions both before and after Hincmar's consecration (845), the number of monks and servants, the details of the properties disposed of in his own time, the people to whom they were transferred, and the reasons for having

---

[22] *Annales de Saint Bertin*, ed. Felix Grot, Jean Viellard and Suzanne Clemencet, with introd. and notes by Leon Levillain (Soc. de l'histoire de France, Paris, 1964, 43–5 and 172–4 (*annis* 842, 843 and 870).
[23] *Nithard: Histoire des fils de Louis le Pieux*, ed. P. Lauer (Les classiques de l'histoire de France, 1962), Bk iv, Ch. 5. Translation in Bernhard W. Scholz, *Carolingian Chronicles* (Ann Arbor, 1972), 171.
[24] F. L. Ganshof, 'Zur Entstehungsgeschichte und Bedeutung des Vertrags von Verdun (843)'. *Deutsches Archiv*, 12 (1956), 313–30.

done so. All this was to be done so exactly that the king's commissioners (*missi dominici*) would be unable to find any mistakes in it.[25] Such a survey, endorsed by public authority, would presumably have provided a title as effective as any entry in Domesday Book, but the preparations necessary before it was completed must have given the landlord a very anxious time, since one of the implications of the questions could have been that the land in question was held at the pleasure of the king and could be resumed by him if he thought it desirable to do so.

The distinction between public and private surveys is so basic, that it is strange to find that one cannot always be certain as to which of the two types a particular survey belongs. Those of which we can be certain start with an account of the circumstances in which the survey was made and give the names of the bishops, abbots or counts who made them. It sometimes happens, however, that the opening passages of a survey are missing, the first and last folios of a manuscript being the most easily lost or damaged, as in the case of the polyptych of the Abbot Irmino. But in these cases, it may still be possible to classify a survey as 'public' if it gives clear reference (as in *Irmino*) to the sworn inquests on which its evidence was based, so that the survey could be seen to have some independent authority at law.

The second distinction is between those surveys which give details of the lands distributed as benefices to vassals, those which merely record the names of the places and vassals concerned, and those which give no information about benefices at all. These variations are in sharp contrast with the regular pattern of Domesday Book, whose compiler took enormous pains to arrange his material for each county under the entry or *breve* of the correct tenant-in-chief. He was able to do this because William the Conqueror, having conquered the whole country, had rewarded his followers with the lands of the dispossessed Anglo-Saxons, who were not given any opportunity to get a protest entered in the text of Domesday Book. In the Carolingian empire, however, many churches felt that they had been despoiled by the king or emperor in order to provide for his vassals, and (as we have already seen) their continued resentment could show through even in a survey.

The third distinction concerns the details given of the individual estates surveyed. Some surveys state no more than the name of each villa or manor and the number of *mansus* or *huben* (the continental equivalents of the English hide) in it. Usually, but not always, there will also be a statement of the dues (in money or kind) and services owed. Such entries, though not similar, are more or less in the same category as the entries for individual manors in Domesday. In other surveys, however, we are given not only the services and payments due from each *mansus* but also the names of the peasants (*coloni*) who held them, together with the names of their wives, and the names and ages (if under sixteen) of their children, so that there is none of the difficulty experienced by Domesday scholars of determining the size of the average family. In this detailed counting of heads it is tempting to see,

[25] Flodoard: 'Historia Remensis Ecclesie', in *MGH, Scriptores*, xiii. 552.

as many historians have tried to see, a continuation of the Roman *census* system through the Merovingian period.[26] If this were so, the differences in the types of information given in the various Carolingian surveys might theoretically reflect various regional forms of taxation in the Roman Empire. Professor Percival has shown that such regional differences existed, but he has also demonstrated convincingly that any continuity in this respect from the Roman to the Carolingian period, though theoretically possible, cannot be proven.[27]

The fourth distinction is between surveys which are concerned exclusively with landed property and those which include moveable goods also. Very occasionally these moveable goods include animals, as in Little Domesday,[28] but more usually they are confined to the treasures of churches. In Hariulf's account of the survey of the abbey of Saint Riquier, made on the orders of Louis the Pious in 831, he considered the details of landholding too tedious for his attention, but copied out in full the inventory of church treasures and books, which occupies almost seven pages of the printed edition.[29] He probably regarded it as a useful catalogue of what the abbey ought still to possess. One cannot help wondering about the extent to which the emperor or his agents regarded it with covetous eyes. The imperial commissioners of the Carolingian emperors may well have seemed as alarming to the churchmen of the time as were the Domesday commissioners to Robert Bishop of Hereford when he wrote that 'the land was plagued with many disasters because of the collection of the royal taxes'.

Though it has been convenient to distinguish four ways in which Carolingian surveys might differ from each other, it is far from easy to say what those differences signify. It would have been neat if it could have been claimed that the surveys which named the *coloni* and their families were inevitably public and vice versa; or that there was a necessary connection between the public surveys and the treatment given to benefices or moveable goods; or that any of the differences could be pinned down to a particular date. Unfortunately no such claims can at present be made, but this may be because our knowledge of the surviving surveys is still too haphazard. What is needed, above all, is a complete list of the documents concerned in all parts of the countries which formed the Carolingian Empire. In the appendix to this paper I have made a start by listing those which I have been able to find, but I am under no illusion about its failings. Quite apart from the difficulty of tracking down the printed texts and references, there is often a major difficulty in deciding which documents should, and which should not, be classified as surveys. The words 'polyptych' *Urbar* and *Saalbuch* have been

---

[26] Walter Goffart, 'Merovingian Polyptychs: reflections on two recent publications', *Francia*, 9 (1981), 57–78, and 'Old and New in Merovingian Taxation', in *Past and Present*, 95 (1982), 3–21.
[27] Percival (1985), 26–7.
[28] E.g. Fulda, in *Traditiones et Antiquitates Fuldenses*; ed. E. F. Dronke and W. Metz (Fulda, 1844), 125–9.
[29] *Hariulf: Chronique de Saint-Riquier*, ed. Ferdinand Lot (Collection de Textes, Paris, 1894), 87–93.

used loosely by historians to describe surveys which are particularly long and bulky. But there are other surveys, to be found embedded in the texts of charters, and in these cases it is always difficult to be sure how much should, or should not, be included.

This last difference becomes very much greater in the tenth and eleventh centuries, for though the ninth-century surveys were varied in form, those of the tenth and eleventh centuries were very much more so. Looking back from the later centuries one can see that though Charlemagne and his successors had failed to impose a uniform pattern or questionnaire for their surveys, they had nevertheless promoted a general idea. Like the idea of empire itself, it survived longer in the Germanic regions than the French, with surveys embedded in charters for S. Glossinde de Metz (963), S. Arnoul de Metz (967) and Gorze (984), and larger surveys for S. Emmeran of Regensburg (1031) and Corvey (*c.* 1060). In general, however, even these surveys are more suggestive of private feudal enterprise than a survival of the Carolingian Empire. If, as Mr Campbell has rightly suggested, they were known and imitated in the reformed monasteries of tenth-century England,[30] they could hardly have prepared anyone for the fact that the greatest and most systematic of all surveys was to be made in England in 1086.

Domesday Book gives a vast amount of information in a relatively short space. It is unique because it surveys almost every inch of the kingdom, whether it was royal demesne or not. The survey follows the pattern of royal administration, each county being given a separate section of its own. Within the counties the lands are arranged in *breves* under the heads of those who held them, those held by the king himself coming first, followed by his tenants-in-chief, ecclesiastical and lay. We are given no details of knight-service. Instead we are told the name of each manor, who held it in the time of King Edward, subsequently and now (1086), the number of hides in it, the number of ploughs both on demesne and otherwise, the number of villeins, cottars, slaves, freemen and sokemen; the amount of woodland, meadow and pasture; the number of mills and fisheries; what had been added to, or taken away from, the estate; and its annual value in the time of King Edward, subsequently and now (1086). The consistency is such that one has to believe that there was a standard questionnaire from which individual commissions diverged only slightly.

At first sight it is remarkable that the Domesday formula was not immediately copied elsewhere. Such an enormous achievement must have been noticed very widely, and one might have expected other rulers to attempt similar surveys based on a similar set of questions, carried out by similar inquests, and reduced to order in a similar way. In fact no one copied Domesday Book. After 1086 surveys were made at various times, particularly between 1150 and 1300, in various parts of Europe, but they are basically different because they do not address themselves to the same questions. Presumably their compilers considered that Domesday Book provided

---

[30] Campbell, 'Observations on English Government', 39–54, esp. 49–51.

information which for them would have been irrelevant.

In the first place they would have noticed that whereas their own surveys usually stated by whom the various estates had been granted, Domesday Book did not specifically state this at all. Instead it merely stated who held the land in the time of King Edward, afterwards, and in 1086. The assumption is that after the Conquest all land had been at King William's disposal, and that he had given it to whomsoever he wished. True, some Normans might have seized land which had not been granted to them, but Domesday Book provided a check on these by naming the person who had held the land in King Edward's day. If that person was not the current Norman's official *antecessor*, there was trouble in store, as the sections of *clamores*, *invasiones* and *terrae occupatae* show.[31] But in the case of church lands there is no information as to how they had been acquired in the first place; it is stated merely that the church had held them 'then' (in King Edward's day) as well as 'now'. The assumption must be that since William the Conqueror had formally regranted them to the various churches, no other information was required. This would not have satisfied a continental ruler, but then no continental ruler had acquired his whole kingdom by conquest and as the result of a single battle.

Secondly, the Domesday Survey asked no questions about knight-service. In one sense this seems surprising, because a list of knights' fiefs might have seemed a basic requirement for a feudal king. But though we know that in the ninth century both Louis the Pious and Charles the Bald attempted to make lists of those who owed military services in the various counties,[32] and though we have a summary *indiculus loricatorum* for the Italian expedition of Otto II in 981,[33] no systematic list of fiefs can be found in any country before the middle of the twelfth century. The earliest known comes from Norman Sicily and is the earliest part of the *Catalogus Baronum* which was made in 1149–50 and revised in 1167 and 1168.[34] It is followed by our own King Henry II's *Cartae Baronum* in England (1166) and Normandy (1172) and by the so-called *Scripta de Feodis* of Philip Augustus and his successors in France.[35] No detailed account of them need be given here because they are not parallels to Domesday Book, but quite a different sort of record.

---

[31] R. H. C. Davis, 'The Norman Conquest', *History*, 51 (1966), 279–86, esp. 285–6.

[32] F. L. Ganshof, 'A propos de la politique de Louis le Pieux', *Revue belge d'Archeologie et d'histoire de l'Art*, 37 (1968), 48.

[33] 'Indiculus loricatorum Ottoni II in Italiam mittendorum (981)'. This is preserved on a single tenth-century membrane, bound up with the works of St Augustine (Bamberg, B. iii. 11) and is printed in *MGH Constitutiones et Acta publica*, ed. L. Wieland (1983), 632–3.

[34] *Catalogus Baronum*, ed. E. Jamison (*Fonti*, 101, Rome, 1972). The catalogus contains three documents of which the most important is the *quaternus magne expeditionis*, drawn up in 1149–50 and revised in 1167 and 1168.

[35] The English *Cartae Baronum* (1166) are printed in *The Red Book of the Exchequer*, ed. H. Hall (3 vols. *RS*, London, 1896), i. 186–445. The *Infeudationes Militum* of Normandy (1172) are printed ibid., ii. 624–45, but see also the comments of F. M. Powicke in *EHR*, xxvi (1911), 89–93. For Philip Augustus in France, see 'Scripta de feodis ad regem spectantibus et de militibus ad exercitum vocandis', ed. De Wailly, Delisle and Jourdan in *RHF*, 23 (Paris, 1894), 608–728. See also the comments by Sivéry in the article cited in n. 44 below.

Thirdly, Domesday Book is not a record of royal revenue. There are some places where it records rents, renders or customary services, but it does so incidentally. In this respect it stands in sharp contrast to some foreign documents which have sometimes been thought parallel, such as the list of payments due to the emperor as king of the Lombards, c. 1027,[36] or the twelfth-century list of food-rents due to the king of the Romans from Saxony, Franconia, Bavaria and Lombardy.[37] These documents, short enough (one would think) to have been written originally on a single sheet of parchment, are more like memoranda than a survey and cannot be compared to Domesday Book in any way. The nearest one can get to a parallel is in Catalonia, where the counts of Barcelona made a full survey of their demesnes, rights and revenues in 1151–2.[38] It is like Domesday inasmuch as the information was recorded on the spot from named bailiffs and notables who gave their evidence on oath and declared (in those districts which had already been divided into manses) the number of manses on each estate and the revenues and services due to the count. On the other hand, it gives no information about ploughs, villeins, sokemen, freemen, cottars, meadow, pasture, mills, fisheries or previous holders of the land. The survey is restricted to the count's own demesne and reads more like a rental than a land survey. The same is true of the thirteenth-century surveys of the dukes of Bavaria,[39] and of the rulers of Upper and Lower Austria,[40] as also of the early fourteenth-century survey of the lands of the House of Habsburg in Switzerland, Swabia and Alsace;[41] they are all demesne surveys and are concerned primarily with rents and renders.

The contrast with Domesday Book is important, because it stands alone in its insistence on values. In every manor we are told what it was worth (*valuit*) in the time of King Edward, what it was worth subsequently, and

---

[36] 'Instituta regalia et ministeria camerae regum Langobardorum et honorantiae civitatis camerae regis', ed. A. Hofmeister in *MGH, Scriptores*, xxx. 2 (1934), 1444–60. The oldest part of it is c. 1027, but the prologue and epilogue are fourteenth-century additions. No authority for the survey is stated, and there is no suggestion of a jury or sworn inquest.

[37] Printed by Aloys Schulte, 'Das Verzeichnis der Königlichen Tafelgüter und Servitien von 1064/5' in *Neues Archiv*, 41 (1919), 572–4. Schulte's date is no longer accepted. Various dates from 1131–2 to 1185 are now suggested; see refs. in R. C. van Caenegem, *Guide to the Sources of Medieval History* (Amsterdam, New York and Oxford, 1978), 95, n. 4. The document is simply a list of food-rents due to the king of the Romans in Saxony, Franconia, Bavaria and Lombardy.

[38] Thomas N. Bisson, *Fiscal Accounts of Catalonia under the early Count-Kings* (2 vols., Berkeley/Los Angeles/London, 1984), ii. 3ff.

[39] 'Urbarium ducatus Baiuwarium antiquissimum' which should be dated c. 1221–8 (not c. 1240), the 'urbarium secundum' which should be dated c. 1262–7 (not 1180–1), and the 'urbarium tertium jussu Ludovici bavari of 1326. The oldest of these surveys is in German, the two later ones in Latin. All three are printed in *Monumenta Boica*, 36 (1852).

[40] Alfons Dopsch and W. Levec (eds.), *Die Landfürstlichen Urbare Nieder und Oberösterreichs aus dem 13 und 14 Jahrhundert* (Wien und Leipzig, 1904) includes a survey of the Babenberg period (c. 1220–40) in Latin (1–114), of Ottokar of Bohemia (1251–76) also in Latin (115–227) and of the Habsburgs (before 1297) in German (229–52), as well as a fourteenth-century survey of Steiermark (253–332).

[41] R. Maag (ed.), *Das Habsburgische Urbar* 2 vols. in 3, vol. ii. 2 being by P. Schweizer and W. Glättl (*Quellen zur Schweizer Geschichte*, 14 and 15, Basel, 1894–1904). The main survey, which is in German, dates from 1303–8, but there are parts of thirteenth-century lists also.

what it is worth (*valet*) now (1086). There are occasions when Domesday mentions rents and renders, but they are mainly in the 'preliminaries' for each county, the county borough and in some (but not all) of the more important manors of the royal demesne. When Domesday gets to the lands of the tenants-in-chief, it says nothing about their renders, but displays their values prominently at the end of each section.

The purpose of recording the values was presumably to enable the king to assess how much he could charge one of his barons' heirs as a relief, and how much for licence to marry a daughter. The values would also make it possible for him to estimate the amount of profit he could expect when the land of a tenant-in-chief reverted to him, either temporarily (as during a vacancy or wardship) or permanently through forfeiture or escheat. In these cases the king would use his sheriff or other agents to manage the lands and account for the profits at the Exchequer. This, presumably, was one of the reasons why the lands of the tenants-in-chief were not surveyed as single nation-wide honours, but divided into their constituent parts in each county. Each sheriff made his audit separately at the Exchequer, and when he was accounting for lands which had recently come into the king's hands, his statements could be checked against Domesday Book, which was kept in the Exchequer for that purpose. The *Dialogus de Scaccario* explains how the correct entry can be found by turning to the list of the holders of land which comes at the beginning of each county.

> The King's name heads the list, followed by those of the nobles who hold of the King in chief, according to their order of dignity. The list is then numbered, and the matter in the actual text of the book relating to each tenant is easily found by the corresponding number.[42]

The attention paid to the lands of the tenants-in-chief, which account for much the greater part of Domesday Book, was one of the main reasons for the alarm expressed by notables such as Robert Bishop of Hereford when the Survey was being made.[43] It also helps to explain how it was that the Domesday Survey was neither extended to Normandy, nor imitated in any other country. No tenant wants his landlord to make a fresh valuation of his property, and if the new valuation is accompanied by a thorough survey, he is likely to fear that his tenancy may be terminated. We have already seen that the Carolingian surveys often led to a partial redistribution of the land, and that abbeys and churches awaited them with apprehension. But in 1086 the situation in England was different. A vast redistribution of the land had just been completed, and a full survey was more likely to endorse it than undermine it. The very fact that many, if not most, of the jurors on the inquests were Anglo-Saxons, implied a legal recognition by the conquered of the redistribution that had taken place, and the Normans were likely to consider that the advantages of the Survey were greater than its disadvantages. In Normandy, on the other hand, they would almost certainly have

---

[42] *Dialogus*, 63–4.
[43] Printed in W. Stubbs, *Select Charters . . . of English Constitutional History*, ninth ed. by H. W. C. Davis (Oxford, 1913), 95.

objected to a ducal survey of their lands, for there their titles were old, and it would have been difficult to see what purpose a new survey could have had, except to facilitate some future distribution.

The point is important because it underlines the fact that the Domesday Survey could not have been made without the co-operation of the barons. The royal administration was astonishingly efficient in its use of sworn inquests in the hundreds and shires, but it could have been brought to a standstill if the barons had been determined to obstruct it. They might have refused to provide the king with information about their own holdings, prevented their own tenants from doing so, and delayed the judicial proceedings by every legal device. But in the circumstances of 1086 it was not in their interest to do so. Because the Conquest was so recent, they had more to gain than lose by co-operating in the Survey, so co-operate they did. At other times and in other countries the circumstances were different. Philip Augustus did not dare to make a 'Domesday Survey' of Normandy after he had conquered it in 1204, and part of his reason for not doing so was that it would have been impolitic. Instead he simply collected such information as he could find in the ducal archives, out of date though much of it was.[44] Similarly the papacy, when it required a record of the payments due to it from churches far or near, did not attempt a series of inquests in the provinces concerned, but merely researched in its own archives (1192), sometimes with strange results.[45]

However one looks at Domesday Book, one is driven to the conclusion that the essential circumstance which made it possible was the Norman Conquest, and that not because of some extraordinary genius of the Normans, but because of the extraordinary nature of the Conquest itself.[46] No other conquest except the Arab conquests of the seventh century had been so speedy, so complete or so permanent, and as a result of it the Normans adopted a superior attitude to the natives. No matter what the language used in the course of the Domesday inquests, the final verdict was written down in Latin by men who spoke French and knew little, if any, English. From their superior viewpoint they attempted to fit the English

[44] G. Sivéry, 'La description du royaume de France par les conseillers de Philippe Auguste et par leurs successeurs', *Le Moyen Age*, 90 (1984), 65–84, esp. 84, 'l'insuffisance d'agents bien formés et les résistances recontrées dans plusieurs des territoires annexes au domaine ou en voie de l'être suffisant à inciter la prudence'.

[45] *Le Liber censuum de l'Eglise Romaine*, ed. Paul Fabre, L. Duchesne and G. Mollat, 3 vols. (Bibliothèque des écoles françaises d'Athènes et de Rome, 2e serie, 1889–1952). Most errors were the result of the lack of local knowledge, as when the church of *Florentia* was placed in the bishopric of London instead of Liège (i. 224). Nonetheless the *Liber Censuum* was repeatedly revised and remained a working document till the fifteenth century.

[46] The nearest approach to similar conditions was in Spain where, in addition to the survey of the demesne of the counts of Barcelona (above, 151) there were several *repartimientos* recording the resettlement of land reconquered in the thirteenth century, as at Jerez and Seville. Curiously enough the Kingdom of Jerusalem, which was also the result of a conquest, seems to have had no land-surveys, though John of Jaffa's 'Livre des Assises de Hautcour' (*c.* 1266) includes lists of those who had their own courts of justice, lists of knight-service owed, arranged by baronies, lists of aids owed by churches and townsmen, and the number of sergeants owed. *Recueil des historiens des croisades: Lois*, i. 419-27.

into categories which they understood, and they succeeded so well that the great majority of people were classified as freemen, sokemen, villeins, bordars, cottars or slaves. Only on one circuit were the conditions so complex, or the commissioners so lacking in confidence, that the elegant pattern failed to emerge,[47] so much so that the master-mind who supervised the text of 'Big Domesday', made no attempt to reduce these three counties to the normal formulae, but left them alone as 'Little Domesday'. The English probably found 'Little Domesday' much more accurate than 'Big Domesday' which reduced their society to the terms which could be understood by a foreign conqueror.

In comparing Domesday Book with surveys made on the continent, one is constantly struck by the immensity of the book; it is so very much larger than any of its rivals. In consequence some scholars have found it difficult to believe the colophon of Little Domesday which states that the Survey was completed for all counties in 1086. When one considers the immensity of the work one begins to realise that if it had not been completed quickly, it would never have been completed at all. The longer the time spent on the work, the more difficult it would have been to resist the temptation to start again whenever an important tenant died, land changed hands, the whole of one circuit forgot about churches, a town was entered on the wrong folio, or the text was in a muddle. Everything had to be done at speed so that the Survey could be completed before it was out of date. Hence the rapid editorial judgements and the way in which unresolved doubts were parcelled away neatly as *clamores*, *invasiones* or *terrae occupatae*.

As a result Domesday Book is not only immense but also monumental. Folio after folio is laid out in two columns with apparent uniformity, with neat headings and rubrications which make the logical order clear at a glance. Everything about it looks final. In this respect one cannot fail to be impressed by the contrast in the physical appearance of Great Domesday Book with any other medieval survey. Even Little Domesday, neat though it is, lacks the air of finality. In part this is because it includes too many details, particularly the numbers of animals, which detract from the impression of timelessness, but apart from that, all it needs is to be written on a much larger page, divided into two columns, and written in a decisive hand which is, or at any rate seems to be, the same all the way through. Dr Rumble has remarked on the air of finality given by that hand, and it is indeed monumental, giving the same impression of timelessness as the stone inscriptions of the Emperor Vespasian's land survey at Orange. Both were public statements of land settlements which were new but were intended for perpetuity.

Domesday Book is the title-deed of all the Norman conquerors of England. We know that when they first received their lands from King William they were given writs which they showed to the relevant county

---

[47] A good example of their confusion is their account of the sokemen of Earsham Hundred, *DB*, ii. 138b–139b.

courts, but the fact that no such writ has survived suggests that the new landowners had to surrender their writs to the king as part of their Domesday returns. Thenceforward they had no title but Domesday Book. That is why Domesday Book is unique.

APPENDIX

A list of Continental Surveys, 751–1086

751   Pepin III orders church property to be described and divided (*res descriptas atque divisas*. Ref. only. *Annales Guelferbytani, Annales Alamannici, Annales Nazariani s.a.* 751, in *MGH, SS*, i. 26–7.

c. 760 (?)   Abbey of Wessobrünn (Bavaria); a short list of services and renders allegedly of this date, but more probably composed retrospectively in the twelfth century. 'Monumenta Wessofontana', in *Mon. Boica*, 7 (1776), 337–8.

7 Oct. 777   Abbey of Fulda; estate at Hammelburg (*et descriptus atque assignatus inde locus undique hiis terminis, postquam iuraverunt nobiliores terrae illius, ut edicerent veritatem de ipsius fisci quantitate*). Two counts and twenty-one witnesses were involved in the transfer of the land, but what is described is only the bounds of the estate. Edmund E. Stengl (ed.), *Urkundenbuch des Klosters Fulda*, i. 153–4. (*Veröffentlichen der historischen Kommission Hessen und Waldeck*, x. pt. i. (Marburg, 1913)).

768 × 814   Abbey of Fleury (Saint-Bénoît-sur-Loire). Ref. to the *libri politici a temporibus Magni Caroli* (but possibly a mistake for Charles the Bald, 838–77) by Abbo of Fleury (d. 1003). *MPL*, 139, col. 442B.

775   Abbey of Prüm. Charlemagne invites the *fiscalini* of the abbey to answer to the *missi* instructed by him to make an *inquisitio publica*. Fossier, *Polyptyques*, 26 and n, but his ref. to Böhmer–Mühlbacher, *Die Regesten des Kaiserreichs unter den Karolingen*, second ed., 1908, no. 198 (194), is incorrect, and I have failed to find his real source.

before 780   Abbey of Saint-Victor de Marseille. The *poleticum* produced with great effect in a lawsuit, 20 Feb. 780, but now lost. B. Guérard, *Collection des Cartulaires de France*, vols. viii and ix: *Cartulaire de l'abbaye de Saint-Victor-de-Marseille* (2 vols. Docs. inédits, 1858), i. 45 (no. 31).

780 × 800   Abbey of Lorsch. Survey of, *c.* 780–800, ed. K. Glöckner, *Codex Laureshamensis* (3 vols. Darmstadt, 1929–63), iii. nos. 3651–62. But see also 830 × 50. For the date(s) see K. Glöckner in *MIOG*, xxxviii (1919), 381–98; also D. Neundorfer, *Studien zur ältesten Geschichte des Klosters Lorsch* (Berlin, 1920), 93–110.

May 787   Abbey of San Vincenzo al Volturno, ed. Vincenzo Federici, *Chronicon Volturnensi del Monaco Giovanni*, 3 vols., *Fonti* 58–60 (1929–30), i. 204–11, Public survey. No benefices. Peasants named. No *trésor* or moveable goods.

787   Abbey of Saint-Wandrille (Fontanelle). Public survey. Text lost but summarised in W. Loewenfeld (ed.), *Gesta Abbatum Fontanellensium MGH, SRG*, 1886, 45. Benefices included. Manses enumerated but unknown whether or not peasants were named or *trésor* or moveable goods included. (But see refs. to losses of *trésor* on p. 44).

790   Bishopric of Salzburg. *Notitia Arnonis* and *Breves Notitiae* compiled by inquest of monks and laymen with the 'consent and licence' of Charlemagne, P. Willibald Hauthaler (ed.), *Salzburger Urkundenbuch* (four vols., Salzburg, 1898–1933), i. 3–16. Only benefices listed. Names of donors of the lands given, but no peasants named. No *trésor* or moveable goods. See also F. Prinz in *Frühmittelalterliche Studien*, 5 (1971), 10–36.

799 × 832   Abbey of Farfa. List of slaves of the abbey, in Balzani, *Farfensi*, i. 258–77. Probably a private survey. No benefices. Peasants and their sons named, but usually not their wives. No *trésor*. Dated by reference to two items which Duke Winigis (of Spoleto, 789–822) holds.

800 × 811   Abbey of Saint-Bavon, Ghent. Two fragments of a survey, apparently public, ed. A. Verhulst, in *Frühmittelalterliche Studien* (1971), 193–234 (text on 231–4). Two benefices mentioned. Manses listed but peasants not named. Inventory of *trésor* and demesne animals.

800 × 820   *Brevium Exempla* a) *Staffelsee* (Worth). Public survey. No benefices. Manses and their services listed, but no peasants named. Inventory of *trésor* and demesne animals. b) *Abbey of Wissembourg*. Public survey. Benefices included. Manses listed and their (peasant) tenants named. No inventory of *trésor* or animals. c) *Annapes* and four other estates in N. France. Public survey. No benefices, no manses and no *trésor* listed, but full inventory of farm buildings, animals and crops. A. Boretius (ed.), *MGH, Capitularia*, i. no. 28. For discussion see K. Verhein in *Deutsches Archiv*, 10 (1954), 313–94, and 11 (1955), 333–92. For identification of estates, P. Grierson in *Rev. belge*, 28 (1939), 437–61. English translation in H. R. Loyn and J. Percival, *The Reign of Charlemagne* (London, 1975), 98–105, and Duby, *Rural Economy*, 363–6.

801–2   Abbey of Cormery (Indre-et-Loire). Ref. in a lawsuit of 828 to a *descriptionem* of 801–2 which specified the dues from each manse in Attoigné as evidenced on oath by the *coloni* of that time. Guérard: *Irminon*, ii. 344–5.

811 × 29   Saint-Germain-des-Prés (Paris). Polyptych of the abbey's widespread estates under the Abbot Irmino. Public survey. Survey of the benefices now lost. Peasants named, together with their wives and children (in the case of the free manses). No *trésor* or animals. Ed. Guérard: *Irminon*. Extracts transl. in Duby, *Rural Economy*, 366–70.

before 814   Archbishopric of Lyon. Refs. to lists of *colonica*, now lost, in a letter of Archbishop Leidradus to Charlemagne. *MGH, Epistolae Karolinae Aevi*, ii. 544.

814 × 18   Abbey of Saint-Victor de Marseille. A list of the unfree (*mancipia*) who are also called *coloni*. No benefices. *Coloni* listed by estate, and named, as also are their wives and children (whose ages also are stated). No *trésor* or moveable goods. The original doc. is a roll of which part (25 cm × 216 cm) survives in the Archives départementales of Bouches du Rhône. *Cartulaire de Saint-Victor de Marseille*, ed. B. Guérard, ii. 633–54, with introduction in i. xi–xiii.

c. 820   Abbey of Saint Eugendus (*alias* Jurakloster or Saint-Claude-sur-Bienne (Jura)). Text lost, but ref. in *MGH, SS*, xiii. 744, 'Zmaragdus abbas et Teutbertus capellanus, missi dominici domni nostri Ludovici imperatoris, in anno vi imperii eius imbreviarunt res monasterii Sancti Eugendi et invenerunt colonicas vestitas 840, absas 17', i.e. public survey listing manses.

822   Survey for the monastic cells of Saint-Pierre-le-vif, Saint-Jean and Saint-Rémi in Sens to rectify depredations by bishops at the expense of the monks. The *libellus* (now lost) mentioned in a diploma of Louis the Pious (18 May 822) (*RHF*, vi. 529 (no. cvii)) in a passage repeated *verbatim* in a charter of Charles the Bald (*Recueil Charles II*, i. 275–9 (no. 104)), which latter text is cited by Fossier, *Polyptyques*, 31, as a simple list of revenues. The survey was confirmed by a synod of bishops.

830 × 50   Abbey of Lorsch, ed. K.Glöckner, *Codex Laureshamensis* (as in 780 × 800 above), nos. 3671–5 which cover an imperial fisc given to Lorsch at this time. List of manses or *huben*. No benefices, no named peasants, no *trésor* or moveable goods.

831   Abbey of Saint Riquier. Full text lost, but summary in F. Lot (ed.), *Hariulf: Chronique de Saint Riquier* (Paris, 1894), 87–97 and 306–8. Public survey including benefices. Summary includes no named peasants, but Hariulf gives full text of the inventory of the *trésor*.

834 × 45   Abbey of Montier-en-Der (Haute Marne). Private(?) survey of the lands allotted for the monks' food and clothing. No benefices as such, but pp. 110–15 are concerned with *precaria or prestaria* of persons who look like benefice-holders. No named peasants. No *trésor* or moveable goods. *Collection des principaux cartulaires du diocèse de Troyes*, iv, ed. Charles Lalore: *Cartulaire de Chapelle-aux-Planches, Chartes de Montier-en-der*, etc. (Paris, 1878), 89–115.

before 835   Sant'Ambrosio of Milan. Public survey of Limonta; no benefices; no named peasants; no *trésor* or moveable goods, *Inventari*, 21–5. One paragraph translated in G. Duby, *Rural Economy*, 376.

839   Cathedral of Urgel. List of dues from the parishes of the diocese to the cathedral church, discussed in P. Bonnassie, *La Catalogne du milieu du Xe à la fin du XIe siécle* (Toulouse, 1975), 86–7. Drawn up on orders of the Bishop Sisebut.

840   Abbey of Farfa. Remains of a survey listing estates without stating whether they are benefices or divided into manses. No *trésor*. Balzani, *Farfensi*, i. 198–206 (the actual survey, 200, l. 33–205, l. 1).

c. 840   Cathedral of Saint Vincent, Le Mans. *Summa de poleticis vel plenariis*. Full text lost, but summary of renders in money and kind survives. Guérard, *Irminon*, i. 922–3 (no. xvii) from *Gesta Aldrici Cenomanensis episcopi*, c. 52. *MPL*, 115 (1852), 92.

c. 841   Abbey of Niederaltaich. Fragment, or summary of a fragment of a survey of a benefice at Ingolstadt, in a diploma of Louis the German, converting the benefice *in propriam*. *MGH, DRK*, i. 37 (no. 30). No mention of public inquest. No peasants named. No *trésor*.

842   Bishopric of Freising, fragment of a survey relating to Bergkirchen. Unknown whether public or private; no benefices; no peasants named; no *trésor*. Printed, Dollinger, *L'Evolution*, 12, n. 23 from ed. Theodor Bitterauf, *Die Traditionen des Hochstifts Freising* (2 vols., Munich, 1905–9), i. no. 652.

842–3   Bishopric of Chur. Public survey, *Die Bündner Urkundenbuch*, ed. E. Meyer Marthaler und Franz Perret (Chur, 1955), i. 373–96. For the date, see O. P. Claverdetscher in *Zeitschrift Schweizer Geschichte*, 30 (1950) and F. L. Ganshof in *Deutsches Archiv*, 12 (1956), 313–30.

844 × 59   Abbey of Saint-Bertin. *Breviarium villarum monachorum victus*, partial text embodied in Folcuin's 'Gesta Abbatum' and ed. F. L. Ganshof, F. Golding-Ganshof and A. de Sinet in *Méms. de l'Académie d'Inscriptions et Belles-Lettres*, 45 (Paris, 1975), 75–86. Private survey on orders of Abbot Adalard, covering 20 vills; no benefices; peasants named on some (but not all) estates; no *trésor* or moveable goods.

847 × 57   Notre-Dame de Soissons. Public survey (now lost) made by the bishops of Soissons and Laon and the abbot of Saint-Médard-de-Soissons, ref. in lost diploma of Charles the Bald, cited in *Recueil Charles II*, i. 509, no. 109.

c. 850   Abbey of Saint-Rémi de Reims, Guérard, *Reims*. Public survey of twenty-four fiscs and five groups of benefices. Peasants named but normally not their wives or children. No *trésor* or moveable goods. Extracts transl. in Duby, *Rural Economy*, 370–1.

c. 850   Abbey of Hautvillers (Marne). Public survey, now lost. In a letter Archbishop Hincmar orders the monk Anselm to make a full inventory of his monastery including details of properties disposed of (as benefices, presumably) and the numbers of monks and servants, *Flodoard, Hist. Remensis Ecclesie, MGH, SS*, xiii. 552.

856   Abbey of Saint-Martin de Tours. Orders for a survey (now lost) in ed. André Salmon, *Recueil des Chroniques de Touraine* (Soc. archéologique de Tours, coll. de documents, t. 1, Tours, 1854), 43.

858 × 83   Abbey of Montecassino. Private survey lost but quoted by Leo of Ostia, *MGH, SS*, vii. 610–12. Made in the time of Abbot Bertharius. Lands and churches described, but no mention of their inhabitants or of their dues or services. No benefices described as such, no peasants named or enumerated. No *trésor* or moveable goods.

862   Abbey of Saint Columbanus, Bobbio. Public survey. No benefices. No peasants named. No *trésor*. Written on a parchment roll. See 883 for another roll; ed. *Inventari*, 127–44. Excerpt (from p. 200) trans. in Duby, *Rural Economy*, 377.

866   Abbey of Saint-Vaast d'Arras. Public survey made by Guillebertus, Ordericus and Eurebertus, *missi* of Charles the Bald. Text lost, but the monk Aimer who compiled the cartulary in 1170 had it before his eyes. *Cartulaire de l'Abbaye de Saint-Vaast d'Arras*, ed. A. van Drival (Arras, 1875), 2.

866 × 924   Priory of Saint-Symphorien d'Autun, *poleticus de rebus canonicorum et abbatis ipsius loci*, now only a fragment with (private?) surveys of five estates; no benefices; no named peasants; no *trésor* or moveable goods. *Recueil des Actes du Prieuré de Saint-Symphorien d'Autun, de 696 a 1300*, ed. André Déléage (Autun, 1936), 15–16 (no. 4). For comment, Déléage, *Vie rurale*, ii. 1199–1205.

868   Abbey of Lobbes. Public survey by authority of Lothar II at request of John Bishop of Cambrai, to restore the monks' share (for food and clothing) which had been despoiled by the lay abbot, Hubert d'Agaune; ed. J. Warichez, 'Une "descriptio villarum" de l'abbaye de Lobbes a l'époque carolingienne', *Bull. de la Commission royale d'Histoire*, 78 (1909), 249–67. No benefices. No named peasants. No *trésor*, but inventories of livestock.

c. 870 (?)   Abbey of Wissembourg. Fragment of a public survey, included in the *Brevium Exempla* (above, 800 × 820, item b), but dated to 870 by Willhelm Metz, 'Das Kloster Weissenburg und der Vertrag von Metz', *Speculum Historiale*, ed. C. Bauer, L. Böhm and M. Müller (Freiburg/München, 1965), 458–68, esp. 461.

c. 870   Abbey of Saint-Trond. Ref. to lost survey and inventory of *trésor*, in Fossier, *Polyptyques*, 32, n. 36.

before 872   Abbey of Saint Amand. One leaf only of (?public or private) survey covering four benefices in detail, no peasants named; no *trésor* or moveable goods; ed. Guérard, *Irminon*, i. 925–6.

878   Cathedral Chapter of Mâcon. *Memoratorium de mansis que sunt Ymitherii* of 878 with additions of tenth–thirteenth centuries. Public(?) or private(?) survey, mentioning one benefice. No peasants named. No *trésor* or moveable goods; ed. Déléage, *Vie rurale*, i. 1219–20.

878 × 938   Abbey of Saint-Bénigne de Dijon. 'Breve commorantium quod Ademarus rogavit facere' for Etourvy (Aube), Melisey (Yonne) and seven other places. Public(?) survey (*invenimus*); no benefices; no peasants named; no *trésor*; ed. Déléage, *Vie rurale*, i. 1214–19.

879–906   Abbey of Santa Giulia di Brescia. Private survey (beginning and end missing); no benefices; no peasants named (free or slaves); *trésor* of dependent churches and chapels; animals. *Inventari*, 53–94. Extract transl. in Duby, *Rural Economy*, 377–8.

883   Abbey of Saint Columbanus of Bobbio. New survey updating that of 862 (q.v.); ed. *Inventari*, 145–65.

c. 893   Abbey of Prüm. Public survey made soon after Viking incursion of 892; includes list of fief-holders but not of their fiefs (or benefices); no named peasants; no *trésor* or moveable goods. Ed. Beyer, *mittelrhein*, i. 142–201 from the cartulary into which it was transcribed with a running commentary by the ex-abbot Caesarius in 1222. K. Lamprecht argued that the basis was a survey of *c.* 810, revised in 854 and 893, but Perrin, *Recherches*, no. 1, has established that the survey was made soon after 892 by nine commissions working simultaneously in different geographical areas.

899   Abbey of Gorze. Text lost, but ref. to *Hubenliste* in an act of 899. Fossier, *Polyptyques*, 31, n. 34.

ninth cent.   Abbey of Hersfeld. (a) *Breviarium Sancti Lulli* or *Breve Compendium*, *Urkundenbuch der Reichsabtei Hersfeld*, ed. Hans Weirich (Marburg, 1936, Veröffentlichungen der Hist. Komm. für Hessen und Waldeck, xix, pt. 1), i. 68–74 (no. 38). Private survey; no benefices; no peasants named; no *trésor* or moveable goods. (b) A possible survey may also be embedded in a charter of 835 × 63 (ibid., 61–3, no. 35), in which the donor gives his family lands to the abbey. No benefices included. Peasants and their wives named, their children enumerated. No *trésor* or moveable goods. (c) A list of places rendering tithes to the abbey, *c.* 880–99 (ibid., 65–7, no. 37).

ninth cent.   Abbey of Saint Maur de Fossés. Polypticum, ed. Guérard, *Irminon*, ii. 283–8 (no. 1). Public(?) survey; no benefices; many peasants named (with numbers of their children) in sections 17–22; no *trésor* or moveable goods.

ninth cent.   Abbey of San Tommaso di Reggio. Private survey of agricultural equipment, stock and renders of five manors and one benefice; no *trésor*; ed. *Inventari*, 196–8.

ninth cent.   Cathedral of San Lorenzo di Tortona. Record of gifts by the lady Teberga; no benefices; six peasants named; no *trésor* or moveables; ed. *Inventari*, 115–17.

late ninth cent.   Abbey of Werden. Composite private survey. Usually peasants named. No *trésor* or moveable goods; ed. Kötschke, *Rhein Urbar*, ii. 4–87. The passage relating to the lordship of Friemersheim (ii. 15–18) translated in Duby, *Rural Economy*, 374–6.

late ninth cent.   Bishopric of Lucca. Two related surveys, ed. Luzzati in
Inventari, 211–46. (i) (pp. 211–25) is a public(?) survey
(*invenimus*) of the bishop's demesnes. No benefices. Many
peasants named. *Trésor* included. Apparently second half
ninth cent. (ii) (pp. 225–46) a private(?) survey of the ben
of twenty-seven of the bishop's men; some named peasan
trésor or moveable goods (890–900).

ninth–tenth   Abbey of Saint Columbanus at Bobbio, private survey, e
cents.   *Inventari*, 169–75, incl. a few benefices, no named peasant
trésor or moveable goods.

913–14   Abbey of Gorze. Survey of demesne at Quincy embodied
charter by the donor, Count Boso. Text in *Histoire de Me*
les religieux Bénédictins de la congrégation de Saint-Vanne (6 v
Metz, 1769–90), iii. 14. Comment in Perrin, *Recherches*, 1
(no. 5). Private(?) survey; no benefices; no peasants name
trésor or moveable goods.

before 921   Verberie (Oise) ref. in diploma of Charles the Simple, 25
921 – 'tres mansos in Vermeria, quos ipse Hadegerus in ber
jure ex nostro tenebat dare. Et haec sunt eorum nomina q
eosdem incoluerunt mansos ex antiquo, ut est scriptum in
polipdico de Vermeria.' *Recueil Charles III*, i. 263 (no. cix)

925 × 50   Abbey of Saint Peter at Ghent (Blandinium). Private surv
Liber Traditionum Sancti Petri Blandiniensis, ed. A. Fayen (C
1906), 15–21. No benefices; all peasants named; no *trésor* c
moveable goods. F. L. Ganshof in *Rev. belge*, 26 (1948), 10.
thinks that some sections go back to the first half of the n
eighth, or even to the second part of the seventh century.

after 926   Verdun Cathedral. Public survey (*pulepium*) compiled after
Hungarian invasion by Evrard the provost, Bertier the dea
Lanfred and Odilo, archdeacons, with the testimony of a
villeins. Demesne manors of the chapter only; ed. Waitz in
preface to 'Gesta Episcoporum Verdunensium' in *MGH*, S
iv. 38; it includes refs. to earlier surveys. Comment in Per
Recherches, 101–7 (no. 2).

937   Autun Cathedral. Public survey by the bishop, dean, cano
Robert the judge and five other named jurors, of seven vi
their lordship of Champdôtre (C. d'Or). No benefices. N
peasants named. No *trésor*; ed. Déléage, *Vie rurale*, ii. 1207
Excerpt trans. in Duby, *Rural Economy*, 373–4.

c. 940   Abbey of Fulda. Private survey, *Traditiones et Antiquitates*
Fuldenses; ed. Ernst F. J. Dronke (Fulda, 1844), 125–9 (no.
one benefice mentioned; no peasants named; no *trésor* or
moveable goods. Excerpts Guérard, *Irminon*, i. 927–9.

945   Bishopric of Tivoli. List of 257 estates given by named
individuals and now confirmed by papal authority; ed. *Inve*
253–75.

949   Abbey of Saint-Père de Chartres. Private survey transcribed by Paul the monk in the cartulary which he began after the fire of 1078, *Cartulaire de l'Abbaye de Saint-Père de Chartres*; ed. B. Guérard, i. 35–45 (Collections des Cartulaires de France, t i, Docs. inédits, 1840). No benefices; no peasants named; no *trésor* or moveable goods.

c. 950   Abbey of Metlach. Private survey to replace a (?public) polyptych destroyed *c.* 915 × 30. Text in thirteenth-cent. transcript (on a roll), the transcriber adding his own observations, but often unable to decipher the original's abbreviations; ed. Beyer, *mittelrhein*, ii. 338–51 (no. 10). Some excerpts in Guérard, *Reims*, 122–3. Perrin, *Recherches*, 108–40 (no. 3), claims that chapters 1, 3, 4, 5, 7, 9, 18, 21 and 23 are from *c.* 950, the rest being added at various dates into the eleventh cent. No benefices. No peasants named. No *trésor* or moveable goods.

950 × 75   Abbey of Remiremont. Public(?) survey, ed. Perrin, *Recherches*, 693–703. No benefices. Peasants named. No *trésor* or moveable goods. Discussed, ibid., 141–69.

950 × 75   Abbey of Gorze. Survey of Count Boso's lands in Wormsgau, embedded in a charter allegedly of 766 but really a twelfth-cent. forgery; *Gallia Christiana*, xiii, instrumenta, 372. Perrin, *Recherches*, 196–217 (no. 7) thinks that though the charter is a forgery, the survey it quotes is genuine.

before 959   S. Maria di Monte Velate. Private survey of rents and renders (only); no benefices, named peasants or *trésor*; ed. *Inventari*, 14–16.

before 963   Abbey of Saint Glossindis (previously Saint Sulpicius) at Metz. Ref. to the existence of public polyptychs (now lost) when the history of the translation of Saint Glossindis was written, *c.* 963. 'Edicta quoque publica de possessionibus ejusdem monasterii in cunctis scriptis vel polipticis vetusto stylo et calamo editis.' Perrin, *Recherches*, 212, n. 2.

967   Abbey of Saint-Arnoul de Metz. Fragment of a public survey (soon after 942) relating to Morville-sur-Seille, embodied in a charter of 967; ed. H. V. Sauerland, *Die Immunität von Metz* (Metz, 1877), 142 and (facs). *Musée des archives departementales* (Paris, 1878), Pl. 10, no. 14. No benefices. No named slaves. No *trésor* or moveable goods. See Perrin, *Recherches*, 225–39 (no. 8).

968 × 80   Abbey of Saint Vanne de Verdun. Private register compiled in part from records 'in antiquo scripto regali et apostolico', ed. Hermann Bloch in *Jahrbuch der Gesellschaft für lothringische Geschichte und Altertumskunde*, 10 (1898), 447–9, and also Guérard, *Reims*, 115–23. No benefices. No names of peasants. No *trésor*.

975 × 1092	Chapter of Saint-Dié. Survey (on a single sheet of parchment), ed. Chr. Pfister, 'Les revenus de la collégiale de Saint-Dié au Xe siècle, *Annales de l'Est*, ii (1888), 515–17 and iii (1889), 407. Discussed, Perrin, *Recherches*, 269–317 (no. 10). Two benefices included. No tenants named. No *trésor* or moveable goods.
984	Abbey of Gorze. Survey of Brouch in a charter of Count Boso, listing manses and services but no named peasants, no benefices and no *trésor* or moveable goods; ed. Guèrard, *Irminon*, ii. 351–2 (no. 18). Comment in Perrin, *Recherches*, 180–96 (no. 6).
tenth cent.	Abbey of S. Giulia di Brescia. Inventory of the estate at Migliarina (in Carpi, Modena) when given as a benefice; no named peasants or *trésor*; ed. *Inventari*, 203–4.
second half of tenth cent.	Bishopric of Verona. Private(?) survey (beginning lost); no benefices; peasants not usually named; *trésors* of dependent churches; ed. *Inventari*, 101–11.
end of tenth cent.	S. Cristina di Corteolona. Private survey of estates, with bounds; no named peasants, *trésor* or moveable goods; ed. *Inventari*, 31–40.
before first half of eleventh cent.	S. Lorenzo di Oulx. Private survey; no benefices; peasants named, and their wives and children either named or mentioned; no *trésor*, but some agricultural equipment and animals; ed. *Inventari*, 5–9.
tenth–eleventh cent.	Abbey of S. Columbanus, Bobbio. Private survey (*breviarium*); benefices included; some peasants named; no *trésor* or moveable goods; ed. *Inventari*, 178–98.
c. 1027	Pavia. Verbose account of the renders in money or kind due to the kings of the Lombards at Pavia, from tolls, criminal jurisdiction, taxes on trade, crafts and fishing rights, etc., but excluding land. Prologue and epilogue fourteenth-cent. additions; ed. A. Hofmeister in *MGH, SS*, xxx, pt. 2 (1934), 1444–60 as 'Instituta regalia et ministeria camerae regis Langobardorum et honorantiae civitatis camerae regis'.
1031	Abbey of St Emmeran, Regensburg. Private survey made on orders of Abbot Burchard, Arnold the reeve and all the brethren in 1031. No benefices. No peasants named. No *trésor* or moveable goods; ed. Dollinger, *L'Evolution*, 504–12.
1040 × 50	Abbey of Saint-Vanne de Verdun. Private survey with no benefices, no peasants named and no *trésor* or moveable goods, but renders in kind or money from the various manses. Lands of the parish churches included; ed. H. Bloch in *Jahrbuch der Gesellschaft für lothringische Geschichte und Altertumskunde*, 14 (1902), 123–30. Discussed in Perrin, *Recherches*, 243–68 (no. 9).
1052 × 76	Abbey of S. Père de Vilamajor en Vallès. Fragments of a rental said to have followed on from a tenth-cent. survey and to have been ed. (in roneo) by A. Mundo in *Bull. du Musée Fidel Fita d'Arenys de Mar*, Circulaire no. 9, 1961. Information from P. Bonnassie, *La Catalogne du milieu du Xe siècle a la fin du XIe siècle* (Toulouse, 1975), i. 243, n. 109.

1056 × 76   Cathedral Church of Urgel. Unpublished survey parts of which survive in the cathedral cartulary, e.g. for estates at Méranges. Alàs, Err and Ayguatebic. See P. Bonnassie, *La Catalogne*, i. 87, 243–50.

c. 1060   Abbey of Corvey. Private survey by Abbot Saracho. No benefices, but peasants are named. No *trésor* or moveable goods. Extracts in Guérard, *Irminon*, i. 926–7 from Paul Wigand in *Archiv für Geschichte und Alterthumskunde Westphalen* (Hamm, 1826 et seq.).

Postscript

Thanks to the help of various friends, the following additions and amendments can be made to the list of continental surveys given in the appendix.

p. 32 *add* 820-21 Abbey of St Emmeran, Regensburg. See Carl I. Hammer Jr, 'Family and *familia* in early-medieval Bavaria' in *Family Forms in Historic Europe*, ed Richard Wall *et al* (Cambridge, 1983) 217-48.

p. 32 *4 lines from bottom, for* Sant' Ambrosio *read* Sant' Ambrogio.

p. 33 c. 850 Abbey of S Rémi de Reims. *Add* See the new edition by Jean-Pierre Devroey, *La Polyptyque et les listes de cens de Saint-Rémi de Reims* (Reims: Académie nationale de Reims, 1984). Devroey argues that the 18th-cent MS is copied from a (lost) 11th cent codex which amalgamated 3 codices: (i) the primitive polyptych of 15 chapters, of which 5 probably date from c. 810-20 and the remainder after 848; (ii) an amalgamation of 3 surveys of revenues assigned to alms and hospitality, late 10th cent; (iii) up-datings of the primitive polyptych, late 9th or early 10th cent. See Barbara Harvey in *EHR* ciii (1988) 169.

p. 34 *add L'histoire polyptyque de l'abbaye de Marchiennes*, ed B. Delmaire (Louvain-la-Neuve, 1985).

p. 34 868 Abbey of Lobbes. A new edition, *La Polyptyque et les listes de biens de l'abbaye Saint-Pierre de Libbes, IXe-XIe siècles* by Jean-Pierre Devroey ([Brussels, Comm royale d'histoire, 1986) shows that there were in fact two polyptyches c. 868-9 and c. 889 with some later interpolations c. 960-5. See Barbard Harvey in *EHR* cv (1990), 713.

p. 35 c. 893 See now *Das Prümer Urbar* ed Ingo Schwab (Publ der Gesellschaft für Rheinische Geschichtskunde, Düsseldorf 1983) which disputes some of Perrin's views. Perrin is upheld by Y. Morimoto, 'La Polyptyque de Prüm n'a-t-il pas été interpole? À propos sa nouvelle édition', *Le Moyen Age* 92 (1986), 265-76.

11

The Authorship of the Gesta Stephani

THE *Gesta Stephani* is by far the most important source for the history of Stephen's reign, and yet we do not know who wrote it. Till recently we did not even know how it ended, but now, thanks to Professor Mynors's discovery of a new manuscript and its publication by Mr. K. R. Potter, we have a text which continues beyond 1147 to the end of the reign[1]. We are therefore in a position to study the *Gesta Stephani* afresh, and to re-open the whole question of when, where, and by whom it was written.

One of the most striking features of the work, which the new manuscript has revealed, is that while most chronicles get more and more detailed as they proceed, the *Gesta Stephani* peters out, as the following table of contents will show : [2]

Book I

1135 (pp. 1–8)	7½ pages.	The narrative begins only at Dec. 1.
1136 (pp. 8–30)	22½ pages.	
1137 (p. 31)	1 page.	March–December missing.
1138 (pp. 32–47)	15 pages.	Feb.-May and July onwards missing.
1139 (pp. 48–65)	17 pages.	Up to June 24 missing.
1140 (pp. 65–73)	7 pages.	Early summer to end of year missing.
1141 (pp. 73–90)	27 pages.	

[1] *Gesta Stephani*, ed. K. R. Potter (Medieval Texts, ed. V. H. Galbraith and R. A. B. Mynors), London, 1955. Previous editions by R. C. Sewell (1846) and R. Howlett in *Chronicles of the Reigns of Stephen, Henry II and Richard I* (Rolls Series, 1886), iii. 3–136, are based on the printed text of André Duchesne in *Historiae Normannorum Scriptores Antiqui* (Paris, 1619). Duchesne worked from a manuscript which was then in the cathedral library at Laon but has since been lost. It had three *lacunae* in the text and was incomplete at the end, terminating abruptly in 1148. The new manuscript was discovered by Professor R. A. B. Mynors in the municipal library at Valenciennes when Mr. Potter's edition was already in proof. It is part of MS. 792 (not 793), a fourteenth-century collection of works on English (and British) history, which may have been made for Abbot Godfrey (1312–44) who was noted for his attachment to the English alliance, since he celebrated the marriage of Philippa of Hainault to King Edward III of England : Joseph Gennevoise, *L'Abbaye de Vicoigne* (Lille, 1929), p. 40. The text of the *Gesta Stephani* in this manuscript was evidently copied from the Laon MS. before it lost its final folios ; it is therefore significant that Vicoigne, a Premonstratensian house and a noted centre of learning, was a daughter-house of the abbey of St. Martin de Laon.

[2] The page numbers refer to Potter's edition. No references are given to chapter numbers, as the division into chapters has no manuscript authority and is obviously the work of Duchesne. (They are numbered consecutively even where there are *lacunae* in the manuscript).

Book II

1142 (pp. 91–6)	5 pages.
1143 (pp. 96–109)	13½ pages.
1144 (pp. 109–115)	6½ pages.
1145 (pp. 116–121)	6 pages.
1146 (pp. 121–131)	10 pages.
1147 (pp. 132–141)	10½ pages.
1148 (pp. 141–2)	1 page.
1149 (pp. 142–8)	6 pages.
1150 (p. 148)	½ page.
1151 (p. 149)	½ page.
1152 (pp. 149–52)	3 pages.
1153 (pp. 152–8)	6 pages.
1154 (p. 159)	½ page.

A simple explanation of this feature would be that the author was writing a panegyric of King Stephen and therefore had no wish to dwell on his final defeat, but the division of the work into two Books suggests that the author had planned his work at a time when he still believed in Stephen's ultimate victory. Book I relates how Stephen sinned against the Lord by laying violent hands on His anointed (the three bishops), and how the Lord punished him by causing him to be defeated and captured at Lincoln (1141) ; and when at the end it tells of Stephen's release, it finds an Old Testament parallel in the tribulation of King David and expressly states that it was God's will that Stephen be cast down for the moment in order that he might be set more gloriously on high (*ut excelsius postea et mirificentius elevari*, p. 76). We consequently expect to find that while Book I has been concerned with sin and retribution, Book II will be concerned with repentance and its reward. And at first this seems to be the case, for the narrative builds up to one climax with Stephen's capture of Faringdon (1145). .' a famous victory to which God had added the greatest amount of glory and the crown of good fortune ' (p. 121)—and seems to be building up to another in 1147, when it suddenly becomes bleak and perfunctory. The impression given is that the author had been interrupted in his work, and had recommenced it only when the dismal outcome of the reign was known.

It is not difficult to show that the account of roughly the first twelve years of the reign was written as a single literary composition, for the author occasionally anticipates the march of events. At the first mention of Henry of Blois in 1135 (p. 5) he mentions that he was enthroned as apostolic legate of all England, though this did not occur till 1139. In the account of 1136 (p. 16) there is a reference to the death of Miles of Gloucester ' as we shall expound more fully in what follows ' : it occurred on Christmas Eve 1143, and a description of it is found in Book II (p. 106). In 1140 (p. 67) we are told of the induction of an abbot of Ramsey whom God was to punish for his simony, and once again we are promised further details which materialize in Book II with the account of the seizure of the abbey by Geoffrey de Mandeville in 1143–4 (p. 109). An even later date is suggested by the author's promise in 1139 (p. 55) of more information about Henry de Tracy ' as we will depict more fully in their proper places (*suis in locis*) in the present history ', the next two references to him—provided that none was in the missing part of 1140—being in 1143 (p. 99) and 1147 (p. 140). Similarly in the account of 1145 (p. 118) we find a reference to the fact that William of Dover was to die blessedly on crusade, presumably in 1147 or 1148. But on the other hand, the author was apparently unaware that the bishop of Chester, whom he rebukes severely (p. 104), was likewise to redeem his faults, dying at Antioch on 16 April 1148. And there may be some significance in the remark (p. 84) that King David of Scotland, having ignominiously fled from England twice, would do so a third time (from the Rout of Winchester in 1141), for after 1149 the author could have mentioned yet a fourth time which he himself records (p. 143).

It would therefore seem that the account of the first twelve years of the reign was written in about 1148, and it becomes important to discover at what point and at what date the work was taken up again and completed. The date is indicated by the author's reference among the events of 1148 to Henry of Blois's nephew (wrongly named Henry) ' whom we have since seen bishop of Durham ' (p. 142), for he was not consecrated till 20 December 1153, and the author must have been writing after that. But the precise point at which the old narrative ends and the new begins is more difficult to determine. One indication is that from the end of 1147 onwards (pp. 135 ff.), Stephen's rival, the young Henry, is described as ' the lawful heir ' of the kingdom, but it has to be admitted that in some cases this description could have been inserted in a last-minute revision of the text. A more definite indication is given by the author's changing attitude to Ranulf, earl of Chester, Eustace the king's son and Walter de Pinkney the commander of Malmesbury.

In the narrative of 1146 (pp. 129–30) the author states that Stephen was well-advised to arrest the earl of Chester, and justifies his conduct at length ; but at the end (p. 156) we are told that it was the earl's conduct that was justified, since the king had arrested him while under safe-conduct. In 1147 he ' writes up ' Eustace the king's son (pp. 137–8) as if he were to play a glorious and triumphant role ; but subsequently he is mentioned neutrally, and his death is recorded baldly and without emotion (p. 158). Most significant of all, however, is the change of attitude towards Walter de Pinkney. In 1145 he receives favourable notice as the king's commander at Malmesbury ; he is described as ' a man of constancy,

well-tried in the arts of war ', and we are told with regret how he
was captured and handed over to the empress ' who hated him more
unrelentingly than all her enemies ' (p. 118).   When he next appears,
at the end of 1147, he has turned into a villain (pp. 140–1).   We
are told that when he was released from prison by the aid of the
earl of Hereford, he promptly flew to arms and showed that he had
not forgotten ' his old cruelty and wickedness ', his subsequent
death at the hands of one of ' Baldwin's knights ' being described
as a judgment of God.   Nothing is said to remind us that Walter
must still have been fighting for King Stephen, or that the Baldwin
whose knights are mentioned was Baldwin de Redvers, earl of
Devon, who features prominently in the earlier part of the work
as one of Stephen's arch-enemies.[1]   One gets the impression that
the author is practising an ' economy of truth ' in order to cover up
the fact that he himself has now changed sides and is no longer a
supporter of the king.

In these examples the division between the earlier and later parts
of the work has been narrowed down to the closing months of 1147,
at some point between pages 135 and 140.   On pages 135–6 we
have the first two references to Henry as ' the lawful heir ', but
these, since they might be interpolations, seem less significant than
the panegyric on Eustace which is full of optimism and contains
no hint of his death (pp. 137–8).   Finally, on page 140 there is the
passage about Henry de Tracy which might be the second of the
references promised on page 55.   If this is so it would mark the
end of the early part of the work, since it is followed immediately
by the account of Walter de Pinkney's death.   But on this matter
it is impossible to be definite since the author has obviously done
his best to conceal the division.   All that we can say for certain is
that the earlier part of the work stretched from the beginning of
the reign to about the end of 1147, and was written in about 1148 ;
that the narrative from 1148 onwards was written after 1153 ; and
that in the meantime the author had changed his sympathies and
ceased to support King Stephen.

On the question of where the *Gesta Stephani* was written there
has been much confusion.   Howlett claimed, not unreasonably,
that the work showed ' too great a mass of topographical detail to
be the product of a monastic pen ', and Mr. Potter has subsequently
stated that it gives ' no clear indication of any special local attachment '.   But the only sure way of approaching the question is to
draw a map showing all the places mentioned in the work, and it
demonstrates beyond doubt that the author's interests were primarily
in the south west of England, in an area bounded by Hereford,

[1] The identity is established by the fact that Christchurch (Hants.) belonged to him.

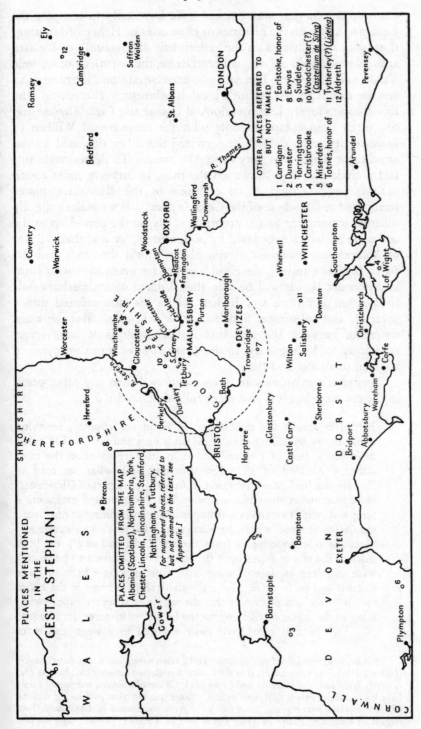

PLACES MENTIONED IN THE GESTA STEPHANI

OTHER PLACES REFERRED TO BUT NOT NAMED

1 Cardigan
2 Dunster
3 Torrington
4 Carisbrooke
5 Miserden
6 Totnes, honor of
7 Earlstoke, honor of
8 Ewyas
9 Sudeley
10 Woodchester(?) (*Castellum de Silva*)
11 Tytherley(?) (*Lidelea*)
12 Aldreth

PLACES OMITTED FROM THE MAP
Albania (Scotland), Northumbria, York, Chester, Lincoln, Lincolnshire, Stamford, Nottingham, & Tutbury. *for numbered places, referred to but not named in the text, see Appendix I*

Oxford, Winchester, and Exeter.[1] We have only to compare the
Gesta Stephani with the histories or chronicles of Henry of Huntingdon (who concentrates on the eastern half of England), of Richard
and John of Hexham (who concentrate on the north), or of Orderic
Vitalis and Robert of Torigni (who concentrate on Normandy), to
see the extent of the author's local attachment. The reason why
this has previously been overlooked is that the *Gesta Stephani* has
too often been compared only with the narrative of William of
Malmesbury who, though he favoured the other side, had a local
attachment which was very much the same. To demonstrate this
fact a circle has been drawn on the map, twenty-five miles round
Malmesbury ; within it lie eighteen of the sixty-three places
mentioned in the whole of the *Gesta Stephani*. If we make a slightly
different experiment and concentrate solely on the period up to the
end of 1142, which is covered by both writers, we find that William
of Malmesbury mentions eleven places within the circle and the
Gesta Stephani twelve ; the complete lists are given in tabular form
in Appendix II. It will be seen that William of Malmesbury fails
to mention Bampton and Radcot where his side suffered minor
reverses, and substitutes Sudeley for Winchcomb. But the main
difference between the two lists is that whereas William refers
repeatedly to Malmesbury, in the *Gesta Stephani* more prominence
is given to Bristol and Bath.

Bristol is not only more often mentioned than any other place
in the country, but it is also more fully described :

> Bristol is almost the richest city of all in the country, receiving
> merchandise by sailing-ships from lands near and far. It lies in the
> most fertile part of England and is by its very situation the most
> strongly fortified of all cities. For just like what we read of
> Brundisium [in Lucan's *Pharsalia,* ii. 610–15] it is a part of Gloucester-
> shire that makes the city, narrowing like a tongue and extending a
> long way, with two rivers washing its sides and uniting in one broad
> stream lower down where the land ends. There is also a strong and
> vigorous tide flooding in from the sea night and day ; on both
> sides of the city it drives back the current of the rivers to produce a
> wide and deep expanse of water, and while making a harbour quite
> suitable and perfectly safe for a thousand ships it hems in the entire
> circuit of the city so closely that the whole of it seems either swim-
> ming in the water or standing on the banks. However, on one side
> of it, where it is considered more exposed to a siege and more

---

[1] It is for this reason that I cannot accept H. E. Salter's suggestion, *Eynsham Cartulary*
(Oxford. Hist. Soc. xlix), i. 415, that the author was Robert Chesney, for he was successively archdeacon of Leicester and (from 1148) bishop of Lincoln, and would surely
have known about events in those districts. Salter was mistaken in thinking that the
Chesney brothers were the only lesser men to be given prominence in the *Gesta Stephani.*
Robert of Bampton, Henry de Tracy and Walter du Pinkney, to name only the first
three who come to mind, receive greater prominence by far.

accessible, a castle rising on a vast mound, strengthened by walls and battlements, towers and divers engines, prevents an enemy's approach (trans. K. R. Potter, pp. 37–8).

There is also a full account of Stephen's half-hearted attempt to besiege the city in 1138, and of his supporters' plan to build a dam across the harbour mouth and flood the city (pp. 43–4). But what is most striking is the fury with which our author writes about the place. He calls it ' the stepmother of all England ', ' the deceiver-ess ' (*impostrix* being a pun on *imperatrix*), and ' the pit of perdition ' (*perditionis barathrum*), and declares that its people ' unrestrained in the commission of every crime ' had ' by open robbery and stealthy thefts thrown the country into confusion ' (pp. 41–3). The place that suffered most from their devastations was naturally the nearest royalist stronghold, which happened to be Bath. It also is de-scribed in detail :

> Six miles from Bristol there is a city where little springs through hidden conduits send up water heated without human skill or ingenuity from deep in the bowels of the earth to a basin vaulted over with noble arches, creating in the middle of the city baths of agreeable warmth, wholesome and pleasant to look upon. The town is called Bath from a word peculiar to the English language signifying washplace, for the reason that the sick are wont to gather there from all England to wash away their infirmities in the health-giving waters, and the healthy to see the wondrous jets of hot water and bathe in them (*ibid.* 38–9).

The author tells how the Bristolians tried and failed to capture the city in 1138, merely losing one of their leaders, Geoffrey Talbot, as a prisoner to the bishop of Bath's knights ; how the Bristolians then invited the bishop to a parley under safe-conduct, and he ' like an innocent believing every word ' went to it only to be seized, insulted, and threatened with hanging until he had ordered Geoffrey's release ; and how, having given into the threats, the bishop nearly lost the friendship of the king (pp. 39–41 and 43). It is a story which is also told by John of Worcester, though more briefly and with less sympathy for the bishop, but the prominence which it receives in the *Gesta Stephani* is hard to explain on any ground but that of the author's special local attachment.

Bath was a place of some importance in the war. It was useful to the king, and hateful to his enemies, because of its nuisance-value to the earl of Gloucester's headquarters at Bristol. But it was always in danger of being surrounded, and we may well imagine that its garrison would have watched with anxiety the fortunes of the castles which controlled its escape-routes. It is consequently significant that the author of the *Gesta Stephani* watches them also, mentioning every one of them. In the north there were Berkeley

(p. 126), Dursley (p. 144), Tetbury (p. 114) and Malmesbury (pp. 62, 65, 113–14, 118, 152–4).[1] The last of these was particularly important because it controlled the main road from Bath to Oxford, and we are told how Stephen captured it in 1139 and how its castellans, notably Walter de Pinkney whom the empress 'hated more unrelentingly than all her enemies', held it against all opposition until 1153.   Further south, the main road from Bath to London was blocked by John Marshal 'that scion of hell and root of all evil' who from 1140 held Marlborough for the empress (pp. 70–1, 111, 144–5).   Nearer Bath and controlling the roads to Winchester and Salisbury was Devizes whose history we are given in the greatest detail ; the king's forces captured it in 1139, lost and regained it in 1140, lost it finally (' to a mob of plain peasants ') in 1141, and made a desperate but unsuccessful effort to regain it in 1149 (pp. 52, 64, 69–71, 77, 89, 144–5, 147–8).   Nearer still to Bath and commanding alternative routes to Salisbury and Poole Harbour was Trowbridge (pp. 61, 62, 64), but the main routes from Bath to the south and south-west were controlled by Castle Cary and Harptree, which were both captured by Stephen in 1138 and figure prominently in the history, as we shall presently see (pp. 44–6, 140).

In the last resort all routes between the south coast and either Bristol or Bath depended on control of Sherborne.   Here was one of Roger of Salisbury's castles, held since 1139 for King Stephen by his steward, William Martel.   But in 1143 William Martel was captured at the battle of Wilton, and in order to gain his release Stephen surrendered Sherborne to the earl of Gloucester.   This was the most dreadful blow for the author of the *Gesta Stephani*. With magnificent hyperbole he calls Sherborne ' the master-key of the whole kingdom ' (*quod una erat totius regni clavis*) and declares that as a result of its surrender the earl of Gloucester was able to put ' almost half of England, from sea to sea, under his laws and ordinances ' (p. 99).   We know that the only two seas to which he can be referring are the English and Bristol channels, but for someone who lived between these two seas the expression would have been pardonable, for the surrender of Sherborne probably did involve the collapse of the royalist cause in Somerset, Dorset, Devon, and Cornwall ; and it is more than probable that if our author still remained in the region of Bath, he would have been living under enemy domination.   It is interesting, therefore, that it is at this very point that he does describe the dominion of the earl of Gloucester :

> This lordship of his the earl very greatly adorned by restoring peace and quietness everywhere, except that in building his castles he

[1] If the identification of *Castellum de Silva* (p. 138) with Woodchester is correct, this would be yet another of the encircling fortresses.   It is on the road from Bath to Stroud, between Dursley and Tetbury.   See Appendix I.

exacted forced labour from all and, whenever he had to fight the
enemy, demanded everyone's help either by sending knights or
by paying scutage. And there was indeed in those regions a shadow
of peace but not yet perfect peace, because nothing more grievously
vexed the people of the country (*compatriotas*) than working not for
themselves but for others and in some sort increasing by their own
efforts the sinews of strife and war (p. 99).

It is a theme on which the author obviously felt strongly, for he
returns to it again (p. 112). But from our point of view its interest
is this. His dismay at the fall of Sherborne and his horror at the
extension of the earl of Gloucester's government from sea to sea
indicate the point of view of a man who is looking at Bristol from
the south ; and this can only be squared with the emphasis which
he places on the fighting at Malmesbury, Devizes and the other
fortresses north and east of Bath, on the assumption that it is at
Bath itself that the author is to be found.

None the less we would agree with Howlett that he could not
have been immured in a monastery, for though his local attachment
is clear, it is certain that he was also familiar with some other parts
of the kingdom. One obvious example is Exeter, for not only does
he describe the city accurately and give a detailed account of its
siege by Stephen, but he also reveals in the course of his narrative
a precise knowledge of the castle with its outer rampart (*pro-murale*)
facing the city and its inner bridge leading up to the gatehouse
(p. 22). He is curiously well-informed about Plympton (Devon)
(p. 23), would seem to have seen the church-tower at Bampton
(Oxon.) (p. 92) and to have been familiar with Oxford and Winchester. He knows that at Pevensey the castle stood within the
walls of a Roman fort, and gives its siege a surprising prominence
(pp. 134–5). He is well-informed about London which he describes
as the capital of the kingdom (*regionis regina metropolis* and *regni caput*
pp. 3, 7), reporting the claim of the citizens to elect the king (pp. 3–4)
and giving a vivid account of their dealings with, and revolt against,
the empress (pp. 80–3). He is deeply interested in Bedford,
mentioning all the occasions on which it changed hands, describing
the siege of 1137–8 in detail, and revealing in the course of it his
knowledge of the rather exceptional plan of the castle, which had a
wall round the summit of its mound with a tower-keep within it
(pp. 31–3, 77, 122, 146, 155).[1] He may also have seen Ely, for he
gives a circumstantial account of its siege in 1140, and his
reference to ' the little castle at the entry of the island ' is an apt
description of Aldreth (pp. 65–7). But these are all particular
places which the author had just happened to visit. There is nothing to suggest that he had travelled over the length and breadth
of England. In general he knows nothing about the north, the

[1] R. A. Brown, *Medieval Castles* (London, 1954), p. 161.

midlands or East Anglia, and his account of the battle of Lincoln suggests strongly that he had not seen the place. The evidence suggests that he came from the west country, that he was particularly interested in the district round Bath, and that he had made occasional visits to London, taking in Ely, Bedford, and Pevensey on his way.

There are several ways in which this general conclusion can be confirmed. In the newly-discovered part of the text, for example, there is a revealing passage in which Stephen's northern campaign is described (pp. 142–4). It is most uninformative until it reaches the point where the young Henry has to flee to the south-west, but then it tells how he went to Hereford, and how on his way from there to Bristol he spent a night at Dursley where he only just escaped an ambush by Eustace the king's son, the story growing more and more detailed as it approaches the region of Bristol (or Bath). More significant still is the fact that while the *Gesta Stephani* either ignores or disparages the great magnates who supported Stephen (for their estates were mostly in the eastern or midland part of the country), it treats one south-western baron, Henry de Tracy, as an absolute hero, though he is not so much as mentioned by any other chronicler. We are told that after the fall of Sherborne in 1143,

> When all in that part of the country were following the Earl [of Gloucester], only Henry de Tracy, maintaining the King's cause, unbendingly resisted all of them and carried on a bitter struggle by constant battles with enemy forces and conflicts with individuals everywhere until, when everyone was almost overcome by the persistence of his unrelenting attacks, he decided to make peace with them for a time until the King was stronger in those regions and the country more obedient to him after the disturbances of war had died down (p. 99).

His history is followed in detail—even his relatives being sought out for special mention—and we are told that the centre of his activities was in North Devon and Somerset, round Barnstaple, Dunster, and Castle Cary (pp. 54–5, 99, 140, 147).[1]

A similarly provincial, or even parochial, outlook can be seen in the author's description of the Scottish army which invaded England in 1138 :

---

[1] The relatives of Henry de Tracy who are particularly mentioned are Robert Fitz Harold (p. 13) and Alured Fitz Joel (p. 24). Robert Fitz Harold (*vir stemmatis ingenuissimi*, p. 13) was descended from King Æthelred II through his daughter Goda, and was connected with the Tracys because his brother, John Fitz Harold, married a Grace de Tracy. For the Tracy pedigree, which is full of problems, see L. C. Loyd, 'Anglo-Norman Families' (*Harleian Soc.*, ciii, 1951), pp. 104–6., A. S. Ellis in *Bristol and Glos. Arch. Soc.* iv. 177, and G. H. White in *Complete Peerage*, xi. App. D., p. 109, *n. l.* In *Hist. et Cart. Mon. S. Petri Gloucestriae* (ed. W. H. Hart, Rolls Series, 1865), i. 180 our Henry de Tracy witnesses a charter for Grace de Tracy's son, William.

To spur him on with frequent urging to create disorder, the King (of the Scots) had with him on the one side the son of Robert of Bampton and his kinsmen, who had been banished from England, as has been said, and had fled to him in the hope of recovering their country, on the other Eustace fitz John a great and influential friend of King Henry . . . (p. 36).

Eustace fitz John, it is true, played an important part in the invasion, but it is somewhat ludicrous to find him linked with an unknown son of Robert of Bampton. The only possible explanation is that the author had a special interest in the two men or their families. It is consequently significant that both men came from Somerset. For though Robert of Bampton got his name from Bampton in Devon, he was also lord of Castle Cary in Somerset, the fortress which (as we have already seen) controlled the routes leading south from Bath.[1]   (He was also a benefactor of the cathedral priory at Bath, having given it the church of Bampton, Devon, and half the tithes of Castle Cary.)   Eustace fitz John had acquired his importance on the Scottish border by his marriage to the heiress of Alnwick and Bamborough, but his family came from the west country and as many as eight of his relatives are mentioned in the *Gesta Stephani*. The genealogical table on page 220 will show who they all were, but for us the most important of them is his brother, William fitz John who, as the *Gesta Stephani* informs us, held Harptree castle against King Stephen in 1138 (p. 44). For if Castle Cary guarded the routes from Bath to the south, Harptree guarded the route from Bath south-westwards to Wells and Bridgwater. We therefore find that our author cannot even describe a Scottish campaign without recalling us to the neighbourhood of Bath.

We must now turn to the question of what sort of man the author was. He was certainly a scholar, for the *Gesta Stephani* is an ambitious literary composition, far grander than the ordinary chronicle. He himself calls it a ' history ' in which events are ' depicted ' (*deflorare* is the word he uses, p. 55), and as if in the literary manner bred he explains that he does not wish to bore the reader with excessive detail (pp. 8, 98, 112). Thus, though he arranges events in their chronological order, he gives hardly any dates, since dates (apparently) would have spoilt the literary effect ; and, as if distressed by the barbarism of English place-names, he

[1] In 1086 Castle Cary was held by Robert of Bampton's father, Walter of Douai (*D.B.* i. 95). Robert would have lost the castle with all his other lands when he was exiled in 1136 (pp. 20, 36), and it was apparently granted by Stephen to Ralph Lovel, who held it in 1138, but lost it in his turn to the king (pp. 44–6). I. J. Sanders in *English Baronies* (1960), p. 27, claims that the castle had been held by Ralph Lovel since 1107 ; but he offers no evidence, and Robert of Bampton's lordship over Castle Cary is proved by his grant of half the tithes to Bath Priory : *Two Cartularies of the Priory of St. Peter at Bath*, ed. W. Hunt (Somerset Rec. Soc. vii, 1893), i. nos. 35, 36, 64.

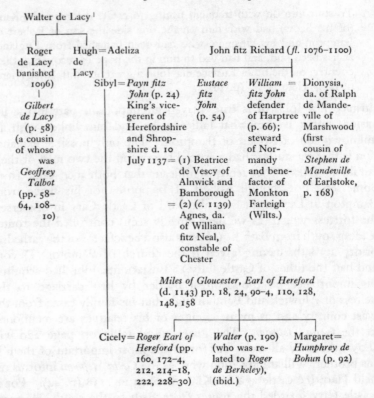

Walter de Lacy [1]

Roger de Lacy banished 1096)

Hugh = Adeliza de Lacy

John fitz Richard (*fl.* 1076–1100)

Sibyl = *Payn fitz John* (p. 24) King's vice-gerent of Herefordshire and Shropshire d. 10 July 1137

Gilbert de Lacy (p. 58) (a cousin of whose was Geoffrey Talbot (pp. 58–64, 108–10)

Eustace fitz John (p. 54)

= (1) Beatrice de Vescy of Alnwick and Bamborough
= (2) (*c.* 1139) Agnes, da. of William fitz Neal, constable of Chester

William = *fitz John* defender of Harptree (p. 66); steward of Normandy and bene-factor of Monkton Farleigh (Wilts.)

Dionysia, da. of Ralph de Mande-ville of Marshwood (first cousin of *Stephen de Mandeville* of Earlstoke, p. 168)

Miles of Gloucester, Earl of Hereford (d. 1143) pp. 18, 24, 90–4, 110, 128, 148, 158

Cicely = *Roger Earl of Hereford* (pp. 160, 172–4, 212, 214–18, 222, 228–30)

Walter (p. 190) (who was re-lated to *Roger de Berkeley*), (ibid.)

Margaret = *Humphrey de Bohun* (p. 92)

often refers to specific places without naming them, a case in poin being Dunster which he actually describes though he does no mention its name (p. 54). The reason for this affectation woulc seem to be that the author was determined to write a history worthy of the ancients. He explains the meaning of Bath (*quod ex Anglica linguae proprietate trahens vocabulum, Balneum interpretatur*, p. 39), pre sumably because the ancient Romans would not have understood it and he thinks he is being helpful when he renders Woodcheste (Glos.) as *castellum de silva* (p. 138). He eschews the technical term of government and the vernacular words of common speech ; in stead he goes to the fountain-head of the classics to discover word which would be suitable for a work of literary distinction. The king's doorkeeper figures as *ianuarum conclusor* (p. 4), the treasure as *thesaurorum custos et resignator* (p. 5), the chancellor as *summu antigraphus* (p. 52), laws as *plebiscita* (pp. 112, 158) and writs a *litterae delegatae* (p. 12). The commanders of towns are callec *praeses* (p. 119), *praeceptor* (p. 77), *primipulus* (p. 118), *commanipulariu* (p. 136) or *summus primas* (p. 156) ; soldiers figure as *legionarii* anc *centenarii* (p. 21), townsmen as *togati cives* (p. 20), and peasants a

[1] For the Lacy part of the pedigree see W.E. Wightman, *The Lacy Family in England and Normandy, 1066-1194* (Oxford, 1966).

oloni (p. 102). Even when men die they come to their last breath classically, *ad extrema deveniens.*

Such learned vocabulary requires a syntax to match, and in the *Gesta Stephani* it gets it. The sentences are long and have dependent clauses enclosed within other dependent clauses, as if constructed on the bracket principle beloved of schoolboys ; and though the subject is sometimes left in air (in the following example it is the bishop of Winchester) the verb invariably turns up at the end.

> Pacis igitur et concordiae foedere in commune peracto cum festiva illam occursione in Wentam civitatem suscepit ; regisque castello et regni corona (quam semper ardentissime affectarat) thesaurisque (quos licet perpaucos rex ibi reliquerat) in deliberatione sua contraditis, in publica se civitatis et fori audientia dominam et reginam acclamare praecepit (p. 79).

The style is nothing if not artificial. Rhymes and assonances abound, and the author delights to juxtapose phrases such as *ut propalatum est* and *dum in propatulo esset* (p. 76). If he knocks off a good phrase he is apt to repeat it, *marino gurgite alluente inaccessum*, for example, being made to do duty for both Dunster and Pevensey (pp. 54, 134). He knows the bible well ; quotations from it are common, and echoes and allusions so frequent that modern editors have not attempted to identify them all.[1] He occasionally drops into the first person singular in order to make some literary explanation or apology, as when he informs the reader that he has read about the battles of Saul and the troubles of the Maccabees, but he never claims to have seen any of the events which he describes.[2] On the contrary, he gives the impression that he is writing about the present as if it were the past, in order to give it the grandeur of antiquity.

None the less it would be wrong to think that his history was in any sense ' dead '. It is vivid because the author, in spite of his stilted Latin periods, is able to express emotion strongly, especially when it concerns the wickedness of men and the suffering which they had to undergo. In this respect he stands out from the general run of twelfth-century writers. The Peterborough Chronicler may give a more terrible picture of the bestialities of the barons, and other chroniclers like John of Worcester may have strong feelings when

[1] There are at least eight on p. 103. Three are noted by Potter. The others are *filii Belial* (1 Kings ii. 12), *tunicam Domini* (John xix. 23), *Hieremie faciem* (Jer. iii. 12), *Moysi frontem* (Exod. xxxiv. 30), *labrum . . . . Salomonis* etc. (2 Chron. iii. 15 and iv. 1.–16).
[2] The only occasions on which the author breaks this rule are when he sees into the future. On p. 33 he sees a sign in the sky, and on pp. 66, 68, 142, he says that ' we have seen ' so-and-so become an abbot, excommunicate or a bishop. The other occasions where the first person plural is used are on pp. 16, 55, 62, 112, 123 and 140 ; the first person singular occurs on pp. 8, 46 (twice), 84, 95, 98 and 104, and on pp. 50 and 137 he emphasizes it with *ego* in order to give a decisive moral judgment.

their own town is burnt, but none of them approaches the author of the *Gesta Stephani* for the sustained horror which he expresses at the sufferings of the common people. Though he reserves his greatest hatred for the cruelties of mercenary turncoats like Robert fitz Hubert who were neither for king nor empress, he is disgusted by all tyranny over the common people (*plebs*) even when it is exercised in the interest of the king (p. 63). He frequently asserts that the endless fighting has reduced the country to a desert (*in solitudinem redigere*), and he is horrified by the ' bestial cruelty ' which led men to burn crops in the fields (p. 145). In his account of the events of 1143 he breaks off to describe the famine which had been caused by the hostilities. He tells us how men ate dogs and horses, and how they died in droves or forsook their homes and went into voluntary exile :

> You could see villages with famous names standing solitary and almost empty, because the peasants of both sexes and all ages were dead, fields whitening with a magnificent harvest (for autumn was at hand) but their cultivators taken away by the agency of a devastating famine, and all England wearing a look of grief and calamity, an aspect of wretchedness and oppression (p. 102).

The author's emotion at what he saw is obviously genuine ; and the horror with which he recollects it almost enables us to see him.

If we proceed to the question of the author's political affiliations, there can be no doubt that he belonged to the party of the king's brother, Henry of Blois, bishop of Winchester, whom he describes as ' a man of inexpressible eloquence as well as wonderful wisdom ' (p. 5). He explains not only his activities but also his motives, defends his conduct in the crises of 1139 and 1141, and disparages the members of the Beaumont family who were, in the early years of the reign, his rivals for the king's favour.[1] As Howlett put it (pp. ix–x) :

> Our author certainly writes like one who stood beside the prelate, explaining on the one hand the story that he persuaded his brother to let the empress reach Bristol, on the other telling us the bishop's stern advice to Stephen, to grant no terms to the Exeter rebels, for their skin was loose and their lips dry, and they must consequently be soon driven by thirst to unconditional surrender.

---

[1] Thus Waleran of Meulan is represented as the most evil of the king's counsellors (pp. 49, 51), and it is pointed out that he fled from the battle of Lincoln without striking a blow (*antequam manus consererent*) (p. 74), and that he was attacked by both the king and the (pro-Angevin) earl of Hereford in 1152 as a neutralist (p. 151). Hugh le Poer, earl of Bedford, is represented as lax and effeminate (pp. 33, 77). Roger, earl of Warwick, is twice mentioned as a supporter of the empress—and a willing one—in 1141 (pp. 77, 85), and otherwise is not mentioned again till his death in 1153 (p. 155) when he was on Stephen's side. Robert, earl of Leicester, the brother of Waleran of Meulan, who was one of the most important men in the realm, is not so much as mentioned till his death in 1153 (p. 155).

This much is indisputable. But doubts have always been expressed, and rightly so, about Howlett's further theory that the author was Henry's chaplain. For it is hard to see how a mere chaplain could have censured his master so magisterially as the author censures Bishop Henry (and two other bishops also) for forgetting his episcopal office so far as to behave like a robber-baron (p. 104). The author writes not like an underling but as a man of stature, and pronounces moral judgments as if his opinion were one that mattered —*ego autem fixe et audacter pronuncio* (p. 50). His concern for the suffering of the people suggests a pastoral care ; and his learning is such that it must surely have marked him for promotion, at any rate in the eyes of Henry of Blois, who was not only the greatest patron of the arts in England but also the greatest dispenser of ecclesiastical patronage.

We might also remark that the author is quite exceptionally conscious of, or even obsessed with, the exalted nature of episcopal orders. He describes bishops as the ministrants of God's holy altar, the venerable sources of all men's faith and religion, the stewards of the grain in the Lord's granary who carry in their breast the ark of God and the divine manna, the pillars that hold up God's house, the small lions that support Solomon's laver, and the bases that hold up the table of the shewbread. They were ' a shield of defence against the enemies of catholic peace ' and ' a wall before the house of Israel ', and it was their duty to take up the weapons with which the Apostle heedfully armed and equipped the man of the Gospel, to wield the very stern sword of excommunication, and to remove evil-doers from the threshold of the Church in order that they might be stricken with the lash of divine vengeance (pp. 40, 50–1, 68, 103, 105, 125, 141). There is a whole homily on the duty of bishops in the strictest Hildebrandine language, and Robert, bishop of Hereford, is singled out for praise because of the courage with which he defended his church's property by excommunicating Miles, earl of Hereford (pp. 103–5). The very structure of the history as originally conceived is based on the author's conception of the sanctity of the episcopacy, for its division into two books was to emphasize, as we have already seen, that Stephen's defeat and captivity in 1141, so far from being a freak of fortune, was a judgment of God. When his enemies had disarmed him, Stephen ' kept on crying out in a voice of humbled complaint that this mark of ignominy had indeed come upon him because God avenged his injuries ' (p. 75) and our author leaves us in no doubt that the injury in question was the arrest of the bishops, which he had previously described as ' a monstrous sin against God himself '.

Hence also the Lord says, in the word of the prophet ' He that toucheth you toucheth the apple of mine eye ', and in the Gospel

' He that despiseth you despiseth me '. And to inflict dishonour so rashly and recklessly, or dishonourable extortion, on the ministrants of the holy altar he thus forbids them in the words of the prophet, saying ' Touch not mine anointed '. For my part I proclaim firmly and boldly that God himself cannot be more swiftly or more grievously offended by anything, than by any man's offence, in word or deed, to those appointed to serve at his table (pp. 50–1).

This sounds, not like the voice of a bishop's chaplain, but like the voice of a bishop himself.

If we concede that our author could have been a bishop, a lot of facts fall naturally into place. For bishops had to travel about the country in order to attend the royal court or one of the numerous ecclesiastical councils which were held in Stephen's reign, and yet they were localized in dioceses where they exercised a pastoral care. There was a diocese of Somerset, which stretched almost 'from sea to sea ' between the Bristol and English channels, and whose bishop's see was fixed (in this period) at Bath. Its bishop during Stephen's reign was Robert of Lewes (1136–66) who was renowned as a staunch supporter of the king and the first of Henry of Blois's protégés. It looks as if he might possibly be our man, and we will therefore investigate his career in detail.

We learn most about him from the *Historiola de primordiis episcopatus Somersetensis* which was written soon after 1175, and which introduces him as follows :

> Immediately on the death of Henry the King and the succession of Stephen, ROBERT became bishop of Bath. This Robert was a monk of Lewes, whom Henry Bishop of Winchester, of worthy memory, had somehow taken thence and sent to Glastonbury, that he might put the affairs of the abbey in order. He was descended of illustrious parents, a Religious man, and was ' made all things to all men ' (*vir religiosus et omnibus omnia factus*).[1]

We are told that he rebuilt his cathedral church at Bath (and much of the cathedral priory too), that he got papal confirmation for the change of his title from bishop of Wells to bishop of Bath, and that ' counselled and assisted by the illustrious King Stephen and the venerable Bishop Henry, at that time the legate of the apostolic see ', he instituted a thorough-going reform in the church of Wells, giving it a new constitution, organizing its estates into prebends, rebuilding it, and virtually refounding it. We can therefore see that he was a reformer in the tradition of Henry of Blois, who likewise was a monk but made a point of reforming collegiate

---

[1] Ed. J. Hunter in *Ecclesiastical Documents* (Camden. Soc., 1840), p. 23. ' All things to all men ' was (in contrast to its modern usage) a high compliment in the Middle Ages, being a quotation from 1 Cor. ix. 22. John of Worcester (ed. J. R. H. Weaver), p. 38 says that Robert was *Flandrensis genere, sed natus in partibus Angliae*. There is no evidence for the view that he had once been prior of Winchester.

churches on the prebendal system ; and there is no difficulty in supposing that he would have shared his ultra-episcopal views also.

But it is when we come to the evidence of dates and places that the case for identifying our author with the bishop is strongest. For if our deductions about the date of the *Gesta Stephani* are correct, the author after being an ardent supporter of King Stephen, must have changed sides at some date *after* 1148, for the main part of the work (which would have been written *in* 1148), still expresses confidence in the king's ultimate victory. The only time before that at which he would seem to have followed the empress, though reluctantly, would have been in 1141, when his history concentrates on her movements as if he were at her court, and when he vigorously defends Henry of Blois's change of sides also. It is therefore significant that Bishop Robert of Bath, though he joined Henry of Blois in receiving the empress at Winchester on 3 March 1141, is known to have been an ardent supporter of King Stephen, is known to have been still loyal to him in 1148, and is known to have been reconciled to Duke Henry before 9 April 1153, when he is found in his court at Stockbridge.[1]

So far as places are concerned, we saw that outside the district round Bath, our author was acquainted with Exeter, Plympton, Bampton (Oxon.), Oxford, Winchester, London, Pevensey, Bedford, and Ely ; and scanty though our information about Bishop Robert's movements is, we can explain his knowledge of all these places except Ely.[2] On 26 September 1137, soon after the siege of Exeter, he gave the last rites to William Warelwast, bishop of Exeter, who on his deathbed was received into the priory of Plympton. In January 1138 he was at the siege of Bedford. Oxford we would expect him to have visited often, for the king held many courts there, but we know that he was at Godstow, only two miles away, for the dedication of its abbey church in January 1139. Bampton, like many other places mentioned, was on the route from Oxford to Bath. We know of at least two, and probably three, occasions when he was at Winchester, and five when he was at London or Westminster. Pevensey was close to his former monastery of Lewes, which he is known to have revisited in 1147, just exactly at the time of Richard fitz Gilbert's revolt and the siege of Pevensey, so fully described in the *Gesta Stephani* (pp. 133–5). If we add to all this that as bishop of Bath he would naturally have been pre-occupied with the military situation round his own cathedral city, and that in 1150 he was particularly commissioned by the pope to see that Malmesbury Abbey, sore troubled by the neighbouring castellans, should be protected by papal authority, it must be

[1] See Appendix III.
[2] Full references are given in the Outline Itinerary, Appendix III.

admitted that the coincidence between his and our author's local knowledge is complete.[1]

But we can go further. Robert de Bethune, bishop of Hereford, who is so highly praised in the *Gesta Stephani*, is known to have been a friend of our bishop's, and to have assisted him at the dedication of the church of Wells.[2] There may also have been some connection between Henry de Tracy, the hero of the *Gesta Stephani*, with the church of Wells, for his son, Oliver de Tracy, gave it the church of Bovy Tracy as a prebend.[3] William fitz John who lost Harptree to Stephen, and whose family interested our author so greatly, gave lands to a Cluniac priory dependent on Lewes, at Monkton Farleigh (Wilts.), his charter being witnessed, not unnaturally, by our bishop ;[4] and later his son gave East Harptree Church to Wells as a prebend.[5] Robert of Bampton, who figures so prominently in the early pages of the *Gesta Stephani*, would have been known to our bishop on two counts, for besides being a benefactor of Bath Priory, to which he gave the church of Bampton (Devon), he was a despoiler of Glastonbury Abbey, from which he had taken Uffculme.[6] Geoffrey Talbot, whose history seems originally to have been followed with animosity in the *Gesta Stephani*, was the man responsible for the capture of our bishop of Bath.[7]

This brings us to the heart of the matter, for if Robert, bishop of Bath, is to be identified as the author of the *Gesta Stephani*—and

---

[1] *Registrum Malmesburiense*, ed. J. S. Brewer (Rolls Series, 1879), i. 381, where the initials of the bishops are given wrongly. *Cf.* Jaffé, *Regesta Pontificum Romanorum* (2nd edn. 1885–8), nos. 9466–7.

[2] In a letter to William Prior of Llanthony, *c.* 1147–50, Hilary, bishop of Chichester, alludes to himself, Symon of Worcester and Robert of Bath as *nos enim et alii amici patris vestri defuncti* (sc. Robert de Bethune), P. R. O. C.115/A1 (Llanthony Cartulary), vol. i, section vi, no. xix. His presence at the consecration of the church of Wells (usually stated to have been in 1146) is mentioned in the *Historiola*, ed. Hunter, p. 25.

[3] *Calendar of the MSS. of the Dean and Chapter of Wells*, by W. H. Bird (Hist. MSS. Comm., 1907), i. 490. For Oliver's relationship to Henry de Tracy see *Monasticon* (1846), v. 198.

[4] *Monasticon* (1825), v. 27. The original charter is in the British Museum, Campbell Charter xiii. 12. Since Robert witnesses with Eustace the archdeacon, the charter must date from the earlier years of his episcopate. The founders of the priory were Humphrey de Bohun II and his wife Maud (*c.* 1120), and Humphrey de Bohun III and his wife Margaret (who was related to the Fitz Johns, as is shown in the genealogical table). *V. C. H. Wilts.* iii. 262.

[5] *H[ist.] M[SS.] C[omm.], Wells*, i. 68.

[6] Henry of Blois himself wrote an account of this affair of the estate of Uffculme ; it is printed in Thomas Hearne's edition of *Adam de Domerham, De Rebus Gestis Glastoniensibus*, ii. 310, and it gives the only account of Robert of Bampton's revolt apart from that of the *Gesta Stephani*. Unless we are mistaken about the authorship of the latter, it would seem that Robert of Bampton's revolt need not have been of more than local importance, and for this reason I cannot accept the ingenious theory of H. P. R. Finberg in W. G. Hoskins and H. P. R. Finberg, *Devonshire Studies* (1952), pp. 59–78.

[7] He figures on pp. 38–40, 43, and 72. In the last case the author is obviously building up to an account of his death in a skirmish near Bath on 22 Aug. 1140, but unfortunately two folios of the manuscript are missing at this point.

a study of his entourage has failed to produce any other candidate [1]—
it must follow that the account of his capture is autobiographical.
It is not easy to prove that this is in fact the case because our author,
as we have already seen, was endeavouring to write a history worthy
of the ancients, and cultivated an impersonal style, in what he
imagined to be the Roman manner. But it is undeniable that the
account of the bishop's capture is told at far greater length than any
other incident which does not concern the king or the empress
themselves ; and it is decidedly partial to the bishop. If we compare it with John of Worcester's shorter account of the same
incident we find a remarkable discrepancy, for John of Worcester
does not suggest that the bishop was actually captured by the men
of Bristol, but simply that he was terrified by a message which they
sent, threatening to hang him if he did not release Geoffrey Talbot
at once.

> Therefore (continues John of Worcester) the bishop, in the manner
> of a mercenary (*vice mercenarii*) fearing for himself and his men, had
> Geoffrey brought out from custody and handed over to them.
> When this reached the King's ears his anger flared up against the
> bishop as an abettor of his enemies, and he might perhaps have
> deprived him of his pastoral staff, even though in so doing the King
> would have given himself over to discord rather than peace. But
> because the bishop had acted unwillingly and under coercion, the
> king ' gave place to his wrath ' on which, according to the word of
> the apostle ' it is sinful to let sun go down '.[2]

Given this account, it is possible to see why the bishop, if he were
relating the incident himself, would stress just those details which are
stressed in the *Gesta Stephani*. For the actual capture is described
with a wealth of corroborative detail, and though we are given to
understand that the bishop might have been ' innocent ' in trusting
to the enemy's safe-conduct, it is made abundantly clear that there
was no thought of treachery and that the treatment meted out to him
by his captors made it ' politic and well-advised ' for him to purchase his liberty at the price of releasing Geoffrey Talbot. Moreover we find that having made his defence once, the writer is not
able to leave well alone, but has to hark back to the subject a few
pages later. He describes how the king came to Bath soon after.

> The bishop, who had been forewarned of his arrival, came to meet
> him as he approached the town. And though at the beginning of
> their conversation the King showed annoyance with the bishop for
> having let Geoffrey, a plotter against himself, and a destroyer of
> peace and his country, leave his custody thus unhindered and un-
> harmed, the bishop satisfied the King, with the support of witnesses,
> that he had been insultingly outraged, nearly hanged, and despitefully

---

[1] See Appendix IV.
[2] *The Chronicle of John of Worcester, 1118–1140*, ed. J. R. H. Weaver (1908), p. 50.

used by the violence of scoundrels ; and having at length appeased him and restored their wonted friendship he brought him into Bath (p. 43).

This is the only record of a private conversation in the whole of the *Gesta Stephani*, and it seems altogether too much of a coincidence that it concerns Robert of Lewes, bishop of Bath. For he has all the qualifications required of our author. He was a bishop, and a zealous one, was situated at Bath, was a close friend of Henry of Blois, changed sides at the same dates as our author, and shared his local knowledge, both about places and people. He had no literary fame, for panegyrics of Stephen were not appreciated in King Henry II's reign, but there can be little doubt that he is the man we have been looking for.[1]

APPENDIX I

A note on the map

The following places, marked with numbers on the map, are referred to in the text, but not named :

1. Cardigan ; it is the battle of Cardigan which is described on p. 11.
2. Dunster, described on p. 54.
3. Torrington, almost certainly the castle captured by Henry de Tracy from William Fitz Odo (p. 55). In 1086 it was held by William Fitz Odo's father, Odo fitz Gamelin (*D.B.* i. 116ᵛ).
4. Carisbrooke, Baldwin de Redvers's castle on the Isle of Wight, mentioned on p. 29.
5. Miserden, almost certainly the castle of Robert Musard, referred to on p. 123. In 1086 it was known as Greenhampstead and was held by Hascoit Musard (*D.B.* i. 169ᵛ). By 1191 its name had changed to *La Musarderie*. There are still some remains of the castle. (A. S. Ellis in Trans. of the Bristol and Gloucestershire Arch. Soc. iv. 186.)
6. Totnes, the author shows great interest in the lords of this honor, Alvred Fitz Joel (p. 24) and Roger de Nunant (p. 85).
7. Earlstoke was the head of Stephen de Mandeville's honor. Stephen de Mandeville is presumably singled out (p. 112) because of his proximity to Bath.
8. Ewyas. This castle was held by Robert Fitz Harold, and is presumably the one referred to on p. 13. Round, *Studies in Peerage and Family History*, (p. 156).
9. Sudeley, of which also Robert Fitz Harold was lord : A. S. Ellis, *Trans. Bristol and Gloucestershire Arch. Soc.* iv. 177.
10. Woodchester, with which I would identify *Castellum de Silva* (p. 138). The attraction of this identification is that it is a literal translation of the English name (*Vdecestre, D.B.* i. 164 or *Widecestre, D.B.* i. 170ᵛ). [But now (1990) I prefer Silchester (Berlin) where the Roman amphitheatre was fortified in the 12th cent. (Michael Fulford in *Antiquaries' Journ.* lxv (1985), 77-8.)]

---

[1] I wish to thank Professor and Mrs. V. H. Galbraith, Mr. H. Mayr-Harting and Professor R. A. B. Mynors for the help they have given me with this article.

11. Tytherley, with which I would identify *Lidelea* (p. 138). Tytherley (*Tiderlege, Tiderlei, Tederlege, D.B.* i. 42, 48v and 50) is situated between Winchester and Salisbury and would have been important, as Salisbury was held by the imperialists.

12. Aldreth, the castle at the entry of the Isle of Ely (p. 67). See the *Liber Eliensis* in H. Wharton, *Anglia Sacra* (1691), i. 620–1, or in the new edition being prepared for the Camden Series by E. O. Blake.

Note : *Burtuna* which is mentioned on p. 136 must (from the context) be Purton near Cricklade, and not Black Bourton (Oxon) as suggested by Howlett and Potter.

APPENDIX II

List of places within twenty-five miles of Malmesbury and mentioned by name in William of Malmesbury's *Historia Novella* or the *Gesta Stephani*, Dec. 1135–Dec. 1142. The page-references are to K. R. Potter's edition of the two works in Nelson's *Medieval Texts*.

	William of Malmesbury	*Gesta Stephani*
Bampton (Oxon.)	—	92
Bath	44	39–43, 45, 47
Bristol	24, 35, 36, 50, 61, 65	37–8, 42–5, 58–9, 69, 75–6
Calne	35	—
Cerney	36, 42	62–3
Cirencester	76	91–2
Devizes	25, 27, 29, 43, 61, 71	52, 64, 69–71, 77, 89
Gloucester	35, 36, 48	63, 67–8, 75
Malmesbury	25, 27, 36, 38–40, 43–4	62, 65
Marlborough	44	70
Radcot	—	91–2
Sudeley	42	—
Trowbridge	36	61–2, 64
Winchcomb	—	63

APPENDIX III

Outline Itinerary of Robert Bishop of Bath

1136	Easter	Westminster : appointed bishop Bath.[1]
1137		(?) Eye (Suff.)[2]
1137	26 Sept.	Exeter and/or Plympton[3]

Notes to Appendix III

1. W. Hunt (ed.) *Two Cartularies of the Priory of St. Peter at Bath.* (Som. Rec. Soc. vii. 1893), i. no. 60.

2. *Monasticon* (1846), iii. 405. Robert figures as a witness to Stephen's charter in favour of Eye which is alleged to have been given at Eye. But the original diploma was certainly written by the beneficiary, and there is a difficulty over the witnesses since they include Gilbert, bishop of London, who died in 1134.

3. Annales Plymptonienses in Liebermann, *Ungedruckte Geschichtsquellen*, p. 27. Obiit Willelmus episcopus Exoniensis VI Kal. Oct. Qui in infirmitate extrema positus et anulum et baculum episcopo Wintoniensi Henrico reddidit, sicque ab episcopo Roberto Batonie crismatus, canonicorum habitum petiit et accepit a Gaufrido priore Plimtoniensi. Cujus etiam corpus in capitulo nostro Plimtonie quiescit sepultum.

1138	Jan.	Goldington, ' at the siege of Bedford '.[4]
1139	8 Jan.	Canterbury : consecration of Archbishop Theobald.[5]
1139	Jan.	Godstow (by Oxford) : consecration of church.[6]
1139	29 Aug.	(?) Winchester.[7]
1141	3 March	Winchester : reception of empress.[8]
1141	24 June	(?) London.[9]
1143		Winchester.[10]
1146		(?) Wells.[11]
1147	April/June	Lewes : consecration of the church.[12]
1147	3 Aug.	Canterbury : consecration of Hilary of Chichester.[13]
1148	14 Nov.	London.[14]
1151	24 June	Bath.[15]
1153	9 April	Stockbridge (Hants.) with Duke Henry.[16]
1153	Dec.	Westminster : treaty between Stephen and Henry.[17]
1154	Late Feb.	Haselbury (Somerset).[18]
1154	10 Oct.	Westminster : consecration of Roger Archbishop of York.[19]
1154	9 Dec.	Westminster : coronation of Henry II.[20]

4. Witnesses royal charter in favour of Glastonbury, ed. A. Watkin, *The Great Chartulary of Glastonbury* (Som. Rec. Soc. lix, 1947), i. 129–30.

5. He was present at Archbishop Theobald's consecration, according to his own statement in a letter to Eugenius III, Haddan and Stubbs *Councils and Ecclesiastical documents relating to Great Britain and Ireland* (1869), i. 352–3. cf. A Saltman, *Theobald Archbishop of Canterbury* (1956), p. 13.

6. Notification by Alexander, bishop of Lincoln, announcing the dedication of Godstow Abbey Church. *Monasticon* (1823), iv. 362. no. 1. Also present was Archbishop Theobald who was consecrated on 8 Jan., and who left for Rome with Simon bishop of Worcester and Robert bishop of Exeter (who were also present) soon after 13 Jan. (ed. J. R. H. Weaver, *The Chroinicle of John of Worcester* (1908), p.54).

7. According to William of Malmesbury, *Historia Novella*, Sect. 471 (ed. Potter, p. 29), ' almost all the bishops of England ' were at the council of Winchester summoned by Henry of Blois to discuss the arrest of the bishops of Salisbury, Lincoln, and Ely.

8. He was present at the reception of the empress in Winchester, with the bishops of Winchester, St. David's, Lincoln, Hereford and Ely. William of Malmesbury, *Historia Novella*, Sect. 491 (ed. Potter, p. 51).

9. I presume he would have gone to London for the empress's intended coronation, since he was now committed to her. The *Gesta Stephani* mentions specifically that some bishops were present (p. 83).

10. Thorne's Chronicle, ed. Twysden, *Historiae Anglicanae Scriptores Decem* (1652), col. 1803, trans. A. H. Davis, *William Thorne's Chronicle* (1943), p. 75.

11. Charter by Bishop Robert given in (or possibly after) 1146 in the chapter house at Wells, confirming a gift made to Bruton Priory. J. H. Round, *Calendar of Documents preserved in France* (1899), p. 173, no. 486.

12. See the charter of William, earl of Warenne, in *Early Yorkshire Charters* (ed. Clay), viii. 84. This was in 1147, probably in April but certainly before June.

13. Saltman, *Theobald*, pp. 100–1.

14. *Chartulary of the High Church of Chichester*, ed. W. D. Peckham (Sussex Rec. Soc. xlvi), no. 299. 15. *Registrum S. Osmundi* (Rolls Series), i. 268.

16. Agreement between Duke Henry and Jocelin, bishop of Salisbury. *Sarum Charters*, ed. W. D. Macray (Rolls Series), p. 23.

17. He is one of the witnesses of the treaty. *Foedera*, i. 18, &c.

18. He arrived at Haselbury after Wulfric's death which occurred on 20 Feb. *Wulfric of Haselbury by John Abbot of Ford*, ed. M. Bell (Som. Rec. Soc. xlvii, 1932), p. 129

19. Saltman, *Theobald*, p. 123. 20. *Ibid.* p. 41.

The *Familia* of Robert of Lewes Bishop of Bath, 1136–66

	after 1141	2	3	4	5	1146	7	8	1148 (14 Nov)	10	1150	1153	1156 (21 Jan)	14	15	16	17	18	1159	20	21	1156 (March)	23	1165/6
	1	2	3	4	5	6	7	8	9	10	11	12	13	14	15	16	17	18	19	20	21	22	23	24
Deans of Wells																								
Ivo (1140/3–1163)			+			+	+	+	+		+			+	+	+	+		−	+	+	+		
Richard (c. 1163–74)																	+	+	+	+	+	+		
Robert sub-dean		+	+	+		+	+	+			+	+	+	+	+		+	+	+		+	+		+
Reginald precentor	+	+	+	+		+	+	+		+	+			+	+			+	+	+	+	+	+	+
Eustace archd. Wells *ultra*	+		+			+	+	+		+	+			+	+			+	+		+	+	+	
Robert archd. Wells																				+	+			
Martin archd. Bath																					+			
Thomas archd. Bath																								
Baldwin archd. Bath *ultra Perret*																								
Hugh of Tournai archd. *ultra Perret*																								
Samuel vice-archd. Wells																								
Master Eustace			++											+++	+	+	+++	+++			++	++	+	
Master Martin	+	+		+	+			+	++	+				+			+	++	+					+
Master Arnold de Cokes				++						+	+			+++			+	+						
Master Alvred			+	+						+	+				+		+				+	+		
Canons: Alvred *ultra*																								
Stephen, 'my relative'	+	+			+	+	+	+	+		+	+		+	+	+		+	+	+	+	+	+	+
Edward																					++	+		
Mauger																					+			
Paris																								
William de Sancta Fide																								
Ralph Martre																								
William de Atebera																	+				+			
Odo																+								
Anschetil chaplain																								
Nicholas chaplain										+	+													
Clerks: Ralph							++													+	+			
Richard of Montacute																								
Hubert of Ilchester								++																
Geoffrey, of Wells																+	+			+	+	+		+
Hamo 'my nephew'																+				+				+
Hamund 'my brother'																								+
Richard 'my brother'																			+	+	+			+
Priors of Bath																								
Benedict (fl. 1156) *ultra*										+	+		+								+			+
Peter (fl. 1159)																								

Notes to Appendix IV

1. *Bruton Cartulary* (Som. Rec. Soc. viii), no. 54.
2. *Bath Cartulary* (Som. Rec. Soc. vii), i. no. 70.
3. *Stogursey Charters* (Som. Rec. Soc. lxi), no. 4.
4. *Monasticon* (1846), v. 27.
5. Cirencester Cartulary, (Reg. A), fo. 158ᵛ. I have to thank Dr. C. D. Ross for lending me photostats of this cartulary which he is editing.
6. *Bruton Cartulary*, p. 11. (no. 51), confirming a grant made in 1146.
7. *Athelney Cartulary* (Som. Rec. Soc. xiv), no. 187, given at (Bishop's) Lydeard, Somerset, probably *c.* 1146.
8. *Bath Cartulary*, i. no. 61, wrongly dated as 1135.
9. *Cartulary of the High Church of Chichester* (Sussex. Rec. Soc. xlvi), no. 299, dated 14 Nov. 1148.
10. *Bath Cartulary*, i. no. 66.
11. *Two Beauchamp Registers* (Som. Rec. Soc. xxxv), p. 57.
12. *Bath Cartulary*, i. no. 67. Charter of William Earl of Gloucester, 1153.
13. *Bath Cartulary*, i. no. 75., dated 21 Jan. 1156.
14. H. M. C. *Wells*, i. 430.
15. *Bruton Cartulary*, no. 122.
16. H. M. C. *Wells,* i. 52. (no. clxxii).
17. *Bruton Cartulary*, no. 83.
18. *Bruton Cartulary*, no. 182.
19. H. M. C. *Wells*, i. 27 (no. lxxxi).
20. *Bruton Cartulary*, no. 136 B.
21. H. M. C. *Wells*, i. 19 (no. xlvii).
22. *Historiola*, in Hunter, *Eccl. Docs.* p. 27, and H. M. C. *Wells*, i. 39 (no. cxxi), which gives the date, 15 March 1165 (by modern reckoning).
23. Cirencester Cartulary (Reg. A), fo. 159ᵛ.
24. Cirencester Cartulary (Reg. A). fo. 159. Cf. J. Armitage Robinson, *Somerset Historical Essays* (1921), pp. 80, 90.

12

What Happened in Stephen's Reign, 1135-54

STEPHEN'S REIGN presents great difficulties for the constitutional historian, for though it was obviously a reign of great importance, nobody is quite sure why. The reason for this curious state of affairs is that historical work on the reign has been dominated by a book whose technical skill has forced historians to accept a thesis which they find it impossible to believe in. The book is *Geoffrey de Mandeville* by J. H. Round (London, 1892), and if we are to make a fresh approach to Stephen's reign, it is vital to clear our minds about it. If its thesis is correct we must believe in it; if we cannot believe in it, we must show where it is wrong.

An initial difficulty lies in the fact that J. H. Round very rarely expressed a general historical thesis in explicit terms. He was nature's born researcher, so excited by his own discoveries that he assumed that everyone would see their bearing at a glance. In the case of *Geoffrey de Mandeville* a clue was given in the sub-title 'A Study of the Anarchy', and in the preface Round explained that the reason why he had constructed his book round the career of one baron was that that baron, Geoffrey de Mandeville, was 'the most perfect and typical presentment of the feudal and anarchic spirit that stamps the reign of Stephen'. He thought that when Henry I died, the barons welcomed the fact that there were two claimants to the throne, because it gave them the opportunity to sell their support to each claimant in turn, and demand concessions which were fatal to any centralized form of royal government. He thought that they resented the way in which Henry I had curbed their independence, and that they were determined to regain it by having, not one king who would rule them, but two rivals whom they could play off against each other.

That, at any rate, was what Geoffrey de Mandeville was supposed to have done. According to Round he detained Stephen's queen and daughter-in-law in the Tower of London early in 1140, was created Earl of Essex by Stephen later in the same year, went over to Matilda shortly before June 1141, came back to Stephen's service by September of the same year, went back to Matilda before the following June, was arrested in the King's Court (though how he came to be there is not explained) in September 1143, was released after he had surrendered his castles, revolted again, and was finally killed at the siege of Burwell in August 1144. It is a story that could hardly have failed to make a deep impression on contemporaries, and it is therefore astonishing to find that it is not related by any chronicler. We do not even find that Geoffrey was singled out by any chronicler as a man of treacherous reputation. Round's story is based almost entirely on charters and inferences drawn from charters. On their evidence it must stand or fall.

It may be thought that charters are a more reliable source of information than chronicles, but this is not always so. Charters are only reliable if they can be proved to be genuine and if they can be dated. In the case of Geoffrey de Mandeville there are four charters at issue, and though their genuineness is not in question, their dates are. Round gave a great deal of attention to them, but his whole chronology was based on the assumption that the charters had to be arranged in 'ascending scale', with the smallest grants first and the largest last. This was a mistake, for the extent of a grant does not necessarily have any connection with the date at which it was given; a man could be given a single manor years after he had been given a whole county. Even if the 'ascending scale' were a valid chronological guide, it would still have to be objected that Round's whole argument was a vicious circle, for starting from the assumption that the larger a grant was the later it was, he ended by 'proving' that the later it was the larger it was.

If one attempts to re-date the charters without reference to the doctrine of 'ascending scale', one finds that it is not difficult to reconcile them with the evidence of the chronicles. A detailed study of the sureties shows that the second charter given to Geoffrey by Matilda should be dated, not to the first half of 1142 but to the last week of July 1141;[1] and the detention of Stephen's queen and daughter-in-law in the Tower of London should probably be moved forward from 1140, for which there is no evidence, to 1141.[2] Instead, therefore, of having to postulate that Geoffrey revolted against Stephen four times, in 1140, 1141, 1142 and 1143, we are left with the two revolts which are recorded in the chronicles, one in 1141 when Stephen was in captivity, and the other in 1143 after Stephen had arrested him.[3] It may seem odd for a man to have revolted after he had been arrested, but the chronicles are unanimous in stating that Geoffrey was arrested while peacefully attending the king's court, that no formal charge was made against him, that he was allowed to purchase his liberty with the surrender of his castles, and that he then revolted in fury at the treatment which he had received.

There is a similar ending to the career of Ranulf Earl of Chester, the only other example of a persistently treacherous baron that Round could produce in support of his general thesis. Round thought that he had

---

[1] R. H. C. Davis, 'Geoffrey de Mandeville reconsidered', *English Historical Review*, April 1964; see below, pp. 203-11.
[2] *ibid.*
[3] *Historia Novella*, ed. K. R. Potter (Nelson's Medieval Texts, London, 1955), para. 499, and *Gesta Stephani*, ed. K. R. Potter (Nelson's Medieval Texts, London, 1955), pp. 106-10.

changed sides seven times in the civil war, but here again he was mis-taken.[4] Ranulf rebelled against Stephen at the end of 1140 and was soon regarded as his worst enemy, since it was while besieging him that Stephen fought, lost, and was captured at, the battle of Lincoln on 2 February 1141. But there is good evidence to suggest that, so far as self-interest was concerned, Ranulf soon found that he was on the wrong side, and did his best to rejoin the king. We know that he tried to join the king's army at Winchester in 1141 and that the king's army would not receive him.[5] We know that he did eventually make terms with Stephen in 1146 and that he was apparently restored to favour, but that within the year he was suddenly arrested in the king's court at Northampton, to which he had come suspecting nothing.[6] As in the case of Geoffrey de Mandeville, no formal charge seems to have been made against him, and he was allowed to purchase his liberty with the surrender of his castles. Like Geoffrey de Mandeville, he was then driven to a fury of rebellion.

Both these arrests were sufficiently unusual to receive detailed atten-tion in contemporary chronicles. Henry of Huntingdon makes a special feature of them, linking them with the arrest of the three bishops at the king's court held at Oxford in midsummer 1139. He was particularly well-informed about this latter arrest since his patron, Alexander Bishop of Lincoln, was one of the victims. It is therefore noteworthy that he complains, not of the injury done to the liberty of the Church, but of the actual manner of the arrest.

> It was [he says] an affair noted for its infamy and contrary to all custom. For after receiving Roger Bishop of Salisbury and Alexander his nephew in peace, the king arrested them violently in court, although they had refused no justice and were devoutly demanding a fair judgement.[7]

He makes the same complaint about the other arrests also, describing that of Geoffrey de Mandeville in particular as 'more according to the retribution of the wickedness of the earl than according to the law of nations, more out of necessity than honesty'.[8] In a similar way William of Newburgh states that in arresting Ranulf Earl of Chester Stephen was 'unmindful of his royal majesty and honesty (*regiae majestatis et honestatis immemor*)'.[9]

If one attempts to analyse what it was that was unkingly, dishonest, and infamous about the arrests, one is bound to be struck by two facts. First, no specific charges were made against the persons arrested, which

---

[4] R. H. C. Davis, 'King Stephen and the Earl of Chester revised', *E.H.R.*, lxxv (1960), 654-60; see below, pp. 213-19.
[5] John of Hexham, in *Symeonis Monachi Opera Omnia*, ed. Thomas Arnold (Rolls Series, 1885), ii. 310.
[6] *Henrici Archidiaconi Huntendunensis Historia Anglorum*, ed. Thomas Arnold (Rolls Series, 1879), p. 279.
[7] *ibid.* p. 265.   [8] *ibid.* p. 276.
[9] *Chronicles of the reigns of Stephen, Henry II and Richard I*, ed. Richard Howlett (Rolls Series, 1884), i. 49.

is presumably the reason why they were released as soon as they had surrendered their castles. Secondly, Stephen welcomed his victims to his court and gave them his peace, but none the less arrested them while they were still his guests. This was an outrageous breach of hospitality, and it was aggravated considerably by the fact that the offence was committed by the king and in the king's court. Any crime committed there was far more serious than one committed elsewhere, because everyone and everything in the king's hall was protected by the king's peace. It was the king's duty to protect his peace; if he broke it he was violating his own majesty. That is why the author of the *Gesta Stephani* claimed that he had hesitated for a long time before arresting Geoffrey de Mandeville, fearing 'lest the royal majesty be disgraced by the foul reproach of treachery',[10] and why he eventually admitted that Ranulf Earl of Chester had just cause to hate Stephen, because he had been arrested in the king's court which he had entered 'confident in the peace bestowed upon him' (*de pace sibi indulta securus*).[11]

Nor was this all. Aelred of Rievaulx informs us that in 1138 Stephen arrested Eustace fitz John at court in exactly the same way and with exactly the same result.[12] William of Malmesbury says that many people thought it wicked (*iniquum*) that in 1140 Stephen, having let the earls of Chester and Lincoln depart from his court in peace 'without any suspicion of rancour', should immediately attempt to surprise them in the city of Lincoln.[13] He also tells how Stephen attempted to ambush Earl Robert of Gloucester when he was at peace with him (1137); and how, when the ambush was discovered, the king thought to proceed by subtle means 'and tried to diminish the enormity of his crime by a genial countenance and an unsolicited confession'.[14] As Richard of Hexham remarked, Stephen always managed to look cheerful (*vultu hilaris*), even in adversity, and laughed off (*deridebat*) his losses as if he did not feel them.[15] But one could not trust his smiling face; he would greet a man with his customary geniality and suddenly arrest him. 'I am going to court', said the abbot of St. Albans to a holy recluse, 'but of my return I know nothing, for I fear the inconstancy (*levitatem*) of the king.'[16]

That is why it is impossible to accept Round's interpretation of the reign. The barons could not possibly have followed a persistent policy of auctioning their services to each side in turn unless both Stephen and Matilda had been exceedingly gullible;[17] yet Stephen, as the above incidents show, was suspicious and sly, while Matilda was renowned

---

[10] *Gesta Stephani* (ed. Potter), p. 107.   [11] *ibid.* p. 156.
[12] 'Relatio de Standardo', ed. Howlett, *op. cit.* iii. 191.
[13] *Historia Novella* (ed. Potter), para. 487.   [14] *ibid.* para. 466.
[15] 'De Gestis Regis Stephani et de Bello Standardii', ed. Howlett, *op. cit.* iii. 145.
[16] *The Life of Christina of Markyate*, ed. C. H. Talbot (Oxford, 1959), p. 171.
[17] The Peterborough Chronicler (*The Anglo-Saxon Chronicle*, trans. G. N. Garmonsway (London, 1953), 263) did describe Stephen as a 'good-humoured, kindly and easy-going man who inflicted no punishment', but the context of the sentence, which comes immediately after 'he put them all in prison until they surrendered their castles', suggests that he was simply referring to the fact that Stephen did not mutilate prisoners as Henry I had done.

as a termagant. We must therefore turn to the contemporary chroniclers for an interpretation of the reign. What they say is, not that the civil war was part of an attempt by the barons to overthrow all royal government, but that it was a war about the succession to the throne. Stated in its simplest terms, the issue was whether the crown was 'elective' or hereditary. If it was hereditary, there could be no doubt that it was Matilda's by right, for she was the only surviving legitimate child of Henry I, and the barons had all sworn to accept her as his heir. If they wished to object to her because she was a woman or because they hated her husband, they had no option but to reject the hereditary principle and choose (*eligere*) an alternative. In the event, this is what they did. Stephen was king because he was 'elected' and consecrated. In a famous charter he described himself as *Ego Stephanus Dei gratia assensu cleri et populi in regem Anglorum electus et a Willelmo Cantuariensi archiespiscopo et Sancte Romane Ecclesie legato consecratus, et ab Innocentio Sancte Romane Sedis pontifice confirmatus.*[18] Matilda claimed that he had been wrongfully 'elected' because, quite apart from the fact that Stephen himself had sworn the oath to accept her, she was the rightful heir. In her charters she was always careful to describe herself as *Regis Henrici filia*, because that was the one and only claim which she had to the crown. Similarly we find her son Henry styling himself *Henricus filius filie Regis Henrici et rectus heres Anglie et Normannie.* In his view England and Normandy were his inheritance; there could be no question of anyone 'electing' or choosing a king; the kingdom was his birthright.

It is sometimes forgotten that in the first half of the twelfth century the hereditary system was still insecure. All monarchies wanted it for themselves, but the only one to have attained it beyond question was that of France, where father had been succeeded by son since 987 and where, in 1131, Louis VI had been able to have his son anointed and crowned in his own lifetime. In Germany, on the other hand, the opposition to hereditary monarchy was both determined and strong. Matilda herself had reason to know this, since on the death of her first husband, the Emperor Henry V, in 1125, the nobles had deliberately rejected his next-of-kin, even though he had been designated, in order to elect a man of another family. In England the hereditary principle, if not opposed in theory, had been consistently ignored in practice. Edward the Confessor, Harold Godwinson, William the Conqueror, William Rufus and Henry I had all been 'elected' king, although they had none of them been their predecessor's nearest male heir. It is true that they were all of royal or quasi-royal blood; but it is one thing to say that no man could be a king unless he had kingly blood in his veins, and quite another to insist on a definite rule of descent whereby a king's eldest son was obliged to succeed his father on the throne, no matter what he, his father, or anyone else wanted. In this

---

[18] Stephen's Oxford charter of liberties, 1136, printed W. Stubbs, *Select Charters* (9th ed., 1913), 143.

respect Stephen's reign marked the end of an era. Stephen himself was 'elected' like his predecessors, but at the end of his reign he made Duke Henry his heir by hereditary right (*jure hereditario*) and undertook to maintain him as his son and heir (*sicut filium et heredem*).[19] Thereafter the strict rule of the hereditary system has been applied to the English monarchy, almost without a break, until the present day.[20] It was one thing which was decided by the civil war of Stephen's reign.

The reign was equally decisive for the nobility. Though the Norman barons had long considered their lands and titles hereditary, it was not until 1154 that they had been able to make their position secure. The Conquest had, as Maitland put it, thrown into the hands of the Norman kings 'a power of reviving the element of precariousness which was involved in the inheritance of a *beneficium* or *feodum*'. Because of the Conquest, and as expounded on every page of Domesday Book, all land belonged to the king, and the barons were merely his tenants or sub-tenants. In theory therefore they could not hold their lands by hereditary right. In practice the king normally allowed his barons to be succeeded by their sons, because every refusal involved a serious risk of revolt, but (to quote Maitland again) 'there is hardly a strict right to inherit when there is no settled rule about reliefs and the heir must make the best bargain he can with the king'.[21] William Rufus charged the sons of deceased barons such heavy reliefs that they complained that he was making them buy back (*redimere*) their fathers' lands, and Henry I in his coronation charter promised, along with many other promises which he did not keep, that he would stop this practice and charge only a 'just and lawful relief'.[22] It may be noticed that of the grants which Henry I made to laymen, only about half (and those mainly in the second half of the reign) were stated to be hereditary, and it still remained the practice that whenever a lord founded a monastery on 'his' land, he needed a charter from the king, since the land was really the king's and could only be alienated by him.

There were various ways in which the king could interfere with the normal rules of inheritance. The first was by forfeiture, the penalty exacted for treason. Since revolts were numerous, especially when Duke Robert was disputing the succession with William II and Henry I, the amount of land involved in forfeitures was large. In the sixty years between 1075 and 1135 forfeitures included the great fiefs of Roger de Breteuil son of William fitz Osbern (1075), Ralph Guader Earl of Norfolk (1075), Odo of Bayeux (1088), Roger de Mowbray nephew of Geoffrey Bishop of Coutances (1095), Robert of Bellême, Roger of Poitou and Arnulf of Pembroke, the three sons of Roger de Mont-

---

[19] Treaty of Westminster, 1153, printed in *Foedera* (1704), i. 13, and *H.M.C. Twelfth Report, App. ix* (1891), 119–21.

[20] In the present context the most important exception was John, but he, even though he had been designated by his predecessor, found it necessary to murder the lawful heir.

[21] Sir Frederick Pollock and Frederic William Maitland, *The History of English Law before the time of Edward I* (Cambridge, 1895), ii. 19.

[22] W. Stubbs, *Select Charters* (9th ed., 1913), 118.

gomery (1102), William son of Robert Count of Mortain (1106), Robert de Stuteville (1106) and Robert de Lacy (1115); the total value of their land amounted to about one eighth of all the land surveyed in Domesday Book. The king did not keep all these forfeitures in his own hand; while he did so, it would have been thought that there was still a possibility of his pardoning the offender and restoring his lands. When he wanted the forfeiture to be irrevocable—as the forfeitures mentioned were—he would give the land to one or more of his barons, for he could trust them to see that the forfeited man recovered nothing at their expense, even if, as was likely, he pursued them with an implacable feud.

A less obvious method of interfering with the hereditary system was by means of escheats and exchanges. A fief escheated to the king when one of his tenants died without an heir; but feudal genealogies were complicated, and it was for the king to decide whether there was an heir or not. It could therefore happen that a baron thought he ought to have inherited land which had escheated to the king; in 1141, for example, Geoffrey de Mandeville was claiming as his right (*ut rectum suum*) the land of Eudo *Dapifer* which had escheated in 1120.[23] Half-way between a dubious escheat and an exchange was the way in which Henry I dealt with the earldom of Chester after the death of Earl Richard in the White Ship (1120). Earl Richard had left no direct male heir, but his cousin Ranulf de Meschin had a claim through the female line, his mother being Earl Richard's aunt. Henry I granted him the earldom, but only in exchange for other lands which he held already; Ranulf found himself obliged to surrender first the large estates of Lucy his wife (though in doing so he disinherited his stepson, William de Roumare, who not unnaturally revolted), and secondly the honour of Carlisle which was his 'own', and which it became the lifelong ambition of himself and his son to regain.[24]

Orderic Vitalis is full of stories about exchanges and forfeitures and the feuds which derived from them. One of the most striking concerns the castle of Brionne in Normandy and is worth quoting because of the vivid light which it throws on the conflicting doctrines of tenure and inheritance. The trouble started in 1090 when Count Robert of Meulan insolently demanded the restoration of the castle of Ivry, which his father had exchanged with the Duke of Normandy for Brionne. When reminded of the exchange, he said he did not agree with it, and insisted on having Ivry as his rightful inheritance. The duke put an end to the argument by imprisoning him in the castle of Brionne itself under the custody of Robert fitz Gilbert. There he kept him until, by the efforts of his father, he was not only pardoned, but allowed to buy back his castle. That was where the complications began, for when the duke ordered Robert fitz Gilbert to surrender Brionne to his former prisoner,

[23] J. H. Round, *Geoffrey de Mandeville* (London, 1892), pp. 167, 173.
[24] *Orderici Vitalis . . . Historiae Ecclesiasticae Libri Tredecim*, ed. Augustus Le Prévost, 5 vols. (Sociéte de l'histoire de France, Paris, 1838–55), iv. 422, 442.

he refused, claiming that he himself had an even better hereditary right
to it. His answer to the duke (according to Orderic) ran as follows:

> If it be your desire to have Brionne as your father [William the Con-
> queror] had it in his own demesne (*proprietate*) I will make no difficulty in
> delivering it to you; but otherwise I will keep my inheritance and will hand
> it over to no one while I live. It is well-known to all the natives of the pro-
> vince that Richard the elder, duke of Normandy [966–96], granted Brionne
> with its whole county to his son Godfrey, and that he on his death left it to
> his son Gilbert. Then, when Gilbert was cruelly murdered by wicked
> men [1040] and his sons' tutors had together with the boys fled for fear of
> their enemies to Baldwin [V] of Flanders, your father [William I] attached
> part of my grandfather's county to his own demesne and divided the rest
> at his will among strangers [e.g. the Counts of Meulan]. A long time
> afterwards, when he married the daughter of Baldwin of Flanders, the
> duke [William I] at his request restored Meules and Le Sap to my father,
> Baldwin [fitz Gilbert], and gave him his aunt's daughter in marriage; re-
> storing also Bienfaite and Orbec to his brother Richard [fitz Gilbert]. At
> length by your favour, my lord, whom it is my desire to obey in all things,
> I am now [1090] in possession of Brionne, the principal town of my
> grandfather, and, God supporting my right, I will keep it to the end.[25]

The speech burns so fiercely with the indignation of the expropriated
that it is hard to remember that the Counts of Meulan felt just as
strongly about Brionne themselves. They had held it for the previous
fifty years, even if Robert fitz Gilbert's family had held it for the fifty
years before that; and they too regarded it as their inheritance.

Such cases were not uncommon, but there were many more which
had been caused not by the direct, but by the indirect action of the
king. This was particularly true in the reign of Henry I, when the 'new
men' whom he had 'raised from the dust' were creating their family
fortunes. Professor Southern has recently studied the rise of these 'new
men', which he compares with the 'rise of the gentry' in the sixteenth
century, and he has shown that Henry I managed to reward them
without noticeably reducing the royal demesne, because he gave them
the lands of other people.[26] Those of his servants who were loyal could
rely on him to turn a blind eye if, like Richard Basset, they appropriated
lands which had been granted to them only in wardship. Nigel
d'Aubigny, the king's chief agent in the North, confessed, when he thought
he was dying, to having disinherited in whole or in part Robert de
Cambos, Robert de Witville, William fitz Warin, Ralph de Paveli,
Ralph de Buce, the sons of Anseis, Hugh of Rampan, Butin, Gerald,
Burnulf, Humphrey de Hastings and Russell de Langford. Geoffrey
de Clinton, who was the king's chief treasurer as well as one of his
justices, succeeded in founding and endowing the abbey of Kenilworth

---

[25] *Orderici Vitalis*, iii. 339–40.
[26] R. W. Southern, 'The Place of Henry I in English History', *Proc. of the British Academy*,
xlviii (1962), 127–69, from which I have taken the following details.

with other people's land. The methods of expropriation were generally gradual, but they were none the less effective. If we make a test of the 193 baronies listed by Dr. I. J. Sanders as having been in existence in 1135, we find that only 102, or less than 52·9 per cent, had descended in the male line since 1086. In the course of fifty years 47 (or 24·3 per cent) had suffered escheat or forfeiture, 21 (or 10·9 per cent) had changed dynasty because of the marriage of heiresses, and 23 (or 11·9 per cent) had been formed out of royal demesne or other people's lands (2 of them in the reign of William II and the remaining 21 in the reign of Henry I).[27]

In these circumstances it was inevitable that there should be endless family feuds over the inheritance of land. Professor Southern quotes the case of William Maltravers who was murdered almost as soon as the death of Henry I was known, so that Ilbert de Lacy could recover the honour of Pontefract which Henry I had taken from his father.[28] This case was peculiarly dramatic, but as a feud it was otherwise typical. In every county examples could be found of families with rival hereditary claims to the same honour or fief, and in the civil war they automatically joined opposing camps. An amusing example is provided by the inheritance of the other, or Herefordshire, Lacys, which was disputed between Miles of Gloucester and Gilbert de Lacy. Up till 1139 Miles was for Stephen and Gilbert for Matilda, but in that year Miles changed sides and went over to Matilda; Gilbert promptly went over to Stephen.[29] The earldoms of Huntingdon and Northampton were claimed by both Henry son of the King of the Scots and Simon de Senlis; Henry was for Matilda and Simon for Stephen. The Marmions and the Worcestershire Beauchamps had rival claims to Tamworth; Marmion supported Stephen and Beauchamp Matilda. Robert de Montfort, who supported the Angevins, claimed (but never got) the honour of Haughley which was held by Stephen's successive constables, Robert de Vere and Henry of Essex. Stephen himself had a feud with Richer de l'Aigle to whom Henry I had given the honour of Pevensey when he had given Stephen most of the other lands of the Count of Mortain. Ranulf Earl of Chester considered himself the heir of Robert Malet whose lands Henry I had bestowed on Stephen; but he was never sure where his real interest lay for he also considered Cumberland to be his, and that had been given by Matilda to her uncle David, the King of the Scots. Most involved of all were the rival claims to the earldom of Hereford which Roger de Breteuil, the son of William fitz Osbern, had forfeited in 1075. Orderic Vitalis tells how his sons, Robert and Reginald, were still alive and hoping to regain their inheritance; but Stephen granted the county, if not the earldom, to Robert Earl of Leicester who had

---

[27] I. J. Sanders, *English Baronies: a study of their origin and descent, 1086–1327* (Oxford, 1960).
[28] Richard of Hexham, ed. Howlett, *op. cit.* iii. 140.
[29] R. H. C. Davis, 'Treaty between William Earl of Gloucester and Roger Earl of Hereford', in *A Medieval Miscellany for Doris Mary Stenton*, ed. Patricia M. Barnes and C. F. Slade (Pipe Roll Soc., New Series xxxvi, 1960), p. 140; see below, p. 256.

married fitz Osbern's granddaughter.[30] Matilda parried by granting the
earldom to Miles of Gloucester who, as one of Henry I's 'new men', had
made his fortune out of other people's lands, disinheriting in the process
Emmelina de Ballon of her honour of Abergavenny. It was not sur-
prising that her hand was sought and won by Roger de Breteuil's son,
Reginald fitz Count, who had come over from Normandy to support
Stephen, in the hope that Stephen might grant him 'his' earldom of
Hereford now that Robert of Leicester was lapsing into neutrality.[31]

Wherever we turn, the politics of Stephen's reign seem to dissolve
into family history. Round noticed the fact and commented on 'the
tendency, in this reign, of the magnates to advance quasi-hereditary
claims often involving, as it were, the undoing of the work of Henry I'.[32]
Round called them *quasi*-hereditary because he thought that they were
nothing more than an excuse for making hereditary demands of the
king, but when he came to disentangle the genealogies he proved that
they were real. They were, in fact, the heart of the matter. According
to both William of Malmesbury and the *Gesta Stephani*, the turning-
point in Matilda's career was when, with Stephen in captivity, she
thought that she could rob his son of his inheritance, refusing to let him
have the counties of Boulogne and Mortain, and perhaps even promising them to supporters of her own.[33] It was this attempted disinheritance that turned Henry of Blois against her and persuaded
Stephen's queen to renew the war. When the war was eventually
brought to an end by the Treaty of Westminster (1153), it was agreed
that Duke Henry should have the kingdom by hereditary right, and that
Stephen's son William should have all the lands which Stephen held
before he became king, and all the lands which his wife had inherited
from the Earl of Warenne. It was specifically stated that those lands
which were in Normandy, and therefore under Duke Henry's control,
were to be returned to William together with their castles, and there
was even a clause to say that he should have the honour of Pevensey,
that part of the Count of Mortain's fee which Henry I had given, not
to Stephen, but to Richer de l'Aigle.[34]

Similar security was given to Stephen's supporters. There was no
disinheritance except in the case of William Peverel who was accused
of having poisoned Ranulf Earl of Chester. On the contrary everything
was done to preserve the *status quo*. Gilbert de Lacy, a most vigorous
supporter of King Stephen, kept his inheritance in spite of the expressed
determination of the Earl of Hereford to disinherit him. The earldoms
of Huntingdon and Northampton were divided between the King of
the Scots and the family of Senlis. Robert Earl of Leicester who went

---

[30] Orderic Vitalis, ed. Le Prévost, ii. 264–5; H. W. C. Davis, 'Some Documents of the
Anarchy', in *Essays Presented to Reginald Lane Poole*, ed. H. W. C. Davis (Oxford, 1927), 172–6.
[31] J. H. Round, *Studies in Peerage and Family History* (London, 1901), 201–6.
[32] *Geoffrey de Mandeville*, 154; cf. 313.
[33] *Historia Novella* (ed. Potter), para. 498, and *Gesta Stephani* (ed. Potter), p. 81.
[34] Treaty of Westminster, see n. 19.

over to Duke Henry in 1153 made his inheritance secure by obtaining a charter for his son as well as a charter for himself, and recovered his wife's inheritance in Normandy, the Norman lands of Roger de Breteuil, even though the earldom of Hereford was left to the 'new' family of Miles of Gloucester. Robert fitz Harding, a zealous supporter of Duke Henry, not only received separate charters for his son and himself but also made a double marriage alliance with Roger de Berkeley who claimed the same inheritance; and his descendants are still in possession of his lands more than 800 years later.

By such compromises most of the disputed inheritances could be settled, but there were bound to be some intractable cases where marriage alliances or tacit agreements were impossible. In these cases rival branches of a family, or two separate families, might continue to nurse their grievances and revive the feud at the first possible moment, as when Robert de Montfort successfully accused his rival, Henry of Essex, of cowardice in the face of the Welsh when he was the king's standard-bearer (1163). But such cases ceased to be common, since after 1154 the King and his agents were no longer going out of their way to create or inflame rival hereditary claims; they had learnt by the bitter experience of Stephen's reign that the proliferation of such claims merely ensured the continuance of civil war. Henry II and his successors made no attempt to behave as if all land was the king's, and all the barons merely tenants. They began to respect the right of every family to its own property and were sparing in their forfeitures; only three of the baronies listed by Dr. Sanders were forfeited between 1154 and 1204. More important still, however, was the elaboration by Henry II of the doctrine of *seisin*. One advantage of this doctrine was that it cut short the argument about proprietary right and protected the man in actual possession at some stated date in the recent past. But seisin was more than mere possession; it implied not only the enjoyment of property but also its *lawful* enjoyment. It provided the lawyers with a convenient transition from the notion of feudal tenure to that of hereditary ownership. As Professor S. E. Thorne has recently shown, the use of it in the assize of *mort d'ancestor* (1176) marked the decisive stage in the establishment of the hereditary principle.[35] Thenceforward the king could no longer pretend that a baron's son succeeded to his father of mere grace, or that the solemn re-granting of the land by the king was anything but a formality. He recognized that it was the right of every heir to inherit his ancestor's land. Just as the crown had become hereditary, so had the nobility.

That was what had happened in Stephen's reign. In one sense it could still be held that the reign was, as Round had claimed, an inevitable reaction against Henry I's rule. But whereas Round thought that the barons were reacting against centralized government, the truth

---

[35] S. E. Thorne, 'English Feudalism and Estates in Land', *Cambridge Law Journal*, 1959, 193–209.

would seem to be that they were reacting against the notion that their lands were merely tenements which they held at the king's pleasure. They wanted their lands to be their own, so that they could become lords of a particular place, have an ancestral castle or seat, and blazon their shields with heraldic devices which proclaimed the bond between family and fief. They demanded that the King should recognize their hereditary right in specific and unambiguous terms, declaring as he declared to Geoffrey de Mandeville, *quod ipse et heredes sui post eum hereditario jure teneant de me et de heredibus meis.*[36] That was what the barons fought for in Stephen's reign, and that is what they won.[37]

[36] *Geoffrey de Mandeville*, 52. The same emphasis may be noted in all four charters.
[37] My thanks are due to Messrs. G. D. G. Hall and M. Maclagan and Professor V. H. Galbraith for helpful suggestions and vigorous criticism.

13

Geoffrey de Mandeville Reconsidered

In a famous historical study, J. H. Round reconstructed the career of
Geoffrey de Mandeville as ' the most perfect and typical presentment
of the feudal and anarchic spirit that stamps the reign of Stephen '.[1]
He showed, or attempted to show, that in the civil war Geoffrey
consistently sold his support to the highest bidder. He claimed that
Geoffrey was created earl of Essex by Stephen between June and
December 1140, went over to Matilda in the summer of 1141 for a
confirmation of his earldom with additional grants, back to Stephen
later in the same year for a higher price, and back to Matilda before
June 1142 for a higher price still, finally being arrested by Stephen in
September 1143. Such a rapid change of sides, involving grants
from the opposing parties every six months between 1140 and 1142,
assumes not only a complete lack of loyalty on Geoffrey's part, but
also the most astonishing gullibility on the part of both Stephen and
Matilda. It is only natural to ask whether Round's reconstruction
of events was correct.

The evidence on which Round based his work was derived from
charters. As he himself put it (p. v):

> The headings of my chapters express a fact upon which I cannot too
> strongly insist, namely, that the charters granted to Geoffrey are the
> very backbone of my work. By those charters it must stand or fall:
> for on their relation and their evidence the whole narrative is built.

There were four of these charters, two granted by King Stephen and
two by the Empress Matilda. Round's first task was to date them
and put them in chronological order. This was no easy matter—
Dugdale and Eyton had already attempted the problem and come to
different conclusions—but Round had the advantage of a new
method. He decided *first* to put the charters in order, and *then* to
determine their dates (p. 43):

> To determine from internal evidence the sequence of these charters,
> we must first arrange them in an ascending scale. That is to say,

---

[1] J. H. Round, *Geoffrey de Mandeville* (London, 1892). All page references given in
the text are to this book.

each charter should represent an advance on its immediate predecessor. Tried by this test, our four main charters will assume, beyond
dispute, this relative order

    (1) First charter of the King [$S1$]
    (2) First charter of the Empress [$M1$]
    (3) Second charter of the King [$S2$]
    (4) Second charter of the Empress [$M2$]

This ' relative order ' is the major assumption of Round's thesis, but
it is not justified. The extent of a grant made by a king to one of his
barons is indicative not of the date, but of the favour with which he
regarded that baron. Some barons rose in favour, others fell, and
some both rose and fell, or fell and rose again. There is therefore no
necessary connection between the ' ascending scale ' and the chronological order of the grants. Round simply assumed that there was,
and arguing in a vicious circle, proceeded to ' prove ' that each
successive grant was larger than the one before.

We must therefore dismiss the theory of the ' ascending scale '
and attempt to date the charters individually. Fortunately two of
them can be dated with confidence. $M1$, ' the first charter of the
Empress ' was issued at Westminster and must therfore be dated
about midsummer 1141, the only occasion in the reign when she was
there. $S2$, or Stephen's ' second charter ' must be subsequent to the
king's release from capitivity (1 November 1141) since it refers to
' the day on which I (the king) was ensnared and captured at Lincoln '
(p. 140) and has the appearance of a formal reconciliation with
Geoffrey de Mandeville. Round dated it ' Christmas 1141 ', and
this, or a date very close to it, would be hard to dispute. The real
difficulty lies with the two other charters.

The one about which Round himself felt that 'there could possibly
be a question ' was $S1$, but the date which he suggested, though it
may be revised in detail, was probably not far off the mark.[1] Its
absolute limits of date are wide. It cannot be earlier than December
1139, for it makes Geoffrey an earl; and in a writ which referred to
' the day on which Bishop Roger of Salisbury was alive and dead '
(4/11 December 1139) Geoffrey was addressed, not as an earl, but as
plain *Gaufrido de Magnavilla* (p. 46). On the other hand it cannot be
later than Geoffrey's fall about September 1143. These are the
closest limits which can be fixed with certainty, though there is a

---

[1] One reason for his hesitation may have been that his dating of this charter involved
the re-dating of Stephen's second seal. *A priori* one would have expected (as previous
historians and antiquaries had done) Stephen's change of seal to have been
connected with his captivity in 1141. Round gave reasons for thinking that the change
had in fact occurred earlier, at the time of the arrest of the bishops in June 1139, and
these seem to be sound. Even if we ignore $S1$ there are two originals of
Stephen's charters with fragments of his second seal which must be earlier than the
battle of Lincoln. (Round, *Ancient Charters (Pipe Rolls Soc.* x, 1888), no. 23, and *Sir
Christopher Hatton's book of Seals,* ed. L. C. Loyd and D. M. Stenton (1950), no. 110.)

strong probability that the charter is also prior to Stephen's captivity, and therefore to his departure from London for Lincoln in December 1140. Though we have to reject Round's argument from the ' ascending scale ' of the charters, his argument from the terms of the creation (p. 97) seems valid; and it may be added that the presence of Robert of Neufbourg as a witness is also suggestive (though not proof) of a date before the battle of Lincoln.[1] At the other end of the scale, however, Round's argument for a date later than ' June or August 1140 ' is inadmissible, because it is based on the date which he attributed to another charter in the mistaken belief that Richard de Luci did not witness in England before the summer of 1140.[2] *S1* should therefore be dated December 1139–September 1143, and most probably before December 1140.[3]

It may be remarked in passing, that in connection with *S1*, Round complicated matters unnecessarily by his treatment of the story of Geoffrey's alleged detention of Constance of France, the bride of Eustace the king's son (pp. 47–48). Round took the story from William of Newburgh (who was writing almost sixty years after the event) and attempted to date it by assuming that Constance had come to England immediately after her betrothal in February 1140, and that it was actually on her arrival in England that she was detained by Geoffrey. In fact William says nothing about Constance's arrival in London; he merely says that she was (*erat*) there at the beginning of his story, and the most plausible date that can be suggested for it is not 1140 but 1141.[4] If we guess that Stephen had left his queen and daughter-in-law in London when he marched north to Lincoln at the

---

[1] Robert de Neufbourg was certainly on Stephen's side in 1138, witnessing a charter of his at Goldington during the siege of Bedford in Jan. 1138 (Watkin, *Great Chartulary of Glastonbury*, i. 129–30), and acting as one of Stephen's justiciars at Rouen on 18 Dec. 1138 (Haskins, *Norman Institutions*, p. 92). He was subsequently very active in the service of Geoffrey of Anjou in Normandy (Haskins, pp. 145–9) his earliest attestation for Geoffrey being earlier than 1144–5: (Bourrienne, *Antiquus Cartularius Ecclesie Baiocensis,* i. 24 (no. xvii). Bourrienne wrongly attributes this deed to Henry rather than Geoffrey; it is necessarily earlier than no. xxxix which can be dated 1144–5). It is natural to assume that Robert changed sides in 1141.

[2] *Geoffrey de Mandeville* p. 49, cf. pp. 146 and 201 n. An unpublished charter of Stephen's in favour of William de Corbeil, archbishop of Canterbury (d. 21 Nov. 1136) shows Richard de Luci attesting at Oxford before that date: Lambeth Palace, MS. 1212, p. 25. In Oct. 1138 he was in Normandy, as Stephen's commander of Falaise: *Orderic Vitalis,* bk. xiii, ch. 38. He was back in England in 1139, for he witnessed a charter of Stephen's at Reading which, when compared with its companion-piece by Stephen's queen, must be dated Oct. 1138–Sept. 1139, after the arrival of William of Ypres and before the defection of Miles of Gloucester. The charter is printed in *Monasticon* (1823), vi. 843, Lees, *Records of the Templars,* p. 177, and Leys, *Sandford Cartulary,* i. 34.

[3] A curious feature of *S1* is that though it is a charter of creation it is not witnessed by any bishops or earls, and not even by William Martel or Robert de Vere who, as steward and constable, were the king's most frequent witnesses. On the other hand, four of the fifteen witnesses were, as Round showed, Geoffrey's own sub-tenants. It is hard to find a convincing explanation for all these facts, but William of Malmesbury (*Historia Novella,* para. 486) noted that when Stephen spent Whitsun 1140 (26 May) at London, the only bishop to attend his court was the bishop of Séez.

[4] I owe this suggestion to Professor H. A. Cronne.

end of 1140, the story as a whole will fit neatly into the months between February and November 1141, when Stephen was in captivity and Geoffrey (at least from mid-June to early September) on the side of the Empress. The passage may be translated as follows :

> . . . And she [Constance] was with her mother-in-law in London. And when' the queen wished to move with her daughter-in-law to some other strong place, this Geoffrey (then in charge of the Tower) withstood her. He took the daughter-in-law from her mother-in-law, who resisted might and main, and kept her in custody, allowing the mother-in-law to go away in ignominy [before June 1141]. Afterwards [on his release in November] the King her father-in-law, concealing for the time-being his legitimate rage, asked for her back, and Geoffrey reluctantly surrendered his prize.[1]

With this chronology the story is at least plausible, even if it does nothing to improve Geoffrey's reputation.

A far more serious problem is involved in the dating of *M2*. At first sight it seems straightforward. Since it was issued at Oxford it must belong to the period when the empress held that city (February 1141–December 1142); since it is witnessed by Miles earl of Hereford it must be subsequent to his creation as earl (25 July 1141); and since it was also witnessed by Robert earl of Gloucester it must be earlier than the end of June 1142, when he left England for Normandy, never to enter Oxford again.[2] Round claimed that even narrower limits could be fixed:

> From internal evidence (he wrote) it is absolutely certain that this charter [*M2*] is subsequent to that dealt with in the last chapter [*S2*]. That is to say it must be dated subsequent to Christmas 1141 (p. 163).

One reason for his ' certainty ' was the doctrine of the ' ascending scale' of charters, which we have dismissed. A second, and seemingly more formidable, reason was that Stephen's second charter [*S2*] was ' expressly referred to ' in *M2* (p. 43) ; but though it is indisputable that in *M2* the empress did refer to charters of King Stephen and his queen, it is to be doubted whether those charters can be identified with *S2*. The basis for my doubt is no longer the same as in 1964 (see Postscript on p. 211). I accept that there are three grants in *S2* which occur also in *M2* with riders that they had originally been granted by King Stephen and Queen Matilda 'as their charters testify', but I do not agree that this amounts to a 'clear reference' to *S2*. On the contrary, the reference is to the charters in which the grants were

c [100] libris, et Writelam pro vi.   ildis Regina ei dederunt.
xx [120] libris, et Hadfeld pro
quater xx [80] libris

---

[1] Quoted in *Geoffrey de Mandeville*, p. 47, n. 2, from *Chronicles of the Reigns of Stephen, Henry II and Richard I*, ed. R. Howlett (Rolls Series, 1884), i. 45.

[2] William of Malmesbury, *Historia Novella*, paras. 518 and 521–3; *cf. Geoffrey de Mandeville*, p. 163.

orginally made. *S2* is not a series of new grants but a systematic catalogue of all the grants and charters which the King had given to Geoffrey during his reign and which, after the turmoil of 1141, he wished to confirm. It is also a charter by the King alone, while the references in *M2* are to charters of the King *and Queen*, which would most naturally suggest charters of the Queen for her Honor of Boulogne with confirmations by her overlord the King. Twenty-three of her honorial charters survive, many of them with the King's confirmation; and though none of them are for Geoffrey de Mandeville, it is a fact that of the grants confirmed to him in *M2* and *S2*, six concern manors, and three knights of her Honor of Boulogne, all of them indicated in Round's footnotes. Round ignored these indications, preferring to hypothesize that there had been a charter issued by the Queen around August 1141 when she was acting as regent, and that it must have been comprehensive, containing most, if not all, of the items confirmed in *S2*. This double assumption provided him with the 'proof' he needed for his theory, but he never drew attention to the fact that we have no example of any charter issued by Queen Matilda as regent anywhere.

If *M2* need not be later than *S2*, then Round's date of 'January-June 1142' for *M2* is not 'certain' but merely conjectural; and as a conjecture it has difficulties. It is hard to see why, having twice transferred to the winning side in 1141, Geoffrey should suddenly have gone over to the empress at a moment when her cause was, as Round put it, 'desperate' (p. 163); it is difficult to understand why, having gone over to her cause, he did nothing to help her; and it is simply incredible that after the empress had given him this charter (a veritable treaty with twenty-five 'hostages' or witnesses), Geoffrey could have kept it dark from Stephen, not just for a few weeks, but for more than a year. During that period, the *Gesta Stephani* tells us that he was exercising the most extensive powers in Stephen's name (*ubique per regnum regis vices adimplens*),[1] and he was evidently attending court, for it was at court that Stephen took him unawares and arrested him; and yet we are asked to believe that all this time he had the empress's charter in his pocket, and that none of Stephen's other followers had noticed his disappearance to the enemy camp at Oxford. If his treason had been as specific as Round suggested, we would have expected to find traces of some specific accusation in the chronicles. In fact the *Gesta Stephani* is distinctly non-committal in its reference to treason, and suggests that the real reason for the arrest was simply that Geoffrey had become an overmighty subject.[2] William of Newburgh has to look back as far as the detention of Constance of France to find a motive for Stephen[3]; and Henry of Huntingdon declares that the arrest was made *magis secundum*

---

[1] *Gesta Stephani*, ed. K. R. Potter (London, 1955), p. 107.
[2] *Ibid.* pp. 106–7. [3] See p. 206, n. 1.

retributionem nequitiae consulis quam secundum jus gentium, magis ex necessitate quam ex honestate.[1]

There is nothing here to suggest treason, which would certainly have been a breach of the ' law of nations ', nor anything to contradict the account of the arrest given in the *Liber de Fundatione* of Walden Abbey, of which Geoffrey was the founder:

> Geoffrey Earl of Essex, a knight well tried in arms, was at that time in faithful obedience to the King's party against his rival [the empress].   At length, however, some of the greater men of the kingdom, spurred on by envy, said wicked things about him, and secretly and mendaciously denounced him to the King as a traitor to the King and betrayer of his country.   After a short time in fact, when a council was assembled at St. Albans, this noble man alone, when everyone else was leaving, was arrested by trickery (*fraudulenter*), being detained by guards who had been posted to prevent his departure.   And though many of his friends bore it ill that such things should be done to him unjustly and appealed to the king on his behalf, he could in no wise escape, although he unwillingly gave up his castles.   He surrendered the Tower of London, Walden and Pleshey with immense rancour of spirit, and thus without a castle left, went forthwith away [to avenge himself by rebellion].[2]

It seems that Stephen's arrest of Geofrey de Mandeville, like his arrest of the bishops in 1139 and of the earl of Chester in 1146, was made not on any specific evidence, but rather in nervous anticipation of the danger of over-powerful subjects.   If the accusation had really involved the charge of receiving this charter [*M2*] from the empress, we may wonder why the hostages and witnesses named in it did not share in Geoffrey's disgrace.   One of them, Gilbert earl of Pembroke, remained in favour at the king's court until 1146.

If there are difficulties in dating *M2* after Christmas 1141, we should explore the possibility of dating it earlier.   In this case it would have to be before 14 September 1141, by which date Geoffrey was back on Stephen's side and fighting for him at the battle of Winchester[3]; and since the charter was issued at Oxford, it would also have to be earlier than 1 August by when the empress had left that city for the siege of Winchester.[4]   That leaves only one week when the charter could have been granted, since its earliest possible date (as we have already seen) is 25 July.   This is roughly the date which Eyton suggested, though Round did not discuss it.[5]   Can it be substantiated?

---

[1] *Henrici Archidiaconi Huntendunensis Historia Anglorum,* ed. T. Arnold (Rolls Series, 1879), p. 276.

[2] *Monasticon* (1823), iv. 142.   There is no complete edition of this chronicle, though a translation of it by Hubert Collar is to be found in vols. 45–47 of the *Essex Review* (1936–8).   [3] William of Malmesbury, *Historia Novella,* para. 499.

[4] The date is given by the Gloucester continuator of Florence of Worcester (ed. Thorpe, ii. 133), *appropinquante festivitate Sancti Petri quae dicitur Ad Vincula.*

[5] Quoted by Round, *Geoffrey de Mandeville,* p. 41.

It suits the list of witnesses, even without the hostages, admirably. Six of the ten, Robert Earl of Gloucester, Robert fitz Regis, Brien fitz Count, John fitz Gilbert, Robert de Courcy and Ralph Paganel, witnessed the charter creating Miles of Gloucester earl of Hereford on 25 July 1141, at Oxford. Miles himself, as Earl of Hereford was a seventh witness, and two of the remaining three were extremely rare, the complete list of their attestations for the Empress anywhere being as follows:

Miles de Beauchamp	Robert fitz Hildebrand
Reg. iii 68 at Oxford, last week of July, 1141, for William de Beauchamp	*Reg.* iii 274 at Westminster, Mid-summer 1141, *M1*, for Geoffrey de Mandeville
	Reg. iii 378. No place-date (but *Reg.* iii 377 suggests Oxford, June/July 1141) for Haughmond
Reg. iii 64 at Oxford, Creation of Aubrey de Vere	*Reg.* iii 634 at Oxford, Creation of Aubrey de Vere
Reg. 275 at Oxford *M2*	*Reg.* 275 at Oxford, *M2*

The last two are bracketed because, as Round explained, they were ' not only granted simultaneously, but formed the complements of one connected whole ' (p. 179). It is hard to imagine that they do not also belong to July 1141.[2]

Such a date would suit the general tenor of the charter and make sense of its references to London. At the end of July, when they had both fled from London, it would not have been unnatural for the empress to have offered Geoffrey the sheriffdoms and justiciarships of London, Middlesex, Essex and Hertford, the castle of Bishop's Stortford (if she could persuade the bishop to give it up) and another castle on the River Lea. From the empress's point of view the Londoners simply had to be prevented from joining the king's supporters in the Midlands, and the only man who could possibly save the situation for her was Geoffrey de Mandeville. She was inviting him to reduce the city of London and its northern approaches to obedience, and she was giving him *carte blanche*. That was why she had to provide hostages for her good faith, for she was merely promising to let him keep things which he would have to win for himself. That would also seem to be the reason why she promised Geoffrey that she would not make peace with the Londoners ' because they were his mortal enemies ' (*quia inimici eius sunt mortales*, p. 168). It is hard to see how she could possibly have made such a statement

---

[1] In *Calendar of Documents preserved in France* (London, 1899), no. 999, Round prints *Willelmo de Sablaillo,* but the MS. (Archives d'Eure-et-Loir, H. 1374, fo. 49) reads *Wid one] de Sablaill[o].* It may also be noted that Wido de Sablé has to be distinguished from William Diffublato; they are two different people.

[2] Round made considerable use of Aubrey's comital style for the dating of charters. It is therefore important if Aubrey was made an earl, not in 1142, but in 1141.

after 14 September 1141, when Geoffrey de Mandeville and the
Londoners had fought in alliance against her at Winchester.

As Round pointed out *M2* contains two references to *M1* (p. 167,
line 9 and p. 168, line 18), but their casualness—*sicut . . . per aliam
cartam meam confirmavi* suggests, not that the two charters were far removed in time, but that they were complementary to each other. *M1*
was a simple grant by the empress to Earl Geoffrey; *M2* was more in
the nature of a formal treaty (*convencionem et donationem*, p. 170, line 12)
with guarantees. If, in the interval between them, Geoffrey had
deserted the empress and returned to the service of the king, we might
have expected some hint of the affair. Instead we find that in *M2*
Geoffrey and his men are granted the assarts which they had made
usque ad diem qua servicio domini mei Comitis Andegaviae et mea adhesit (p.
168, line 22). It was not thought necessary to state whether the day
intended was the day when Geoffrey had *first* or *last* adhered to the
empress; presumably she knew of only one occasion, and only one
day, when he had come over to her cause.

If these arguments are accepted, the order of the charters granted
to Geoffrey de Mandeville will have to be revised as follows:

(1) First charter of the King [*S1*], probably Dec. 1139–Dec. 1140
(2) First charter of the Empress [*M1*] c. 22 June 1141
(3) Second charter of the Empress [*M2*] 25 July–1 Aug. 1141
(4) Second charter of the King [*S2*] Christmas 1141

The importance of this re-arrangement is that it destroys Round's
conception of Geoffrey as a professional turncoat. If we are correct,
Geoffrey's revolt of 1143–4 would have been due not to any calculated plot on his part, but to a natural impulse to avenge the wrong
which Stephen had done him by arresting him without due cause.
The one occasion on which he deliberately went over to the empress
would have been in 1141 when the king was in captivity and his
cause seemed lost. Even then Geoffrey reverted to his former
loyalty at almost the first opportunity, and his conduct—except for
his infamous treatment of Stephen's queen—could be represented as
no worse than that of a very large number of bishops and barons,
including the king's own brother, Henry of Blois. If Geoffrey
was a typical baron, he was not typical in the way which Round
suggested.

Our view of Stephen's conduct must also be changed. He excused Geoffrey's desertion in 1141, as he excused the desertion of his
own brother, but though he restored him his lands and his powers,
he was evidently wary of him. As William of Newburgh put it,
' the king cautiously disguised the injury which he had been done by
him, and waited for a favourable moment when he could avenge
himself '.[1] So far from being gullible, he was nervous and distrust-

ful, forgetting nothing and forgiving nothing. He might be sly in the way in which he took his revenge, but he did not allow his barons to desert him with impunity.[1]

[1] I would like to thank Professor H. A. Cronne and Dr. H. Mayr-Harting for valuable criticisms and suggestions.

Postscript

As a result of the debate between Mr J.O. Prestwich and myself in *E.H.R.* cii (1988) 288-312 and 960-67, and *ibid* cv (1990) 670-72, I have rewritten the paragraph which runs over from p. 206 to p. 207 because the figures in my original version were incorrect and had to be removed. I have also revised the first paragraph on p. 207 because the witness-list can now be dated securely without recourse to the hostages, whose actual presence Prestwich is reluctant to accept.

14

King Stephen and the Earl of Chester Revised

How often did Ranulf Earl of Chester change sides during the civil war of Stephen's reign? J. H. Round claimed that it was seven times, which may be listed as follows: [1]

(1) The revolt against Stephen in 1140, which culminated in the battle of Lincoln (2 Feb. 1141).

(2) Reconciliation with Stephen in 1142.

(3) Revolt against Stephen later in 1142—or 'armed neutrality'.

(4) Reconciliation with Stephen early in 1146.

(5) Revolt against Stephen late in 1146, because Stephen had arrested him and forced him to surrender his castles.

(6) Reconciliation with Stephen in 1149.

(7) Revolt against Stephen in 1153.

For the first, fourth and fifth items on this list there was unequivocal evidence from contemporary chronicles, but all the other items were the result of elaborate arguments from the evidence of three charters. It is time that these arguments were reviewed.

The review is most conveniently started with the sixth item, the alleged revolt of 1149, because Dr. A. L. Poole has already demonstrated that in this case the newly discovered portion of the *Gesta Stephani* is wholly destructive of Round's view.[2] Round's argument had been based on an undated charter of King Stephen which made lavish grants to Earl Ranulf.[3] Assuming that no such grant could have been made except as the price of a change of sides, he looked for an occasion on which Ranulf's support could have been bought, and he picked on the year 1149 because in that year the northern expedition of Duke Henry and David King of the Scots failed because (as John of Hexham put it) 'Earl Ranulf did none of the things he had promised' (*nichil eorum quae condixerat prosecutus*).[4] He took these words to imply that Ranulf had changed sides; but the new evidence of the *Gesta Stephani* shows that he did not.

[1] ' King Stephen and the Earl of Chester ', *EHR* x (1895), 87–91. *Cf.* his article on Randulf in *Dict. Nat. Biog.* xvi. 729–31.

[2] *Gesta Stephani*, ed. K. R. Potter (London, 1955), pp. xvi–xxii.

[3] Text printed in Foster, *Registrum Antiquissimum*, i. 287, W. Farrer, *Lancashire Pipe Rolls and Early Charters* (1902), pp. 367–8.

[4] John of Hexham in *Symeon of Durham* (R.S.), ii. 323.

It is not necessary to repeat the detailed arguments of Dr. Poole, but it must be stressed that once Ranulf's alleged change of sides in 1149 has been disproved, there is no evidence to suggest that Ranulf was ever on Stephen's side after his arrest in 1146. How then can it be held that Ranulf ' changed over ' to the Angevins in 1153? The only evidence that Round could produce was a charter in favour of Earl Ranulf which was given by Duke Henry at Devizes, apparently early in 1153.[1] This time it is not the date but the interpretation of the charter which is in question. It is a grant to Ranulf of his inheritance in Normandy and England together with several other lands, most of which Ranulf had already acquired, but some of which he was allowed (in certain circumstances) to acquire in the future. Round once again assumed that no ruler could possibly have made so large a grant except as a bribe to change sides, and he therefore assumed that in 1153 Ranulf did change sides; it fitted neatly with what he thought had happened in 1149. But in fact the charter need not imply a change of sides on Ranulf's part; it need not be anything more than the price of more active and whole-hearted military support. We know that at some date during the period 1149–53 Ranulf had tried to limit the scope of the civil war in the North Midlands by making a treaty with Robert Earl of Leicester.[2] It had provided, amongst other things, that ' if it shall be necessary for the earl of Chester to go upon the earl of Leicester with his liege lord he may not bring with him more than twenty knights ', and it is perhaps because of this that the *Gesta Stephani* records no fighting in the North Midlands in 1150, 1151 or 1152. In 1153, after the grant of Duke Henry's charter, the position changes, and we read about Ranulf's ' intestine hatred and unrelenting strife against all the King's (Stephen's) men '.[3]

If we now turn to the second and third items on Round's list, the alleged changes of side in 1142, we will find a rather similar situation. The two changes were inferred from a single undated charter which was given by King Stephen at Stamford. It was a grant in favour of William de Roumare earl of Lincoln (Ranulf's half-brother), which must certainly belong to a period when Ranulf was supporting King Stephen since he was the first of its witnesses. But what was its date? Round claimed that it belonged to 1142, and did so not only because he thought that the witness-list suggested it, but also because he thought (at one time) that the Anglo-Saxon Chronicle demanded it.[4] He was referring to its statement that the

---

[1] Text printed in Rymer's *Foedera* (1704), i. 12, Ormerod's *Cheshire* (1882), i. 23, W. Farrer, *Lancashire Pipe Rolls and Early Charters* (1902), pp. 370–1, G E. Cokayne, *Complete Peerage*, new edn. (1916), iv Appendices 163–4.

[2] Text in F. M. Stenton, *The First Century of English Feudalism* (1932), pp. 285–8 and 249–55.

[3] *Gesta Stephani*, ed. Potter, p. 156.

[4] J. H. Round, *Geoffrey de Mandeville* (1892), p. 159.

king and Earl Ranulf were ' reconciled at Stamford, and swore oaths and plighted their troth that neither of them should deceive the other ',[1] but he was mistaken in thinking that it either stated or implied any particular date for the incident. When he discovered that both Howlett and Miss Norgate had thought it referred to 1146, he withdrew this part of his argument completely.

> The chronology at the close of the Peterborough chronicle, he wrote, is unfortunately so confused that one cannot positively say to what date it assigns the Stamford meeting, which it places just after Stephen's release (1141) and before his seizure of Randulf (1146) but also before the siege of Oxford. All I contend is that my charter, from the names of its witnesses, certainly seems to belong to the beginning of 1142.[2]

Do the names of the witnesses bear out his claim? They certainly belong to a period between 1139 and 1146, because Gilbert Clare is styled earl of Hertford (a title bestowed on him after 1138), and he and his uncle Gilbert earl of Pembroke (d. 1148) were in revolt against Stephen from 1147 onwards.[3] One would therefore, in the normal course of events, have assigned the charter to one of the years in that period when Earl Ranulf was known to have been on Stephen's side—1139, part of 1140, or 1146. But Round did not consider these possibilities. He plumped instead for 1142 on the ground that the witnesses suggested ' a close connection in date ' with a charter granted by Stephen to Geoffrey de Mandeville at Canterbury at Christmas 1141. But here we must beg to differ. There are six witnesses (not seven as he stated) common to the two charters, but one of them, William Martel, is so frequent a witness as to be valueless for dating purposes; and if we print the two lists in parallel columns, which Round did not do, the coincidence between them is hardly remarkable:

Canterbury Charter. Christmas 1141.	Stamford Charter.
(*Geoffrey de Mandeville.* 143–4)	(*ibid.* 159)
Queen Matilda	Earl Rannulf (of Chester)
Henry Bishop of Winchester	*Earl Gilbert of Pembroke
William Earl Warenne	*Earl Gilbert of Hertford
*Earl Gilbert of Pembroke	*Earl Simon
*Earl Gilbert of Hertford	Earl Roger of Warwick
William Earl of Aumâle	*Earl Robert de Ferrers
*Earl Simon	*W(illiam) Martel

[1] C. Plummer and J. Earle, *Two Saxon Chronicles Parallel* (1892), p. 267, and G. Garmonsway, *The Anglo-Saxon Chronicle* (1953), p. 267. The chronicle gives no dates between 1140 and 1154 and makes no attempt to preserve the chronological order of events. It should be noted that in the manuscript it is all in one paragraph from the annal for 1140 to the end.

[2] *EHR*, x, 89.

[3] *Gesta Stephani*, ed. Potter, p. 133.

Canterbury Charter. Christmas 1141.	Stamford Charter.
(*Geoffrey de Mandeville.* 143–4)	(*ibid.* 159)
Earl William of Sussex	*Bald(win) fitz Gilbert
Earl Alan	W(alter) fitz Gilbert
*Earl Robert de Ferrers	Richard de Camville
William of Ypres	Richard fitz Urse
*William Martel	Eustace fitz John
*Baldwin fitz Gilbert	Ralph de Haia
Robert de Vere	H(ugh) Wake
Pharamus (of Boulogne)	W(illiam) de Coleville
Richard de Lucy	
Turgis of Avranches	
Adam de Belnai	

Twelve of the eighteen witnesses at Canterbury do not witness at Stamford, and nine of the fifteen Stamford witnesses do not occur at Canterbury. The truth of the matter is that the Canterbury witnesses are just a good representative list of Stephen's supporters who could easily turn up in other charters, even when there was no ' close connection in date '; seven of them, for example, occur in a charter of Easter 1136.[1] What is far more remarkable than the coincidences between the two lists, is the fact, duly noted by Round, that the Stamford charter was something of a family affair, being a grant in favour of Ranulf's half-brother, witnessed by Ranulf, four of Ranulf's relatives and four of Ranulf's tenants.[2] It does not suggest the composition of a typical Christmas court, which the Canterbury charter does, but seems to be an entirely different kettle of fish. It could easily belong to either 1140 or 1146, when Stephen was bidding for Ranulf's support. But Round dated it 1142 and argued from it that Ranulf *must* have been on Stephen's side in that year.

From chronicle sources we know that Ranulf was supporting the empress in 1141, 1143, and 1144.[3] In order to maintain that in 1142 Ranulf was on Stephen's side, Round was therefore forced to postulate that Ranulf changed sides twice in a year, once to Stephen and once back again. One might have thought that such astounding conduct would at least have been mentioned by a chronicler, but we find no word of it; William of Malmesbury whose *Historia Novella* continues to December 1142 is silent, so is John of Hexham, so is Henry of Huntingdon, and so is the *Gesta Stephani*. The *Gesta Stephani* indeed gives a distinct impression that Ranulf had not been

[1] *Geoffrey de Mandeville*, pp. 262–3.
[2] The relatives were Gilbert earl of Pembroke, Gilbert earl of Hertford, Baldwin fitz Gilbert and Walter fitz Gilbert; the tenants Eustace fitz John, Ralph de Hay, Hugh Wake and William de Coleville.
[3] For 1141 (after the battle of Lincoln), John of Hexham, p. 310 and William of Malmesbury's *Historia Novella* (ed. K. R. Potter, 1955), p. 59. For 1143, John of Hexham, p. 315. For 1144, *Gesta Stephani* (ed. Potter), p. 111, Henry of Huntingdon (R.S.), p. 277.

reconciled to Stephen at any time between 1141 and 1146. When describing the reconciliation of 1146, it says that Ranulf

> supplex et mansuetus regem adiuit, crudelitatisque et perfidiae, quam in eum egerat cum et manus in Lincolnensi captione in regem et dominum extendit, . . . tandem poenitens.[1]

In 1146, that is to say, Ranulf was begging pardon for his conduct at the battle of Lincoln (1141). Why was this necessary if he had already been restored to favour? And if he had committed treason a second time, in or after 1142, why did he not need forgiveness for that?

Finally we may wonder how or when Ranulf is supposed to have rejoined the empress. Round, in an attempt to get the best of both worlds, wrote:—

> My view is that during the period since the beginning of 1142 [until 1146] the earl had occupied a position of armed neutrality, not siding with either party, and with no wish to oppose the King so long as he was left in possession of Lincoln and of the other portions of the crown demesne of which he had obtained possession.[2]

But this, as we have already seen, was not the view of the chronicles which portray him as actively belligerent; and Round's wording leaves one with the suspicion that he was uncomfortably aware of the fact that in 1144 Ranulf had been besieged in Lincoln by King Stephen himself.[3]

If we reject Round's hypotheses about 1142, 1149 and 1153, we are left with the chronicle evidence that Ranulf revolted against Stephen (though with some hesitation) in 1140, and except for the temporary reconciliation of 1146, remained in revolt till his death in 1153. He was not so much a professional turncoat, as a rather unsteady, or hesitant, supporter of the empress. His conduct seems to have been governed by two natural but incompatible considerations, one of which inclined him to the empress and the other to King Stephen. On the one hand, since his wife was the daughter of Robert earl of Gloucester, the first of the empress's supporters, his natural loyalty lay with her. On the other hand his territorial ambitions made him the natural enemy of King David I of Scotland who was the empress's uncle and, after Robert of Gloucester, her most valued supporter.

The reason for Ranulf's hostility to King David is well-known.[4] Before his accession to the earldom of Chester in 1120, Ranulf's father had held the honour of Carlisle. Henry I had deprived him of it, perhaps (though this is no more than surmise) as the price of

---

[1] *Gesta Stephani* (ed. Potter), pp. 121–2.   [2] *EHR*, x, 89.
[3] Henry of Huntingdon (R.S.), p. 277.
[4] See H. A. Cronne, ' Ranulf de Gernons, Earl of Chester 1129–53 ', *Trans. Roy. Hist. Soc.*, 4th ser., xx (1937), 103–34. I should add that I am personally indebted to Professor Cronne for much help and friendly criticism.

being recognized as heir to the earldom. Ranulf still wanted it back and probably regarded it as rightfully ' his '. He did not hesitate to show his anger when, in February 1136, Stephen granted the honour to King David's son as the price of Scots neutrality. But if Ranulf could not have Carlisle, he was still interested in extending his power towards it, and therefore wished to acquire the honour of Lancaster, which consisted of Lancashire north of the Ribble. This, as it happened, formed part of Stephen's lands even before he became king, and so it was his to bestow on Earl Ranulf if he so wished. But it was also claimed by King David I as part of the old earldom of Northumbria, and it was a foregone conclusion that the empress would maintain his claim. It followed, therefore, that if Ranulf followed his natural loyalty and adhered to the empress, he would lose all hope not only of the honour of Carlisle but also of the honour of Lancaster. If, on the other hand, he sacrificed his natural loyalty and supported Stephen he might, when David abandoned his neutrality, get both.

In these circumstances it is hardly surprising that Ranulf hesitated about his initial revolt in 1140. He started, apparently, by seizing Lincoln castle, in consequence of which Stephen hurried north.[1] This was before Christmas, and we are told both that Stephen made peace with Ranulf again and that he heaped honours on him.[2] It is to this occasion that we would refer the charter which Round wrongly ascribed to 1149; it gave to Ranulf, amongst other things, the castle and city of Lincoln and the honour of Lancaster (*totam terram Rogeri Pictauis a Northamptona usque in Scotiam excepta terra Rogeri de Monte Begonis in Lincolnshira*).[3] Then Stephen, thinking he had lulled Ranulf into security suddenly marched on him which, as William of Malmesbury put it, ' to many people seemed wicked '.[4] Ranulf, taken by surprise, enlisted the support of his father-in-law, Robert, earl of Gloucester, and defeated and captured Stephen at the battle of Lincoln (2 Feb. 1141). He was now necessarily a supporter of the empress. But so alas! was King David I who, abandoning all pretence of neutrality, came to spend the summer at the empress's court and obtained possession of the honour of Lancaster.[5] This must have been a bitter pill for Ranulf, and it is not surprising to find that he would have returned to Stephen's side if he could have persuaded the king's supporters to receive him.[6] As it was, he had to support the empress and it was not till 1146 that he made his

---

[1] This is the sequence of events established by Cronne, *op. cit.*

[2] *Gesta Stephani* (ed. Potter), p. 73, William of Malmesbury, *Historia Novella* (ed. Potter), p. 46.

[3] See note 3, p. 213 above.

[4] *Historia Novella* (ed. Potter), p. 47.

[5] His possession of the honour at this date was proved by J. Tait in *Medieval Manchester and the Beginning of Lancashire* (1904), pp. 165–9 and by G. W. S. Barrow, ' King David I and the Honour of Lancaster ', *EHR*, lxix (1955), 85–9.

[6] John of Hexham in *Symeon of Durham* (R.S.), ii. 310.

peace with the king; and even then the reconciliation was not lasting because the king's supporters, still unwilling to believe that Ranulf could be genuinely on their side, persuaded the king to arrest him. He was forced to surrender his castles in order to regain his liberty, and then enraged (as we would suppose) at the king's second act of perfidy, burst into revolt, and never attempted to make peace with Stephen again. In spite of the fact that her uncle David held the honours of both Carlisle and Lancaster, he had to support the empress. If at times his support was little more than nominal, or if his hand ' as we read of Ishmael, was against every man, and every man's hand against him ',[1] it was hardly a matter for wonder. For no matter who won the civil war, Ranulf was bound to lose.

This reconstruction of the events may be less dramatic than that proposed by J. H. Round, but it is in accordance with the evidence of both charters and chronicles. Had the final chapters of the *Gesta Stephani* been discovered before Round wrote, he would never have made the mistakes which he did. Now that we have this fuller evidence before us, we need no longer believe that Stephen and Matilda were so gullible as to let Ranulf change sides seven times in fourteen years.

[1] *Gesta Stephani* (ed. Potter), p. 156.

Postscript

The charter which, on p. 218 and n. 3, I ascribed to Christmas 1140, should now be ascribed to 1146 when Earl Ranulf submitted to King Stephen. It is printed in *Regesta Regum Anglo-Normannorum* vol. iii, no. 178 where reasons for the redating are given. This redating does not affect the main argument of my article.

15

An Unknown Coventry Charter

THE charter which we print below is a grant of Coventry to Robert Marmion by Ranulf earl of Chester (1129–53). It has never been published or noticed before. It is in the possession of Colonel A. Gregory-Hood of Loxley Hall, Warwick, having descended to him from his ancestor Arthur Gregory of Stivichall who seems to have acquired it in the 1570s. (See the Appendix contributed by Mr. Robert Bearman.) It poses considerable problems, because it is necessary to explain how it came about that Earl Ranulf gave Coventry to a family which was noted for its hostility to him, and also, since it mentions no division of the town, how it relates to 'the Coventry forgeries' whereby the cathedral priory claimed half of the town as if by gift of Earl Leofric, Lady Godiva, and Edward the Confessor.

One glance at the mid-twelfth century handwriting of the charter is sufficient to establish a presumption in favour of its authenticity. It has not been possible to find another charter of Earl Ranulf II in the hand of the same scribe, but it has been possible to find others very like it.[1] The formulae are correct, the witnesses can all be identified as followers of either Earl Ranulf or Robert Marmion, and at one point the text has been altered (as will shortly be explained) by another twelfth-century hand. These indications are sufficient to outweigh the fact that the seal is a forgery, showing an equestrian

1. The following originals of Earl Ranulf's charters may be compared: Manchester, John Rylands Library, Rylands Charters 1807, with seal (facs. in *Hist. Soc. of Lancs. and Cheshire*, lxxxvii (1935) 97–112; Lincoln Cath., DiJ/86/1/1, facs. in *Registrum Antiquissimum*, ii. 7; P.R.O., DL 25/36; DL 34/1/1; DL 36/2, pp. 61 and 74; B.M. Cotton Ch. xvi. 36; Cotton MS. Nero C iii, fo. 178; Huntington Library, Hasting Ch. no. 375; Staffs. Rec. Office, marquis of Anglesey, no. 14; Salisbury Cath., Box E. 5; and facsimiles in Nichols' *Leicestershire*, iv, pl. lxi, and *Chester Arch. Soc.*, N.S., vi (1899), frontispiece.

figure caparisoned in the manner of the late-thirteenth or early-fourteenth centuries. It does not seem possible that anyone could have composed and written so correct a text, and then used a seal which was so anachronistic. We therefore assume that the original seal was broken and lost, and that the present seal is a forger's replacement. The text is as follows:

> Ran(ulfus) comes Cest(rie) constab(ulario) suo et dapifero et omnibus baronibus suis et hominibus atque amicis clericis ac laicis Francis et Anglis tam presentibus quam futuris salutem. Notum sit vobis omnibus me dedisse Rob(er)to Marmion Coventreia(m) in feudo et hereditate sibi suisque heredibus, tenendam constanter de me ac de meis heredibus cum omnibus pertinentiis in burgo et in villa in bosco et in plano in aquis et molendinis et in omnibus rebus. Quare volo et jubeo quatinus sic bene et quiete ac libere et honorifice et in pace et eisdem libertatibus teneat quibus tenebam quamdiu erat in meo dominio, et eisdem conventionibus que prescripte sunt inter me et ipsum, videlicet hac conventione *quod mihi serviat contra omnes homines et o(mne)s mulieres.* His etiam testantibus et cartam confirmantibus, Hugo(n)e Wac, Ric(ardo) de Ca(m)villa, Sim(one) fil(io) Will(elm)i, Hugo(n)e de Cuill(i), Will(elm)o de Redza(m)i, Will(elm)o fil(io) Rad(ulfi), Rob(er)to Potario.

> [Equestrian seal (legend defaced) in white wax on a tongue with a yellowish silk seal-bag]

> [The words in italics are written in a later hand over an erasure]

Before proceeding to discuss the date of the charter, it should be pointed out that the text makes it clear that it is only one part of a transaction or series of transactions. The earl of Chester grants that Robert Marmion is to hold Coventry 'according to the same agreements (*conventionibus*) which have been written down between me and him, viz. that agreement (conventione) . . .'. Unfortunately it is at this point that a later forger has erased some words and written instead 'so that he serve me against all men and all women'.[1] As a result we do not know the terms of the agreement, but the very fact of its existence is interesting. The famous treaty which Earl Ranulf made with the earl of Leicester between 1149 and 1153 was called a 'conventio . . . et finalis pax et concordia',[2] and we must be alive to the possibility that in the present charter Earl Ranulf is referring to a similar transaction with Robert Marmion.

But which Robert Marmion? The Marmions were an important family, being lords (amongst other things) of the castle of Tamworth, but in almost every generation the senior member was called Robert.

1. We can only speculate what the original words were. The forger has had to squeeze up his writing so as to fit his new phrase into the space provided, so it is certain that the original was shorter. It may have read something like 'hac conventione que facta est apud . . .'. or it may have referred to some awkward condition which the forger wished to remove.

2. F. M. Stenton, *The First Century of English Feudalism* (2nd ed., Oxford, 1961), 286, no. 48.

During Earl Ranulf's lifetime there was Robert Marmion II (d. 1144) and his son Robert Marmion III (d. *c.* 1181), and it is important to determine which of them it was that our charter was given to. The first reaction is to attribute it to Robert Marmion II, for though he was a notorious enemy of Earl Ranulf, he was well-known for his dealings with Coventry where, in or before 1144, he expelled the monks from the cathedral priory and turned it into a fortress. William of Newburgh tells the story as follows:

Robert Marmion, a man of war almost unequalled for ferocity, astuteness and audacity in his time, since he was already famous for many successes ranging far and wide, profaned the church (of Coventry) by shutting out the servants of God and putting in it the hirelings of the Devil; and he harrassed the earl of Chester, to whom he was particularly opposed, with frequent heavy attacks. When the earl approached (the city) with enormous forces, he (Robert) went out to attack him, but when he was riding proudly on his foaming steed in full sight of both his own men and of the enemy he forgot the craft with which he had covered the field with ditches to impede the enemy and keep them at a distance. It was by the Judgment of God, I say, that forgetting his own craft and labour, he 'is fallen into the ditch which he made' (*Psalm* vii. 15). Because he had broken his thigh he was unable to get up; and while everyone was watching, a menial of the enemy army hacked his head off. It was on almost the same day as the Judgment of God was celebrated on Geoffrey de Mandeville (16 Sept. 1144).[1]

At first sight we might consider that our charter was earlier than this incident, and imagine that Earl Ranulf, having given Robert the charter, nonetheless refused to surrender his castle of Coventry, and that consequently Robert attacked it, using the fortified priory as a siege-work.[2] But in this case our charter would have to be earlier than 1144, and this is impossible.

The most important clue to the dating of the charter lies in the identity of the witnesses. Two of them are the earl of Chester's men, and five of them Marmion's. Neither of the earl of Chester's two seems to have witnessed before 1144, for Hugh Wake (d. 1176) seems to have taken the place of Robert Grevesac *c.* 1145, and Simon fitz William de Kyme, though a frequent witness, does

1. William of Newburgh in *Chronicles of the reigns of Stephen, Henry II and Richard I*, ed. Richard Howlett (R.S., 4 vols., 1884–9), i. 47.
2. The site of the earl's castle is not known, though it is thought to have been somewhere between Broadgate Street and Bailey Lane. D. F. Renn (*Norman Castles in Britain* (London, 1968), p. 160) considers that there was no permanent castle, but only the cathedral priory as fortified by Marmion and Earl Ranulf II's siege-castle of 1147, but Earl Ranulf II's charter for the burgesses (*c.* 1153) expressly exempted them from pleas in the castle, and we find an 'Yvo constable of Coventry' witnessing another charter for the earl *c.* 1144–6 (printed by G. Barraclough in *A Medieval Miscellany for Doris Mary Stenton* (Pipe Roll Soc., lxxvi, 1960), p. 28). The situation in Coventry would therefore have been very similar to that in Hereford in 1140 when Geoffrey Talbot fortified the cathedral in an attempt to capture the neighbouring castle (*Gesta Stephani*, ed. K. R. Potter (London, 1955), p. 72).

not appear earlier than *c.* 1144–6.[1] Most of Marmion's witnesses are more difficult to date,[2] but it can at least be said that no connection between Richard Camville and the Marmions is known before 1144, though soon after that date he established a very strong connection by marrying Robert Marmion II's widow.[3]

A further clue lies in the description of the charter as part of an agreement or *conventio*. Since the Marmions seem to have been consistent in their support of King Stephen, and Richard de Camville was one of his chief advisers,[4] it may be assumed that this agreement was made while Earl Ranulf was not actively hostile to Stephen, that is to say in one of the following three periods: 1135–40, or September 1141 (when he tried to join the king's supporters at Winchester but was rebuffed), or 1145–6 (between his reconciliation with the king at Stamford and his arrest at Northampton.)[5] The last of these three periods is the only one which is consistent with the witnesses of our charter, and is also the only one which is followed immediately by a period when the earl of Chester is known *not* to have held Coventry.[6] It must therefore be the date we are looking for.

1. These conclusions emerge from a study of forty of Earl Ranulf's charters. For printed texts see G. Barraclough in *A Medieval Miscellany for Doris Mary Stenton* (Pipe Roll Soc., lxxvi, .1960), pp. 25–36 (nos. 1–7); *Hist. MSS. Comm. Duke of Rutland*, iv. 147, 167; F. M. Stenton, *Danelaw Charters* (British Acad., London, 1920), nos. 496–7; Stenton, *First Century of English Feudalism* (2nd ed., Oxford, 1961), pp. 271–2, 285–6 (nos. 23–4, 47–8); W. Farrer, *Lancashire Pipe Rolls* (Liverpool, 1902), pp. 277, 278, 326; J. Tait, *Chartulary of St. Werburgh* (Chetham Soc., N.S., vols. 79, 82), nos. 9–12, 15, 20, 349, 352; *Hist. MSS. Comm., R. R. Hastings*, i. 66; *Cal. Charter Rolls*, iv. 235 and v. 102; Ormerod, *Cheshire*, i. 25; J. Nichols, *Leicestershire*, iv. 411 (pl. lxi); *Staffs. Rec. Soc.* p. 61 (1937), p. 11 (no. 14); *Registrum Antiquissinum* ii (Lincs. Rec. Soc. 28), 7 (no. 316); *Monasticon* (1846), iv. 313 and vi. 1024; I. H. Jeayes, *Muniments and Charters of the Marquis of Anglesey* (Staffs. Rec. Soc. 1937), no. 14.

2. Hugh de Cuilli and William de Rezem attested a charter of Robert Marmion II *c.* 1139–46 for Polesworth (C. F. R. Palmer, *History of the Baronial Family of Marmion* (London, 1875), p. 37. William fitz Ralph was a benefactor of Stoneleigh Abbey and held a knight's fee of Robert Marmion in 1166 (*Sir Christopher Hatton's Book of Seals*, ed. D. M. Stenton (Oxford, 1950), no. 194, and *Red Book of the Exchequer*, ed. H. Hall (R.S. 1896), i. 327. Robert Potarius was presumably related to Ralph Poter who attested for Robert Marmion *c.* 1170–5 (ed. H. E. Salter, *The Boarstall Cartulary*, Oxford Hist. Soc. lxxxviii, 1930), 4.

3. Richard de Camville was a minor baron at Middleton Stony in Oxfordshire in 1130, but was richly rewarded by Stephen during the civil war, particularly with the lands of John de St. John who adhered to the empress (*Pipe Roll 31 Henry I*, p. 5, and H. E. Salter, *Oxford Charters* (Oxford, 1929), no. 61). He had married, and had a son by, Milicent widow of Robert Marmion II by the time he founded Combe Abbey in 1150 (*Monast.* v. 584(i)).

4. For Richard de Camville, see R. H. C. Davis, *King Stephen* (London, 1967), p. 70. The Marmions were not only opposed to the earl of Chester at Coventry, but also to William de Beauchamp of Elmley, to whom in 1141 the empress 'gave' the Marmion castle of Tamworth (*Reg.* iii, no. 68).

5. J. H. Round thought that Ranulf changed sides much more often than this, but I have explained in detail why his theory must be rejected, see below, pp. 255–63.

6. *Gesta Stephani*, ed. K. R. Potter (London, 1955), p. 132. It is probable that Earl Ranulf did not recover Coventry till 1153 – Duke Henry was in the town in about June 1153 (*Reg.* iii. 841), subsequent to his undertaking to restore Earl Ranulf's in-

It would be tempting to go still further and conclude that our charter was issued after the earl's arrest (28 August 1146), since we know that he purchased his freedom by surrendering all his castles.[1] But there is another charter which suggests a connection, not so much with the arrest at Northampton as with the preceding reconciliation at Stamford. This is a grant by Earl Ranulf in favour of Robert earl of Leicester, another prominent supporter of King Stephen. Though published by the Historical Manuscripts' Commission in 1928, it has not received the attention it deserves. It reads as follows.

Ran(nulfus) comes Cestr(ie) constab(ulario) dap(ifero) ministris vic-(ecomitibus) et omnibus ballivis suis Francis et Anglis salutem. Sciatis me dedisse et concessisse Roberto comiti Legrec(astri) in feodo et hereditate sibi et heredibus suis de me et de heredibus meis Cerneleam et omnes boscos adjacentes juxta forestam suam Legre(castri) tam meos proprios quam eos de feodo meo, excepto parco meo de Barow, ad habendum eos in foresta de me ita bene et libere et plenarie sicut melius tenet forestam Legre(castri) de rege. Excepto hoc solo, quod retineo in boscis illis aisiamenta maneriorum juxtapositorum sine wasto et sine venditione. Et praeter hoc dedi ei hereditarie quicquid habeo in civitate Legrec(astri) in dominio et feodo. Et de hac tenura fidem mihi fecit sicut domino de quo tenet. Quare volo et precipio quod bene et in pace et libere teneat, et prohibeo ne quis ei quicquid de rebus istis forisfaciat. Testibus Alexandro episcopo Linc(olnie), et Rogero episcopo Cestr(ie), et comite Willelmo Linc(olnie), et comite Simone Norhant(onie), et Radulpho de Haia, et Hugone Waac, et Willelmo Coleville, et Simone filio Willelmi, et Turstano Banastre, et Hugone Bard(olf), et Hugone Ostrac(ario), et Ricardo Pincerna, et Gaufrido Disp(ensatore), et Ivone fratre suo, et Rogero de Turre, et Hugone Maleb(isse), et Roberto filio Nigelli, et Johanne de Stuteville, et Willelmo Burdet, et Roberto de Creft, et Gaufrido Abbate, et Radulpho de Normanville, et Fulcone Trussell, et Roberto Puher, et (*sic*) agris deinter Legrec(astrum) et Monte Sorel.[2]

In spite of its charter form this is obviously a peace-treaty concluded in neutral territory in the fields between Leicester (which belonged to Earl Robert) and Mountsorel (which was Earl Ranulf's). It must be distinguished from the more famous 'disarmament treaty' or 'non-aggression pact' made between the two earls *c.* 1149–53,[3] first because it is earlier – necessarily before Bishop Roger

---

heritance (*Reg.* iii. 180). It may be added that Lincoln, a still more important castle of the earl's, was held by the king's men from the time of Earl Ranulf's arrest until the Treaty of Westminster in Dec. 1153 (*Reg.* iii. 272).

1. *Gesta Stephani*, pp. 128–31. The date comes from the *Annales Cestriae*, ed. R. C. Christie (Record Soc. of Lancs. and Chesh. xiv, 1886), p. 20.

2. MS., Huntington Library, San Marino, Calif., U.S.A. (original); printed in *Report of the MSS. of the late Reginald Rawdon Hastings Esq. of the Manor House, Ashby de la Zouche* (Hist. MSS. Comm., 1928), i. 66–67. The places referred to are Charley and Barrow-upon-Soar (Leics.), the forest 'of Leicester' being Charnwood.

3. F. M. Stenton, *The First Century of English Feudalism* (2nd ed., Oxford, 1961), pp. 286–8 (no. 48).

of Chester (or Coventry) departed on crusade in May 1147 – and secondly because, unlike the later treaty, it is very one-sided. In it the earl of Chester is obviously purchasing peace; it is he who makes all the grants, and yet he gets nothing in return except that the earl of Leicester 'will do him faith as to a lord from whom he holds'. Once again the circumstances of 1145–6 are indicated, but this time there can be no connection with the earl's arrest, for he is clearly at liberty and in the field with a secure castle behind him. It looks rather as if he were still negotiating for peace with the king, and 'clearing the ground' by purchasing the goodwill of his most prominent supporters. It is significant that of the charter's witnesses Earls William and Simon, Ralph de Hay, Hugh Wake, and William de Colville were with the earl when he made his peace with Stephen at Stamford[1]; and that two of those present on that occasion, Hugh Wake and Richard de Camville, also attested our Coventry charter.

When J. Horace Round wrote about the Anarchy of Stephen's reign, he invariably suggested that the greater barons could change sides at will, virtually selling their support first to one side and then to the other. We now know that he was mistaken both in his general thesis and in the particular instances which he adduced to support it. The present charters underline the difficulties faced by anyone who wanted to change sides, since he had to make his peace not only with the king or empress, but also with his, or her, supporters. These latter were the men who bore the brunt of the day-to-day fighting, and who suffered most from the fortunes of war. They would not want their enemies to be reconciled with the king unless they were first given satisfaction for all that *they* had suffered. That, presumably, was why Earl Ranulf experienced such difficulty in making peace with Stephen, and why it was not Stephen's queen but her army which refused his assistance in September 1141.[2] Similarly the *Gesta Stephani* tells us that after Stephen had made peace with the earl at Stamford in 1145, it was his barons and counsellors who continually filled his mind with suspicion until he agreed to go back on his word and arrest the earl. If our interpretation of the charters is correct, this was in spite of the fact that Earl Ranulf had purchased the support of Stephen's leading noble supporter, Robert earl of Leicester, and of one of his most prominent 'new men', Richard de Camville. But of course the number of barons whom Earl Ranulf had despoiled was legion; we know specifically that they included Earl Alan of Richmond, John count of Eu, William Peverel of Nottingham, William d'Aubigny *Brito*, William Clerfaith, and Gilbert de Gant who was shortly to become

1. *Reg.* iii. 494. *Cf. Reg.* iii. 178, and J. H. Round, *Geoffrey de Mandeville* (London, 1892), pp. 159–60.
2. John of Hexham in *Symeon of Durham* (R.S.), ii. 310. *Cf.* my *King Stephen*, pp. 93–95.

earl of Lincoln. Were they all to receive *douceurs* in the name of war reparations? And if not, how were they to be placated? Ranulf earl of Chester would surely have laughed at Round's notion of the civil war, for he had learnt by experience that changing sides was difficult, dangerous and, as our Coventry charter shows, very expensive.

II

So far we have concentrated on those aspects of our charter which concern Earl Ranulf and the general circumstances of Stephen's reign, but it also has a bearing on the history of Coventry, and particularly on the famous 'Coventry forgeries'. These are a series of charters which were fabricated in the twelfth century for the benefit of Coventry Cathedral Priory with the object of establishing that its 'liberties' had been bestowed upon it by its founder Earl Leofric of Mercia (d. 1057), the husband of Lady Godiva. These 'liberties' included several conventional exemptions from royal and episcopal control, but linked them with the grant of half the city. As a result, Coventry was divided for about two centuries into the 'prior's half' which was coincidental with the parish of Holy Trinity on the north, and the 'earl's half' or parish of St. Michael on the south, which was held by the earls of Chester as (so it was thought) the heirs of Earl Leofric.[1] Historians are all agreed that these charters are forgeries, but the date at which they were concocted is still open to question. Miss Joan Lancaster, who examined them in detail, considers that sufficient of them had been made to cause the division of the town by 1113, and that the rest were no later than 1139.[2] If this view is correct, considerable doubt must be thrown on the earl of Chester's grant to Robert Marmion, for though we have dated it 1145–6, it implies that Coventry was as yet undivided. If we wish to maintain that his charter is genuine, we must re-examine the Coventry forgeries in order to see if they could not have been fabricated at a later date than Miss Lancaster has supposed.

It will be simplest if we first enumerate the documents concerned, starting with those (nos. 1–4) which are known only from cartulary copies and ending with those of which we have pretended originals:

1. Earl Leofric's foundation charter, including the grant of 24 vills and half Coventry.

[1]. Strangers to Coventry are apt to muddle the two halves. The old cathedral was destroyed in the sixteenth century. When Coventry was made a bishop's see again in 1918, the parish church of the 'earl's half' (St. Michael's) was made the cathedral. Therefore the present cathedral is in the 'earl's half.'

[2]. Joan C. Lancaster, 'The Coventry Forged Charters: A Reconsideration' in *Bulletin of the Institute of Historical Research* xxvii (1954), 113–40. *Cf.* her contributions to the *Victoria County History of Warwickshire*, viii (published in 1969), 2, 256, and her *Godiva of Coventry* (Coventry 1967), pp. 37–38.

2. Pope Alexander II's license for Leofric to found the monastery, which is exempted from episcopal control.
3. Edward the Confessor's confirmation of Earl Leofric's foundation charter (including the grant of half Coventry).
4. Pope Alexander II's privilege addressed to Edward the Confessor, exempting the monks from episcopal control and granting them the right to elect 'abbots or deans' without papal interference.
5. Edward the Confessor's Anglo-Saxon writ confirming Earl Leofric's grant and adding that no-one should administer the house but the abbot and brethren (British Museum, Add. Ch. 28657).
6. William the Conqueror's writ confirming the grants of Earl Leofric and the charters of Edward the Confessor (British Museum, Add. Ch. 11205).
7. William the Conqueror's writ granting exemption from castle work (*omnia opera castelli*). The first $2\frac{1}{3}$ lines of this writ may be genuine, though the substantive portion is a forgery (British Museum, Harley Charter 43 C. 10).

In Miss Lancaster's opinion these forgeries were made in two separate stages, a 'first' version being produced by Bishop Robert de Limesey ('possibly in 1107 or 1111'), and a 'second' by the prior and monks some years after Bishop Robert's death in 1117 but before 1139. She deduced the existence of an earlier and later version from the fact that there were two separate manuscript traditions for the four charters whose texts were known only from cartulary copies. She dated the 'first' version before 1113 because she discovered evidence that the church of the Holy Trinity (whose parish was 'the prior's half') was in existence by then, and therefore connected the 'first' forgeries with Robert de Limesey's removal of his episcopal see from Chester to Coventry in 1101/2.[1] She dated the 'second' version after Bishop Robert's death (1117), preferably 'in the late 1120s or 1130s', and postulated that it was produced by the prior and convent, who 'took the opportunity of inserting clauses which would preserve their independence against Robert's successors as bishops of Coventry'. Finally the forgeries were put up for confirmation by King Stephen *c.* 1147, 'thus making doubly secure a position already accepted by both pope and king'.[2]

Any criticism of Miss Lancaster's thesis must start with an examination of her central postulate, that the two versions of the charters in cartulary copy (nos. 1–4) indicate two separate stages in the production of the forgeries, the first being made in the interest of the bishop, the second in the interest of the prior and convent. The weakness of the theory lies in the fact that the difference between

---

1. Lancaster, pp. 129, 138.   2. Lancaster, in *V.C.H. Warwicks*, viii. 2.

the two versions does not seem to be as significant as Miss Lancaster thought. The exemptions from episcopal control should, in her view, be stronger in the 'second' version than the 'first'. But in fact the reverse is the case, for the 'first' version gives them in two letters of Pope Alexander II, and the 'second' in only one (for it omits the pope's license to Earl Leofric). It seems incredible that Bishop Robert de Limesey, who was reviled by the monks of Coventry (as William of Malmesbury tells us) for having stripped their abbey of its wealth,[1] should have gratuitously forged a papal letter stating that 'no bishop or powerful man should presume to have (the monastery) under his law or authority' (*ut nullus episcopus vel prepotens homo sub jure aut ditione illum habere presumpsere*).[2] Yet this letter appears *only* in Miss Lancaster's 'first' version of the forgeries. Is it not simplest to assume that it was omitted in the 'second' version simply because of a copyist's error?

The only other major difference between the two versions is that in the 'first' there is no mention of the grant of half the town of Coventry in Earl Leofric's charter, while in the 'second' there is. This would have been a serious matter if there had been no mention of this grant in any of the charters of the 'first' version, but in fact it is found in Edward the Confessor's confirmation of Earl Leofric's charter, in the 'first' version as well as the 'second'. What we are faced with, therefore, is not a stepping-up of the convent's demands, but a curious textual discrepancy. It need not worry us too much if we remember that the texts in question are all cartulary copies or copies of cartulary copies. The most likely explanation is that the scribe of the 'second' version, was simply a copyist who was trying to be helpful, inserting a few words, which he presumed his predecessor to have omitted in error, so as to make Earl Leofric's charter agree with the king's confirmation of it.[3]

If we ignore the differences between the two versions as being of no historical significance, it still remains to examine the grounds which led Miss Lancaster to believe that the forgeries must have originated in the time of Bishop Robert de Limesey (d. 1117). In her view the period 1102–7 offered the greatest opportunity for the production of the forgeries, since just at the time when Bishop Robert was moving his see from Chester to Coventry (1102), the earl of Chester (who is thought to have held the whole of Coventry at this date) was a minor, Earl Hugh having died on

---

1. William of Malmesbury, *Gesta Regum*, ed. W. Stubbs (R.S., 1889), ii. 388–9.

2. Lancaster, p. 140.

3. The 'first' version of Leofric's charter is printed in Lancaster 140, the 'second' in *Monasticon* (1846), ii. 191 (iii). Comparing the two texts, the additions made by the second version are as follows: (1) *In Lancaster l. 7, after* Has igitur viginti et quatuor villas *add* una cum medietate villae in qua fundata ipsa ecclesia. (The words seem to have been taken direct from Edward the Confessor's confirmation of it); (2) *In Lancaster, l.13, for* Has autem terras dedi *read* Has autem villas cum medietate praedictae villae trado.

27 July 1101 and his son Richard not being invested with the earldom till about 1107 when he was thirteen. Unfortunately, however, the earl was a tenant-in-chief, and during a minority his lands would have been managed by the king's sheriff, who would have had a direct financial interest in exploiting them to the full. It is hard to imagine that he could have been cheated any more easily than an adult earl.

In addition to this general consideration, however, there was the 'proof' that 'somewhere between 1101 and 1113 the priory added to its possessions the parish of Holy Trinity – the "prior's half" '. In comparing continental Bede Rolls of 1101, 1113 and 1122, Miss Lancaster found that whereas in 1101 the abbey church was referred to as *S. Mariae Coventrensis Ecclesiae*, in both 1113 and 1122 the references were to *T(itulus) Sanctae Trinitatis et Sanctae Mariae Coventrensis ecclesiae*.[1] To many it may seem that the most obvious reading of the entries is that the dedication of the abbey (or cathedral) church had been amended, but even if it were right to consider that the reference was to the parish church of Holy Trinity, it still would not follow that because the priory 'owned' the church it also owned the land and secular jurisdiction with its parish.

Finally there was the evidence of a charter given by King Henry II in 1155 which granted to the then bishop of Coventry all liberties and customs 'as the charter of King Henry [I] my grandfather testified that Bishop Robert vindicated them in his court at Portsmouth'.[2] One is tempted to suspect that this reference could have been a magnificent 'plant' in the interest of the forgeries, since no text of the alleged charter of Henry I can be found, but even if we assume that it did exist and was genuine, it does not seem to have been very significant. If the liberties it recognized were the same as those recited in the confirmatory charter of Henry II, they were a very

---

1. Lancaster 138, with refs to *Archaeological Journal*, cvi, supplement (1952), 40–53.
2. I print the text from a confirmation of Edward I in 1280, as given in the Lichfield cartulary in the Bodleian Library, Oxford, Asmole MS. 1527, fo. 25: 'Henricus rex Anglorum et dux Normannorum et Aquitanorum et comes Andegavorum archiepiscopis, episcopis, abbatibus, comitibus, justiciariis, baronibus, vicecomitibus, ministris et fidelibus suis Anglie, salutem. Precipio et concedo quod Walterus episcopus de Coventr(e) habeat omnes libertates et consuetudines suas in bosco et plano, in pratis et pascuis, in aquis et molendinis, infra burgum et extra, et in omnibus locis, et socam et sacam et tol et theam et infangenetheof, et hallemotum suum in omnibus terris suis, ita bene et in pace et libere et plene et quiete sicut ecclesia sua melius habuit tempore regis Edwardi et Leouvrici comitis, ipsius ecclesie edificatoris, et sicut carta regis Henrici avi mei testatur quod Robertus episcopus illas libertates disrationavit in curia sua apud Portesmudam. Testibus Joh(anne) episcopo Wygorn(ensi), et R(oberto) episcopo Lincoln(iensi), et Thoma canc(ellario), R(oberto) comite Legrec(estrie), R(eginaldo) comite Cornub(ie), H(ugone) comite de Norfolca, Ric(ardo), de Hum(eto) conest(abulario), Guar(ino) fil(io) Ger(oldi) cam(erario), et Mann(assero) Biset. Datum apud Westmonasterium'. [The date of the charter is fixed by the fact that John bishop of Worcester died on 31 Mar. 1157 and that Henry II was on the continent from Jan. 1156 till Apr. 1157].

conventional lot indeed. They certainly contain no hint of anything like the 'prior's half'.

In fact the earliest dated reference to the division of the town between earl and prior is in the Pipe Roll of 1175,[1] though an undated charter of Earl Hugh's which recites the bounds of the two 'halves' of the town could well be a few years earlier (*c.* 1161–79).[2] Miss Lancaster thought that the division of the town could be detected earlier still, because a privilege of Pope Innocent II, which is dated 18 April 1139, confirms the grant made by Bishop Roger de Clinton of (amongst other things) 'half the rent of Coventry (*dimidium census Coventrensis*) and the church of Holy Trinity in that town'. Miss Lancaster took this to mean the 'prior's half', but if so it occurs in a curious position in the list of properties, after £100 pounds' worth of land in five named villages and before the mill at Olton, where it hardly looks like the monks' most prized possession. Indeed since the purpose of the privilege was to confirm the division of revenues between bishop and convent, the most natural interpretation of the passage would be that the bishop was surrendering to the convent half the rents which *he* had in Coventry. No-one would doubt that he had some rents in the town, but that is very far from saying that he or the prior held one half of the town.

Having thus cleared away the undergrowth, we can approach the question of the date of the forgeries afresh. The most significant item which they grant to the monks is the 'prior's half' of the town. We know from Domesday Book that the monks did not have this in 1086, and we know from the Pipe Rolls that they did have it by 1175. At some point between these two dates the charters must have been forged, but there is no need to postulate a whole succession of forgeries, each improving on the one before. It is simpler to assume that they were all made at the same time.

In these circumstances it is best to start by an examination of the three which have survived as so-called 'originals'. Two of these (nos. 5 and 6 on our list) are complete forgeries, while the third (no. 7) may have a genuine basis though the forger has added to it considerably. The two complete forgeries are supposed to be writs of Edward the Confessor and William the Conqueror, but since Miss Lancaster wrote, Mr. Bishop and Dr. Chaplais have shown

---

1. *Pipe Roll 21 Henry II* (Pipe Roll Soc. 22), p. 93: 'Homines Comitis Cestrie de Covintrea reddunt computum de x marcis pro concelatione terrarum inimicorum Regis. . . . Homines Prioris de eadem villa reddunt compotum de x marcis pro eodem forisfacto.' *Cf. Pipe Roll 26 Henry II* (Pipe Roll Soc, 29), p. 102: 'Pars Comitis Cestrie in villa de Covintre reddit compotum de x marcis quia negaverat quod postea recognovit.'

2. *Cal. Charter Rolls*, v. 101 (no. 9). Edmund had ceased to be archdeacon of Coventry by 1179 (*Magnum Registrum Album*, ed. H. E. Savage (Wm. Salt Arch. Soc., xlviii, 1924), p. 247.

that both were written by a scribe who wrote as many as ten documents in favour of Westminster Abbey, seven of them in the name of Edward the Confessor, two of William I, and one of Stephen! They also found that the forged seal of William the Conqueror on no. 6 was from a matrix which they associated with Abbot Gervase of Westminster (1137–57).[1] Dr. Chaplais has subsequently shown that the text of Edward the Confessor's privilege (our no. 3) which survives only in cartulary copies is in the style of Osbert de Clare who was a monk at Westminster *c.* 1121–61.[2] All these facts suggest that the most likely date for the Coventry forgeries would have been in the reign of Stephen.

To be more precise than that with the evidence hitherto available would have been almost impossible, but if it is conceded that Earl Ranulf's charter to Robert Marmion is a genuine grant of 1145–6, then it must follow that the division of the town was made after that date. In that case the prime instigator of the forgeries would have been Prior Laurence (*c.* 1144–   ), who has always been regarded with some suspicion in this respect. He would undoubtedly have found it convenient that for more than two years he was left without a bishop, for in May 1147 Bishop Roger de Clinton left England on crusade, where he died, and his successor, Walter Durdent, was not consecrated till 2 October 1149. Bishop Walter would have been naturally sympathetic to any claims of the cathedral priory, for his previous position had been prior of the cathedral priory at Canterbury.

The main difficulty facing Prior Laurence was that Coventry was held either by the earl of Chester or by Robert Marmion III (or his guardians). The *idea* of a division might well have been fostered by the events of 1144 when Robert Marmion II expelled the monks from the cathedral and turned it into a fortress against the earl of Chester, but it still cannot have been easy to revive this accident of war as a permanent legal right. We know that Robert Marmion III made gifts both to the cathedral priory and to the bishopric 'pro satisfactione et salute anime patris dicti Roberti pro irrecuperabilibus dampnis et enormis injuriis que idem pater dicti Roberti quondam multipliciter et malitiose intulit ecclesie nostre',[3] and perhaps he might also have conceded the 'prior's half', though he could hardly have done so by charter since the forgeries claimed that the monks had had it since 1043. Alternatively Earl Ranulf could have bought the prior's support against Robert Marmion III by promising him

1. T. A. M. Bishop and P. Chaplais, *Facsimiles of English Royal Writs to 1100* (Oxford, 1957), p. xxii.

2. P. Chaplais in *A Medieval Miscellany for Doris Mary Stenton*, ed. Patricia Barnes and C. F. Slade (Pipe Roll Soc., lxxvi, 1960), p. 92.

3. *The Boarstall Cartulary* ed. H. E. Salter (Oxford Hist. Soc., lxxxviii, 1930), pp. 4, 8. He also, and for the same reason, gave Thornton church to Lichfield (*Mag. Reg. Album*, no. 513).

half the town if he could help him to regain it (which he had done at any rate by 1153). Or perhaps again the prior might have taken possession of his 'half' on Earl Ranulf's death (16 Dec. 1153) before the confusion of the civil war had abated sufficiently for royal government to be effective. The possibilities are many enough, and there is no need to guess which of them is correct. In the present context it is sufficient to say that the Coventry forgeries were made in the second half of Stephen's reign, *c.* 1145–54, in the school of forgery which flourished at Westminister Abbey under Abbot Gervase.

Arthur Gregory and the Coventry charter

Nothing is known of the Coventry charter between the time it was granted and the 1570s, when it came into the hands of Arthur Gregory of Stivichall, who endorsed it and copied it into a cartulary he was compiling.[1] Arthur's father, Thomas Gregory, had moved from Asfordby in Leicestershire to Coventry in about 1528 to take up the post of town clerk. From the mid-1530s, when he, and later his son, began to purchase lands in the Coventry area, large quantities of mediaeval deeds came into their possession. These fall into four main categories: those acquired in 1542–4 with the manor of Kingshill formerly belonging to the abbey of Stoneleigh, those relating to the bishop of Coventry's manor in Stivichall which the Gregorys purchased in 1563–5, the mediaeval deeds for Combe Abbey which came with the purchase of Brinklow manor in 1588, and deeds relating to the Ferrers' manor in Stivichall acquired when Arthur Gregory married Jane Ferrers in 1573.[2] As the Coventry deed apparently bears no ecclesiastical endorsement, it is more likely to have derived from the last of these sources. Arthur Gregory, writing in the 1580s,[3] asserted that he held the Coventry charter as a lineal descendant of Robert Marmion, the original grantee. This ancestry, traced (rather tenuously) through the Ludlow, Dimmock and Malin families, was approved by the College of Arms in 1581,[4] and Arthur was permitted to quarter the Marmion arms. Be this as it may, the appearance of the Coventry charter in the Gregorys' muniments is more easily explained by their connection with the Ferrers.

If the Marmions retained possession of the Coventry charter it could well have been kept at Tamworth castle, the 'caput' of their barony. When,

1. Stratford-upon-Avon, Shakespeare Birthplace Trust, G[regory-]H[ood] collection no. 1409, fo. 38.
2. This is necessarily a simplified account of the establishment of the family in Warwickshire. I am writing a fuller account of the Gregorys in the sixteenth century to be published shortly.
3. G-H, no. 1408.
4. G-H, no. 2071. For the Gregory coat of arms, see *Visitation of Warwickshire 1619* (Harleian Soc., xii, 1877), p. 154, where the arms, quartered sixth, are not identified as Marmion because they differ slightly from the accepted version.

on the death of Philip Marmion in 1291, the barony was partitioned, Tamworth was allotted to Alexander Freville who had married one of Marmion's co-heiresses.[1] As the Coventry charter no longer related to any part of the barony, it would have probably remained among the muniments at the castle. The Frevilles were also lords of a manor in Stivichall and they retained this and Tamworth until 1423, when, on the failure of the male line, the two manors and the castle passed to the Ferrers family.[2] When the muniments were divided, both in 1291 and 1423, there would have been no reason to give the Coventry charter to any of the heiresses.[3] Instead it descended with the castle as a residual item and thus came into the Ferrers' possession.

The Ferrers held their manor in Stivichall until 1573 when it passed to Arthur Gregory by settlement on his marriage to Jane Ferrers.[4] Associated with this manor were four Coventry chief rents which had been allotted to the Ferrers in 1423 and which they had continued to collect down to 1573. By this time it was probably thought that the Coventry charter was in some way connected with these rents and the adjoining manor in Stivichall, and it was therefore handed over to the Gregorys.

For some years Arthur made no use of the charter. Rentals down to 1579 show that he was collecting eight or nine rents in Coventry. Some of these he had inherited from his father and the remainder were those acquired on his marriage. The next surviving rental, dated 1585, is far more impressive. It is headed 'Marmion's manor in Coventry' and includes about fifteen additional rents.[5] Arthur is known to have purchased several since 1579[6] but they cannot all be easily accounted for. The probable explanation, however, is to be found in Arthur's current relations with the municipal authorities. Since at least 1572, the Corporation had been trying to establish that Arthur and his Stivichall tenants owed suit of court at their manor of Cheylesmore. It was a difficult point, for though custom apparently supported the Corporation's claims, Arthur was able to assemble some evidence to suggest that he was both exempt from Cheylesmore's jurisdiction, and entitled to hold his own court leet in Stivichall. In 1574 Arthur had succeeded his father as clerk of the statute and coroner in Coventry, but the Corporation had allowed him to continue in this office only if he gave up his right to this court in Stivichall.[7] In retaliation, Arthur began a campaign to re-establish what he believed were his rights in Stivichall and to extend his influence there at the Corporation's expense. The municipal authorities countered this by removing Arthur from his official position in Coventry in 1578, and three years later they brought a case of forgery against him in the Court of Star Chamber.[8] Most of the charges were vague or could not be proved and it seems clear that the real intention of the Corporation in bringing together these disconnected allegations, was to put an end to Arthur Gregory's activities. In this struggle the Coventry charter became a useful

1. *V.C.H. Warws*, iv (1947), p. 246.   2. G-H, no. 1316.
3. There is no doubt that these divisions took place. The deeds for the Freville estates allotted to the Willoughby family in 1423 are now in the Middleton MSS. deposited at Nottingham University.   4. G-H, nos. 805–9.
5. G-H, no. 2558.   6. G-H, nos. 423, 426–7.   7. G-H, no. 1870, fo. 64ᵛ.
8. P.R.O. Star Cha. 5/48/C7; 5/59/C13; 5/69/C30. See also *Coventry Leet Book* (Early English Text Society, 1907–1913), pp. 815–19 and 831, n. 3.

weapon and the reason for the revival of 'Marmion's manor' during this period is therefore easily understood. Many of Arthur's claims, however, appear to have had little basis: his successors abandoned their claim to most of the Coventry rents and nothing further is heard of Marmion's manor.

ROBERT BEARMAN

Postscript

For subsequent discussion of the charters printed on pp. 223 and 225 see the third edition of my *King Stephen* (London, 1990), Appendix vii.

16

The College of St Martin-le-Grand and
the Anarchy, 1135-54

THE College of St Martin-le-Grand is chiefly remembered because it has given its name to a London street. Its church, of which nothing remains, stood on the site now occupied by Courtaulds, Ltd, and its precinct included the greater part of the Old and New General Post Offices. But though its buildings have been destroyed, its records have survived, preserved in the muniment room of Westminster Abbey, to which in 1503 the College was appropriated as part of the endowment of King Henry VII's Chapel.

For the reign of King Stephen these records are important because they are remarkably complete. Some of them were published in 1825 by A. J. Kempe in his excellent *Historical Notices* of the College,[1] and others were discussed at length by J. H. Round in *The Commune of London* (1899), but no one has yet attempted to publish them in full, or to arrange them in chronological order. In the case of Round this was not altogether surprising since the muniments of Westminster Abbey had not then been catalogued, and one of his personal feuds prevented him from entering the room where they were kept. He worked instead from a manuscript in the British Museum (Landsdowne MS. 170), which is a seventeenth-century transcript of a sixteenth-century transcript[2] of the College's fifteenth-century cartulary (Westminster Abbey Muniment Book 5). Round did not know that at Westminster Abbey a large number of the original documents still survived, or that there was also a fuller and earlier cartulary of the thirteenth century, in the form of a parchment roll (W.A.M., 13167). Consequently he did not realise that, for the period of Stephen's reign, St Martin-le-

[1] A. J. Kempe, *Historical Notices of. . . St. Martin-le-Grand* (1825).
[2] The sixteenth-century transcript is *Liber Fleetwood* in Guildhall Library.

Grand had a longer series of royal charters and writs than any other religious house in England. Abingdon had only 14, Westminster 17 (5 of them blatant forgeries), Bury St Edmunds 24, St John's, Colchester 25, Lincoln Cathedral and its bishop 31 and Reading Abbey the same. The Collegiate Church of St Martin-le-Grand had a total of 41.[1] How was it able to get so so many?

In order to answer this question a rather lengthy inquiry will be necessary, and it is best to start with an account of St Martin-le-Grand itself. In the later Middle Ages it was chiefly famous as a special sanctuary where both criminal and political offenders could find a permanent asylum: in 1470, for example, when Henry VI was restored to the throne, the precinct was full of Edward IV's supporters, and rents were correspondingly high. But whatever the lawyers might claim, this privilege was of no great antiquity. Miss Thornley has shown that, like the special sanctuary right of Westminster Abbey, it was probably a creation of the late fourteenth or early fifteenth century, and that in the twelfth century St Martin-le-Grand could offer no sanctuary more permanent than the forty days' asylum to be had in any church.[2] It did, however, possess a soke (the soke of St Martin-le-Grand), which was larger in area than the sanctuary precinct of the fifteenth century and which undoubtedly had the status of a franchise or immunity. This privilege it owed to a grant made by William the Conqueror in 1067, and confirmed by his charter of 1068.[3] In this charter, which has been the object of much specialist study, it was stated that the College had been built and endowed in the reign of King Edward the

[1] *Regesta Regum Anglo-Normannorum* (henceforth cited as *Reg.*), III (1968), 521–61.

[2] Isobel D. Thornley, 'Sanctuary in Mediaeval London', *Journal of the British Archaeological Association*, n.s. XXXVIII (1932–3), 293–315. For the sanctuary boundaries, see Marjorie B. Honeybourne, 'The Sanctuary Boundaries and Environs of Westminster Abbey and the College of St Martin-le-Grand', *ibid.* pp. 316–22. Her plan of the college and its environs accompanies this present paper, p. 11.

[3] W. H. Stevenson, 'An Old-English Charter in favour of St Martin-le-Grand, London', *E.H.R.* XI (1896), 731–44, where the text is better than that printed by Kempe, *op. cit.* pp. 173–6. For the date see J. H. Round. *The Commune of London* (1899), pp. 28–36.

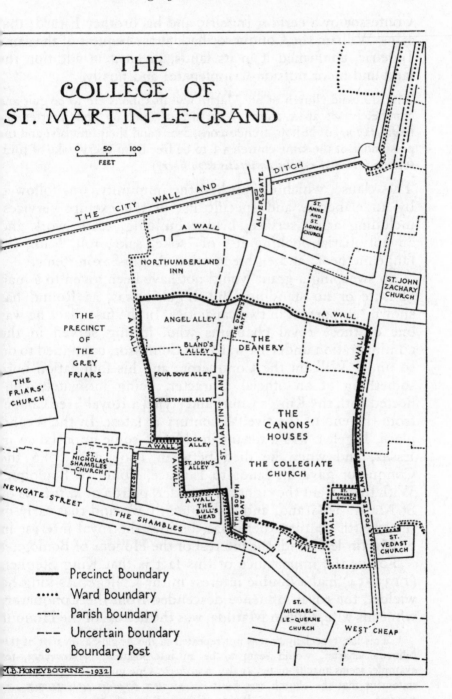

THE COLLEGE OF ST. MARTIN-LE-GRAND

0   50   100
FEET

DITCH

THE CITY WALL AND

ALDERSGATE

ST. ANNE AND ST. AGNES CHURCH

A WALL

NORTHUMBERLAND INN

ST. JOHN ZACHARY CHURCH

A WALL

THE PRECINCT OF THE GREY FRIARS

A WALL

ANGEL ALLEY

THE DEAN'S GATE

BLAND'S ALLEY

THE DEANERY

THE FRIARS' CHURCH

FOUR DOVE ALLEY

CHRISTOPHER ALLEY

ST. MARTIN'S LANE

THE CANONS' HOUSES

THE COLLEGIATE CHURCH

COCK ALLEY

A WALL

ST. NICHOLAS SHAMBLES CHURCH

PENTECOST LANE

ST. JOHN'S ALLEY

A WALL

ST. LEONARD'S CHURCH

FOSTER LANE

NEWGATE STREET

A WALL THE BULL'S HEAD

THE SOUTH GATE

THE SHAMBLES

A WALL

A WALL

ST. VEDAST CHURCH

ST. MICHAEL-LE-QUERNE CHURCH

WEST CHEAP

——— Precinct Boundary
••••• Ward Boundary
------- Parish Boundary
– – – Uncertain Boundary
○ Boundary Post

M.B. HONEYBOURNE – 1932

Confessor by a certain Ingelric and his brother Eirard; that King William the Conqueror had, at the request of the same Ingelric, confirmed it in its lands, given it in addition the land and moor outside Cripplegate; and finally,

The aforesaid church of St. Martin and its canons are to be quit and completely set apart from every sort of exaction and interference (*inquietudine*) of bishop, archdeacons, deans and their officials; and the possessions of the same church are to be free from every yoke of royal service (*ab omni regalis servitutis iugo libere*).

This clause, which established the immunity, was followed by an elaborate and specific list of the exempt services, including army service, bridge building, castle work and an antiquarian-looking list of 'soke, sake, toll, team, in-fangennetheof' and eighteen other Anglo-Saxon items.[1]

So sweeping a grant would not have been given to a man of little or no standing. But Ingelric was, as Round has shown,[2] important in two capacities. In the first place he was one of those royal chaplains who, having served in the administration under Edward the Confessor, continued to do so under William the Conqueror: and his foundation bore something of an official character, being intimately connected with the King's Court and styled a Royal Free Chapel from the end of the twelfth century at latest. In the second place, Ingelric was a tenant-in-chief of some importance in Essex, and when he died between 1068 and 1086 the Conqueror gave his lands to Eustace, Count of Boulogne. With them went the rights of founder, patron or *advocatus* of St Martin-le-Grand, and consequently we find that early in the twelfth century there was, besides the royal interest in St Martin-le-Grand, the interest of the Honour of Boulogne.

For us the importance of this fact is that King Stephen (1135–54) had a double interest in the College. As king he wielded the royal influence descended from the Conqueror, while his wife, Queen Matilda, was the heiress of the Honour

[1] This list, especially as it is not repeated in the Anglo-Saxon part of this bilingual charter, would seem to be an interpolation. *Miskennynge*, for example, seems anachronistic, as also *weardwite*. One might also question the statement that the church was built *canonicalem regulam imperpetuum servandam*.   [2] Round, *Commune*, pp. 28–36.

of Boulogne and so enjoyed the rights of patron. St Martin-le-Grand, therefore, was not only royal, but also firmly attached to the cause of King Stephen as opposed to that of the Empress Maud. It is not in the least surprising to find that, at the first opportunity, Stephen gave its deanery to his own brother, Henry of Blois, even though he was already Bishop of Winchester, Abbot of Glastonbury and (for full measure) Papal Legate. It was for his benefit that at least 33 of the 38 writs in favour of St Martin-le-Grand were issued.

But that is to anticipate. At the beginning of the reign it was not Henry of Blois but another formidable figure, Roger of Salisbury, who was Dean. Roger, of course, was also a bishop, and a statesman and politician of the first rank. King Henry I had raised him up from the dust and had made him first his Chancellor (1101–2) and then head of the royal administration; and Roger himself had raised his family, so that by the beginning of Stephen's reign one of his nephews, Alexander, was Bishop of Lincoln and another, Nigel, both Bishop of Ely and royal Treasurer, while his natural son, Roger le Poer, was the King's Chancellor. As is well known, the power of these episcopal civil servants alarmed King Stephen. He heard that they were plotting his overthrow and consequently arrested them at his midsummer court in 1139 and only released them when they had surrendered their castles.

This break with Stephen's official administrators is usually said to be the turning-point of the reign, but for us its importance lies in the fact that the man who was most active in Roger's defence was also the man who succeeded him as Dean of St Martin-le-Grand. Henry of Blois had just received his commission as Papal Legate when the arrests were made, and he used it to summon an episcopal council to sit in judgment on the King. Henry of Blois held that the King had erred most grievously in arresting the bishops, who should have been subject only to the law of the Church, and according to William of Malmesbury Henry actually declared that he would have preferred to see great damage to his own person and possessions rather than witness such an insult to the exalted office (*celsitudinem*) of bishop. But none the less he pocketed Roger's deanery of St Martin-le-Grand.

The only question is when. Dr Lena Voss thought that the
date was between Roger's arrest on 24 June and his death
on 11 December 1139, but she did not apparently realize
that in this case Henry would have been guilty of a major
breach of canon law. In fact the royal writs make it clear that
he waited till Roger was dead.[1] But the speed with which he
then moved was indecorous and does nothing to remove the
suspicion that the deanery had been promised him in advance
as a peace-offering from the King.

Henry of Blois' appointment coincided approximately with
the opening of the civil war, and the subsequent writs, thirty
in number, are valuable for the light which they throw on the
extent of 'anarchy' that then prevailed. Thirteen concern the
London property of the College, and though allowance must
be made for the repetitions which are characteristic of any
long series of writs, their cumulative effect is considerable.[2]
In 1139, for example, the Justiciar of the City, Osbert
Eightpence, was ordered to re-seise the canons of St
Martin's of the land and houses of which the sons of Hubert
the Youth had recently disseised them unjustly and without
judgment. The King had already commanded the return of
the property by another writ, and soon afterwards he ordered
that the canons were to hold their lands and stalls in peace, as
he had already granted in his charter. The canons were in
particular to hold their church of St Botulf (Aldersgate), and
were not to be impleaded about it until their Dean returned
from Rome, whither he had gone by permission of the King
and at the Pope's command. They were also not to lose their
soke so long as they were not lacking in justice, and they
were to hold as well their soke of Cripplegate, as the King
had already ordered by his writ. Further, the stones which
had fallen from the city wall were to be piled up so as not to
obstruct the road beside the wall; garbage was not to be

---

[1] Lena Voss in *Heinrich von Blois* (Historische Studien, Heft 120 (Berlin,
1932)), p. 100, argued that the writ *Reg.* III, 527, was prior to Roger's death But
her argument was one from silence. It is most likely that the writs *Reg.* III
526–7 were issued by King Stephen on his way to Salisbury to clear up affairs
after Roger of Salisbury's death. See Round, *Geoffrey de Mandeville* (1892),
pp. 46–7; and *The Chronicle of John of Worcester* (ed. J. R. H. Weaver, 1908),
p. 58.   [2] *Reg.* III, 523–35.

dumped on the land outside Cripplegate – the chief culprits being probably the neighbouring butchers of the parish of St Nicholas Shambles in Stinking Lane; and the canons, having proved their right by charter in the Husting Court, were permitted to make further dumping impossible by enclosing the land in question. When, apparently in 1141-3, these walls and curtilages were destroyed by mob violence in despite of the King's writ and peace, the Justiciar and Sheriff were commanded to see that the canons were allowed to rebuild them in peace and sue the malefactors lest the King's justice (*rectum*) be forgotten; and to make assurance doubly sure, Henry of Blois in his capacity of Papal Legate himself addressed two separate letters to the citizens, reminding them of the sentence of excommunication which had been decreed in Council against the plunderers of church property.

It is undoubtedly an impressive catalogue of woe, and one writer, Miss Reddan, has thought it suggested a condition of 'utter anarchy'; but in truth the grievances, though undoubtedly numerous, were not exceptional in their nature. Cases of *novel disseisin* were always occurring even under the strongest of kings, while the stink of the butchers' garbage, so far from being peculiar to the reign of King Stephen, remained a source of civic complaint for more than 200 years, till the slaughterhouses were moved out to Knightsbridge.[1] What is remarkable is that it should have been in 1141–3, three of the darker years of Stephen's reign, that St Martin-le-Grand should have attempted to improve its land outside the City by enclosing and reclaiming what had previously been a rubbish dump. It was an attempt which admittedly ran into trouble, but the very existence of the writs is sufficient to show that the Dean and canons stood their ground and defended their property not by force but by recourse to the law.

It is this reliance on legal form which is, perhaps, the most remarkable feature in the history of St Martin-le-Grand. Even on the canons' country estates, which were all in Essex and uncomfortably close to those of Geoffrey de Mandeville,

[1] V.C.H., *London*, 1, 560. Cf. John Stow, *Survey of London* (C. L. Kingsford's edition, 1908, 1, 316–17).

they were usually capable of producing the correct writ for the correct occasion, and extricated themselves from the most desperate situations by their capacity for invoking the aid of the right authority. Three examples may perhaps be given of the different sorts of situation which they had to face and of the way in which they dealt with them.

First, and most straightforward, was the case of their estate at Good Easter, which suffered severely from its proximity to Geoffrey de Mandeville's manor of High Easter. At first, while Geoffrey was at the height of his power, there was nothing that the canons could do against him, and they did not even seek a writ of protection from the King, presumably because it would have been useless. But when Geoffrey was ill and on his deathbed, their opportunity came. They procured from him a general charter of restitution (which has been printed in part by J. H. Round),[1] and a specific writ to Ælard de Guerris, ordering him to restore the corn and everything else which he had taken from them at Good Easter.[2] But that did not entirely end their troubles, for subsequently they were persecuted by officials of the Honour of Boulogne, one of whom was known as Walter de Guerris; and they required a writ from their patron, the Queen, to call her servants to order.[3]

Secondly, there was a more involved case at Maldon, where St Martin-le-Grand owned the church and its appurtenant lands. These lands were held from two Honours, those of Boulogne and of William Peverel of London, which were both in the King's hand at the beginning of Stephen's reign, the one because it belonged to the Queen, and the other because it had escheated to the Crown. From this coincidence endless confusion arose, for the borough belonged to the royal demesne and was given by Stephen in 1137 as a peace-offering to his brother, Count Theobald of Blois.[4] He in his turn confused (to his own advantage) the

---

[1] Round, *Commune*, p. 118; and Kempe, *op. cit.* p. 61.
[2] Kempe, *op. cit.* p. 61.   [3] *Reg.* III, 557.
[4] *Ibid.* p. 543; and Round, *Geoffrey de Mandeville*, p. 102; and Robert de Toringi in *Chronicles of the Reigns of Stephen, Henry II and Richard I* (ed. R. Howlett, Rolls Series, 1885), IV, 132.

royal demesne with the two Honours in the King's hand, and disseised St Martin-le-Grand of its holding. Consequently, at the turn of 1139–40, the canons mobilized the royal authority with a writ ordering Geoffrey de Mandeville, as Sheriff of Essex, to re-seise them. Eighteen months later, however, Geoffrey himself, having changed sides in the war, was given all Count Theobald's land in Maldon by the Empress Maud; and he must have interpreted the grant as liberally as his predecessor, for when at last he fell, in 1143, St Martin-le-Grand had still not recovered its land and was still procuring writs for its recovery. In 1147 there were more difficulties, this time because Osward the (borough) Reeve had disseised the canons of land which they held from the Honour of Peverell, and it was necessary to invoke the testimony both of the Hundred Court and of the men of the Honour of Peverell.[1]

An interesting feature of this case is that the Queen ordered the Justiciar and Sheriff of Essex (Richard de Lucy and Maurice de Tiretot respectively) 'not to tolerate interference with the alms of St. Martin by Ailward the Archdeacon or any other official'. Ailward, Archdeacon of Colchester, also played a prominent part against the canons in the affair relating to the Chapel of Bonhunt which will serve as the third of our illustrations. The fullest account of it is to be found in a letter of Richard de Belmeis II copied on to the thirteenth-century cartulary roll. In translation it reads as follows:

Richard de Belmeis Archdeacon (of Middlesex) to his venerable lord and father R(obert de Sigillo), by the grace of God bishop of London, greeting with faithful obedience.

The canons of St. Martin assert that they have been oppressed by their witnesses being corrupt and spirited away by guile. At their request, therefore, we have taken care to write the truth of the matter to you, according to what we have seen and heard. For we were at (Saffron) Walden in Chapter with the prior of that vill when Ailward the Archdeacon, having summoned the parties before him, we heard a certain man called Philip contending at length with the canons of St. Martin about the chapel of Bonhunt. At last this Philip asked them if they would give him an adjournment since he had only come with

[1] *Reg.* III, 547–8.

few [supporters]. But the canons opposed him, saying that they were being unjustly troubled by him since the case had been terminated by judgment a long time ago. And they had their witnesses present there, and wanted to produce them in the midst. As the archdeacon was not willing to hear them, the canons approached us, and we went apart to hear what their witnesses wanted to testify. And we heard two priests of venerable age, Aylmer of Newport and Turbert of Littlebury, who gave their testimony and were prepared to prove it. They said that in the church of Wenden, in chapter before the Archdeacon Cyprian, they had heard the chapel of Bonhunt given in judgment to the church of Newport and judged not to belong to the church of Wicken, the parson of Newport then being Adam and that of Wicken Geoffrey. And this is the truth which we then heard there from these witnesses. Farewell![1]

What the motives of Ailward the Archdeacon were we cannot pretend to know, though it is perhaps significant that Geoffrey de Mandeville had lands at all the places – Newport, Bonhunt and Maldon – involved in his opposition. But what we can observe, and indeed admire, is the efficiency with which St Martin-le-Grand invoked alternative or superior authorities to counter Ailward's action. A rival archdeacon was found conveniently on the spot and he, though *ultra vires* (for he was not in his own archdeaconry) held a secessionist court on his own and sent his findings to the bishop. At the same time, and at a higher level, the Dean of St Martin-le-Grand was complaining to the Archbishop and inducing him to take direct action to make Ailward hold up the lawsuit, apparently irrespective of anything that the Bishop of London might say.

This double-checking and appeal to every possible authority is one of the most characteristic features of the College's external policy in Stephen's reign. Whoever it was who gave them legal advice was clearly a man of exceptional thoroughness and thought out every possible contingency. Even in simple matters no risks were taken. An excellent example is afforded by the documents which concern the foundation of a tenth prebend for a tenth canon by Queen Matilda.[2] The endowment was to be provided by giving the

---

[1] Westminster Abbey Muniments, 13167, no. cxxxii.
[2] *Reg.* III, 539–42.

church of Witham to St Martin-le-Grand, and so Matilda addressed a writ to the priest who served Witham, ordering him to submit to the canons. At the same time the King addressed a similar writ in support. The Queen in another writ then notified the Archbishop of the fact. The King did so too, and finally the Archbishop notified the whole of England.[1] A simple affair perhaps, but it involved at least five writs at a time when every writ cost money.

It so happens that three of this particular series have survived in the original, and they are worthy of special consideration. So far as can be seen, they are all written in the same hand. In the case of two of them, the initial writs from the King and the Queen to the priest of Witham, this is hardly surprising, since both writs were addressed from Windsor and were apparently drawn up at the same time; but the third writ is the general notification by Archbishop Theobald, and in this case we should certainly not have expected to find the same scribe. When we find that he was also responsible for six, and possibly seven, more writs by Stephen, and for one letter of Henry of Blois, all of them in favour of St Martin-le-Grand,[2] we can no longer conceal our dismay.

We are faced with the fact that six, or possibly seven, of the thirteen royal writs which we possess in the original were the handiwork of a single scribe whose interests were apparently confined to St Martin-le-Grand. Are we to assume that we are dealing with forgeries on a large scale? If so, they are very special forgeries, for the texts of the writs are good, and contain none of the anachronisms, conflations or inflations that were the stock-in-trade of mediaeval forgers. The witness lists are both varied and chronologically possible; the writing is a court hand; and the parchment, and the way in which it is cut, help to give the documents the external appearance of authentic royal writs. But if they are not ordinary forgeries, some alternative explanation must be found for the single hand that wrote them. Were any of the canons men who might in the normal course of events

[1] A. Saltman, *Theobald, Archbishop of Canterbury* (1956), no. 170.
[2] T. A. M. Bishop, *Scriptores Regis* (1961), p. 8; and *Reg.* III, xiv–xv.

have drawn up official documents not only for the King but also for the Archbishop and Henry of Blois?

The first step in any such inquiry must obviously be to discover who the canons were. Fortunately this is not difficult since in 1158, only four years after the end of Stephen's reign, their names were all recorded in a new prebendal constitution.[1] They were as follows:

> [Henry of Blois, Dean]
> Richard de Montacute (Q)
> Robert of the Castle (*de Castello*)
> Theoldus
> Robert de Cornevilla (K)
> Robert de Limesi (W)
> Augerius the chaplain
> Robert de Boulogne (K)
> Master Bernard de Boulogne (K)
> Ralph the Lotharingian (Lotharus or Lotaringus).

Of these canons, we can say without hesitation that one, Robert of Limesi, had earlier been appointed to a canonry, and had served as chaplain to Henry de Blois in his capacity of Bishop of Winchester: we have not only the charters which he witnessed but also the letter in which Henry as Dean demanded that the canons should give Robert de Limesi the next vacancy.[2] Another canon in the list, Richard de Montacute, was apparently a chaplain or clerk to Queen Matilda towards the end of the reign; and as many as three were chaplains or clerks to the King. Robert de Cornevilla is so described by the writer of the Battle Chronicle in 1148, while Robert de Boulogne and his brother Bernard were given leave of absence from the College at the request of the King. Robert of Boulogne's father, Richard, had been both a royal chaplain and a canon of St Martin's, and it is probable that Adam the King's clerk is to be identified with Adam the clerk of St Martin's.[3]

---

[1] Voss, *op. cit.* p. 151.   [2] *Reg.* III, xi–xiii.
[3] FitzStephen in *Materials for the History of Thomas Becket* (ed. J. C. Robertson, Rolls Series, 1875–8), III, 15; and *Reg.* III, 541. Cf. Saltman, *op. cit.* p. 167.

It would therefore seem that there was a reasonably close connection between the canons and the King's court. But what was their connection, if any, with Archbishop Theobald's household? Here it must be admitted that we have no direct evidence, at any rate so far as the canons of 1158 are concerned; but fifteen or twenty years before the case might well have been different, and if a tentative suggestion may be permitted it is that a link might be found in the two brothers of Boulogne, Baldwin the Archdeacon (of Sudbury) and Master Eustace, who introduced Thomas Becket to the Archbishop. We are told that they were the *familiares* of the Archbishop or of his household. They had also a connection, as their name suggests, with the Honour of Boulogne, and witnessed a charter of Queen Matilda (*c.* 1143–7), which was in favour of St Martin-le-Grand. One might add that it was one of the five documents that concerned the foundation of a tenth prebend for a tenth canon, the series which first attracted our attention to the work of a single scribe. Whether or not the original of this charter was written by him we cannot tell, since unfortunately it is one of the two which are lost so we know it only from a transcript.

It would seem quite possible that the canons of St Martin-le-Grand were so closely connected with the households of the King, Archbishop and Papal Legate that their scribes could be employed in writing writs for all three of them. But if we are to establish a really intimate connection between the King's court and St Martin-le-Grand, it will be necessary to approach the problem of its deanery. In the thirteenth and fourteenth centuries this belonged, as Professor Tout has proved, 'almost by hereditary right to the clerks of the King's Wardrobe',[1] and the question which naturally occurs is whether there was not a somewhat similar connection in the twelfth century also. Our most suitable starting point is the list of Deans given by Miss Reddan in her scholarly article in the *Victoria County History*.[2] The list reads as follows:

[1] T. F. Tout, *Chapters in the Administrative History of England* (1923–35), I, 279.
[2] V.C.H., *London*, I, 564.

1. Ingelric, the first Dean
2. Geoffrey, (?) occurs 1077
3. Roger, Bishop of Salisbury, appointed *temp*. Henry I, died 1139
4. Fulcher
5. Henry of Blois, Bishop of Winchester, appointed *temp*. Stephen, occurs 1158
6. William, son of Count Theobald, *c.* 1160
7. Godfrey de Lucy, appointed 1171, occurs 1177, promoted 1189
8. William de Ste. Mère l'Eglise, appointed 1189, promoted 1199
9. Richard Briger, appointed 1199.

Of these Deans, the last three present little difficulty. In King John's letter of appointment he described Richard Briger as *fidelis clericus noster*.[1] Wiliiam de Ste. Mère l'Eglise was a clerk of the King's Chamber;[2] and Godfrey de Lucy, the son of Richard de Lucy, served Henry II as an itinerant justice. What of the earlier Deans?

It must be admitted that the earlier names in the list are not at first sight promising. But is the list correct? Miss Reddan herself put a question mark against the name of Geoffrey; but that was too modest for she had in fact demonstrated that he was a fictitious character, created by the misreading of Godfrey for Geoffrey in a bull wrongly attributed to Pope Alexander II instead of Alexander III. He is merely Godfrey de Lucy mis-dated by a century!

A second name which may be deleted, though with less certainty, is that of William, son of Count Theobald. He was the nephew of Henry of Blois, was also known as William of the White Hands, and ultimately had a distinguished ecclesiastical career in France, being elected Bishop of Chartres in 1165, Archbishop of Sens in 1168 and Archbishop of Reims in 1176. His connection with the College of St Martin-le-Grand emerges from a letter which he wrote in 1159 or 1160 to inform the canons that both the King and

[1] Westminster Abbey Muniments, 13155.
[2] *D.N.B.*

Henry of Blois wished him to have the deanery.[1] It is clear, however, that at that time he had been neither elected by the canons nor installed by the King; and it must remain an open question if he ever was, especially as by November 1160 Henry II was once again at war with his brother, Count Theobald the Younger.

A further emendation concerns one of the more interesting names on the list, that of Fulcher. We know of him only from the solitary writ which the Empress Maud issued in favour of St Martin-le-Grand. The writ declared that Henry of Blois was to hold certain houses and lands pertaining to the deanery 'as Roger, Bishop of Salisbury, Dean of the same church [of St Martin-le-Grand], and Fulcher were seised of them on the day on which they were alive and dead'.[2] But if Fulcher was thus clearly a Dean of St Martin's, it is also clear that he cannot have been Roger's successor since Henry of Blois succeeded Roger immediately. It would therefore follow, as Dr Lena Voss pointed out, that he must have been his predecessor. Our revised list of the early Deans would then read as follows:

1. Ingelric, alive in 1068 but dead by 1086
2. Fulcher
3. Roger of Salisbury, d. 1139
4. Henry of Blois, 1139–(?)1171
5. Godfrey de Lucy, 1171(?)–1189.

Ingelric as we have already seen was a chaplain and administrator of William the Conqueror, Roger of Salisbury was almost everything from Chancellor to Chief Justiciar, Henry of Blois was King Stephen's brother and the 'Kingmaker' of the period, and Godfrey de Lucy was a civil servant and itinerant Justice. Who was Fulcher?

With nothing to build upon but a single name it might be thought rash to make any attempt at identification, but we cannot refrain from commenting that King William Rufus had a chaplain named Fulcher, and an important one too. He was the brother of Ranulf Flambard and acted in association with him (as we know both from the official acts

---

[1] W.A.M., 13167, no. cxlix.   [2] *Reg.* III, 529.

of the reign and from the testimony of Orderic Vitalis) as one of the chief ministers of the King.[1] In June 1102 this Fulcher was rewarded with the bishopric of Lisieux, and on 29 January following he died, thus disappearing from the scene at the very moment when Roger of Salisbury, successor as Dean, was being promoted in the royal service from the Chancery to an even higher position.[2]

In short, the more one looks at the early history of St Martin-le-Grand in London, the more closely it seems to have been associated with the royal court. There is, for example, the generous grant of William the Conqueror to be considered. Did he really, within two years of the conquest of England, create an *entirely new* immunity in the City of London for the benefit of his chaplain Ingelric? And why did he find it necessary to have the document witnessed in a quite exceptional way, not only by the great men of the kingdom but also by a group who look singularly like the whole of the Chancery staff – Arfast the Chancellor and eight chaplains? The answer may be ready to hand: the precinct of St Martin-le-Grand occupied the probable site for the royal palace of Anglo-Saxon London after King Ethelbert's conversion.[3] It was not till the reign of Edward the Confessor (1042–66), probably *c.* 1060, that the Court moved out of the City to the new palace at Westminster; and it was in Edward's reign also that Ingelric 'founded' the College of St Martin-le-Grand. Is it not possible that Ingelric's College was really a re-foundation, on the site of an old royal one? Such an explanation would explain the extraordinary liberties of the College and why, as a sanctuary in the London area, it was equalled only by Westminster Abbey itself. It would explain also why all the

[1] *Reg.* 1, 464, 480; and Orderic Vitalis, *Historia Ecclesiastica* (ed. A. Le Prévost, 1838–55), iv, 116.

[2] R. W. Southern, 'Ranulf Flambard and Early Anglo-Norman Administration', *Royal Hist. Soc. Trans.*, 4th Series, xvi (1933), 95–128; and *Reg.* ii, ix.

[3] An earlier royal palace, that of King Ethelbert, was probably on the west side of Aldermanbury. See R. E. M. Wheeler, *London under the Saxons* (1935), pp. 103–4; and W. Page, *London, its Origin and Early Development* (1923), pp. 279–80.

royal chaplains witnessed William I's charter, for they
would have been interested parties in a scheme which erected
a new College on the site of their former one. Further, it
would explain the stories, traceable back to the thirteenth
century, which attribute to St Martin-le-Grand a legendary
antiquity that it had been founded by the Britons in memory
of Cadwalla.[1] It would, moreover, explain the dedication to
St Martin, which is always considered to denote an early
origin, and is paralleled exactly at Canterbury where, before
the arrival of St Augustine, Ethelbert's Queen Bertha
worshipped in a church thus dedicated and surely not far
from the royal palace.[2]

The College of St Martin-le-Grand would seem, in short,
to have been a sort of 'proto-Westminster', founded on a
royal site and endowed with royal privileges. By the twelfth
century it had developed into a college of civil servants, its
Dean was the King's chief minister, many of its canons were
clerks of his Chancery or Chamber, and its school, where the
young Becket may perhaps have studied,[3] could easily have
served as the natural training ground for the royal service.
The College was an almost detached part of the King's court
and was the natural home of ecclesiastics trained in the tradition of Roger of Salisbury. Consequently it procured many
royal writs in Stephen's reign, for in a time of civil war
everyone was naturally reduced to self-help: barons built
castles, bishops excommunicated their enemies, and the
King fought for his kingdom. The canons of St Martin's,

---

[1] An alternative version, believed by the canons in the fifteenth century,
was that their founder was Wihtred, King of Kent (690–725), but this
opinion was probably due to confusion with the church of St Martin-le-
Grand, Dover. For both legends see Wheeler, *op. cit.* p. 100 n.

[2] Bede, *Historia Ecclesiastica*, ch. 25 (C. Plummer's edition, 1896, I, 47).

[3] Becket was educated at Merton Abbey and at one of the three schools in
London (*in scholis urbis*). Factors suggesting that this was St Martin-le-
Grand are (1) that his introduction to Archbishop Theobald was effected by
Baldwin and Eustace, the two brothers 'of Boulogne' (above, p. 21); and
(2) that he seems in some sense to have been a protégé of Henry of Blois as
well as of Archbishop Theobald, for it was on the instance of both of these
men that he was appointed Henry II's Chancellor (FitzStephen in *Materials*,
III, 17).

having no power but that of their clerkly hands, simply issued more writs. It is not suggested that the resultant documents were forgeries, for so far as can be seen they were issued in the proper form. They should be regarded simply as a monument to the faith retained by the King's clerks, even at the height of the anarchy, in the remedial power of red tape. They knew that on the final day of reckoning, whenever it might be, their writs would prevail. So they busied themselves with their pens, and addressed their formal writs to every authority that could possibly be useful.

If this interpretation is correct, there is one final problem to be faced. Why was Henry of Blois, the Cluniac high churchman and Papal Legate, so anxious to be Dean of this college of civil servants? It is easy to fall into the trap of thinking that Church and State were opposing ideals, and that no man could possibly have served both. In reality the medieval ideal was that Church and State were one, and it was Henry of Blois' ambition to be, at one and the same time, a sort of resident Pope Gregory VII and papalist Roger of Salisbury. For in spite of the fact that he later found it his duty to sit in judgment on the King, in the earlier years of the reign he undoubtedly acted as chief political adviser to the Crown. Henry aspired, it would seem, to be the first minister of both *regnum* and *sacerdotium*. Is it not possible that in accepting the deanery of St Martin-le-Grand he was hoping to establish control over both the conscience of the King and also his administration? If so, it would have been his aim not only to help formulate the general lines of royal policy but also to supervise the daily business of government, so that the family of Roger of Salisbury would be replaced by that of Blois.[1] This suggestion cannot as yet be substantiated but it emerges from the records of St Martin-le-Grand and is an invitation to further research.

[1] See John of Hexham, *Symeonis Monachi Opera Omnia* (ed. T. Arnold, Rolls Series, 1882–5), II, 331, on the treaty between King Stephen and Duke Henry [of Anjou] in 1153: 'Confirmatumque est inter eos, quod Henricus dux negotia regni disponeret, haeresque regni post regem Stephanum haberetur, idemque Henrico episcopo Wintoniensi ut patri acquiesceret de causis agendis in regno.'

17

The Treaty between William Earl of Gloucester and Roger Earl of Hereford

This treaty, which has not been printed before, is basically a renewal of the treaty made by the two earls' fathers, Robert earl of Gloucester and Miles of Gloucester earl of Hereford, between 25 July 1141 and 24 December 1143. The earlier treaty was printed by J. H. Round from a transcript by Dugdale,[1] and subsequently by Lady Stenton with a reproduction of the seventeenth-century facsimile of it in *Sir Christopher Hatton's Book of Seals*[2], the volume which was presented to her husband on his seventieth birthday. It is therefore a special pleasure to print the sequel in a volume printed in her own honour.

Its date, as explained in the note at the beginning of the text, must be later than the death of earl Robert of Gloucester (31 October 1147), and earlier than the accession of Henry of Anjou to the duchy of Normandy (1150), but all the indications are that it is early in the period. Quite apart from the problematical death of William de Berkeley (? before 9 March 1149), the natural assumption would be that this treaty followed quickly on the death of earl Robert of Gloucester, since it was his death which made it necessary. In the earlier treaty earl Miles of Hereford (d. 24 December 1143) had bound his son and heir, Roger, as well as himself. But the earl of Gloucester had not bound any of his sons to it, so that on his death it automatically lapsed. If the alliance between the earls of Gloucester and Hereford was to continue, it had to be made afresh.

A study of the later treaty is best begun by comparing it with its predecessor. It is immediately apparent that, though cast in the same general form, it is a great deal more precise. In the first place it defines the relationship between the two earls; they are lord and man. The earl of Hereford is to aid the earl of Gloucester '*sicut domino*', and the earl of Gloucester is to aid the earl of Hereford '*sicut homini*'. From William of

---

[1] J. H. Round, *Geoffrey de Mandeville*, 1892, 381-3.
[2] *Sir Christopher Hatton's Book of Seals*, ed. Lewis C. Loyd and Doris Mary Stenton, Oxford, 1950, no. 212.

Malmesbury and John of Worcester we know that the relationship was the same between the two earls' fathers,[1] but in the earlier treaty it was not specifically stated.   In the second place it states categorically which side the two earls were supporting in the civil war, for they both refer to the young Henry as their liege-lord.   Surprisingly enough, there was no comparable declaration in the earlier treaty in which the two earls' fathers had merely promised not to make separate truces or separate peace 'particularly concerning the war which now is between the empress and King Stephen.' One would have expected two supporters of the empress to remember that her proper title (since 8 April 1141) was *domina Anglorum*; and since in the same breath they allowed Stephen his title of king, one can only imagine that they were themselves uncertain of the future.

A third respect in which the later treaty is more precise concerns the benefits to be received by the earl of Hereford.   In the earlier treaty the earl of Gloucester promised to help him to protect those of his inheritances, tenements and conquests which he already had, and to conquer those of his inheritances which he did not then have.   In the later treaty we are told that what this involved in particular was the disinheriting of Gilbert de Lacy.   The point was that earl Roger and Gilbert de Lacy both claimed the inheritance of Hugh de Lacy (d. before 1121), Roger through his wife whose maternal grandmother was apparently Hugh's sister, and Gilbert through his mother who (according to Giraldus Cambrensis) was another sister.   We may suspect that Gilbert's was the better claim, but it was certainly Roger who, through his father Miles of Gloucester, had the greater influence, and in December 1137 his right to the inheritance was recognized by king Stephen.[2]   Gilbert promptly rebelled; we know that in the summer of 1138 he was fighting for the earl of Gloucester in company with his kinsman Geoffrey Talbot II (presumably another claimant though he died conveniently in August 1140).[3]   He may well have imagined that Matilda and the earl of Gloucester would both press his claims.   But alas ! in September 1139 Miles of Gloucester and his son Roger changed sides and were treated with the highest favour by the empress.   Gilbert's only chance was then to change sides himself and regain his inheritance from Stephen.   That was not easy because Stephen had already given Roger's share of the Lacy inheritance to a supporter called Gocelin de Dinan.[4]   But luck favoured Gilbert when Gocelin was unwise enough to desert to the empress   in 1141 .   Gilbert rallied to Stephen, upheld his cause with energy in Herefordshire, and by 1146 had recovered most of his lands.[5]   That was why, in 1147-9, earl Roger was so anxious to disinherit him.   But though he tried hard, as we know from

---

[1] William of Malmesbury, *Historia Novella*, ed. K. R. Potter, Nelson, 1955, 35, '*Recepit illam [imperatricem] postea in Gloecestram Milo, qui castellum eiusdem urbis sub comite habebat tempore regis Henrici*' ; *The Chronicle of John of Worcester*, ed. J. R. H. Weaver, 1908, 56, '*Milo constabularius regiae maiestati redditis fidei sacramentis, ad dominum suum comitem Glaucestrensem . . . se contulit.*'

[2] *Ancient Charters*, ed. J. H. Round, O.S. X, no. 21.

[3] *Gesta Stephani*, ed. K. R. Potter, Nelson, 1955, 39.

[4] H. W. C. Davis, 'Some documents of the Anarchy', *Essays in history presented to R. L. Poole*, ed. H. W. C. Davis, 1927, 173.

[5] R. W. Eyton, *Antiquities of Shropshire*, 1854-60, V, 248-52.

both the letters of Gilbert Foliot[1] and the agreement which he made with William de Braose,[2] he was not successful; even in Henry II's reign it was Gilbert de Lacy who had the inheritance.

A fourth point to be noticed in the treaty between the two earls is the reference to another treaty which had already been made between the earls of Hereford and Leicester, with the earl of Gloucester as a hostage. But for this one reference we would know nothing of this treaty which secured the earl of Leicester's south-western estates in the same way as his treaty with Ranulf earl of Chester secured his north-western estates.[3] To earl Roger of Hereford it was important because the earl of Leicester had himself a claim to the earldom of Hereford (his wife being a great-granddaughter of William fitz Osbern) and in 1140 Stephen had actually given him the whole county, excepting only the estates of two churches and four named supporters.[4] The earl of Leicester had therefore a personal interest in opposing earl Roger, as well as a duty to oppose the enemies of the king; but he was prepared to be bought off, for though he wanted to be loyal to the king, he wanted also to preserve his family estates in Normandy, and Normandy had, since 1144, been lost irrevocably to the Angevins. He was obviously preparing to change sides, though he did it in a seemly manner by first withdrawing into a sort of neutrality.

The most remarkable feature of the treaty as a whole is that the conditions which it stipulates are all in the interest of the earl of Hereford. It is true he admits in passing that he is a vassal (or like a vassal) of the earl of Gloucester, but he only does so on terms. He promises to serve the earl of Gloucester if the earl of Gloucester will help him to disinherit Gilbert de Lacy; and he points out that he has made it impossible for the earl of Gloucester to ask him to attack the earl of Leicester. Though the treaty is called a 'treaty of love', it suggests hard bargaining, as if the earl of Gloucester had had to pay for the continued love and goodwill of the earl of Hereford. Why was the treaty necessary, and why did it have to be guaranteed by twenty-nine hostages, unless there had been reason to doubt their natural friendship?

Earl Roger's father, Miles of Gloucester, was so renowned for his single-minded loyalty to the empress that it has often been assumed that his son was equally loyal. But the newly-discovered portion of the *Gesta Stephani* has shown that this was not so. It recounts how, in 1152 when Stephen's forces were in the ascendant, the earl of Hereford

> 'sent messengers under some pretext and made a secret proposal to the king, saying that he wished to enter upon a pact of inviolable peace and

---

[1] *Gilberti Foliot epistolae*, ed. J. A. Giles, 1845, letters 131, 138, 142. Letter 135 which dates from the vacancy in the see of Worcester (20 Mar. 1150—4 Mar. 1151) and refers to the first of three incidents which embroiled earl Roger with the church, suggests that letters 131, 138 and 142 (which must be subsequent to archbishop Theobald's legatine commission which he had received by March 1150) date from 1151. (Thanks are here due to Professor C. N. L. Brooke).

[2] Hereford cathedral, charter 790, printed by Z.N. and C. N. L. Brooke in *Cambridge Historical Journal*, VIII, 185. The numerous deletions and insertions in the document, together with the French forms of the witnesses' names, show that it is not the original document but a copy of the thirteenth century or later.

[3] Sir Frank Stenton, *The first century of English feudalism*, Oxford, 2nd ed. 1961, 250-3, 286-8.   4 See *n* 4 on p. 256.

friendship with him and fight steadfastly and loyally on his side against his enemies, on condition however that the king would besiege with him, and hand over to him the castle of Worcester, which at that time the knights of the count of Meulan had seized by trickery, capturing and humiliating in close confinement William de Beauchamp, its former possessor who had sided wholeheartedly with the earl of Hereford'.[1]

Roger earl of Hereford was evidently a specialist in treaties of conditional love, having one with the earl of Gloucester, one with the earl of Leicester, and a third with Stephen.   It is hardly surprising that Henry II regarded him with more suspicion than favour.   After his coronation he allowed him to keep the castles of Hereford and Gloucester,[2] but soon he began to have second thoughts about them and the earl rebelled, declaring that he would 'rather undergo all the perils and hardships of rebellion than subject his lordship of the tower of Gloucester and castle of Hereford to the king's authority'.[3]   It is true that he was soon induced to submit and surrender the castles.   But he became a monk and died in the same year, and it is noticeable that his brother and heir, Walter, though he inherited the family estates (without the Lacy lands) was not permitted to inherit the earldom of Hereford, which was deemed to have become extinct.

Since earl Roger's treaty with earl William of Gloucester reflects little credit on his name, it is desirable to reconsider the earlier treaty between earl Miles of Hereford and earl Robert of Gloucester.   Though it is not as specific as the later treaty, it is equally one-sided; J. H. Round who noticed 'the absence of any provision defining the services to be rendered by earl Miles' thought (wrongly) that Dugdale's transcript, from which he was working, must have been incomplete.[4]   In fact earl Miles' part of the bargain was clearly stated; he was to surrender his son Mahel to the earl of Gloucester, for him to keep as a hostage 'until the war between the empress and king Stephen and Henry, son of the empress, be finished.'   In return for that one concession earl Robert was prepared to help earl Miles keep his territorial honour and castles, to defend him against his enemies, and to help him conquer those of his inheritances which he did not then have. He was paying lavishly for the right to secure earl Miles' loyalty with a hostage.   Would he have thought the price worthwhile unless he had serious doubts of earl Miles' intentions ?

---

[1] *Gesta Stephani*, 150-1.

[2] The charter granting him these castles (and other lands) is printed by T. D. Hardy in *Rotuli chartarum in turri Londoniensi asservati*, I, i, 53 and 61.   It probably dates from January 1155 and must be earlier than earl Roger's rebellion in March 1155, because it grants the castles which he subsequently lost.   The fact that it does not include a grant of the Lacy inheritance may have been a further reason for earl Roger's rebellion.

[3] *Historical works of Gervase of Canterbury*, ed. W. Stubbs, Rolls Series, 1879, I, 161-2.   For his becoming a monk, see his brother's charter in *Historia et cartularium monasterii sancti Petri Gloucestriae*, ed. W. H. Hart, Rolls Series, 1863, I, 331.   Was it at the king's insistence ?

[4] *Geoffrey de Mandeville*, 379.

Earl Miles, it must be remembered, was a *parvenu*, one of king Henry's servants who had been raised, if not from the dust at any rate from moderate circumstances. His career has recently been studied by Dr. Walker, and there can be no doubt that if he was richly rewarded by Henry I, he was equally richly rewarded by both Stephen and the empress.[1] He did not lose by the civil war. On the contrary he gained by it, and the first reason for his success was that, unlike the earl of Gloucester, he rallied to Stephen at the very beginning of his reign. The reward for his promptitude was the formal confirmation not only of his existing honours of Gloucester and Brecknock but also of the custody of Gloucester castle 'to hold for the same "farm" as he rendered in the time of king Henry, as his patrimony'.[2] The remarkable thing about this grant is that in Henry's reign Miles had held Gloucester castle, not direct from the king, but under the earl of Gloucester, as William of Malmesbury explicitly states.[3] Miles was therefore improving his own position at the expense of the earl of Gloucester, and it is not surprising to find that when the earl rebelled (May 1138), Miles remained loyal to the king. The most important of the earl's supporters were Miles' enemies, his rivals for the Lacy inheritance, Geoffrey Talbot and Gilbert de Lacy.[4]

Logic and self-interest suggest that Miles should have remained opposed to the earl of Gloucester throughout the civil war. Why then did he rally to the empress in October 1139 ? Was it simply due to the dramatic effect of her arrival in England ? A more potent reason may be suggested by the frequency with which the name of bishop Roger of Salisbury is found in company with that of Miles of Gloucester.[5] The two men must have known each other well. Both were *curiales* who had been raised to greatness by Henry I; both had supported Stephen from the very start of his reign; and both had taken over royal castles. Their positions were very similar, and when Roger of Salisbury and his nephews were suddenly arrested (24 June 1139), Miles might well have felt his own security threatened too. In that case, self-interest would have combined with devotion in prompting Miles to adhere to the empress, in spite of the earl of Gloucester. That he served her loyally is well-known, but there is evidence enough to suggest that his relations with the earl remained cool. He boasted to the Gloucester chronicler that the empress 'had received neither provisions nor service for her table for a single day except by his own munificence and forethought', as if earl Robert had done nothing for her.[6] William of Malmesbury, on the other hand, thought that all the empress' successful activities were directed by earl Robert (to whom he dedicated his book), and his silences about Miles are eloquent. Earl Robert, he

---

[1] David Walker, 'Miles of Gloucester earl of Hereford,' *Trans. Bristol and Gloucestershire Archaeological Society*, LXXVII, 66-84, and 'The "honours" of the earls of Hereford in the twelfth century', *ibid.*, LXXIX, 174-211.

[2] *Geoffrey de Mandeville*, 13 *n*, reading '*firma*' for the transcript's '*forma*.'

[3] *Historia Novella*, 35. This fact also explains, *pace* Round, why Stephen made his agreement with Miles '*sicut rex et dominus.*'

[4] *Gesta Stephani*, 39 ; *Geoffrey de Mandeville*, 284-5.

[5] The names occur together most often in charters and writs of Henry I, but see also *Ancient Charters*, no. 22, and the writs by Stephen and Roger of Salisbury in favour of St. Guthlac's, Hereford, Balliol College, Oxford, MS. 271, items 415 and 439.

[6] *Florentii Wigorniensis monachi chronicon ex chronicis*, ed. B. Thorpe, 1849, II, 132.

declared, was 'alone or almost alone' in serving the empress without self-interest, her other adherents being 'either followers of fortune who change as it changes or having already made great gains, fight for justice in the hope of yet richer rewards'.[1]   Miles of Gloucester, one feels, was intended for this second category; from Stephen he had received Gloucester castle (1136), and the daughter of Pagan fitz John (complete with the Lacy inheritance) as a bride for his son (1137), while his subsequent fight for empress and justice brought him the castle of St. Briavel's and the forest of Dean (1139), the earldom of Hereford (1141) and the honour of Abergavenny.[2]   He was a powerful man whose support was essential to the Angevin cause, but it may well have been that his support could not be had for nothing.   The earl of Gloucester had reason to know his man.   He demanded the privilege of taking a hostage, and paid for it.

1

In the 35*th Report of the Deputy Keeper of the Public Records*, 2, this document is summarized and erroneously dated '1154'. The outside limits of date are the death of earl Robert of Gloucester (31 October 1147) and the accession of Henry to the duchy of Normandy (1150). Narrower date limits are suggested by the appearance of William de Berkeley among the list of hostages, since he seems to have died before 9 March 1148-9 when his cousin and heir, Roger de Berkeley III, was received by the monks of Kingswood as their founder (*Monasticon Anglicanum*, Record Commission, 1817-30, V, 427 (x), where the relevant charter is dated '*sexto idus Martii anno ab incarnatione* 1148'); as Kingswood was a Cistercian house, and the Cistercians usually calculated the beginning of the year from 25 March after Christmas, the year would probably have been 1149 by our reckoning.

Hec est confederacio amoris inter Willelmum comitem Gloec' et Rogerum comitem Herefordie. Rogerus comes Herefordie affidavit et juravit Willelmo comiti Gloec' quod ei fidem tenebit et auxilium feret sicut domino contra omnes homines nisi contra corpus domini sui Henrici. Et Willelmus comes Gloec' affidavit et juravit Rogero comiti Herefordie quod ei fidem tenebit et auxilium feret sicut homini suo contra omnes homines nisi contra corpus domini sui Henrici et nominatim ad exherandum Gillebertum de Lasci. Salvo hostagio in quo Rogerus comes Herefordie posuit Willelmum comitem Gloec' erga Robertum comitem Legrecestrie. Et prescripte confederacionis firmiter tenende inter eos ad posse suum sunt isti sui homines obsides per fidem ita quod si aliquis eorum comitum inde exiret et se eorum admonitu infra quadraginta dies nollet corrigere, in eorum serviciis utilitatem non haberet donec se corrigeret. Et isti sunt obsides ex parte Rogeri comitis Herefordie per fidem:—Walterus frater comitis Heref', Badero de Munemua, Elyas Giffard, Walterus de Clifford, Rogerus de Stantona,[3] Alanus filius Main, Rad[ulfus] de Baschervilla, Willelmus de Berchelai, Hugo forestarius, Rad[ulfus] Avenel, Ricardus Talebot, Robertus de Cha[n]dos, Robertus de Bask[er]villa, Hugo de Heisa. Et isti sunt obsides

---

[1] *Historia Novella*, 64.
[2] *Geoffrey de Mandeville*, 56, 123 ; *Ancient Charters*, no. 26. The honour of Abergavenny was given by Brien fitz Count with the empress' approval perhaps in return for the numerous sorties which Miles made to relieve Brien in Wallingford.
[3] Corrected from *Santona*.

ex parte Willelmi comitis Gloec' per fidem:—Robertus frater suus, Hugo de Gunn' constab[ularius], Gregorius filius Roberti, Rogerus de Berchelai, Rad[ulfus] de Hastingis, Ricardus de Sancto Q[u]intino, Willelmus filius Johannis de Molariis, Symon de Sancto Laudo, Fulcho filius Guarini, Willelmus filius Elye constab', Hubertus dapifer, Robertus de Alm[er]i dapifer, Rogerus dapifer, Robertus Norr[eis] vic[ecomes], Mauricius de Lundoniis. [31 October 1147-1150, probably 31 October 1147—9 March 1149].

HEC EST COMPOSICIO AMORIS

Size : 7⅞″ x 7⅛″; the document is a chirograph. This is the upper part, and consequently the tongue for the seal of one of the earls is at the top. The seal is missing.

Endorsement : *Confederacio amoris inter Willelmus com[item] Glouc[estrie] et Rogerum com[item] Hereford[ie]*. [14th century; the remaining endorsements are modern].

Public Record Office, Duchy of Lancaster, Ancient Deeds, Series L (D.L.25)4.

2

Treaty between Robert earl of Gloucester and Miles earl of Hereford [25 July 1141—24 December 1143, probably June 1142]. Reprinted from *Sir Christopher Hatton's Book of Seals*, ed. L. C. Loyd and D. M. Stenton, Oxford, 1950, no. 212. The names of hostages who occur in the later treaty are in italics.

Noscant omnes hanc esse confederationem amoris inter Robertum comitem Gloecestrie et Milonem comitem Herefordie. Robertus comes Gloecestrie assecurauit Milonem comitem Herefordie fide et sacramento, quod custodiet illi pro toto posse suo et sine ingenio suam uitam et suum membrum et terrenum suum honorem, et auxiliabitur illi ad custodiendum sua castella et sua recta et sua hereditaria et sua tenementa et sua conquisita que modo habet et que faciet et suas consuetudines et rectitudines et suas libertates in bosco et in plano et aquis. Et quod sua hereditaria que modo non habet ei auxiliabitur ad conquirendum. Et si aliquis uellet inde comiti Hereford' malum facere uel de aliquo decrescere si comes Hereford' uellet inde guerreare quod Robertus comes Gloecestrie cum illo se teneret et quod ad suum posse illi auxiliaretur per fidem et sine ingenio. Nec pacem neque trewias cum illis haberet qui malum comiti Herefordie inferrent nisi per bonum uelle et garantum comitis Hereford'. Et nominatim de hac guerra que modo est inter imperatricem et regem Stephanum se cum comite Hereford' tenebit et ad unum opus erit et de omnibus aliis guerris. Et in hac ipsa confederatione amoris affidauit comitissa Gloecestrie quod suum dominum in hoc amore erga Milonem comitem Heref' pro posse suo tenebit et si inde exiret ad suum posse illum ad hoc reponeret. Et si non posset legalem recordationem si opus esset inde faceret ad suum scire. Et de hac conuencione firmiter tenenda ex parte comitis Gloecestrie sunt hii obsides per fidem et per sacramenta erga comitem Hereford', hoc modo quod si comes Gloecestrie de hac conuencione exiret dominum suum comitem Gloecestrie requirerent ut se erga comitem Heref' erigeret, et si infra xl dies se nollet erga comitem Heref' erigere, se comiti Heref' liberarent ad faciendum de illis suum uelle, uel ad illos retinendum in suo seruitio donec illos quietos clamaret, uel ad illos ponendum ad legalem redempcionem ita ne terram perderent. Et quod legalem recordationem de hac conuencione facerent si opus esset Guefridus de Walteriuill, Ricardus de Greinuill', Osbernus Octdeners, Reinaldus de Cahagnis, *Hubertus dapifer,* Odo Sorus, Gislebertus de Unfranuill', *Ricardus de Sancto Quintino.* Et ex parte Milonis comitis Heref' ad istud confirmandum concessit Milo comes Hereford Roberto comiti Gloecestrie Mathielum filium suum tenendum in obsidem donec guerra inter imperatricem et regem Stephanum et Henricum filium imperatricis finiatur. Et interim si Milo comes Heref' uoluerit aliquem alium de suis filiis qui sanus sit in loco Mathieli filii sui ponere recipietur. Et postquam guerra finita fuerit et Robertus comes Gloecestrie et Milo comes Hereford' terras suas et sua recta rehabuerint, reddet Robertus comes Gloecestrie Miloni comiti Hereford' filium suum. Et tunc de probis hominibus utriusque comitis considerabuntur et capientur obsides et securitates de amore ipsorum comitum tenendo in perpetuum. Et de hac conuencione amoris Rogerus filius comitis Heref' affidauit et iurauit comiti Gloecestrie quod patrem suum pro posse suo tenebit. Et si comes Hereford' inde uellet exire Rogerus filius suus inde illum requireret et inde illum corrigeret, et si comes Heref' se inde erigere nollet seruitium ipsius Rogeri filii sui prorsus perdet donec se erga comitem Gloecestrie erexisset. Et de hac conuencione ex parte comitis Heref' sunt hii sui homines obsides erga comitem Gloecestrie per fidem et per sacramenta hoc modo, quod si comes Heref' de hac conuencione exiret dominum suum comitem Heref' requirerent ut se erga comitem Gloecestrie erigeret, et si infra xl dies se nollet erga comitem Gloecestrie erigere, se comiti Gloecestrie liberarent ad faciendum de illis suum uelle, uel ad illos retinendum in suo seruitio donec illos quietos clamaret, uel ad illos ponendum ad legalem redempcionem ita ne terram perderent. Et quod legalem recordationem de hac conuencione in curia facerent si opus esset Robertus Corbet, Willelmus Mansel, *Hugo de Lahese.*

18

An Oxford Charter of 1191 and the Beginnings of Municipal Freedom

THE charter shown on Plates I & II is the earliest charter extant to have been given by the city of Oxford, and its seal is the earliest municipal seal in Great Britain. It was given to Oseney Abbey, in whose archives it presumably remained until the dissolution of the monasteries. After the dissolution nearly all the Oxford charters of Oseney Abbey went to Christ Church, but this one was obviously a collector's piece. By the 19th century it was in the possession of the Willes's of Newbold Comyn (Warwicks.). Whichever member of the family bought it would probably have bought also the charter of the Empress Matilda for Bordesley Abbey (now Brit. Mus., Add. Ch. 75724) which was certainly owned by William Willes in 1875, and like the Oxford charter, has a remarkable seal in a damask seal-bag. Both these charters were sold by Mr. E. J. Willes at an auction at Sotheby's on 10 July 1968, and the Oxford charter was bought by the city. It is now displayed in the plate-room at the Town Hall. Its text runs as follows:

> Notum sit tam presentibus quam futuris quod Nos Cives Oxenefordie de Communi Civitatis et de Gilda Mercatoria, pro salute nostra ac nostrorum, et pro animabus parentum et antecessorum nostrorum, concedimus et presenti carta nostra confirmamus Ecclesie Sancte Marie de Oseneia et canonicis in ea Deo servientibus donationem quam antecessores nostri eis fecerunt de Insula de Middeneia cum omnibus pertinentibus ejus. Ita ut singulis annis ad festum Sancti Michaelis reddant ipsi canonici dimidiam marcam argenti pro hac eadem tenatura ubi nos jusserimus, sicut testatur cirographum antecessorum nostrorum quod eis de donatione ejusdem insule fecerunt. Preterea quia nos cepimus in manu pro nobis et pro heredibus nostris warantandi predictam insulam eisdem canonicis ubique et versus omnes homines, ipsi pro hac

---

* The following abbreviations are used:
Ogle: Octavius Ogle, *Royal Letters Addressed to Oxford and now existing in the City Archives*, Oxford, 1892.
O.H.S.: Oxford Historical Society.
Oseney Cart.: The Cartulary of Oseney Abbey, ed. H. E. Salter, 6 vols. (O.H.S., 1929–36).
Oxford Charters: Facsimiles of Early Charters in Oxford Muniment Rooms, ed. H. E. Salter, Oxford, 1929.
Regesta: Regesta Regum Anglo-Normannorum, iii (1135-54), ed. H. A. Cronne and R. H. C. Davis, Oxford, 1968.
S.F. Cart.: The Cartulary of the Monastery of St. Frideswide at Oxford, ed. S. R. Wigram, 2 vols. (O.H.S., 1894–6).

warantatione solvent nobis et heredibus nostris singulis annis ad Pascha
aliam dimidiam marcam quam tradent cui nos jusserimus, et nos et heredes
nostri fideliter warantabimus eis predictum tenementum per servitium
predicte marce annue pro omnibus rebus et pro omnibus servitiis.   Hanc
nostram concessionem et confirmationem fecimus nos communi consilio
Civitatis, et communali sigillo nostro confirmavimus.   Hii sunt autem qui
hanc concessionem et confirmationem fecerunt: Nigellus tunc Decanus
Oxenef(ordie); Joh(anne)s Kepeherm, et Henr(icus) filius Segrini, tunc
alderma(n)ni; Laur(encius) Kepeh(er)m, et Thom(as) de Thademartona,
tunc pretores; Petr(us) fil(ius) Gaufridi, Will(elmu)s fil(ius) pretoris,
Will(elmus) fil(ius) Rad(ulfi), Thom(as) fil(ius) Ailrici, Henric(us) fil(ius)
Simeonis, Laur(encius) fil(ius) Hardingi, Rad(ulfus) Padi, Walt(erus) fil(ius)
Viel, Will(elmus) fil(ius) Kniht, Segar mercator, Rog(erus) fil(ius) Sewi,
Joh(anne)s fil(ius) Ailnod, Malger(us) vinitari(us), Adam Rufus, Barthol
(omeus) Grosmarchie, Rog(erus) fil(ius) Burewoldi, Gileb(ertus) fil(ius)
Buroldi, Jocelino (*sic*) fil(io) Safari, Rad(ulfus) Coleman, Will(elmus) fil(ius)
Rog(eri) fil(ii) Siwardi, et Hug(o) fr(ater) ejus, Alvredus Delmeleia, Owein
et Rob(ertus) filius ejus, Beneit fil(ius) Ailnod, Rad(ulfus) filius Bur',
Henr(icus) de Chaudre, et Lambertus frat(er) ejus, Will(elmus) Pilet,
Walt(erus) Pille, Will(elmus) fil(ius) Amfridi fil(ii) pretoris, Rad(ulfus
Cordewanarius filius Simonis Cordewan(arii), Henr(icus) de Lisewis, Hug(o)
aurifab(er), Ric(ardus) fr(ater) ejus, Petr(us) fil(ius) Joh(ann)is, Joh(anne)s
aurifab(er), Nichol(aus) fil(ius) Sewi, Walt(erus) Halgod et Rad(ulfus)
fr(ater) ejus, Rad(ulfus) Kepeh(er)m, et Beneit frat(er) ejus, Adam
vinitari(us), Joh(anne)s fili(us) Henr(ici) cl(er)ici, Nichol(aus) fil(ius)
Will(elm)i fil(ii) Rad(ulfi), Henr(icus) fil(ius) Gaufr(idi) fil(ii) Bodini, et
Ric(ardus) fr(ater) ejus, Will(elmus) Husari(us) de Osen(eia), et Hug(o)
fili(us) ejus, Henr(icus) cl(er)icus tunc clericus pretorum, Ric(ardus) fili(us)
Hardingi, Rob(ertus) fil(ius) Wimarc, B(e)n(e)dict(us) fil(ius) Paulini,
Rob(ertus) fil(ius) Gaufr(idi) fil(ii) Bodini medarii, Thom(as) fil(ius)
Eadwini, et Henr(icus) fr(ater) ejus, Rog(erus) fil(ius) Fulconis, et totum
Commune Civitatis Oxoneford(ie).[1]

Discussion of the charter starts best with the seal which the evidence of this
charter establishes as the oldest municipal seal in Great Britain.   It had a long
life, being used as the common seal of the city until the 17th century; Twyne
made a drawing of it from an impression on a lease of 1638,[2] and its destruction
in 1662 is recorded in the Council Acts:

The seal which, for many years past has been used as the common seal of the
City is now thought ' by reason of its absurd, ill and unhandsome cutting to be
dishonourable to the Cittie and unfit to be used '.   The Mayor, with the con-

[1] A shortened version, with only the first 6 of the 63 witnesses, from the Oseney Cartulary (B.M.,
Cotton MS., Vitellius E. xv) was printed in *Osen. Cart.*, iv, 88 (no. 63), and discussed by James Tait in
The Medieval English Borough, Manchester, 1936, 235.
[2] Bodleian Lib., Twyne MS. 3, f. 127.   An impression from a deed of 1384 in the archives of
Magdalen College is illustrated as the frontispiece of *Oxford City Charters*, ed. H. E. Salter (O.H.S.,
1926).

sent of his brethren, has had a new seal cut ' with the Armes of the Citty together with the supporters and Crest thereunto belonging ', which seal being shown to a full meeting of the council is approved by them.   It is agreed that this new seal is henceforth to be used as the Common Seal of the City and the old seal broken as soon as the keykeepers meet to open the chest, and the new seal is to be committed to the custody of the Mayor and the key-keepers according to custom.   Until the old seal is broken, which will be this afternoon or nine o'clock tomorrow morning (in the presence of the viewers now named and as many of the house as care to come) the new seal is committed to the care of the Mayor and Mr. Ald. Harris.[3]

There were five keykeepers with five keys.   The reason why so many people were involved was that once the seal was affixed to a document it was legally binding on the whole city.   Possession of a common seal was the most obvious way of demonstrating that the citizens had formed themselves into a corporate body, so that they could be regarded as ' the city ' rather than a chance collection of citizens.   Anyone who wished to abolish the liberties of a corporate body had to destroy its seal, as happened at Salisbury in 1304 and St. Albans in 1332.[4]

The seal depicts a complete walled city whose identity is established by the superimposition of an ox passant (from dexter to sinister, and not from sinister to dexter as in later times).   Inside the city are three cylindrical towers with conical roofs which do not resemble any of the existing towers in Oxford.   It is possible that the central (and tallest) one, which is adorned with large chevrons, may be intended as the original tower of St. Martin's at Carfax, since (according to a charter of 1172) it was in the cemetery of that church that the portmanmoot met.[5]   The legend, which is damaged on the present impression, is known from other impressions, and read: +SIGILL' COMMVNE OMNIVM CIVI͞V CIVITATIS OXENEFORDIE, ' the common seal of all the citizens of the city of Oxford '.

About the turn of the 12th and 13th centuries several towns acquired seals of this general type, with a representation of a town or part of a town, or, in the case of a port, a ship.   The most prominent examples, with the earliest dates at which they occur, may be listed in two groups according as their legends refer to people (citizens, burghers or barons) or places (towns, cities or boroughs):

York   Sigillum Civium Eborac. Fideles Regis (Aug. 1191–1206).[6]
Winchester   Sigillum Civium Wintoniensium.

3 *Oxford Council Acts* (1626–66), ed. M. G. Hobson and H. E. Salter (O.H.S., 1932), 290.
4 Tait, *Medieval English Borough*, 236–7.
5 *Oseney Cart.*, II, 550 (no. 1097).
6 *Early Yorkshire Charters*, I, no. 298.

Worcester	Sigillum Commune Civium Wigornie.
Gloucester	Sigillum Burgensium de Gilda Mercatorum Gloucestrie (1200).
Scarborough	Sigillum commune burgensium de Scardeburg.
London	Sigillum baronum Londoniarum (1219).
Ipswich	Sigillum Communitatis Ville Gypewic (1200).[7]
Exeter	Sigillum Civitatis Exonie (1208).[8]
Southampton	Sigillum Ville Suthamtonie.
Taunton	Sigillum commune Burgi Tantonie.

To some people it has seemed puzzling that the city should have a common seal before it received the grant of the fee-farm in 1199, because the grant of fee-farm is often spoken of as if it ' made ' a borough. In fact most towns became corporate bodies by a very gradual process. What the grant of the fee-farm did was to establish the royal dues as a fixed annual sum, and authorize the townsmen to collect it through their own reeves without the intervention of the sheriff; in the formal language of King John's charter for Oxford in 1199 the King granted the town to the burgesses, to be held of the crown in chief and in perpetuity for an annual ' farm ' of £63 0s. 5d.[9] It did not ' make ' the town a corporate body, but recognized that it already was one, so that the King could hold it corporately responsible for its dues.

The importance of the charter which we are studying is that in its text, and in the background of its text, we can trace something of the slow process by which the citizens of Oxford became a corporate body. In the very first line they describe themselves as ' We the citizens of Oxford of the commune of the city and of the Guild Merchant '. What did these words mean? Some of them are straightforward. ' Citizen ' (*civis*), for example, is used in chronicles, charters and Pipe Rolls as the exact equivalent of ' burgher ' (*burgensis*); the two words are interchangeable and denote a townsman of the ruling class, as opposed to mere labourers who did not count as citizens. The term ' Guild Merchant ' (or guild *of* merchants) is also unambiguous. According to Henry II's charter, no one who was not of the guild could engage in merchandise in the city or suburb except (presumably) during the midsummer fair of St. Benedict.[10] It is easy to see that if the trade of the town was confined to guildsmen, no one who was not a guildsman could possibly be a leading

---

[7] Charles Gross, *The Gild Merchant*, Oxford, 1890, 117.
[8] The matrix of this seal has an inscription recording that it was presented by William Prudum who flourished, not (as was once thought) *c.* 1170, but in the first quarter of the 13th century. (See Ethel Lega-Weekes, ' Prudum, Prodom, etc. of Exeter, and the first city seal ' in *Report and Transactions of the Devon Assoc.*, XLVIII (1915), 248–56.)
[9] Ogle, 5–6.
[10] Ogle, 4–5; Stubbs, *Select Charters* (9th ed., 1913), 198–9.

townsman, i.e. ' citizen ' or ' burgher '. For that reason historians have often been confused by the distinction, or lack of distinction, between Guild and Town; and in the case of the present charter it will be seen that the terms are virtually synonymous. But we must not forget that some members of the guild, who might also call themselves citizens, would not have been townsmen in our sense of the word. A few of them could be secular or ecclesiastical lords who lived outside the city but needed its trading facilities; in 1147, for example, the chief man or ' alderman ' of the guild was an important baron called William Chesney who was, amongst other things, castellan of Oxford castle.

The term ' commune ' is more difficult, since it was a word which aroused strong emotions. In its proper sense it denoted a conjuration, that is to say a group of people who had taken an oath to unite, and remain united, in a single corporation; and hence it could be viewed as the ' body politic ' of a guild or town. Glanvill, for example, in explaining how a villein could make himself free, said that he could do it by residing for a year and a day in a privileged town, ' provided that he is received into their commune, that is to say their guild, as a citizen ' (*ita quod in eorum communam, scilicet gildam, tanquam civis receptus fuerit*).[11] It was a fact, however, that on the continent the earliest communes had been established by rebellions of the townsmen. With Cambrai, Ghent or Milan in mind the word acquired a revolutionary flavour. Many people thought of communes as established ' against ' their lords in order to abolish established authority. The classic exposition of this view in England came from the pen of a monk of Winchester when he wrote about the grant of a commune to London in 1191 :

> Now in the indulgence of this conjuration for the first time London knew that there was no King in the kingdom, for neither King Richard himself nor his predecessor and father [King] Henry would have let such a thing happen for a thousand thousand silver marks. How great indeed are the evils that derive from a conjuration can be seen from its very definition which is this: a commune is a tumult of the people, the terror of the kingdom, and the tepidity of the Church (*tumor plebis, timor regis, tepor sacerdotii*).[12]

In this sense it is probably true that there were no communes in England before the death of King Henry II. But if we accept the word in the unemotional context which Glanvill gives it, the case is different. In Stephen's reign there are clear references to a commune not only in London but also in Oxford.[13]

---

[11] Glanvill, ed. G. D. G. Hall (Nelson's Medieval Texts, London, 1965, 58.)

[12] *The Chronicle of Richard of Devizes*, ed. J. T. Appleby (Nelson's Medieval Texts), London, 1963, 49. The point of the word *tepor* was in its alliteration with *tumor* and *timor*, but the force of its meaning is clear in *Revelation*, iii, 16: ' So then because thou art lukewarm (*tepidus*), and neither cold nor hot, I will spue thee out of my mouth.'

[13] R. H. C. Davis, *King Stephen*, London, 1967, 58–9.

In the Oseney Cartulary there is a copy (unfortunately incomplete) of a charter of 1147 which is the exact counterpart of the charter which we are now studying, since it records the original grant which the charter of 1191 confirms, and likewise describes the grantors as ' We the citizens of Oxford of the commune of the city and of the Guild Merchant '.   It has been printed by Salter, but its importance in the present context is such that we must print it again

Cyrographum burgensium Oxon de Middeleye

Notum sit cunctis fidelibus Sancte Ecclesie tam presentibus quam futuris quod nos cives Oxenefordie de commun(i) civitatis et de gilda mercatorum, pro stabilitate totius regni et statu et incolumitate regis nostri et regine et filiorum suorum, necnon et pro nostra salute omniumque nostrorum et pro animabus patrum nostrorum et matrum et omnium antecessorum nostrorum, damus et concedimus in perpetuam elemosinam ecclesie Dei et Sancte Marie de Osen(eia) et canonicis ibidem deo servientibus insulam nostram que vocatur Middeleya, cum omnibus ad se pertinentibus, in terris et pratis et pasturis cum omnibus eisdem libertatibus et consuetudinibus quas ibi antecessores nostri habuerunt liberalibus concessionibus regum, et nos post ipsos; ita tamen ut singulis annis reddant ipsi canonici dimidiam marcam argenti pro hac eadem tenura, ubi nos jusserimus.   Hanc donationem et concessionem fecimus communi consensu in portmanmot, et hanc eandem fecimus in capitulo de Osen(eia) coram canonicis ejusdem loci et in presentia Will(elm)i de Cheneto aldermanni nostri, et per eum, et postea cum ipso supra altare cum textu obtulimus.   De hac donatione et concessione est testis Everard(us) abbas de Thama etc.[14]

The essential differences between this charter and that of 1191 are that it contains no mention of a common seal, and that at the last moment it introduces an element of doubt as to who made the gift   Why did the citizens declare that having made the grant with the consent of the portmanmoot ' we have made it again in the Chapter of Oseney before the canons of that place, and in the presence of William de Chesney our alderman, *and through him*; and *with him* we have offered it on the altar with the charter ' ?   Why did they have to involve William de Chesney, and what did he do?

The short answer would seem to be that unlike the ordinary citizens he was a baron—he was in fact the commander of the royal garrison—and that unlike the commune he had a seal.   He could produce a charter which the King's court would consider valid; and this is what the canons of Oseney wanted, and got.   Its text reads as follows:

---

[14] *Oseney Cart.*, IV, 86 (no. 62), from the cartulary at Christ Church, f. 32.   The date is provided by the Oseney Annals (ed. H. R. Luard, in *Annales Monastici*, IV (R. S., 1869), 25: ' Eodem anno (1147) donata insula Middenia ecclesiae nostrae a civibus Oxoniae.'   This is consistent also with the witnesses of William Chesney's charter.

Cunctis fidelibus Sancte Ecclesie tam pre*sentibus quam futuris* Willelmus de Cheneto salutem. Sciatis *quod ego Willelmus de Cheneto* qui sum aldreman de gilda *mercatorum Oxenefordie, pro* salute regis Stephani et regine et *Eustachii filii* sui et mea atque meorum et pro animabus patris *mei et Rogeri* fratris mei et omnium parentum meorum et *antecessorum, do* atque concedo in perpetuam elemosinam ec*clesie Dei et Sancte* Marie de Oseneia et canonicis ibidem Deo *servienti*bus insulam que Middeleia vocatur, quam cives Oxenefordie de communi civitatis et de gilda mercatorum michi in perpetuum feudum consesserunt; et hoc facio predictorum civium consensu et voluntate; reddendo singulis annis dimidiam marcam argenti, de qua eos omni anno acquietabo, in escambio decimationum molendinorum meorum que sunt juxta castellum Oxeneford. Hanc concessionem *et* dationem, prout concessum a civibus fuerat in portmanimot feci in capitulo de Oseneia coram ejusdem loci canonicis super textum, et in presentia Everardi abbatis de Thama et Aluredi [abbatis] de Dorchcestreia super altare cum textu obtuli, et pl[ures] ex eis civibus mecum qui ad hoc ipsum [ab] aliis fu[erunt] missi. Quapropter volo atque precor ut bene [et in] pace et honorifice prefatam insulam p[refata ecclesia] teneat sicut unquam ipsi cives aut eorum antecessores melius et honestius et liberius ten[uerunt de] liberalibus concessionibus regum. Testibus predictis [abbatibus] Everardo de Thama, et Aluredo de [Dorch-cestreia], et Roberto fratre meo archidiacono de Leicestria, [Hugone] de Cheneto, et Willelmo de Stratfort, et Azor [vicecomite], et Willelmo de Glinton, et multis aliis.[15]

The legal device is that the citizens are said to have given Medley to William Chesney in perpetual fee, so that he in his turn could give it to Oseney in free alms. In the course of the transaction William made a little profit for himself, for he acquitted the canons of the annual rent (6s. 8d.) which they owed the city for Medley, in exchange for their acquitting him of the tithes which he owed them from his mills by the castle. In strict fairness he should then have paid the 6s. 8d. a year to the city himself, but it is hard to believe that he did so.

In any case there was a much greater complication in the fact that the citizens had already given Medley to someone else. Some nine years before, in the course of a dispute with the Priory of St. Frideswide, they had secured from King Stephen a writ ordering the removal of some stalls belonging to the priory in the city. The priory had claimed compensation, since the revenues from the stalls maintained a light in its church; and as a result the citizens were forced to give it Medley in exchange. This was confirmed by a royal writ in 1138-9, but we may suspect that the citizens were already plotting to recover

---

[15] *Oseney Cart.*, IV, 87 (no. 62 A). In the present text I have shown the elements from which Salter reconstructed the text. The basis is the cartulary of *c.* 1200 (B.M., Cotton MS., Vitellius E., xv, f. 89) which was badly damaged in the Cottonian fire of 1731. Words in italics are supplied from the transcript made by Twyne in the 1640s (Bodleian Lib., Twyne MS. 22, p. 291), but this is incomplete and stops with the words ' super textum '. Words printed in square brackets are conjectural.

Medley, since it was not specifically named in the writ but described in a splendidly roundabout way as ' a meadow . . . , that is to say that island which borders on (*continet*) Fenneit and Cripley '.[16]   It is hard to believe that when in 1147 they gave Medley to Oseney, they were not acting, in part at least, from spite of St. Frideswide's.   Oseney was in favour because it was outside the city; St. Frideswide's was out of favour because it was inside the city and enjoyed rights which could well interfere with the citizens' aspirations.

Naturally St. Frideswide's was not prepared to accept the loss tamely.   It took the matter to law, and we next hear of it in a remarkable letter written to Archbishop Theobald by Atsur (or Azor) who was both sheriff of the shire and a citizen of the city.   He had previously attested William Chesney's grant of Medley, but now (1150–2) he had to dance to a different tune.   Translated his letter runs as follows:

> To Theobald by the grace of God archbishop of Canterbury, primate of all England, and legate of the Apostolic See, Atsur sheriff and citizen of Oxford with all the other citizens of that city, greetings as to their father and lord. We testify before God and yourself that at the command and adjuration of the King we have assembled the portmanmoot (*portmannimot coadunavimus*), and have recalled that the church of St. Frideswide was in possession of a certain island called Medley (*Middeleit*) when Prior Robert of the said church set out for Rome, but that when he came back he found that his church had been despoiled of it without judgment.   And immediately on this same day we have returned to the King and testified to this fact in the presence of him and his barons.   Farewell in Christ.[17]

The reason why the sheriff was reporting to the archbishop was presumably because the case had been taken up in the ecclesiastical as well as the royal court—the Oseney Annals tell us that in 1151 Abbot Wigod went to Rome, ' provoked by Robert prior of St. Frideswide's '[18]—but for us the main interest lies in the light which the letter throws on the organization of the city.   This time there is no mention of commune, guild, or alderman.   It is the sheriff who has assembled the citizens in the portmanmoot and who leads the delegation that bears its testimony to the king.   It is true that he was also a citizen, but the stark fact was that Church and King had intervened to undo the injustice which the citizens had done.   In a royal writ King Stephen confirmed

[16] *Regesta*, III, no. 638, which also explains the dispute about the stalls.   Cf. *Wood's History of the City of Oxford*, ed. A. Clark (O.H.S., 1889–1899), II, 500–01.
[17] Text in *S.F. Cart.*, I, 33 (no. 30), which follows the MS. in writing Thomas for Theobald as the addressee, and has consequently misdated the letter.   The archbishop's titles show not only that it must be Theobald but also that it must be in the period 1150–9 or 1160–1.   Azor the sheriff, who is known from other sources also (e.g. *Cartulary of Eynsham Abbey*, ed. H. E. Salter (O.H.S., 1907–08) I, 104, 414, and II, 43–4) cannot have been sheriff later than 1152.
[18] *Annales Monastici* (R.S.), IV, 27.

Medley to St. Frideswide's, though allowing that the citizens rented it for 5s. 8d. a year.[19] The city had failed in its attempt to assert itself.

Under Henry II the citizens could not hope to make much progress, for that king kept a very strict hand on all English towns, refusing even to recognize the grant of the fee-farm which his grandfather, Henry I, had granted to London. In 1155 he gave Oxford a charter, but the liberties which it granted were those which the city had enjoyed in the reign of Henry I, specifically the Guild Merchant, the right to serve the king with the Londoners at his coronation, and the right of appealing to the customs (or laws) of London.[20] These were not the sort of liberties which would have satisfied the citizens of a continental commune, but while Henry II was alive they were about as good as could be got.

After his death (6 July 1189) the situation changed dramatically. Richard I was in urgent need of money for his crusade, and within a few weeks had sold grants of perpetual fee-farm to five towns (Northampton, Bedford, Hereford, Worcester and Colchester). While he was on crusade London acquired, first (1190) the restoration of the fee-farm which Henry I had granted, and secondly, as a result of the civil war between the justiciar, William Longchamp, and Count John the king's brother, the grant of a commune.[21] This was on 8 October 1191 and was one of the steps which marked the restoration of peace, but there can be little doubt that a commune had existed *de facto* for some months before.

It is in this context that we must see the Oxford charter of July 1191. It is the product of a revolutionary year. It is defiant from beginning to end, the opening ' We the citizens of the commune of the city and of the Guild Merchant ' being matched by closing attestation of ' the whole commune of the city of Oxford '. More than half the text (almost 14 of its 25 lines) is taken up by the names of the citizens who formed the commune, and the document is authenticated with ' the common seal of all the citizens of the city of Oxford '. The message is clear, but what makes it even more interesting is that we can reconstruct with some plausibility the steps leading up to its issue.

The essential point to realize is that the dispute over Medley must have acquired a symbolic importance out of all proportion to the value of the place as a meadow. St. Frideswide's denied the validity of the city's grant to Oseney, and in so doing would have insisted that the ' commune ' of citizens which had made the grant was legally a non-existent body. If the citizens wanted St.

---

[19] *Regesta*, III, 639. The date given there is " 1138–52, and probably *c.* 1138–9 ', but in view of Azor's letter it should now be amended to 1150–2.

[20] Ogle, 4–5; Stubbs, *Select Charters* (9th ed., 1913), 198–9.

[21] For the correct chronology, see Tait, *The Medieval English Borough*, 181.

Plate I:
The City of Oxford's
grant of Medley to Oseney, 1191.

(*City of Oxford*)

Plate II:
Enlargement of the seal. (*City of Oxford*)

Frideswide's to recognize the commune, they had to persuade it that the commune's grant of Medley to Oseney was valid; and in that case St. Frideswide's would claim that since Medley had been given to it in exchange for the stalls of which it had been deprived in the city, those stalls should now be restored. The citizens were therefore caught on the horns of a dilemma, from which they were able to extract themselves only by means of a complicated and costly ' package deal '.

The first stage of the settlement was marked by a final concord in the King's court on 4 July 1191. This concerned the subject of Medley, which the citizens were allowed to hold from St. Frideswide's at an (increased) rent of 8*s.* a year. As if to emphasize that none of the larger questions had been settled by this final concord, St. Frideswide's demanded, and got, from the citizens a written undertaking about the rent in the form of a charter ' sealed with the seal of the alderman of the guild '.[22] In other words there was no mention of a commune or a common seal of the city. That was reserved for the second stage of the settlement, for which the citizens had to pay more dearly.

In it St. Frideswide's and the citizens exchanged charters before a large body of witnesses. St. Frideswide's charter was simple since it merely confirmed the terms of the agreement about Medley as they had just been stated in the final concord.[23] The citizens' charter, on the other hand, was long and complicated.[24] It started by confirming the agreement about Medley, and then proceeded to make concessions which amounted to a general settlement with the priory. First they conceded that among the liberties of St. Frideswide's was the right of holding all pleas in the city during the fair of St. Benedict (10–16 July); the citizens undertook to hold no pleas in the city or suburb during this period. Secondly, they came to a complicated agreement about St. Frideswide's town properties, undertaking that no citizen should gain possession of any tenement of St. Frideswide's by purchase, mortgage or perpetual lease unless he had St. Frideswide's permission; that if St. Frideswide's wished to refuse this permission it could do so, provided that it itself took over the purchase, mortgage or perpetual lease at the price which had been offered; that property which did change hands by sale, etc. did not thereby lose its obligation to pay rent (*census*) to St. Frideswide's; and that amercements from pleas by the attachment of the city's reeves or bailiffs should (in the case of these properties) go to St. Frideswide's.

At first sight all this may seem very one-sided; the citizens make comprehensive concessions to St. Frideswide's, and in return get nothing but the right

---

[22] *S.F. Cart.*, I, 38 (no. 35); *Oseney Cart.*, IV, 89 (no. 63 B).
[23] *Oseney Cart.*, iv. 90 (no. 63 C).
[24] *S.F. Cart.*, I, 36 (no. 34). Its 23 witnesses include all the 18 witnesses of St. Frideswide's charter.

to continue holding Medley, though at an increased rent.   There is, however, more to it than that, for the charter was issued by the citizens as a corporate body.   It is true that they did not use the emotional word ' commune ' but described themselves as the *universitas* (or commonalty) of the citizens of Oxford,[25] but at the end they state explicitly that in order to make the charter valid they have sealed it with their common seal.[26]   If St. Frideswide wanted the privileges which the charter granted, it had to concede that that seal was valid, and that the commonalty, ' body politic ', or commune which owned it was a lawful institution.

Having won this recognition, it is hardly surprising that the citizens made use of it to confirm their gift of Medley to Oseney, undertaking to warrant it to the abbey in any court ' and against all men ', and making the charter a public declaration of their communal existence.   Not only did they affix their common seal but they also recorded themselves all, individually and by name, as witnesses—there are sixty-three of them.   This is one of the facts that makes the charter so fascinating.   It is always baffling to read in chronicles or documents of consent being given by the ' whole kingdom ', or ' all the men of the land ' or a ' whole commune '.   Commonsense may prevent us from thinking in astronomical terms, but nonetheless it is not easy to guess how small a number could have seemed complete and total to a medieval writer.   Too often we talk of urban ' oligarchies ' in order to evade the fact that we have no idea how many citizens attended a portmanmoot or formed a commune, but now we know that for Oxford in 1191 the answer was sixty-three.   They are very far from being all the inhabitants of the town, but they are all the citizens and all the members of the Guild Merchant.

The list is worth looking at with care.   It is headed by an ecclesiastic. There is nothing surprising about this, because it was customary to put ecclesiastics before laymen, but it must be pointed out that Nigel the (rural) dean was in a special position.[27]   Like his father before him he was rector of St. Martin's Church at Carfax and played a large part in secular affairs, presumably deriving much of his importance from the facts that the guild hall was just opposite his church and that the portmanmoot met in his churchyard. Next follow the principal officers, two aldermen and two praetors.   Alderman was the normal English word for the head man of a guild, but whereas in 1147 the alderman (as we have already seen) was a baron, now there are two aldermen, both of them townsmen.   This had also been the case in 1182 when the

[25] ' Omnibus Sancte Matris Ecclesie filiis ad quos litere presentes pervenerint, universitas civium Oxoneford salutem.'   *Universitas* has not yet acquired its specialized meaning of ' university '.

[26] ' Ut autem hec omnia premissa rata sint et firma, hoc presens scriptum sigillo nostro communi roborare curavimus.'

[27] *Oxford Charters*, 77n.

two aldermen, Lambert and Amfrid, issued a certificate to attest a transfer of seisin, though in that case they had felt it necessary to mention the assistance of the King's sheriff also.[28]   Now in 1191 there is no mention of sheriff or baron; the two aldermen were capable of standing on their own feet.   John Kepeharm indeed was a man of substance; when he died (1204) his widow gave the King 100 marks and 2 palfreys that she might marry whom she wished, almost as if she were the widow of a baron.[29]

The title ' praetor ' was a rare classicism for the officers who came next in seniority and were responsible for the administration of justice; in many charters of this date they are called by the more normal title of ' praepositi ' or ' reeves ' which eventually superseded the classical title entirely.   Though it is impossible to compile a complete list of officers for this early period,[30] we know that there was a normal *cursus honorum* whereby men became praetors before they became aldermen; Henry fitz Segrim, for example, who was the second alderman in 1191, had been praetor in 1183 and 1189, and Laurence Kepeharm who was a praetor in 1191 was to become both an alderman and the first mayor of the city.   There is plenty of evidence that the praetors or reeves held a court, but in the earliest mentions they seem to be associated with either a justice of assize (*c.* 1169–81),[31] or the sheriff (*c.* 1182–4).[32]   The earliest mention of them acting as judges in the portmanmoot without the assistance of royal officers may be dated shortly before Michaelmas 1190.[33]   When they began to act independently of the royal officers it would have been necessary for them to have a clerk, and in fact the 56th witness of our charter is ' Henry the clerk, then clerk of the praetors '.   It is probably fair to describe him as the earliest recorded town clerk, and put him at the head of Mr. Graham Pollard's list.[34]

It would have been nice to imagine that Henry the clerk wrote the charter in his own hand, but in fact that cannot have been the case.   The handwriting is that of an Oseney scribe who not only wrote charters for his abbey, but also compiled (*c.* 1196) the first part of the abbey's cartulary.[35]   It would seem that for a charter as important as this it was essential to get the services of a scribe

[28] *Oxford Charters*, 89.
[29] H. E. Salter, *Medieval Oxford* (O.H.S., 1936), 38.   The man whom his widow chose as her second husband was the tenth witness in the list, Henry fitz Simeon.
[30] The best list (by Salter) is in the preface to *Oseney Cart.*, III.   It shows that amongst the witnesses of this charter Henry fitz Simeon, Walter Pille, Owein, and Adam Rufus were all to become praetors.
[31] *Oxford Charters*, 88.
[32] *Oxford Charters*, 91.
[33] *Oxford Charters*, 90.
[34] *Oxoniensia*, XXXI (1966), 43–76.
[35] *Oxford Charter*, 93 is in his hand, and is there identified by Salter as the first hand of Cotton MS. Vitellius E. xv.

who would produce, not the small and cramped type of charter which was usual for a townsman, but a charter which in size and spaciousness could be taken for that of a lord.   Oseney was the friend of the city and the beneficiary of the charter, and it was only natural that one of its canons should help the city to produce a document which was worthy of its newly-acquired status.   One glance at the charter is sufficient to show how well he succeeded.[36]   It gives the ' citizens of the commune of the city and of the Guild Merchant ' all the appearances of a corporate baron.   To them it must have seemed something like a Declaration of Independence.

[36] For example, I first saw this charter by accident when (in 1966) it was deposited in the Warwickshire Record Office.   It was lying on top of a boxful of deeds, and I picked it up thinking it might be a charter of King John.

19

The Ford, the River and the City

IT is well known that Oxford means ' the ford of the oxen ' ; the name is first recorded in the *Anglo-Saxon Chronicle* for the year 912 as *Oxna forda*. Because the city's coat of arms displays an ox paddling idly in a river, it is easy to forget that in the early Middle Ages oxen were beasts of burden, used for hauling heavy loads. An oxen's ford, therefore, would be one through which oxen could draw heavy freight carts. In other words it would have to be on a main road at a spot where the river was shallow and had a hard gravelly bottom. Where was it ?

The first condition for any proposed site must be a road which was genuinely important. The ford was not called after the town, but the town after the ford, and it must therefore be presumed that the town came into existence because of the ford and not *vice-versa*. For this reason it is hard to believe that the ford could have been on an east-west route, because such routes could, and did, avoid any crossing of the Thames by keeping either to the north or the south of it. In particular there would have been little point in a ford between Port Meadow and Binsey Green, though this is one of the sites which have been suggested, since having crossed the river the oxen would have had to haul their carts to the top of Wytham Hill, only to descend to a second crossing of the river at Eynsham. It is hard to see how anyone would have wanted to use such a route, any more than tney would have wanted to cross the Cherwell at Magdalen Bridge, unless the town was already in existence.[1]

The obvious facts of geography are that the biggest river at Oxford is the Thames, and that since it flows from west to east the traffic crossing it would be going from north to south or south to north. For this reason it used to be assumed that the most likely site of the ford was near Folly Bridge, but in 1928 H. E. Salter published evidence which convinced him that the old route to the south started out from the west gate and crossed the river on that side of the city.[2] The evidence consisted of a charter of 1352 and a plea of 1376. The charter, which survives in the original, is a grant by Roger Brekebek of various properties including a close (*hamma*) ' between the meadow of the Prioress and Convent of Studley on the north side, and the ford called Oxenforde near the bridge leading to North Hinksey on the south side '.[3] From these indications Salter was able to locate the spot with precision ; it was on the line of the present footpath from Oseney Mead to Hinksey at its crossing of the Bullstake stream. Its antiquity was specifically claimed in the plea of the mayor and citizens as recorded in the Abbot of Oseney's reply :

[1] Neither of these suggestions was ruled out of court by Andrew Clark in his discussion of the possible sites in his edition of the *Survey of the Antiquities of the City of Oxford composed in 1661–6* by Anthony Wood (O.H.S. xv (1889), i, 46).

[2] H. E. Salter, ' The Ford of Oxford ', *Antiquity*, ii (1928), 458–9.

[3] *Cartulary of Oseney Abbey*, ed. H. E. Salter, ii, 161 (O.H.S. xc, 1929).

Item, as for what the mayor and commonalty say that there is a place called Oxenford, from which the town takes its name, and which is a parcel of the same town, the abbot says that the said place is within the franchise and hundred of the Northgate, and does not belong in any way to the town or its franchise.[4]

I have quoted this passage in full because it is important to recognize that it is not a historical statement but an *ex parte* claim.　It comes from a lawsuit in which the burgesses were claiming that the abbot should have no jurisdiction in the Isle of Oseney since that island was really part of the town ; and one of their ' proofs ' was that the Oxenford was on the far side of the isle.　How could that ford have given its name to the town, they argued, unless the town was on the island ?　True, but they lost the case.[5]　The judge (who was the Bishop of Lincoln) can hardly have been convinced about the site of the ford, and there may be some suspicion that the citizens had decided to call this particular ford ' Oxenforde ' simply in order to stake a claim to the island.　It is certainly strange that the only two documents to mention the place should come within 24 years of each other, some three centuries after the ford had gone out of business.

It is also strange that there is no solid evidence for the other stages of Salter's route to the south.　What he claimed was that it left Oxford by the west gate, crossed four or more branches of the river (including the Bullstake stream) on its way to Ferry Hinksey, and went up Harcourt Hill (past Westminster College) to Little Bradley Farm, where it joined the main road from Cumnor to Abingdon. It is admittedly a possible route but, as Mrs. Lambrick demonstrated in this journal, its use can only be attested for pedestrians and individual horsemen. So far as the written evidence goes, all the heavy traffic, whether southbound or westbound, seems to have left the city by the south gate and proceeded along the Abingdon road to the top of Hinksey Hill where the roads for the south and the west diverged.[6]　We will therefore start with an investigation of river-crossings on this route.

Before the end of the 17th century, Folly Bridge was known as ' the great bridge ' (*magna pons* or *grand pont*).[7] According to the *Abingdon Chronicle* it was built by Robert d'Oilli, the first Norman lord of Oxford, who died in 1091 or 1092.　But in the 12th century most major buildings were attributed to the Normans, and it may well be, as Salter has argued, that Robert d'Oilli did little more than repair an earlier bridge.[8]　Be that as it may, the important point to realize is that this was not just a single bridge crossing one big river, but the largest bridge in a causeway which extended for a mile or so, and which in the 17th century had a grand total of 42 arches.[9]　The present main stream has been

---

[4] *Medieval Archives of the University of Oxford,* ed. H. E. Salter, 1,200 (O.H.S. LXX, 1917).

[5] The bishop merely adjusted the boundary on the east side of the isle, awarding Warham Bank (Fisher Row) to the city. *Oseney Cart.,* II, 477.

[6] Gabrielle Lambrick, ' Some Old Roads of North Berkshire ', *Oxoniensia,* XXXIV (1969), 78–92.

[7] The name ' Folly Bridge ' first occurs in 1695, the ' folly ' being the tower on the bridge which was known as ' Friar Bacon's study '.

[8] *Chronicon Monasterii de Abingdon,* ed. Joseph Stevenson (Rolls Series, 1858), II, 15 and 25.　The first of the statements (which refers to ' the great bridge to the northern bank [of the river] at Oxford '—*ad septemtrionalem plagam Oxoniae*) dates from the 13th century ; the second (which calls it more soberly *pons Oxenfordis*) dates from the 12th.　For the possible pre-Conquest origin of the bridge, see H. E. Salter, *Medieval Oxford* (O.H.S., C (1936), 15).

[9] *Wood's City of Oxford,* I, 416.

deliberately canalized and deepened, both by dredging and by the construction of weirs to keep the water back.   Before this had been done the various branches of the river, whose courses can be traced without difficulty, would have been more equal in size.   In winter they would doubtless have flooded a large area round Oxford, but in summer they would have been very shallow.   Crossing the river might then have been described as ' island-hopping ', the main difference between a crossing on the west and the south being that on the south the islands were larger.

To trace the route in detail, the first stream on the north would have been the Trill Mill Stream which crosses St. Aldate's beneath the road between Brewer Street and Rose Place ;[10] it can be seen emerging into the open on the far side of the Christ Church Memorial Gardens.[11]   The second was the Shirelake stream so called because it formed the boundary between Oxfordshire and Berkshire—a fact which suggests that it may once have been the main stream ; it was bridged by the Denchworth Bow, just north of Folly Bridge, and then continued across the middle of Christ Church meadows—which is why the meadow floods still rise from the centre.   The third was the present main stream at Folly Bridge, but even here the presence of a small island called Ailrich's Eyot meant that the crossing could be done in two stages.   After this came the island of Grandpont which took its name from the great bridge or causeway, and which was divided from Hinksey by the small stream which flows past Eastwyke Farm and the north side of Hinksey Park.   Hinksey was a large island (nowadays the railway and the reservoir make it look smaller that it is), and the final crossing was from Hinksey to Kennington.   To make this crossing the Abingdon Road used (before the building of the new by-pass) to take a marked bend to the right, or south-west.   Most motorists thought that the only object of the bend was to enable the road to bridge the railway, but in fact, it also bridged the last two branches of the Thames (here known as the Hinksey stream), one on each side of the railway.

It may at first seem that so many islands and so many crossings would have made the route more difficult than one which crossed the river in fewer stages, but on reflection it will be appreciated that multiple crossings and a large number of islands suggest a shallower river with a firmer bottom.   Historically we have evidence for the existence of the two southernmost fords in the middle of the tenth century ; they are mentioned in the (Anglo-Saxon) bounds of charters in favour of Abingdon Abbey, and are called *Maegtheford* (Mayweed ford) and *Stanford* (stone ford), the latter name suggesting a made-up road.[12]   From Abingdon we

[10] I use the current names for streets, but St. Aldate's (which in the Middle Ages was ' Fish St.') used to end at the South Gate (ie. by Brewer Street), its continuation being known as Grandpont.

[11] I have myself made the passage of the Trill Mill Stream in the 1930s and Mr. Hassall reports it still passable, having navigated it in 1971.   The covered channel starts between Paradise Street and Oxpens Road and continues all the way to Christ Church Meadow.

[12] W. de Gray Birch, *Cartularium Saxonicum* (3 vols. and index, London, 1885–99) no. 906, Cf. nos. 366 and 102.   Both fords are mentioned in the description of the bounds which are discussed by G. B. Grundy in the *Berkshire Archaeological Journal*, 27 (1922), 100–2, and 30 (1925), 55–9.   The (Latin) charters to which the (Anglo-Saxon) bounds are appended purport to date from the 9th and 10th centuries, but the 9th century one is not genuine. See P. H. Sawyer, *Anglo-Saxon Charters : An Annotated list and Bibliography* (London, 1968), nos. 183, 567 and 663.

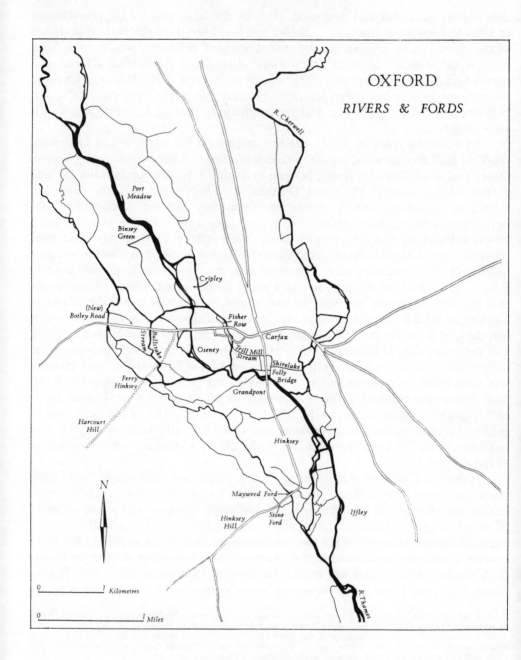

FIG. I
The topography of Oxford.   Drawing by David Sheard.

also have evidence for the northern end of the crossing, since in the time of Abbot Faritius (1100–1117) there was a mill at Oxford bridge which was suggestively called Longford (*molendinum Langeford . . . apud pontem Oxeneford positum*).[13] Further to the north, but just south of the Trill Mill Stream, recent excavations have uncovered a clay bank which ' could have been used as a roadway into Oxford on the south ' and is thought to go back ' at least to the early 9th century '.[14]

It is submitted therefore that the original oxen's ford was indeed on the line of St. Aldate's and the Abingdon Road, but that it did not consist of one particular ford, but of a whole series of fords which could be negotiated by heavy ox-carts. Though presumably the easiest possible ford of the Thames, it would have been by far the most serious obstacle for traffic on the route from Northampton to Southampton, and it is not in the least surprising to find that it was eventually converted into an elaborate causeway. What one has to remember is that as the causeway was improved, so the nature of the river would have been changed. In order to prevent the causeway from acting as a dam when the river was in flood, it would have been necessary to ensure that a sufficient rate of water could pass under the various arches and bridges, and the easiest way of doing this would have been to deepen and enlarge some of the channels. It has been suggested, for example, that the straight reach below Folly Bridge, along the college barges and boathouses, is an artificial cutting made to divert the main-stream from the Shirelake when the bridge was built.[15]

But whatever the precise details may have been, it is clear that once the causeway and bridges had been built, it would have been necessary to deepen the river at the points where it had been shallowest. In this way the fords would have been destroyed and in consequence it would be pointless to look for them now.

II

The building of the causeway would not have been the only factor which led to the deepening and canalization of the river. Another would have been the construction of water-mills. These had been virtually unknown to the Romans but were introduced into England in the middle or late Saxon period.[16] An early example on the Thames has been excavated at Old Windsor and apparently dates from the 9th century, but it is not until the middle of the 10th century that references become common, the earliest mention of a mill near

---

[13] *Chron. Mon. de Abingdon*, II, 123.

[14] T. G. Hassall, *Oxford : the city beneath your feet, Archaeological Excavations in the City 1967–72* (Oxford, 1972), 10. See also his forthcoming article in *Archaeometry*.

[15] I owe this suggestion to Mr. David Sturdy. Mr. Hassall tells me his excavations revealed ' rapid silting on the up-stream side of the clay bank in St. Aldate's suggesting it may have acted as a dam ' as here suggested.

[16] H. R. Loyn, *Anglo-Saxon England and the Norman Conquest* (London, 1962), 356–7, and Marc Bloch, ' The Advent and the Triumph of the Watermill ', translated (from *Annales* VII (1935), 538–63) in his *Land and Work in Medieval Europe* (London, 1967), 137–168. According to Richard Bennett and John Elton, *History of Corn-Milling* (4 vols. London, 1898–1904) the earliest references to mills in Anglo-Saxon charters (blatant forgeries apart) date from 762, 814 and 838 (J. M. Kemble, *Codex Diplomaticus Aevi Saxonici*) (6 vols, London 1839–48), nos CVIII, CCVII and CCXXXIX.

Oxford being at Abingdon, *c.* 954–63.[17]   When a mill was built it was necessary not only to dig a millstream or leat, but also to construct a weir and build up the river banks so as to hold a sufficient mass of water above the mill.   As a result, if a whole series of mills was built on one river, that river would become both deeper and slower and therefore more suitable for navigation.   To quote Andrew Clark :

> The benefits conferred on the navigation of the Thames by mill-weirs may thus be stated.   When the river ran in its natural channel, it passed through alternate series of sharp shallow streams and long deep pools.   In summer many of these rapids were too shallow to float a barge.   Now it was just at these shallow places that mills were generally constructed because the descent in the level of the ground which caused the rapids on the river furnished also the fall necessary for working a mill-wheel.   The mill-weir, which kept back the water and forced it over the mill-fall, of course deepened the water for some distance above.   Also, when a barge was approaching from below, the miller would open his weir and let a rush of water through sufficient to tide the barge over the shallows.   This rush of water was called . . . ' a shoot '.   For the benefit of this shoot, the barge paid the miller a fee, the original of our modern payments at locks.[18]

It follows from this that soon after we begin to hear of mills in large numbers we should also be hearing of navigation.   The first reference we have comes from Abingdon a few years before the Norman Conquest, but in its details it implies that navigation was already on quite a large scale.

> In the time of Abbot Ordric (1052–66) the river ran on the other side of the church's land (which its inhabitants call Barton) close by the hamlet of Thrupp. This caused the oarsmen no little difficulty, for the land below rose more steeply than the land above, often causing the river to run dry.   For this reason the citizens of the city of Oxford (for it was their shipping which made the passage most often) besought that the course of the river should be diverted through the church's meadow, which lies below it on the south, on condition that for the rest of time 100 eels should be paid as a custom to the monks' cellarer by each one of their boats.   The request was granted, the terms agreed, and the promised custom is paid to this day.[19]

Another reference in the same chronicle makes it clear that the 100 eels from each boat had to be paid between 2 February and Easter and served as a sort of season-ticket for the year,[20] but the real significance of the affair is that the abbey considered that the number of boats would be sufficient to justify the major works involved in the diversion of the river.   The original course had been the so-called ' Swift Ditch ' on the far side of Andersey Island, while the new course used the bed of the River Ock from the north end of the Ditch to the town, then

[17] *Med. Arch.* II (1958), 183–5; *Chron. Mon. Abingdon*, II, 278–9. Cf. the interim note on ' A Saxon Water-Mill in Bolebridge Street ', in the 5th Report of Excavations at Tamworth, Staffs., by P. Rahtz and K. Sheridan, *Trans. S. Staffs. Arch. and Hist. Soc.*, XIII (1971–2), 9–16 ; but it should be noted that though this excavation revealed a mill of some sort, the evidence for its being a *water*-mill is not absolutely secure.

[18] Andrew Clark in *Wood's City of Oxford*, I, 431 n.I.

[19] *Chron. Mon. de Abingdon*, I, 480–1 ; cf. II, 282.   The author was a monk who entered the abbey before 1117 and was still alive in the reign of Henry II.

[20] *Ibid.*, II, 119–20.

turned down the new cut (which is still so called) which ran in a straight line to the south end of the Ditch, a distance of about half-a-mile.[21]

We next hear of navigation in 1110–11 when the Oxford boatmen were accused of trying to evade the custom due to Abingdon. The abbot sued them successfully before the King's sheriffs in Oxford and had his right to the custom reinforced by a royal writ.[22] In 1163 the abbot had a major dispute with the men of Oxford at Wallingford about his right to a market, the judgment which was finally given being that he could have the fullest type of market, except that it could not be used by the freight barges which plied the Thames (*navibus onerariis per aquam Tamisiae currentibus*) though he could use his own boats for his own affairs.[23]

In 1205 King John granted to William son of Andrew ' that he might have one ship going and returning upon the Thames between Oxford and London ', free of toll and with permission to load his ship wherever he wished on the Thames. His father, Andrew, had permission for a boat plying between Abingdon and London but he, in accordance with the judgement of 1163, could only carry ' corn, victuals and other necessaries for the support of himself [presumably the abbot] and his men '.[24]

After the early years of the 13th century, however, evidence of an effective navigation on the Thames is hard to find, and by the 14th century it seems certain that (as Thorold Rogers demonstrated) it was not Oxford but Henley which was ' the furthest point to which [the Thames] was ordinarily navigable '. When stone was being transported from Taynton (near Burford) for the building of Eton College in 1456, it was not shipped down the Thames from Oxford but was carted overland to Henley, and shipped from there.[25] Something had happened to make the river less navigable than it once had been.

It is surprising that this fact has received little attention from historians, for the evidence is singularly clear.[26] In 1197 (and again in 1199) Richard I ordered all weirs in the Thames to be removed because of the ' great detriment and inconvenience ' they had caused to the city of London. In 1215 clause 33 of Magna Carta declared that all kydells (or fish-weirs) were to be pulled down in the Thames and Medway. In 1227 Henry III appointed justices to inspect and measure all weirs which had been heightened and increased to the detriment of vessels passing through them. In 1235 it was ordered that weirs should not be higher, nor with narrower openings than in the reigns of Henry II, Richard I and John. In 1253 the sheriff of Middlesex had all weirs destroyed for the whole

---

[21] Fred S. Thacker, *The Thames Highway* (2 vols. 1914–20 ; repr. Newton Abbot, 1968), I, 13 and II, 144.

[22] *Chron. Mon. de Abingdon*, II, 119.

[23] *Ibid.*, II, 229.

[24] *Rotuli Litterarum Patentium*, ed. T. D. Hardy (London, 1835), vol. I, pt. i, 38 and 52.

[25] Douglas Knoop and G. P. Jones, ' The Building of Eton College, 1442–60 ', *Transactions of the Quatuor Coronati Lodge*, xlvi (1933), 84.

[26] The evidence is collected in Thacker, *op. cit.*, vol. I ch. ii and Appendix ii. In the latter he disputes Thorold Rogers' conclusion about Henley as the head of navigation, without apparently noticing that all his evidence was early, and all Rogers' late. Neither writer seems to have considered the possibility that the river had deteriorated between the 12th and 15th centuries, though all their evidence pointed in that direction.

length of the river to the west of London.[27]   In 1274 the water of the Thames was to be so widened ' that ships and great barges might ascend from London to Oxford '.   But complaints and injunctions continued ; we read of them in 1278, 1281, 1294, 1316, 1320, 1351, 1352, 1358, 1364, 1369, 1371, 1376, 1377, 1388, 1391, 1399 and on into the 15th century.   The complaint was always the same ; weirs were being increased in such a way as to make the river impass-able, and only too often the remedy proposed was to abolish them all.

The abolition of all weirs would in fact have been disastrous since (as we have already seen) it would have brought navigation to an end.   But it was nonetheless possible to have too many weirs.   Before the construction of pound-locks (which, though invented in Italy towards the end of the 15th century, were unknown on the Thames before 1624, rare till the end of the 18th century, and not universal till the 20th) boats did not go *past* weirs but *over* them, by means of a flashlock.[28]   A flashlock was simply a section of the weir which could be opened by raising the paddles (or ' spades ') so as to allow the water to rush through.   This rush of water was called a ' flash ' and going down-stream the boatmen would ' shoot ' it like a waterfall.   Going upstream they would need a longer ' flash ', waiting until the level of water had been somewhat reduced, before attempting to haul their boat up with a winch and tackle.   As John Strype put it (1720) :

> Some of these locks are extraordinary dangerous in passing.   The going up the Locks were so steep, that every year Cables had been broken that cost 400 l. and Bargemen and Goods drowned.   And in coming down, the Waters fell so high, that it sunk the Vessels, and destroyed Corn and Malt wherewith they were laden.[29]

As if the danger was not enough, there was also the expense and the delay. Millers often charged enormous sums for a ' flash ' (30 shillings at Sutton Courtenay in the 18th century), and when the weir had been surmounted the boat might have to wait a long time for the water to rise again, since the ' flash ' might have drained a whole stretch of river.

III

If this account of the development of the river is correct, it would follow that Oxford should have become a ' boom town ' when the river first became navigable, and should have slumped when the navigation began to fail.   There is every indication that this was in fact the case.   When we first hear of Oxford in 912 it was one of the West Saxon *burhs*, and from the figures given in the Burghal Hidage (*c.* 911–19) we know that the circuit of its walls cannot possibly have

[27] *De Antiquis Legibus Liber*, ed. Thomas Stapleton (Camden Soc., 1846), 20.
[28] Thacker, *op. cit.*, I, 67–8. Cf. I, 125 and II, 489. The last flashlock in use on the Thames was Hart's weir near Eaton Hastings, which Thacker himself last shot in 1911 (*ibid.*, II, 48–9). Poundlocks, how-ever, had been in use on the Exeter Canal as early as 1563.
[29] Quoted from Thacker, I, 46.

exceeded 2062½ yds.[30]   The circuit which we can trace today is about 600 yds more than that, but it is clear that the extra length is due to the extension of the city eastward of what are now Radcliffe Square and Oriel Street, the actual points at which the newer walls joined the old being indicated by a marked change of direction.   The date at which this extension was made is not known, but it must have been before 1086, since in Domesday Book the church of St. Peter-in-the-East is inside the city.   Most probably it was before the Norman Conquest.

In the first half of the 11th century Oxford figures largely in the *Anglo-Saxon Chronicle*, and its prosperity is attested by the fact that numismatists have calculated that during the reign of Edward the Confessor, its mint must have been about the fifth most important in the kingdom, since it had at least seven moneyers working at the same time.   Canterbury had the same number and the only towns with more were London (21), York (12), Lincoln and Winchester (8 or 9 each).   A similarly prominent position is given to Oxford if a calculation is made of the number of burgesses or houses recorded in Domesday Book. Though London and Winchester are not included in the Survey, Oxford comes fifth of the towns that are, after York, Norwich, Lincoln and Thetford.[31]   It is true that at this same time many of Oxford's houses were ' destroyed and waste ', but this seems to have been a temporary disaster, since the town was well to the fore again in the 12th century.

In the Pipe Roll of 1130 Oxford was one of the six towns mentioned as having guilds—and it had two, one for the weavers and another for the shoemakers.[32] Judged by the size of aids paid to the King in 1130 and 1156, Oxford would have ranked equal sixth among English towns, behind London, Winchester, York and Norwich, and about equal with Exeter and Canterbury.[33]   It was also in the front rank of those towns which were seeking political liberties for themselves. It attempted to form a commune in 1147,[34] and though the attempt failed, it succeeded in getting a generous charter from Henry II in 1156.   By this charter the men of Oxford were to have the ' customs, liberties and laws which they have

---

[30] The number of hides attributed to each burh represented the number of men required to man the walls on the basis of 4 men for every 5½ yds of wall.   The most convenient text of the hidage is in A. J. Robertson, *Anglo-Saxon Charters* (2nd ed., Cambridge, 1956), 246–9, but important emendations have been made by David Hill, ' The Burghal Hidage : the establishment of a text ' *Med. Arch.*, XIII (1969), 84–92.   It should be noted that earlier writers (including H. E. Salter and E. M. Jope) have been misled by Gale's edition which gave the number of hides dependent on Oxford as 2,400.   This was an error ; the various manuscript readings give 1300 and 1500.   Mr. Hill suggests that the correct figure was 1400, and subsequent excavations on the W. line of the Anglo-Saxon ditch suggest that the resulting circuit of 1925 yards will be established.   See T. G. Hassall in *Oxoniensia*, XXXV (1970), 18, and XXXVI (1971), 34–48.

[31] For both sets of figures see F. M. Stenton, *Anglo-Saxon England* (3rd edition, Oxford, 1971), 537–8.

[32] The other towns with guilds were London, York, Lincoln, Winchester and Huntingdon.

[33] F. W. Maitland, *Domesday Book and Beyond* (Cambridge, 1907), 175.

[34] R. H. C. Davis, ' An Oxford Charter of 1191 and the Beginnings of Municipal Freedom ', *Oxoniensia*, XXXIII (1968), 53–65; see above, chapter 18, pp. 265-79.

in common (*habent communes*) with the citizens of London ', the right of serving the King on his festival with the men of his butlery (i.e. the Londoners), and the right of trading in London in common (*communiter*) with the Londoners.   If they were ever in doubt or dispute over any judicial matter, they were to send their messengers to London ' and hold firm and fast by the judgement of the Londoners ... because the citizens of London are of one and the same custom, law and liberty '.35   When, in 1191, London declared itself a commune, Oxford did so too.   The municipal seal of Oxford, which was produced in that same year, is the earliest known in England.36

But if Oxford was an important town (as opposed to university-town) in the 12th century, it was not to remain so for long.   The poll tax returns of 1377 suggest that so far as population was concerned it had sunk to sixteenth place among English towns,37 and its decline was to continue further.   According to H. E. Salter, the wealth and population of the city were shrinking perpetually from 1250 to 1350.   He reached this conclusion from a detailed study of almost all the tenements in the city, many of which seem to have been deserted in the later Middle Ages.38   He found that, in spite of the general inflation, shops in the Cornmarket fetched a higher rent in 1200 than three centuries later ; that the rent of Broadgates Hall (on what is now part of the Brasenose frontage in High Street) fell from 11 marks in 1293 to 8 in 1339, to 6 in 1357 and as little as 3 in 1480 ; and that there was a general disposition to pull down houses and use the sites as gardens.   The extent to which this de-urbanization of the city took place can be appreciated visually in the garden of Merton which is on the site of ten or twelve deserted houses ; or in the vast area covered by New College whose site, acquired in the 1370s, was formerly occupied by more than thirty houses.   Even in the case of Oriel which was less far from Carfax, we know that the site of the college covers 17 properties, only 3 of which were inhabited when the college acquired them, and most of which were simply added (in the first place) to the college garden.39

If it had not been for the university Oxford might have been reduced to a fraction of its former size.   That was what made it so congenial to the poor scholars of the Middle Ages.   They had no need of heavy barges on the Thames but did need a town in a central position with so many empty houses that rent and accommodation would be cheap.   Oxford provided just what they wanted, thanks very largely to the river.   The town had come into existence because of the ford across the river.   It had become rich and had expanded when the

35 Octavius Ogle, *Royal Letters Addressed to Oxford and existing in the City Archives* (Oxford, 1892), 4–5. For the service in the butlery see J. H. Round, *The King's Serjeants and Officers of State* (London, 1911), 172.
36 See note 34.
37 J. C. Russell, *British Medieval Population* (Albuquerque, 1948), 142.
38 H. E. Salter, *Medieval Oxford*, 87.   Cf. his *Survey of Oxford*, ed. W. A. Pantin and W. T. Mitchell, 2 vols., O.H.S. new series, xiv (1960) and xx (1969).
39 *Oriel College Records*, ed. C. L. Shadwell and H. E. Salter (O.H.S., xci (1926), 113).

construction of weirs had made the river navigable. And when there were so many weirs that the river ceased to be navigable its fortunes declined, the merchants moved out, and the scholars were able to take almost the whole place for themselves.

20

The Content of History*

At present it is unfashionable to discuss the content of history. We change our syllabuses frequently on the assumption that we, or our pupils, should study only such periods or topics as we, or they, may choose. We discuss the aims, objectives and methods of history-teaching and declare our intention of developing our pupils' verbal reasoning, of teaching them how to assess evidence, and of firing their imaginations. But we do not insist that there are any facts that they ought to know. If they do not know that Thomas Becket was a churchman, that Simon de Montfort had something to do with parliament, that Louis XIV was a French king, and Bismarck the name of a statesman as well as of a battleship, we assume simply that they must have 'done' some other period of history. Macaulay would have been horrified. In his view there were some facts which 'every schoolboy' ought to know, and without which intellectual conversation would have been impossible.

This point of view was long accepted as axiomatic. Until the 1960s history syllabuses in British universities conformed to a broad general pattern, of which the Oxford syllabus was typical. It consisted of English History from 'the beginning' to 1914, examined in three papers; a period of English Constitutional History (one paper); a period of foreign history (two papers); Political Theory, based on Aristotle, Hobbes and Rousseau (one paper); a Special Subject (two papers); a general paper and, if one wished to do it as an optional extra (which I did), a dissertation. In other universities there could be differences of detail, and a slightly different emphasis, but the basic structure was the same; and it conformed to the state of historical studies generally.

When I went up to Oxford in 1937, the great novelty was *The Oxford History of England*; five of its volumes had been published, three of them in 1936. It was that year also which saw the publication of the final volume of *The Cambridge Medieval History*, a monument to the concepts of what we then called the 'pre-war' world. A good deal of progress was being made in religious history; Powicke was the Regius Professor; the knowledgeable sought out volumes of *The Downside Review* for essays on monastic history by a monk called David Knowles; and in 1937 the first volume of 'Fliche-et-Martin', the great co-operative history of the Church, was published in France. Economic history was on the threshold; the *Economic History Review* had been founded in 1927, Eileen Power gave the Ford Lectures in 1939, and the first volume of *The Cambridge Economic History of Europe* was to be published in 1941.

*A presidential address given at the 74th annual conference of the Historical Association at Loughborough in April 1980.

The basic assumption, even though it was beginning to be questioned, was that history was narrative and national. This was evident in the _Oxford History of England_, though the most noticed, and most ludicrous, examples of the mode were to be found in _The Cambridge Medieval History_ which divided the history of the empire into separate chapters on 'Germany' and 'Italy', written by different authors with virtually no coordination, so that the anxious reader had to leap from chapter to chapter every time an emperor crossed the Alps. In 1937 the concept of national history was coming under fire because of the way in which it was being used, or abused, in Nazi Germany, but though we could appreciate the dangers of propaganda and national bias, we did not really question the basic assumptions of national history _per se_.

In retrospect this seems curious, because the most difficult problem of national history concerns those composite nations which, like Yugoslavia, Czechoslovakia or the United Kingdom itself have histories which, as they recede into the past, divide into two or more national histories which are not only different but conflicting. Most people subconsciously believed that the existing nations had been predestined since the beginning of time, almost as if nations had had ' "souls" before their separate political existence had started'.[1] One of the reasons for the great and instant success of the first volume of Pirenne's _Histoire de la Belgique_ (1896) was that it showed the Belgians that though their state had been formed only in 1830, they had a history going back almost to the Romans. By 1900 the history had been recommended to all communal schools as:

> a work whose appearance has been greeted by historians, abroad as well as in Belgium, as a truly scientific event. In it, for the first time, the history of our country is traced, not as that of a conglomeration of duchies and counties with nothing to bind them together except the identity of their feudal lord, but as that of a nation, possessing its own original nature, its distinct personality, a communal civilization which makes our territory a single region of intellectual culture.[2]

Since 1945, and particularly in the 1960s and 1970s, we have seen many other nations discovering themselves through their history. National history, and museums of national culture are _de rigueur_ in most of the more recent states of Asia and Africa, while in the British Isles we have been made much more aware of the national histories of Wales, Scotland and Ireland. A new _Oxford History_ would surely be, not a History of England but of Britain.

No comparison of the intellectual climate of history in 1937 and 1980 can be complete unless it notices the changes of scale. In 1937 a historian was expected to command a wide span of historical learning. Not many people had published works of original research on both the medieval and the modern periods—though this was true of Trevelyan and Oman, and of my own father—but professors and tutors were expected to have a wide

---

[1] Herbert Butterfield, 'Marxist history', reprinted in _History and Human Relations_ (London, 1951), p. 82.

[2] Translated from the citation by Léon Lepage, 21 Sept. 1901, which is printed in Bryce Lyon, _Henri Pirenne: a biographical and intellectual study_ (Ghent, 1974), p. 135.

range of teaching knowledge. At Edinburgh the Professor of History lectured on the whole of British history, and single-volume histories of England were published by G. M. Trevelyan, A. F. Pollard, E. L. Woodward, Keith Feiling and others. The desire for synthesis was overwhelming and everyone was something of a historicist, trying to discover in history the pattern of human development and seeking, either openly or covertly, for some clue as to the future. Arnold Toynbee had begun publishing his *Study of History*.

Now we are narrower. We scoff at our elders for the 'superficiality' of their breadth and proudly boast of the 'depth' of our own studies. 'Depth' does not merely mean 'more detail', it signifies also a shift from political to social history. Now the greatest interest is in the forms of primitive society—kindred and bloodfeud—in the structure of class, particularly in so far as it concerns the peasantry and the urban proletariat, and in social upheavals, especially when they culminate in war or revolution. It is a strange contrast with the quiet and luscious history of the 1930s, but the one has grown out of the other, sometimes through the agency of historians who would have disapproved most strongly of the present state of affairs.

Preeminent in this class was Sir Maurice Powicke. He believed that it was the historian's task to 'get inside' a period, so as to discover not only what it looked like, but how it felt to be alive in it. If one was to achieve that, it was necessary to renounce all foreknowledge. Because those who attended parliament in the thirteenth century could not have known that they were helping to create an institution which was to spread democracy around the world, he insisted that the historian should respect their ignorance. Because people at the time did not know what was to come, the historian should give no hint of it either. Hence his distaste for enquiring into concepts such as 'the origins of parliament'.

> It is the mystery which attends on all beginnings, when men are doing things because they are convenient and do not attach conscious significance to them, still less consider what the distant outcome of their acts may be. The word ['parliament'] was in the air, the materials were to hand. To track down every nerve in the body politic and locate each impulse, as though they carried some secret message, is as futile as to read into the rivulets which compose the upmost waters of the Thames a foresight of the wharves and shipping in its spacious estuary.[3]

As a result his writing was extraordinarily vivid, while the message which it conveyed was mysterious and evanescent. I remember that when *King Henry III and the Lord Edward* was first published, I astonished myself by reading the two volumes in 24 hours, spell-bound to the end, though I could not for the life of me say what was the thesis of the work. What Powicke had given was poetry. He saw 'a world in a grain of sand' and conjured up a vision of

> The cloud capp'd towers, the gorgeous palaces,
> The solemn temples, the great globe itself,

all destined to dissolve and 'leave not a rack behind'.

---

[3] F. M. Powicke, *King Henry III and the Lord Edward* (2 vols., Oxford, 1947), p. 340.

However much one may admire Powicke's poetic evocation of the past, one cannot fail to notice that his insistence on stripping himself of fore-knowledge proved strangely harmonious with very different schools of thought. One would not imagine that Sir Lewis Namier's approach to the eighteenth century would have been very appealing to Powicke, but here also is a 'small society going about its everyday business'[4] and a refusal to interpret it in the light of a later age. The two historians offer a curious comparison as well as a real contrast, for Powicke described his *Henry III and the Lord Edward* as a 'study in social history',[5] though even he recognized that he was using the term in an unusual sense. Namier, on the other hand, was concerned with society in order to explain the structure of politics in a way which our present-day social historians have understood; and he started a fashion of exploring politics, not from the stated ideals of politicians but from their social origins. For this reason the basis of the great *History of Parliament* which he instigated consisted of biographies of MPs, many of which were compiled by research students for whom they provided admirable material for Ph.D. theses. The number of MPs was enormous and there was what seemed an unlimited store of new material deposited by families in the Local Record Offices which had opened in such numbers since the War.

Namierism chimed in well, though unexpectedly, with a historical work which was immensely influential in the thirties, forties and fifties. This was Herbert Butterfield's *Whig Interpretation of History*. Butterfield himself had never intended that his work should cause historians to stop trying to explain history. But because he had demonstrated that the Whig historians had read their own ideas into historical events, lesser historians have felt timid of expressing any ideas at all. In this respect his original observation has been hardened and coarsened or, as he himself put it, 'turned by sheer repetition and rigidity of mind into hard dogmatic formulas'.[6] What he was saying in his book was that each generation had to test the framework of history provided by its predecessors, since the likelihood was that in some vital part of the story it had indulged in wishful thinking. The very last thing he intended was that historians should express no ideas at all. Everything he wrote proclaims his belief that the historian's business is not only to identify missing facts and find them, but also to interpret them. He was insistent that historians should keep their minds flexible so that they could detect not only the existence of new facts, but also the changes which those new facts demanded of the orthodox interpretation. The notion of trying to strip history of interpretation so as to make it a compilation in which new facts were simply added to old, was abhorrent to him and, more importantly, struck him as an impossibility. People could not keep interpretation out of history. They might, like the Whigs, think they were doing so, but a rigorous investigator would soon uncover their underlying assumptions and beliefs.

[4] R. W. Southern, 'Sir Maurice Powicke, 1879–1963', *Proc. Brit. Acad.* 1 (1964), p. 293.
[5] Powicke, *op. cit.* vol. 1 p. v.
[6] Herbert Butterfield, 'The Dangers of History', reprinted in *History and Human Relations*, p. 170.

I have stated this point at some length, because it is important for an understanding of what happened to Namierism. Namier was no Marxist, but the army of research students whom he induced to investigate the family origins and social environment of MPs were naturally anxious to justify their labours in their own eyes. Just what did these accumulations of facts amount to? The simplest answer, though perhaps it was adopted too naïvely, was Marx's doctrine of historical materialism:

> In direct contrast to German philosophy which descends from heaven to earth, here we ascend from earth to heaven. That is to say, we do not set out from what men say, imagine or conceive, nor from men as narrated, thought of, imagined, [or] conceived, in order to arrive at men in the flesh. We set out from real, active men, and on the basis of their real life-processes we demonstrate the development of the ideological reflexes and echoes of their life-processes.[7]

In other words, find out the life-processes of your Members of Parliament and you will be able to deduce their 'ideological reflexes'; the history of politics and political thought is reduced to an appendage of social history.

The pure Marxist is less interested in the higher classes of society than in what he calls 'the real people', and he insists that the prime objective of the historian should be to discover how these 'real people' really lived. This is because of the desire to start, not 'from what men say, imagine (or) conceive', but from 'real active men', and it has led, at any rate since the 1950s, to the study of 'working-class history', the aim of which, to quote one of its exponents is 'to help readers. . . to think and feel themselves into the skins of such "primitive rebels" as [are] described in this book'.[8] In one sense it is a development of 'Powicke-ism', because Powicke wanted to 'think and feel' himself into the skins of medieval people, though in his case it was not the working-class but the élite that attracted him. But it can also be connected with a different tradition.

The object of 'getting inside' the (basic) working-class (man) is to discover the real nature of man by stripping him of his education and culture (which would be considered 'artificial') in order to regard him in his essential nakedness. One notices the pride with which some historians proclaim their ancestry from a peasant or steelworker, as if that ancestry made their history 'purer' and less contaminated by the development of civilization. It has remarkable parallels with the romantic quest for the 'noble savage' and depends on a rather similar set of beliefs.

This can be seen by reference to the nineteenth-century brothers Jakob and Wilhelm Grimm who, at a time when politically speaking there was no Germany, made a major contribution to the revival (or perhaps the creation) of German nationalism, by their efforts to restore the language and customs of their ancestors. To do this they turned their backs on the culture of the élite and collected folktales 'from the lips of peasant women,

---

[7] Quoted from Marx and Engels, *The German Ideology* (1846) in Fritz Stern, *The Varieties of History* (London, 1957), p. 149.

[8] E. J. Hobsbawm, *Primitive Rebels* (London, 1959), p. 175. Cf. Richard Johnson in *Working-class Culture: Studies in History and Society*, ed. John Clarke, Chas. Critcher and Richard Johnson (London, 1979), pp. 41–71.

shepherds, waggonmen, vagrants, old grannies and children'.[9] That, at any rate, was their ideal, and they counted it a piece of great good fortune when they got to know

> an old peasant woman who lived in a small village called Niederzwehrn, near Kassel. . . . She was hale and hearty, and not much over 50 years old. Her face was firm, pleasant and somewhat knowledgeable, and her eyes clear and sharp. She retained the old stories in her head.[10]

It was a remarkable attempt to reach primitive German culture, but it was unfortunate that Katerina Vielmann, the woman they thus described, came in fact 'from a French Huguenot family, grew up speaking French, and took some of her stories straight from Charles Perrault, a 17th-century French writer'.[11]

Attempts to recreate the past, to rebuild their monuments, or to get 'inside their skins' and think and feel as they did, are always vulnerable to this sort of disaster, but that does not mean that attempts should not be made, On the contrary, man will always go on trying to recreate the past, and it is important that historians should keep a check on his efforts. It would be all wrong if historians turned their backs on contemporary thinking, claiming that it was none of their business, since their function was the purely 'scientific' one of 'adding new facts to old ones'.[12] But unfortunately this is what is happening. We are now in the grip of the D.Phil. business where all the emphasis falls upon making no mistakes, thus encouraging the more timid to stick to what in the good old days was known as 'scissors and paste'.

The doctorate system originated in Germany and reached Britain by way of the United States of America. In its origins it was not only harmless but even admirable. It came into being at a time when university posts were rare, and a scholar who wished to organize a research project of magnitude had to rely on a great deal of voluntary labour. If one was to publish the chronicles, charters or laws of a nation such as Germany, one needed a lot of devoted editors who would spend years learning the necessary technical skills before they even began the work of editing, and all this without grants or pay. For them a D.Phil. was a very suitable reward, something like an academic knighthood, to show that they had served the community well in the field of historical scholarship.

What has perverted the situation is numbers. At present there are about 1800 teachers of history in the universities of the United Kingdom alone, and it is normally the rule (though I am one of those who have broken it) that aspirants for university posts should have doctorates. As a result there are between two and three thousand postgraduate students registered for doctoral degrees in history, and the problem is to find enough good subjects to go round. Quite possibly the whole system would have broken down if it had not been for the emergence of Local Record Offices. Rare

---

[9] Quoted by Louis L. Snyder, *Roots of German Nationalism* (Bloomington and London, 1978), p. 42.

[10] *Ibid.* p. 52.

[11] *Ibid.*

[12] Herbert Butterfield, 'Official History: its pitfalls and criteria', reprinted in *History and Human Relations* (London, 1951), p. 207.

creations in the 1920s and 1930s, they grew apace after the Second World War. Their primary object was to house a county's own administrative records, but they soon discovered the need of turning themselves also into repositories where county families could deposit their own records. In this way a vast amount of 'new' material became available to historians, and it was possible to find enough research subjects for aspiring D.Phils., provided that one adopted a Namierite style and 'biographed' every Member of Parliament or (say) every medieval bishop. Since the newly deposited records also included numberless court rolls, account rolls, surveys, charters and leases it was possible to advance on a broad front by 'doing' a manor or the landed possessions of a baronial family or religious house.

There is no harm in this *per se*. Quite the reverse. Where the harm comes in is when this sort of research is mass-produced and attached to a system in which the whole aim is, as is commonly expressed, to get a doctorate 'safely under one's belt'. I do not underrate the merits of the system. To sort out records, reconstruct the administrative processes that went into their making, and draw conclusions from the evidence revealed, is a task requiring great academic skill. In the process of 'doing a doctorate' students not only get a first-class training in the techniques of research but also sort themselves out into academic classes or grades, so that the system serves as an efficient sieve for the academic profession. But what is lost is the purpose of the exercise. The system encourages students to research, not because they have stumbled on some problem which they simply have to solve, but because they want to qualify for an academic job. Moreover, since they and their supervisors realize the importance of getting the qualification in a reasonable time, it is important that the problem undertaken should be one which the supervisor thinks can be 'done' in the time allotted, which is tantamount to saying that he can more or less guess what the broad lines of the 'answer' will be. The thesis, in short, becomes an elaborate form of exam. It is not surprising that the world at large is losing interest in academic history; no one is interested in an answer unless he has recognized the question itself to be interesting.

II

If one turns to history in schools, a parallel development can be detected. When I was at school it was accepted that in the course of a school career every English child should 'do' the whole of English history—with Greece and Rome as a prelude and subsequent excursions into the history of Wales, Scotland, Ireland, Europe, the Empire and America as the circumstances of English history might dictate. The Tudors and Stuarts were popular then as now, for their combination of Italian Renaissance (which was good for a classical education), Protestant Reformation and the doctrines of constitutional monarchy, but a brief survey of the whole course of English history was found to be the best way of introducing pupils of different abilities and backgrounds to the modern political scene; it allowed for diversity of opinion within an agreed framework.

The first doubts about this sort of syllabus were ideological. During the Second World War, British opinion had been virtually unanimous in considering that the Nazis had gained control of the German people through their unscrupulous use, or abuse, of history. They had perverted history for their own ends, with the result that the Germans honestly believed that they were a superior race, with a mission to lead the rest of Europe to their superior civilization by force of arms. After the war, the Allies, through their Control Commission, set about a policy of German re-education and sent parties of school-teachers, especially historians, to discuss educational problems with their German counterparts. I myself took part in two such exercises, in 1948 and 1949, and well remember how we preached the civilising merits of teaching the history of countries other than one's own, until one schoolmaster from Hull let slip the fact that the amount of time which he would devote to German history was 'two periods of 40 minutes each'.

It was not surprising, therefore, that some groups of historians turned their attention to the teaching of history in British schools. First there were those who wished to purge all historical textbooks of nationalist bias. They were particularly active on the International Committee of the Historical Association; G. T. Hankin and E. H. Dance were bitterly disappointed when Council refused to endorse an Anglo-German 'memorandum on the study of Anglo-German relations, 1890–1914' on the grounds that it would be regarded as 'official', cause the Association to be 'represented as having taken sides in a political discussion', and lead to 'an insidious form of censorship'[13].

Secondly there were those historians who, believing that nationalism was one of the main causes of war, and seeing that it was supported, if not created, by national histories, boldly declared that the teaching of World History was a necessary preliminary for world peace. As an ideal this had a great deal to commend it, but in practice there were difficulties. Adequate Histories of the World were not easy to find—H. G. Wells's offering was often unpopular with historians because it reduced man to scale in the history of the universe—and eventually it was realized that any history of the whole world which could be studied in the context of a school curriculum would inevitably be so selective as to re-open the doorway to nationalist bias. On a practical level there was also a difficulty in teaching adolescents about people and places whose names they could neither pronounce nor spell.

Some of those who still continue the battle for World History attempt to meet these difficulties by teaching only contemporary World History in the hope that its 'relevance' will overcome the difficulty of strange names. But that does not solve the problem of bias, while the shortness of the period studied tends to make it a survey of the world without history. Others attempt to cut the Gordian knot by basing a syllabus on selective comparative studies of (say) the peasantry of China and England at some dates in the past, but in my opinion such comparisons are so selective as to omit both history and the world.

Other historians have attempted to take refuge in social history, but so far as bias is concerned, this is no remedy because it is as dangerous to concentrate on social divisions as on national divisions. Consequently there

[13] *History* N.S xxxv (1950), pp. 253–5 and xxxvi (1951), pp. 182–5.

is still a large body of history teachers who rely on the old traditional syllabus, while endeavouring to remove the national bias. Too often the result is spineless. Bias, whether national, religious or social, cannot be removed by being ignored. It has to be exposed to careful observation and analysis. The process may not prove too difficult when the historians analysed belonged to a different age and held beliefs which to us seem quaint or repugnant; we can all have some success at analysing the bias of Macaulay or Froude. But in the case of modern writers whose natural presuppositions coincide with our own, the case is different, and analysis will often be beyond the powers of the fledgling student.

In these circumstances it is not surprising that many history teachers have come to the conclusion that what is needed in the classroom is not great sweeps of history, but local history which the children can research for themselves, so as to discover the secrets of historical method. These teachers are certainly right in thinking that what matters in the end is an attitude of mind and a rational method of approaching problems. But it seems to me that in starting with detailed work, or even research, they are putting the cart before the horse. In other subjects it would be logical to work in this way, but as Butterfield put it:

> In the case of mathematics we start with our feet on the hard earth, learning the simplest things first, firmly establishing them at each point before we go any further, and making our argument good and watertight at each step of the way. In other words, we begin with strong foundations of concrete, and we gradually build our skyscrapers on top of this. In the case of history, on the other hand, we start up in the clouds, at the very top of the highest skyscraper. We start with an abridged story, seen in the large and constructed out of what in reality are broad generalisations. It is only much later, when we reach the actual work of research, that we come down to earth and arrive at the primary facts and primary materials.[14]

In writing this Butterfield was not pleading for a reversal of the usual order of the processes of an historical education. He did not think it wrong to start with the 'skyscraper' and work down to the foundations. On the contrary, he did not think that anything else was possible. The historian could only advance knowledge by questioning existing orthodoxies. If there were no orthodoxies, there would be no questioning and no new discoveries.

Butterfield's *Whig Interpretation of History* has had as big an influence in schools as in universities, and has been equally misunderstood in both. Butterfield did not mean that one should not attempt to see a pattern in history. He delighted in pointing out the fallacies in the pattern which the Whigs thought they had seen, and he was confident that future historians would find a fallacy in his own view. But that did not mean that he thought historians should abandon all attempts to interpret the past. He realized better than the rest of us have done that the patterns of history were determined by the frames we put them in. A view of the past is already framed if one starts a history of the Norman Conquest, as Freeman did, in the fifth century A.D. A history of the Second World War would equally be

---

[14]Herbert Butterfield, 'The Dangers of History', repr. in *History and Human Relations* (London, 1951), p. 168.

framed by its terminal dates if it started in 1919 with the Treaty of Versailles, in 1933 with the advent of Hitler, in 1939 with the western war, or 1941 with the Russian War.

It is impossible to study history without first assuming a framework. That is a fact which we have to accept and there is no harm in it if, as we proceed to an investigation of the foundations, we remember that the whole structure is artificial, a product of our own minds. At all stages, whether in school or university, it is essential to be open about it, because if we pretend either that there is no framework, or that the framework is God-ordained, we will merely harden our belief in our own preconceptions.

III

We can see something of this process if we turn from academic history to leisure history. The providers of mass-entertainment have always appreciated the popularity of the subject and have made full use of it on the stage—as with Shakespeare's historical plays—on cinema, television, radio, and, above all, in the tourist industry. Sometimes the material is presented quite openly as history, as in the recent programmes on *Ireland* (BBC) and *The Troubles* (ITV), but it is also conveyed in the form of plays or in a dramatized version of novels, as in the case of *The Forsyte Saga* and *The Pallisers*.

If we confine ourselves to those TV programmes which are deliberately historical, we must first distinguish between those concerned with the period before, and those after, the invention of the cinema camera. The distinction is important because the whole nature of the programme changes when the historical illustrations are moving pictures rather than static illustrations. The existence of newsreel provides the producer with an enormous opportunity, because it enables him to show real politicians making real speeches, real soldiers fighting real battles, and real rioters rioting. But of course these scenes are only highlights; one is not shown the many hours in which the photographer was waiting for the riot to happen, let alone the days and weeks which he had spent, more or less idle, between assignments. Even in the case of politicans' speeches, the film treats one to only a very short excerpt, because the newsreel editor was only too aware that if he allowed the speech to go on too long, the audience would be bored. The producers of the recent programmes on *Ireland* stated that they had searched the film archives for everyday scenes of 'normal life' in Ireland, but had not been able to find any.[15] Consequently, if they were to make full use of the visual medium, they had to overweight their programmes with films of fighting and rioting. They tried to correct the general impression with the spoken word, but the general impression was nevertheless one of perpetual motion; and the viewer was left bemused.

In the pre-cinema age there is no such difficulty. The only illustrative material is static, whether it be pictures, statues, buildings or landscapes. It is usually beautiful, and the historian stands in front of it, or walks through

---

[15] Statement by Robert Kee and Richard Broad. T.V. programme, B.B.C.2, March 8th, 1981.

it, giving a lecture. This form of presentation was admirably suited to Sir Kenneth Clark's *Civilization* which was mainly concerned with art history, but it has also been used to good effect in many other programmes, notably Alastair Cooke's *History of the United States of America,* Peter Ustinov's *Imperial Europe* and Michael Wood's series, *In Search of the Dark Ages*[16]. The success of them all was due to the fact that they were primarily visual, and that the audience was told about the past by people who were standing in, or walking about, real places which were connected with the events which were being described. It is important to notice, however, that though the narrative often concerned disaster, and though a determined effort was made to portray disaster visually, the overall impression was of sunshine, colour and security. Michael Wood, for example, tramped around fields or towns in brilliant sunshine, discovering places where particular events might have happened; but the fact that the sites of battles or massacres were now green fields, shopping centres, or Ancient Monuments in the care of the Department of the Environment, gave the viewer a subconscious assurance that 'all's well that ends well', or even that 'everything is for the best in the best of all possible worlds'.

One of the features, not only of TV history, but of most coffee-table histories, is that they partake of the nature of a travelogue. The tourist industry is well geared to historic sites, and through them is a major purveyor of popular history. The importance of this is not always appreciated, but it can be witnessed all over the world. To give some simple examples from our own country, the battlefields of Killiekrankie and Culloden are admirably displayed, with museums or exhibition halls in which pictures explain the course of the battle and incidentally spell out the message of Scottish nationalism. An English nobleman's house, on the days when it is open to the public, normally does an excellent 'public relations job' for the English aristocracy. A ruined abbey can promote a feeling for religion, and a 'folk-museum' not only portrays the life of the past but also helps the people of a particular country or province to discover its identity. No one who saw Hitler's Germany or Mussolini's Italy can doubt the propaganda value of historic monuments.

It is an interesting fact that few, if any, historic monuments are objects of hatred. In part this may be because those with the most hateful associations have often, like the Bastille, been destroyed; but it remains true that the most brutal monuments, even the remains of concentration camps, invoke grief rather than hatred. In an attempt to explain this I revert to the Scottish battlefields. The effect they have is to stir up two conflicting emotions. On the one hand there is the excitement of hearing a story at the place where it actually happened and in a manner which makes history 'come to life'. On the other hand there is the beauty of the scenery which dispels all thought of war. What most impresses the tourists who visit the battlefield is the extraordinary peacefulness of the scene.

---

[16] Boudicca, Arthur, Offa, Alfred (1980), Athelstan, Eric Bloodaxe, Ethelred the Unready and the Norman Conquest (1981). In 'Eric Bloodaxe' Michael Wood gave the programme an emphatic 'northern nationalism', commenting on Northumbrian feeling on the death of Eric . . . 'the end of their ancient Kingdom and the liberty they had enjoyed. And of course some of them still feel that way'.

But it need not always be so. The Royal Hill of Tara must have felt equally peaceful before Daniel O'Connell held his 'monster meeting' there in 1843. He activated the place and derived power from it; now it is 'dormant' again. In a mild way, everyone can experience the 'activation' of an ancient monument on ceremonial occasions in (say) Westminster Abbey or St. Peter's Rome. We have also, in our own generation, glimpsed the potential of an object which we might have thought 'dead', when the stone of Scone was stolen from Westminster Abbey by Scottish nationalists.

Burial places have a particular potency, because they have been designed to keep alive the memory of someone who is dead. Napoleon's tomb casts a certain spell even on the descendants of his old enemies, while in our own age the tomb of Lenin is said to be extraordinarily powerful. The experience of visiting it has recently been described by Christopher Booker:

> I had always imagined that a visit to Lenin's tomb was, for the Western visitor at least, just another tourist sight, a curiosity. . . .It is not like that at all . . . I was haunted by the experience of visiting that holy ground at the heart of the Soviet empire as by nothing else since I had come here. The quasi-religious symbolism of that shrine is something that cannot be conveyed to those who have not seen it.[17]

Modern sightseeing has more than a few features of the medieval pilgrimage. In this country our forefathers used to go to Canterbury in the belief that prayer at the shrine of St. Thomas would cure their ailments or cleanse them of their sins. Now we go to Stratford-upon-Avon, thinking that we will understand Shakespeare better if we see his plays performed in the town where he was born.

Left to themselves, most ancient monuments are benign. Visited in ordinary circumstances they promote sympathy, and provided we do not commit sacrilege—for example by denouncing Shakespeare and all his works in the Birthplace house—their potency is not to be feared. Nonetheless the potential is there. That is why medieval heretics were burnt, so that there should be no relics of them and no tomb. For the same reason Charles II had the body of Oliver Cromwell exhumed and hung on Tyburn Tree. No monument was erected to him until the end of the nineteenth century, when his memory was judged no longer to be dangerous, because it had at last been fitted into the framework of national history. When we look at ancient monuments we see those parts of the past which we want to remember. That is why they seem so full of sunshine and colour. As in school syllabuses we have put a frame round the part of the picture which we like.

[17] Christopher Booker, *The Games War: a Moscow Journal* (London 1981), pp. 119, 120, 125.

IV

The conclusion to be drawn from these observations is not that 'history is bunk' but that history is potentially dangerous. It can be used to manipulate people, to play on their emotions and to persuade them to do things which they would not otherwise dream of doing. It might be thought that it should therefore be abolished, but this, as I have tried to explain, is impossible because it is everywhere around us—not only in books, plays and films but also in ancient monuments and scenery. For this reason the only defence against the abuse of history is knowledge. It is only if we understand the ways in which history can be manipulated that we will be able to protect ourselves from pseudo-historical propaganda.

The first lesson which we must learn is that no presentation of history, whatever form it takes, can fail to convey some ideas. Even the barest list of facts, written in note form, conveys ideas, because it is necessarily selective and has to start and end at arbitrary dates. That is why Butterfield insisted that we view the framework first, diagnose its ruling assumptions, and then test them by more detailed research; and in a modest way that is what we must also attempt in schools. It is important that we should teach outlines before we teach special subjects; and it is important that we should teach our pupils to diagnose the 'message' conveyed in the outline and to question it.

When history is used for the purpose of indoctrination, the bias is usually created, not so much by statements which are untrue, as by the omission of facts which are inconvenient. Hitler's history depended largely on the notion of continuity between the three German Empires or *Reichs*, the first of which ended in the thirteenth century though a ghost of it continued till 1806, the second which lasted from 1871 to 1918, and the third which Hitler himself inaugurated in 1933. The art was to pass over the gaps, conveying the idea that since they were not specifically German, they could be treated as irrelevant. It was the same in Fascist Italy, where the ruling idea was the continuity between it and the Roman Empire. Physically this was expressed by the fact that Mussolini's residence was the Palazzo Venezia, adjacent to the Capitol and Forum, but remote from the monuments of christian Rome. In history syllabuses the Fascists had to create the same impression by getting from ancient Rome to modern Fascism as fast as possible. It would have been much easier for them if history in schools had been as narrowly specialized then as it is now; gaps are not so easily concealed from those who, having studied long periods of history, have acquired a sense of chronology.

The essential feature of historical knowledge is that it locates events in time, in the same way as geographers locate them in space or philosophers in logic. The historian must have a sense of chronology. He cannot afford to be unsure whether it was before or after the Romans that the Anglo-Saxons conquered Britain, or whether the Reformation came before or after the Renaissance. This is the sort of groundwork which a historian is expected to have completed before embarking on research, since even if he were researching into nineteenth-century civilization, ignorance or hesitation on these points would lead him into basic misunderstandings in research.

Naturally, the amount of history that can be learnt at school is limited. Though we often underestimate the amount of historical knowledge that is normally absorbed before the age of ten, it remains true that if a long period of time is to be studied, it will be impossible to relate it to a very wide area of the world. In spite of the experiences of the Second World War there may be no harm in this. It has the advantage of explaining the phenomena which the children see around them, and provided that it is explained that the framework is national and that other nations have frameworks which are partly or wholly different, no harm will have been done.

On the contrary, the results will probably be beneficial. In a multiracial society such as ours, it will be possible to maintain social and national cohesion only if our children can communicate with each other. Communication involves not only language, but also a community of ideas, so that terms such as baron, Protestant, Cavalier, Roundhead, Whig, Tory, Trafalgar and Peterloo are not meaningless. If our present trends in history-teaching continue, we will have students at university who have no idea of what or when was Magna Carta or the Armada. This may sound fanciful but I have been assured that in Holland, where the history taught in schools is World History, it is not only possible but has actually happened that a university student, listening spellbound to a lecture on the Revolt of the Netherlands, has had to ask who the revolt was against.

It may, of course, be argued that it would be better to study an area of history which was non-national, such as art history, intellectual history or the history of social classes. In my view there would be no fundamental objection to any of these, provided that they involved the study of a long span of time, and provided that the reasoning behind the framework was explained and its basic assumptions investigated. The great mistake which must be avoided at all costs is to think that history can be taught without conveying any beliefs or assumptions at all. Do what we may, beliefs and assumptions will keep coming in, because nothing else is possible. The honest historian will not attempt to deny their existence, but will do his best to identify them, point them out to his pupils and invite them to examine their validity. In this way history would be defended from abuse; it would also be made a great deal more interesting.

21

Degree Day*

The ceremony in which we are now engaged is one of great antiquity. Its essential features have been the same since the twelfth century, when the first universities came into existence. Its necessary constituents are the chancellor or his deputy, the academic staff on the platform, the graduands, and the public.

I say 'chancellor or his deputy' because this is one of the few occasions on which the vice-chancellor acts, not in his own right, but simply as the chancellor's substitute. When the chancellor is present it is he who confers the degrees, saying to the graduands: 'By virtue of my authority as chancellor, I admit you to the degree of . . .'. Those words are a literal translation of the Latin form used in the Middle Ages, but they offer no explanation of where the chancellor's authority comes from. This is because, even in the Middle Ages, universities were not too keen to admit that the chancellor's authority came from the church. But this was the case. The church had a monopoly of education, partly because it was the guardian of true doctrine, and partly because clerics were almost the only people who could read and write. As a result, the only person who could license a teacher was the bishop of a diocese until, under pressure of other business, he deputed the task to his chief-secretary or chancellor. Academics might complain that the chancellor was not as learned as they, but nonetheless the Church would punish anyone who dared to teach without his licence. As learning spread, teachers wanted a licence to teach not just in one diocese, but everywhere, and the ony person who could give them that was the pope. The chancellor's authority, then, came from the pope. But at the Reformation King Henry VIII assumed for the Crown all the rights which had previously been the pope's in England. That is why all subsequent universities in England have been created by royal charter, in our case a charter of Queen Victoria's. It is for this reason also that in England the chancellor of a university no longer wears ecclesiastical robes, as he would have done in the Middle Ages, but robes similar to those of the Lord Chancellor of England.

*An address given at a Degree Congregation in the University of Birmingham, 12 July 1979.

The second group participating in the ceremony is the academic staff on the platform. In the twelfth century they would all have been called 'masters' or MAs. At that date they were paid no salaries, but hired their own lecture-rooms and charged their own fees. But they also formed themselves into a guild or union, which is what *universitas* originally meant. As in all guilds they were insistent that they, and only they, should determine who should be of their number, and since this involved saying who should be teachers, they soon found themselves in conflict with the chancellor. In the thirteenth century they won a great victory when they persuaded the pope to decree that chancellors were obliged to confer degrees on all those nominated by the masters. That is why the masters examine the candidates, why the dean, acting as their spokesman, reads out the names of those who are to receive degrees, and why the masters on this platform watch to see that the chancellor or vice-chancellor does what is required of him. It may be added, however, that while the pope required chancellors to confer degrees on all those nominated by the masters, he did not divest himself of the authority to confer degrees on other people nominated by himself. In England this authority was transferred, at the Reformation, to the archbishop of Canterbury who still can, and does, confer 'Lambeth' degrees on people of his own choice.

Thirdly the graduands. Up till now I have been talking loosely of degrees being 'conferred' or 'given', but what the vice-chancellor has been saying to the graduands is: 'I *admit* you to the degree of . . .'. The word 'degree' comes from the Latin *gradus*, which means 'a step'. When a student is admitted to the degree of Bachelor of Arts, he moves one step up towards the mastership. When he is admitted to the degree of MA he climbs another step and comes up on a level with the masters, who then receive him into their guild or *universitas*. In the Middle Ages he would then have stayed on the platform, so that his old master could invest him with the symbols of his office. But that was only part of the business. The new master had to deliver an inaugural lecture, entertain the whole guild of masters to dinner, and preside over disputations for forty days continuously. For that reason, taking one's MA was called 'inception', or the beginning of one's career as a master.

The fourth participant in this ceremony is the public, those of you who are seated in the further part of the hall. You also have a function, because the whole point of the proceedings is that they should be seen and heard by valid witnesses. You hear the words of the dean and vice-chancellor, and you see the new graduates dressed in their respective gowns or robes. The gowns are derived from the everyday dress of the medieval clergy. In the Middle Ages they were not open in front but closed like a clergyman's cassock. It was about 1500 that academics had the front opened up so as to display the fine clothes which they were wearing underneath. The hood was the normal medieval headwear, as on a modern anorak, but it soon acquired a coloured lining. By the seventeenth century, if not earlier, these colours were strictly controlled, so that anyone could tell from the colour of a graduate's hood what was his university, and what his degree.

Perhaps you are wondering why we preserve those old forms today. Some people have no use for ceremonies and regard them as a vanity. But for most of us there is a real point in celebrating the major events of our lives in a way which will make them memorable. An eighteenth or twenty-first birthday is remembered as the day on which one came of age, and a wedding drives home the point that two people have made a memorable decision. Today's ceremony commemorates that you, the new graduates, have taken an important step in being admitted to a degree. It is firstly a matter for joy and congratulation, and I do indeed congratulate you. But though you may be thinking of today as the triumphant end of a gruelling course, you should remember that it is really your 'inception' or beginning. Just as when you come of age you become responsible for your debts, so also when you are admitted to a degree you become responsible for the truth. When you were students, you could expect some member of staff to point out your mistakes and correct them. It was he, or she, who took responsibility for seeing that what you learnt was, so far as modern knowledge could ascertain, true. Now that responsibility is yours. You have to stand on your own feet, detect your own mistakes, correct them, and see to it that what you teach is true, however awkward or inconvenient the truth may be.

In this ceremony your teachers have publicly declared their faith in you. Your name has been called by the Dean of your Faculty, the Chancellor or Vice-Chancellor has admitted you to your degree, and you have mounted the steps of this platform so that all can see you in the robes of this university. We have admitted you as one of ourselves, and at the end of the ceremony you join in our procession. When you leave the hall, you carry the honour of this university on your shoulders.

22

Installation of the Chancellor*

In this country, one of the first statements in the charter or statutes of a university is that there should be a chancellor. That is because students go to universities in order to obtain degrees, and degrees can be conferred only by authority of a chancellor. But if one is to understand what else the chancellor is or does, it is necessary to view his office historically, examining in turn the six major stages through which it has passed.

In the first stage, which was in the twelfth century, the chancellor belonged not to a university but to a diocesan bishop. This was because all learning was controlled by the Church. In theory it was the duty of the bishop to examine all those who sought a licence to teach and, when satisfied, to grant them a degree; but in practice he delegated this duty to the head of his secretariat, or chancellor. During the course of the twelfth century the demand for education rose dramatically; teachers overflowed from the cathedral schools, 'set up shop' (as it were) in towns like Paris, and organised themselves into a Masters' Union or *universitas*. When they considered their students competent, they presented them to the bishop's chancellor, and if he refused them a degree, there was trouble; in 1212 the University of Paris persuaded Pope Innocent III, who was one of their own graduates, to rule that the chancellor was obliged to confer degrees upon those nominated by the university. In law this did not prevent him from conferring additional degrees on persons of his own choice, but in practice he was restrained by the fact that the university was a 'closed shop' whose members refused to work with anyone whom they had not themselves admitted into their own society.

If disputes were not to be endless, it was essential for the chancellor to be acceptable to the university. It was for this reason that bishops found it prudent to grant universities the right to elect their own chancellors, subject only to the bishop's confirmation. In this second stage, which in England had begun by 1221, the chancellor belonged to the University and was one of its own masters. He did not wear special robes, but, in the same way as a modern vice-chancellor, continued to wear the gown he had

*An address given at the installation of Sir Alex Jarratt as Chancellor of the University of Birmingham, 21 October 1983.

worn as a professor. His term of office was usually no more than two or three years. In the Middle Ages university teaching was not a career for life but a step towards a benefice in the Church. Ordindary lecturers might expect a vicarage, rectory or canonry. Chancellors usually ended up with a bishopric.

As head of the university the chancellor was responsible for its academic work, but he also presided over its court of justice. Universities were ecclesiastical institutions, and their members, whether masters or students, were subject only to the law of the Church, which was administered in the chancellor's court. This court was originally subject to the bishop's authority, but in the thirteenth century most universities liberated it from this control by persuading the Pope to take it under his direct protection. The universities did this in the name of academic liberty, so as to ensure that the bishop could not circumscribe their teaching. But in addition to academic liberty they gained material privileges because (at any rate in this country) their members could not be summoned in any court other than that of their chancellor. Townspeople naturally resented that it was only in this court that they could sue a university man for debt; and that when scholars started a riot in which buildings were burnt and people killed, they were tried, not in the King's court but in that of the university's chancellor. They must have hated even more the fact that the price of food and lodgings in the town was fixed by the university authorities and enforced by the chancellor's court.

The secular discontent which these privileges aroused brought about the third stage of the chancellorship. Recognising that it would not be easy to defend their privileges, universities decided that the sort of person they now needed as a chancellor was not a promising young academic, but a former graduate who had moved on to a position of power and influence. In practice this meant choosing an influential bishop; at Oxford the first such appointment was in 1461 when the university elected George Nevill, younger brother of Warwick the Kingmaker, already Bishop of Exeter and soon to be Archbishop of York. He was, of course, non-resident, and the day-to-day work of his office passed to the vice-chancellor. But the university could rely on his goodwill and protection.

The fourth stage of the chancellorship came about as a result of the Reformation, which removed English universities from the protection of the Pope and placed them under the authority of the King. There was then no further need for chancellors to be clerics. On the contrary, if patronage was what was required, there were strong arguments for choosing as chancellor someone who had, or was thought to have, the ear of the King. The difficulty, and danger, was that academics were not always the best judges of which way the political winds were blowing. Cambridge's success in picking the 'top men' may be judged by the fact that of the nine chancellors it elected in the sixteenth century, five were beheaded. What was more, while alive and in office, most of these chancellors interfered blatantly in academic appointments, and secured the dismissal of those of the 'wrong' religious persuasion. At Oxford it was considered safer to elect chancellors who were not so much political 'heavyweights' as personal favourites of the monarch, but these men also used their office to forward their own particular interests. When Oxford eventually turned to men of state it chose two chancellors who proved to be real benefactors, though one of them, Archbishop William Laud, was beheaded, and the other, Oliver Cromwell, having died in his bed, was hanged posthumously at Tyburn.

The fifth stage of the chancellorship was less dangerous. It began with the Restoration of the Monarchy in 1660 and lasted until the nineteenth century. In this period all the chancellors died in their beds, many of them after very long periods in office. But the feature which distinguished them all was that, whether religious or secular, they were members of the House of Lords. This enabled them to protect the interests of their universities by presenting petitions to the King in parliament, and by rallying opposition to any bills which might damage their ancient privileges. Because they were members of the House of Lords, they likened themselves to the King's Lord Chancellor and adopted robes like his, which remain to this day the model for all university chancellors in this country. Our chancellor's robes, which we will be seeing in a few minutes' time, were made for our first degree congregation in 1901, and are a particularly fine example.

In the eighteenth century and for much of the nineteenth, the university privileges which were most consistently attacked were those which concerned religious tests. Until 1854 no-one was allowed to matriculate at Oxford or Cambridge without subscribing to the Thirty-Nine Articles. Dissenters were excluded from senior teaching posts even longer, for in Oxford it was not until 1871 that Masters' degrees were conferred without a religious test. That was because in theory the university was still an ecclesiastical institution, with its government controlled by the Masters. Those who were not members of the Church of England endeavoured to found new universities which would be free of all religious constraints. But they found themselves checked by the fact that no institution could confer degrees without a chancellor, and no institution could have a chancellor without the consent of the Crown. The Crown could not be moved without parliament, and the chancellors of Oxford and Cambridge fought a stubborn rearguard action in the House of Lords. It was not until 1836, four years after the Great Reform Bill, that the King gave his assent to the foundation of a University of London, with a chancellor and the right to confer degrees. The chancellor named in London's charter was William Cavendish Earl of Burlington and subsequently 7th Duke of Devonshire. He was a distinguished mathematician with a passion for promoting scientific education. Such was his generosity that other universities queued up to have him as their chancellor also. After serving London for twenty years he moved to Cambridge, for which he built and equipped the Cavendish Laboratory at his own expense. From 1880 he was also chancellor of the Victoria University, for which he made munificent benefactions at Manchester and Leeds.

The sixth stage of the chancellorship belongs to the twentieth century and was inaugurated at Birmingham. The first chancellor of this university was named in its charter, given on 24 March 1900, as 'our trusty and well-beloved Councillor Joseph Chamberlain'. He was obviously the right choice since it was he who had had the vision, he who had raised the funds, and he who, through his position in the government, had secured the charter. But he was the first commoner to become a university chancellor for 240 years and, what was more important, the first university chancellor *ever* not to have been a member of the Established Church. In the Middle Ages it would have been unthinkable for a bishop to receive a degree from an avowed heretic, but that was what happened here in 1909.

Pro-Chancellor,[1] since Joseph Chamberlain was then ill, it was your grandfather who made history by conferring an honorary degree on Bishop Charles Gore. It is now your turn to make history by installing as Chancellor the first of our own students to have been elected to that office.

Sir Alex Jarratt, in the name of the University I welcome you back, I charge you to uphold our charter and statutes, and I wish you a long, happy and successful chancellorship.

---

[1] The pro-Chancellor here addressed was Charles Beale, grandson of Charles Gabriel Beale who, like Joseph Chamberlain, was a Unitarian.

Index